Federal Resume Guidebook

Third Edition

Write a Winning Federal Resume to Get in, Get Promoted, and Survive in a Government Job

Kathryn Kraemer Troutman

JIST Works
America's Career Publisher

Federal Resume Guidebook, Third Edition

© 2004 by Kathryn Kraemer Troutman

Published by JIST Works, an imprint of JIST Publishing, Inc.
8902 Otis Avenue
Indianapolis, IN 46216-1033
Phone: 1-800-648-JIST   Fax: 1-800-JIST-FAX   E-mail: info@jist.com

Visit our Web site at www.jist.com for information on JIST, free job search tips, book chapters, and ordering instructions for our many products!

Quantity discounts are available for JIST books. Please call our Sales Department at 1-800-648-5478 for a free catalog and more information.

To order the *Federal Resume Guidebook* CD-ROM with resume and KSA samples and templates: www.resume-place.com, The Resume Place, Inc., Baltimore, MD, (888) 480-8265.

Acquisitions and Development Editor: Lori Cates Hand
Interior Designer: Aleata Howard
Page Layout Coordinator: Carolyn Newland
Cover Designer: Trudy Coler
Proofreader: Jeanne Clark
Indexer: L. Pilar Wyman

Printed in the United States of America
07 06 05 04 03   9 8 7 6 5 4 3 2 1

Library of Congress Cataloging-in-Publication data is on file with the Library of Congress.

ISBN 1-56370-925-2

Contents

Index of Sample Resumes

Foreword

There are deep rhythms in the history of American public life. One such rhythm is the ebb and flow of the call to public service. Of course, there are individuals of each generation who hear the call and answer, sustaining the nation between the times when the summons is more urgent. But there are other times—difficult times—when a clarion call goes out to a generation of Americans. Citizen servants and citizen soldiers have always answered the call.

The call of the nation and the response of its people has sustained the hymn of our democracy through revolution, civil war, progressive reform, depression and world war, and the dismantling of American apartheid. Today, another call goes out, as urgent and compelling as any before. How many times in the past have those who heard the call said to themselves, "But I am only one person. What could I do that would make a difference in the face of the great forces at work in the world?" And yet, they answered, and together they made a difference. All the difference.

There are many ways to serve. Some of the opportunities today are obvious. A new Department of Homeland Security, assisted by many other Federal departments, confronts the enormous challenge of defending the nation against terrorism while ensuring that the threat of it does not cripple the nation's economy. The demand is clear for skills related to intelligence analysis, law enforcement, customs inspection, immigration processing, food-safety assessment, scientific research, and airline baggage inspection.

But less obvious skills are also in great demand. For example, government reforms mandated by Congress have imposed rigorous requirements on Federal agencies to put their financial books in order. This has opened excellent opportunities for skilled accountants and financial analysts throughout the government. The need for such skills has been strongly reinforced by Federal initiatives to track down the sources of terrorist funds and Congressional mandates for closer oversight of corporate governance.

Likewise, September 11th dramatically revealed the need for Federal agencies to integrate fragmented information systems in order to meet their missions. Bringing these systems into the 21st century is crucial to meeting virtually every major challenge facing the Federal government today.

Contingency planning for biological warfare has exposed the decades-long deterioration of the nation's public health system. America needs dedicated health-care professionals to rebuild it.

Fear is corrosive to a democracy, and the threat to homeland security has generated considerable alarm in America. The nation needs public servants committed to protecting the civil rights and liberties of its citizens in the face of mounting pressure to compromise the fundamental values of our democracy.

Public service is often called a "sacrifice." I have not found it so. True enough, as a Federal employee, you're not likely to be offered a package of options at a favorable strike price. You *will*, however, be offered a competitive salary, a generous health-care package, and an excellent pension plan. And the opportunities for advancement are outstanding. In many agencies, as much as a third of all employees will be eligible to retire in the next five years.

But most importantly, you will be offered *meaningful work*. This is the great attraction of public service: work which engages our heads, hands, and hearts—and those of others—to achieve something of enduring value for ourselves and our children. Hardly a sacrifice.

Read on, follow Kathy Troutman's advice, and answer the call.

Philip N. Diehl
Former Director, United States Mint

About This Book

Federal resume writing is almost a part-time job for everyone inside government because of the growing A-76 studies, reorganizations, base relocation and closure activities, and retirement planning. Private-industry job seekers are writing Federal resumes also, recognizing that the Federal government is the largest employer in the U.S. and that there are thousands of job listings on www.usajobs.opm.gov every day.

Federal Civil Service visionary and Senior Executive Services Consultant and writer Edward J. Lynch, Ph.D., wrote some great advice in *Reinvention Federal Resumes* (published by The Resume Place in 1997) that is still true today:

> *Today's resume focus must be on*
>
> ***Accomplishments and results,*** *not merely a description of the duties and responsibilities that you performed. Include details of your projects or programs.*
>
> ***Programs and policies that serve*** *specific people (customers), not just a generalized public, or functions of job responsibilities.*
>
> ***Developing skills and competencies*** *that will be required in the next century, not limited to serving today's needs. Emphasize skills that you will need in your next position, not simply a list of your present skills.*
>
> ***Describing accomplishments*** *in dynamic terms, demonstrating that you have made a difference in your organization, not merely writing about activities.* Making a Difference

In 1999, the date of the last edition of the *Federal Resume Guidebook*, I was still preaching in my Federal resume and KSA writing workshops, "Now you can edit your 20- to 30-page SF-171 'book' into a focused three-to-five-page Federal resume. The 'fedres' is a great-looking presentation, no longer just an employment form. I'll show you how." In 2000, only 20 percent of the Federal workforce had converted to the Federal resume. Now in 2003, more than 80 percent have converted to the Federal resume (or the OF-612). [OF-612] The big challenge to today's Federal resume writer is to *write a better Federal resume* so that the applicant will stand out and be recognized as "Best Qualified."

Applying for promotions, changing careers, and attempting to move into a new "industry" (government) require top-level sales, marketing, and targeting. Because the Federal and private-industry job markets are so competitive, your Federal resume has to be outstanding, focused toward the particular occupational series, and capable of selling you! This is not easy, especially for a Federal employee who normally doesn't sell or market anything. The Federal employee's strengths are implementing programs and policies, managing teams, disseminating information…not marketing.

The art of writing an outstanding, focused Federal resume. This new edition gives you the samples, tips, information, and inspiration to take your Federal resume to the next level. You've converted from the SF-171 and OF-612 to the "fedres." Now, let's move on to the *art* of Federal resume writing. It's time (or past time) for a promotion or change in occupational series. Play this Federal employment game to the max with the best possible Federal resume and KSA narrative statement you can possibly write. Federal employment can work for you if you are well-prepared!

Electronic resumes are requested in 60 percent of all vacancy announcements. The electronic resume revolution in government is growing by the day. There are several "electronic resumes" in government, including the following: the USAJOBS Resume Builder; the Resumix resume accepted by DoD in the textbox of an e-mail or in a Resume Builder; and the electronic resumes (text format) that you copy and paste into the Quickhire, Avue, and other online builders at more than 100 Federal agencies.

The science of getting "Best Qualified," not just "Qualified." The *Federal Resume Guidebook* has become the standard guide for Federal resume writing in the careers industry, with more than 40,000 copies in print. This third edition contains the cutting-edge techniques needed to be qualified, and "Best Qualified," for your selected position.

Survival of the fittest in commercial activities studies—compete to win! The number-one reason hundreds of Federal employees are reading this book and working on their Federal resumes is the huge commercial activities studies that will occur in government. President Bush is discussing the conversion of 850,000 Federal jobs to commercial jobs!

Acknowledgments

This book is the result of four more years of Federal resume writing and training by Resume Place writers and trainers. The Certified Federal Resume Writers and Coaches (CFRWC) at The Resume Place were important consultants, researchers, and contributors of chapters of this book. I could never have completed the third edition without this excellent writing team, each of whom is dedicated to helping Federal applicants successfully apply for and land Federal jobs.

★ Mike Ottensmeyer, CFRWC, Contracts Management

★ Laveta Casdorph, CFRWC, Career Strategies, Senior Executive Service, and Human Resources

★ Carla Waskiewicz, CPRW, CFRWC, Secretarial and Administrative

★ Mark Reichenbacher, CPRW, CFRWC, Electronic Resume Writing

★ Alan Cross, FJST, CFRWC, Federal Resume Writing Accomplishments

★ Jacqueline Allen, CFRWC, Program and Management Analysis

★ David Raikow, Ph.D., FJST, CFRWC, Science Federal Resumes and CVs

★ Evelin Letarte, CFRWC, Information Technology Specialist

★ Rita Chambers, CFRWC, and Jessica Coffey, CFRWC, CPRW; KSA Writing

★ Diane Burns, CPRW, Military to Federal Resume Writing

★ Christopher Juge, J.D., Plain Language Writing

★ Mike and Debbie Dobson, CareerProofing™

★ Barb Guerra, first Development Editor

★ Sarah Blazucki, CFRWC, Editorial Assistant

My thanks go to my best Federal friends and colleagues for their technical direction and answers to questions on Federal personnel policies: Ligaya Fernandez, Project Manager, Merit System Protection Board; John Palguta, Vice President, Partnership for Public Service; Richard Whitford, Transportation Security Administration; Faith Williamson, Ph.D., Director, Career Training, Federal Drug Administration.

Thank you very much to the Federal employees who have contributed their resumes and KSAs to this edition with permission. You are providing a valuable service to hundreds of job seekers who need good writing samples and inspiration in order to write an excellent Federal resume.

A very special thank you to Philip Diehl, who has inspired me with his successful career as an executive in government. Philip has successfully led change, led people, been results-driven, built coalitions, and proven his business acumen with the rebuilding of the U.S. Mint.

About the Contributors

Author **Kathryn Troutman** is both a resume expert and career consultant with more than 30 years of experience in the specialized Federal job market. She is Founder and President of The Resume Place, a leading resume writing service in Baltimore that originated in 1971. A sought-after trainer of Federal job seekers and HR professionals, Troutman has written six career books and produces www.resume-place.com.

Jacqueline Allen is a Federal Career Consultant and senior resume writer. She has been with The Resume Place for two years. She spent 20+ years in Marketing Management positions in the private sector, directing major Federal proposal efforts for multimillion-dollar contracts. She taught career communications at the college level, and she developed and presented numerous business writing courses to corporate executives and midlevel managers. She also has a book and several magazine publishing credits.

Diane Burns, CCMC, CPRW, IJCTC, CEIP, CCM, is an international career-industry speaker and national writer with dozens of published articles, and resumes published in more than 14 books. With 14 years of experience and as a former recruiter for a major aerospace corporation, she specializes in military conversion, Federal government resumes, and career coaching. Contact her at www.polishedresumes.com.

Laveta Casdorph has more than 28 years of experience in the Federal personnel career field. She has won many awards and was recognized as an expert human resources program manager with the Air Force and the Department of the Interior. She also served as a Federal labor and employment law attorney at Kelly Air Force Base, Texas.

Rita Chambers brings an M.S. degree in Computer Science and more than 15 years of management and technical writing expertise from the IT field. As a hiring manager in commercial industry and Federally related institutions, Rita has often been on the other side of the hiring process and knows what managers are looking for. Rita also has a bachelor's degree, with a double major in Philosophy and Education.

Jessica Coffey, CPRW, is a certified resume writer and experienced career consultant. For more than 10 years, she has provided career-management strategies to all levels of government and private-sector employees. Jessica wrote the interview chapter in Kathryn's *Ten Steps to a Federal Job.* She graduated from Virginia Tech with a B.S. in Business Management and an M.Ed. in College Student Personnel Administration.

Alan Cross is a writer, trainer, and consultant specializing in the Federal job market. For the past six years, Alan has delivered "dynamic, practical, and immediately useful" workshops and classes to participants at Federal agencies, job fairs, and regional and national conventions, and has assisted more than 1,500 job seekers in creating interview-winning GS-5–through–SES Federal application packages.

Philip Diehl is the President and COO of FH|GPC, the government relations and public affairs subsidiary of Fleishman-Hillard. Previously, he served as director of the U.S. Mint, where he led a dramatic agency turnaround. Before the Mint, he held several senior positions in Washington, including Chief of Staff to Treasury Secretary Lloyd Bentsen. He has been recognized with numerous awards, including the Treasury Medal for outstanding public service and *Government Executive's* Federal 100 Award.

Deborah Singer Dobson is co-author of *Enlightened Office Politics: Managing UP!* and *Coping with Supervisory Nightmares.* Specializing in organizational change, she has been VP of Human Resources and Organizational Development for GATX Terminals, an international petroleum and chemical company; Senior Director of Management Development, Training, and Staffing for Giant of Maryland; and Executive Director/Co-Founder of ERIS Enterprises, a national management consulting practice. She is married to Michael Dobson and lives in Maryland with her son, two Shelties, and a Honduran tarantula.

Michael S. Dobson, FSJT, has consulted and advised career seekers in Federal service since 1978 and has written thousands of resumes, SF-171s, KSAs, and other career materials. A nationally known authority on project management, he is the author of eight management books, including *Streetwise® Project Management, Enlightened Office Politics, Coping with Supervisory Nightmares,* and *Exploring Personality Styles,* and two novels, *Fox on the Rhine* and *Fox at the Front.* He can be reached through www.dobsonbooks.com.

Award-winning author, lecturer, and trial attorney **Christopher Juge** has nearly 20 years of professional writing experience in the corporate, legal, and government spheres. He is also a French-English interpreter, a professional portrait artist, the soloist at his church, and a martial-arts student. He is currently a senior executive in the largest foster-care agency in the world.

With a B.A. in English and an M.A. in Higher Education, **Evelin Letarte** has been in higher education since 1996. She has worked directly with students and alumni in a university career center and currently teaches a cooperative-education course that helps students articulate career experiences and earn academic credit for on-the-job learning.

Senior writer **Mike Ottensmeyer** is a resume expert, Senior Executive Writer, and career consultant with more than 29 years of experience in human resources in the Department of Defense, including 12 years overseas. Mike has been writing for The Resume Place since August 2000. He has an extensive background in training managers in the Federal personnel process, and in working one-on-one with Federal job candidates at all levels. He has contributed articles to Air Force publications, as well as *Resume Writers Digest.*

David Raikow received his Ph.D. in Zoology and Ecology, Evolutionary Biology, and Behavior from Michigan State University. An aquatic community and ecosystem ecologist by trade, his scientific work has appeared in *Limnology & Oceanography* and other journals. As a Certified Federal Job Search Trainer, he writes Federal resumes, other Federal application materials, articles for the Web, and books.

Mark Reichenbacher, CPRW, has a distinguished career of more than 25 years of Federal service, having held generalist, specialist, supervisory, and managerial positions at field and headquarters levels in labor-management relations and program management. Currently, he serves as a senior-level Program Analyst and coordinates special projects dealing with workforce-transition issues. He has contributed to two of Kathryn's previous books.

Carla Waskiewicz, a Certified Professional Resume Writer (CPRW), has more than 20 years of professional writing experience. She provides full-service resume writing and career consultation to The Resume Place clients, including private-industry and Federal resumes, KSAs, and Resumix writing and editing services. She holds a B.A. in Communications from Penn State University.

Part 1

Getting Started

CHAPTER 1

What Is a Federal Resume?

A Federal resume is your most important document for starting or advancing your government career. Just as the SF-171 was your "life history," the Federal resume is your marketing piece, career summary, and personal presentation and is critical to your career success and satisfaction. It is not just an outline of your jobs and dates. It is a carefully focused, well-written, clearly organized, and professionally presented career package that can help you earn promotions as you select your jobs, education, and training.

Here are the basics about a Federal resume: It uses a reverse-chronological format (your most recent positions are listed first). It could be two pages to six pages; however, some electronic formats are restricted to three to five pages. A Federal resume is different from a private-industry resume because it is typically longer and contains some basic "compliance" information required by government personnel offices. A full list of this compliance information is on pages 42–43.

The typical section headings in a Federal resume are the following:

PERSONAL INFORMATION

OBJECTIVE

SUMMARY OF QUALIFICATIONS

PROFESSIONAL EXPERIENCE

EDUCATION

TRAINING & AWARDS

PROFESSIONAL MEMBERSHIPS

OTHER QUALIFICATIONS

You can organize, edit, and style these headings many ways, depending on what job you are seeking and what you are trying to do with your career. This chapter includes seven samples of Federal resumes designed to help the applicant make six typical career moves.

> ★ **Note:** The preceding edition of this book focused on converting your SF-171 to a Federal resume. In this edition we assume that at least 80 percent of Federal employees have converted to an OF-612 or Federal resume because the SF-171 was basically eliminated in 1995. We will therefore move on with little discussion or mention of the SF-171. We mention the OF-612 occasionally because some people converted to it from the SF-171. We now recommend, however, that you abandon the OF-612 and move up to a great-looking, focused Federal resume.

A Federal resume can be printed on paper or distributed electronically. The differences between a paper Federal resume and an electronic resume are principally related to their formats. There are samples of both the Federal and electronic resume formats in the appendix at the end of this book. The Federal resume that I talk about in this book is principally for human resources professionals and people who appreciate a nice format and presentation. The electronic resume is unformatted and ready for copying and pasting into resume builders and e-mail textboxes.

This chapter contains samples of before-and-after excerpts and complete resumes for each of five general Federal resume objectives. Because everyone has a different objective, you can draft your resume's content to focus on your most relevant skills, education, and experience. Federal human resources professionals review hundreds of applications, so if your resume features information that is of great interest to these first reviewers, it could increase your chance of being rated "best qualified." The best-qualified packages are referred to the selecting official for consideration for an interview.

Six Resume Formats for the Six Most Common Federal Career Objectives

The six resume formats in this chapter are the following:

- ❏ Federal resumes for career change (occupational series change and advancement)
- ❏ Federal resumes for career change (with new training and education)
- ❏ Federal resumes for lateral moves (new agency, new location, new supervisor)
- ❏ Federal resumes for new agencies with new missions

- ❏ Federal resumes for reinstatement
- ❏ Private-industry resumes converted to Federal resumes

The major differences among the six resumes are the organization of the headings, the content (what's included and what's not), the emphasis on certain accomplishments, and the presentation of education and training.

Every day you read about Federal agency reorganization, military base closures, privatization, merging agencies (for example, the Homeland Security Department), retirement (which is resulting in the "Human Capital Crisis"), employee morale and customer satisfaction statistics, and new recruitment strategies. All of these items affect Federal employees and their careers. When the President talks about public/private competition for 425,000 jobs, that means 425,000 Federal employees will be competing with people in private industries to keep their jobs. It's important for the average Federal employee and Federal job applicant to keep abreast of Federal employment news. You need to know which jobs are being considered as "non-core" for Federal service and therefore are at risk for being privatized in the future.

At the workshops I have taught over the past years, each audience faces a different situation that requires them to write their resumes. The reasons include the following:

- ❏ The organization is relocating to another state but employees are hoping to find new jobs and stay in this area.
- ❏ A certain occupational series is being eliminated and privatized, so the employees need to change occupational series. Some Federal employees return to school in order to change series and grades.
- ❏ Employees want new challenges, a new supervisor, a job closer to home, or to relocate to another state.

❏ An office has either won or lost a competitive bid, which affects some or all jobs.

Regardless of the reason for the change they are facing, all Federal employees need a great resume. The rest of the chapter is dedicated to a discussion and examples of each of the five different Federal resume styles.

Federal Resumes for Career Change (Occupational Series Change and Advancement)

"I'm at the top of my pay scale. I have to change series if I want to make more money." "My series is being privatized and I have to change series to keep a job in government." If these situations apply to you, you'll need to prepare a Federal resume geared toward making a career change. This section shows you how.

PATCO—Federal Job Chart

P
Professional—GS 13–15

Professional in the government—The Professional positions have a positive educational requirement—such as chemist, accountant, doctor, social worker, or psychologist. Candidates for jobs in this category must be educated and certified by a board or institution.

A
Administrative—GS 9–12

Administrative—These jobs usually have the title of Analyst or Specialist. They require a four-year degree or, if the candidate has no degree, he or she must have experience to qualify for the position. This category includes certain law-enforcement positions such as Special Agent, Border Patrol, Customs Inspector, and Immigration Inspector.

T
Technical—GS 6–9

Technical—These jobs are the Technician or Assistant positions. Examples of job titles include Accounting Technician and Accounting Assistant. There is no educational requirement. The main requirement is experience. The Federal Aviation Administration Electronics Technician can be classified as high as a GS-12. Bachelor's degree graduates can qualify for Technician or Assistant positions starting at a GS-7.

C
Clerical—GS 1–5

Clerical—These jobs are clerk positions and have no educational requirement. An Associate of Arts degree graduate can qualify for a GS-3 or GS-4 position.

O
Other

Law enforcement professionals (other than Special Agent), including security guards, police, park rangers, U.S. Marshals, and others.

Strategies for Writing a Federal Resume for Career Change

Here are the essential strategies for preparing your career-change Federal resume:

1. Analyze the basic skills and qualifications needed at the higher level and new position.

2. Demonstrate in your resume that you have the qualifications for the new position, series, and grade.

3. Write a description of your work that clearly defines and demonstrates the skills needed in the new series.

4. Write your duties at a "higher level." In other words, do not feature skills and duties that are clearly at the lower level. Focus on the skills and duties that you have now that also apply to the higher-level position.

5. Are you only minimally qualified for the next level? Then be sure to add hours per week, months, and year for your employment at the previous grade level. And add relevant training, awards, and accomplishments to demonstrate your ability to do the job at the higher grade level.

6. Include projects and accomplishments that will make your resume stand above the competition. If you have received awards, recognitions, or e-mail messages from supervisors or team leaders regarding your outstanding service, these will impress the selecting official.

SAMPLE 1: Occupational Series Change and Advancement

Accounting Clerk (GS 5/8) to Accounting Technician (GS 6)

This is a sample Work Experience section write-up for an Accounting Clerk who is seeking an Accounting Technician position. Moving from the Clerk level to the Technician level is a challenging career change. First you'll see the "Before" version; then you'll see how better organization and formatting can make it more effective in the "After" version.

BEFORE

This description is difficult to read and is not focused on the next grade level and position. This "blurb" of copy has little chance of being found Best Qualified because it focuses on the minute details and is not written at the higher grade level. Because this person has been on the job for seven years, he or she could easily perform similar duties at a higher grade level; however, the resume does not make this clear.

WORK EXPERIENCE

03-1996 to Present; 40 hours worked per week; Accounting Clerk; GS-525-05/08; $13.36 per hour; Commander Navy Region, 517 Russell Avenue, Pearl Harbor, HI; K. Jones, (808) 444-4444 ext 271; may contact supervisor.

Accounting services related to U.S. Navy obligations and contracts. Major accounts include: the Facilities Management Division, Facilities Department, Naval Computer and Telecommunications Area Master Station, Eastern Pacific. Accountable for Class I and Class II Real Property valued at more than $214 million. Established and maintained Plant Property and Minor Property Records for Class III and Class IV items. Duties include: reviewing and screening vouchers, invoices,

---

(continues)

(continued)

---

requisitions, work requests, and contracts; validating information, noting any discrepancies or inaccuracies; reviewing documents for accuracy, proper signatures, funding, and compliance with Defense Finance and Accounting Service (DFAS) regulations; returning items with missing or erroneous information; applying appropriate policies, procedures, directives, and instructions to specific cases; updating and maintaining accounting records and ledgers of all operating targets (OPTARS); monitoring and controlling accounting transactions; tracking customer funds; certifying availability of funds; monitoring accounts receivable and collection of underfunding; identifying problem areas or potential problem areas and providing solutions; preparing and posting journal vouchers; reconciling accounts; validating completeness and accuracy of each invoice and statement; researching and resolving discrepancies; initiating and monitoring corrective action; answering customer or colleague inquiries; serving as liaison between vendors and client commands; closing old accounts after ensuring all activity was completed and verifying all transactions; determining which accounts are handled on a reimbursable basis and preparing appropriate documents for this procedure; preparing cash collection vouchers and obtaining required signatures; conducting periodic physical inventories of property as required; preparing appropriate documents for property transfer or disposition; and keeping supervisor apprised of customer account status.

AFTER

The new electronic resume has been organized into skill sets that the applicant needs to highlight in order to be successful at landing an Accounting Technician position. This new draft is easy to read, looks impressive, and features the higher level of skills so that the applicant will be considered for a grade higher in the accounting profession.

WORK EXPERIENCE

03-1996 to Present; 40 hours worked per week; Accounting Clerk; GS-525-05/08; $13.36 per hour; Code N464, Commander Navy Region, 517 Russell Avenue, Pearl Harbor, HI; K. Jones, (808) 444-4444 ext 271; may contact supervisor.

ACCOUNTING: Accounting services related to U.S. Navy obligations and contracts. Major accounts include the Facilities Management Division, Facilities Department, Naval Computer and Telecommunications Area Master Station, Eastern Pacific. Accountable for Class I and Class II Real Property valued at more than $214 million. Manage accounts in compliance with Defense Finance and Accounting Service (DFAS) policies and procedures.

Established and maintained Plant Property and Minor Property Records for Class III and Class IV items.

ACCOUNT MAINTENANCE: Update and maintain accounting records and ledgers of all operating targets (OPTARS); monitor and control accounting transactions; track customer funds; certify availability of funds; monitor accounts receivable and collection of underfunding.

DISCREPANCY RESOLUTION: Identify problem areas or potential problem areas and provide solutions; prepare and post journal vouchers; reconcile accounts; validate completeness and accuracy of each invoice and statement; research and resolve discrepancies; initiate and monitor corrective action; answer customer or colleague inquiries.

LIAISON AND CUSTOMER SERVICE: Serve as liaison between vendors and client commands; close old accounts after ensuring all activity was completed and verifying all transactions; determine which accounts are handled on a reimbursable basis and prepare appropriate documents for this procedure; prepare cash-collection vouchers and obtain required signatures; verify open obligation documents on a regular basis; determine availability of funds to ensure no over-obligation; inform supervisor of all overruns.

BUDGET ASSISTANCE: Produce Contract Obligation Authority (COA) documents and other funding documents in a timely manner; compile analytical, statistical, and other data or documents; prepare cost-data analysis for the Facility Management Specialist for budget preparation; prepare budget exhibits for submission to comptroller; generate monthly and quarterly financial and administrative status reports; update and maintain funding document files.

INVENTORY CONTROL: Conduct periodic physical inventories of property as required; prepare appropriate documents for property transfer or disposition; keep supervisor apprised of customer account status.

PUBLIC UTILITIES PAYMENTS: Certify more than $30 million in utility invoices for electricity, gas, water, and sewage for several different activities. Monitor and report gas, electricity, and water consumption as well as sewage usage, noting any discrepancies or irregularities. Receive and validate meter readings and compile reports. Also generate reports 5R32 and 5R44 (water & sewage) for facilities department. Keep records used to generate monthly and yearly utility reports for PWC and PACDIV. Prepare funding documents 2275 and 2276 to obligate into FAST DATA system.

SAMPLE 2: Occupational Series Change and Advancement

Housing Management Specialist (GS 1173-12) to Realty Specialist (GS 1170-12)

The U.S. Navy is eliminating the Housing Management Specialist series at most bases worldwide. Private-industry realty firms are taking over the housing and tenant services on military bases. Federal employees are transitioning to other series for which their skills qualify them.

BEFORE

This applicant's 12-year work experience description was unfocused. It will be difficult for a human resources staff to find the relevant skills and experience for another occupational series.

WORK EXPERIENCE:

Housing Management Specialist—Program Manager
GS 1173-12
March 1992 to Present
Engineering Field Activity North East
10 Industrial Hwy. Mail Stop 82
Lester, Pa 19113-2090

Supervisor—Sam Smith, 666-666-6666   40 hrs week, $69,075/yr

Direct and administer the modernization and new construction program. Fiscal manager of design and construction accounts. Prepare and review economic analyses in support of projects. Correct and improve design plans and specifications. Compile budget data, documentation, and justification for use by congressional liaisons in support of projects. Provide briefings to senior management on program execution. Responsible for the administration of facilities management functions such as planning, programming, budgeting, cost reporting, maintenance, repairs, and improvements, and serve as focal point on all facilities management issues for assigned geographic locations. Develop plans for acquisition, out leasing and licensing, and management and disposal of real property. Assist in developing reality-planning reports that include plans for disposal of excess land, improvements, and leasehold interests. Compile data to be used in preparation of environmental documentation, title evidence, appraisals, and congressional notification. Project coordinator on various multimillion-dollar design/build projects at northeast locations. Work on standard design criteria to be utilized by organization on all new housing construction and revitalization projects. Provide oversight and assistance in the day-to-day administration of programs relating to requirements determination, acquisition, resource management, and facilities and manpower management for government facilities. Determine current and long-range resource requirements. Coordinate input for development and presentation of acquisition programming to higher authority to be used in budget preparation. Prepare program briefs and point papers on facilities matters for Command officials, activity commanders and Regional Commanders, and Office Secretary of Defense (OSD) staffers. Participate in on-site reviews of the efficiency, economy and effectiveness of management and make recommendations. Review and investigate congressional, General Accounting Office (GAO), Naval Investigative Service (NIS), and Department of Defense Inspector General (DODIG) inquiries and draft replies answering such inquiries.

AFTER

This Work Experience section is much better targeted to the Realty Specialist, Construction Management, Project Management series. The applicant has had diverse experiences and skills that can be successfully used in other jobs in government.

WORK EXPERIENCE

March 1992 to Present, 40 hours per week, Housing Management Specialist – PROGRAM MANAGER, GS 1173-12, $69,075 per year, Engineering Field Activity North East, 10 Industrial Highway, Mail Stop 82, Lester, PA 19113-2090, Sam Smith 666-666-6666, may contact supervisor.

Direct and administer the modernization and new construction program funded in excess of $30 million per year. Fiscal manager of design and construction accounts. Prepare and review economic analyses in support of projects. Correct and improve design plans and specifications.

FACILITIES MANAGEMENT: Direct all functions such as planning, programming, budgeting, cost reporting, maintenance, repairs, and improvements. Focal point for all facilities management issues on one project consolidating maintenance service contracts at two locations, yielding savings of $500,000. Compile budget data, documentation, and justification for use by congressional liaisons in support of projects. Brief senior management on program execution through oral and written reports.

REALTY MANAGEMENT: Plan acquisition, outleasing and licensing, and management and disposal of real property. Gain knowledge of real estate laws, principles, and practices. Create realty plans for disposal of excess land, improvements, and leasehold interests. Compile realty data for environmental documentation, title evidence, appraisals, and congressional notification.

CONSTRUCTION MANAGEMENT: Project coordinator on multimillion-dollar design/build projects. Write standard design criteria for all new housing construction and revitalization projects. Oversee facilities requirements determination, acquisition, resource management, and facilities and workforce management. Determine resource requirements. Coordinate input of budget requirements for acquisition programs for presentation to higher authority.

MANAGEMENT ANALYSIS: Write program briefs and point papers for command officials, activity commanders and Regional Commanders, and Office Secretary of Defense (OSD) staffers. Review efficiency, economy, and effectiveness of management and make recommendations. Gain knowledge of management principles and processes, and the analytical and evaluative methods and techniques for assessing program development and execution and improving organization effectiveness and efficiency. Review fact-finding and investigative techniques of inquiries by congressional staffs, General Accounting Office (GAO), Naval Investigative Service (NIS), and Department of Defense Inspector General (DODIG). Write replies to these inquiries.

Federal Resumes for Career Change (with New Training and Education)

Many people are returning to college and certifications to change their careers, increase their work challenges, and improve their earning power. Military personnel complete their degrees to begin their private-industry careers. Administrative employees take human resources or contract training to become more specialized in their jobs. Many people go back to school to finish their college degrees so that they can simply be promoted. If you have gone back to school recently, your federal resume should focus on your recent education rather than your most recent job.

SAMPLE 3: Career Change with New Training and Education

Head Operations Analysis Branch (Lieutenant, U.S. Navy) to Supervisory Paralegal Specialist, GS-0950-12

Emily T. Paton
7777 Laytonsville Court, Alexandria, VA 22222
Home: (703) 222-2222
emilypaton111@aol.com

U.S. Citizen, SSN 000-00-0000
5-point Veterans' Preference
Highest Federal Civilian Position: NA

Objective: Vacancy Announcement Number: 02-CRD-068
Supervisory Paralegal Specialist, GS-0950-12, Appellate Section of the Civil
Rights Division, U.S. Department of Justice

Skills & Qualifications:

- **Successful leader and supervisor.** Team leader on projects and programs. Proven track record for effecting positive change and motivating subordinates in new directions. Repeatedly commended for leadership skills and office management initiatives.
- **Skilled paralegal.** Legal research assignments have been progressively difficult and important to significant case management.
- **Strong research skills.** Meticulous in details with comprehensive research and computer skills. Expert in trial preparations and litigation performance.
- **Excellent interpersonal skills.** Active listener with ability to effectively communicate with colleagues, clients and subordinates. Skilled in team building and establishing trust and rapport.

Education:

- **B.S.B.A.,** 2002, Strayer University, Washington, DC. Graduated with honors. **Overall 3.5 GPA; OUTSTANDING SCHOLAR; National Honor Society**
- **Paralegal Certificate,** 2000, Old Dominion University, Fairfax, VA, with honors. Selected Coursework:
  Introduction to Paralegal Studies (3 credits)
  Legal Research and Writing (3 credits)
  Civil Litigation (3 credits)
  Computer Applications for Paralegals (3 credits)
  Administrative Law
  Wills, Trusts and Estates
  Real Estate Law for Paralegals
  Criminal Law and Procedure

Certifications and Professional Skills:

- Certified Paralegal and Notary Public, State of Virginia
  Computer Skills: Windows 2000, Microsoft Word, Microsoft PowerPoint, Microsoft Access, WordPerfect, Harvard Graphics, Westlaw, Nexis/Lexis

Employment History:

U. S. Navy (active duty)   **7/1989 to 1/2000**
Office of Commander, Naval Legal Service Command Rank: Lieutenant
2200 Stoval Street, Alexandria, VA 22332 (10/95 to 01/98)
Supervisor: Captain John Smith, 703-555-5555

Head Operations Analysis Branch
Performed management analysis of 50 legal service field offices. Gathered, reviewed and analyzed field office performance data, identifying potential problem areas and providing recommendations for improving field performance. Conducted research studies; prepared reports, executive summaries, briefs and electronic presentations relating to legal services provided by the Office of the Judge Advocate General. Researched performance of prototype of Trial Service Office and produced report for Judge Advocate General and Chief of Naval Operations.

Prepared documentation and justification for establishment and disestablishment of legal service field offices. Responded to field office inquiries, providing guidance concerning headquarters policies, programs and management initiatives. Conducted outsourcing studies and prepared contractor performance work statements. Drafted implementing directive and administered the Office of the Judge Advocate General's and Commander, Naval Legal Service Command's urinalysis program. Supervised two GS-11 management analysts.

Major accomplishments:
- Received certificate of commendation from Judge Advocate General for development and supervision of the total reorganization of the Headquarters office filing system.
- Implemented cross-training for civilian management analysts to optimize utilization of civilian personnel assets.
- **Led process action team chartered to review and recommend new procedures for transcription of court-martial records of trial in the Naval Legal Service Command.**

Federal Resumes for Lateral Moves (New Agency, New Location, or New Supervisor)

There are many reasons why employees want to change jobs other than the job itself. For personal and professional reasons, they want to move to a new agency with a different mission and program. Or they are relocating because of a spouse or family situation. Sometimes a supervisor can cause an employee to decide to change jobs because they can't change the supervisor. Whatever the reason, this type of Federal resume presents the career experience in the best possible light to help the applicant make a job change.

SAMPLE 4: Lateral Career Move

Natural Resource Specialist, GS-0401-09 to Natural Resource Specialist, Terrestrial Habitat, GS-0401-09
This job applicant wants to change locations but stay in the same job series and agency. This resume presents his experience in a chronological format and includes excellent descriptions of his duties, projects, and skills. His entire resume is included here. This resume was successful in achieving his job change.

MICHAEL P. SMITH
1555 N. Grand St.
Portland, OR 97229
Office: 500-555-5555 ▪ Home: 500-555-5555
E-mail: smoskoff@att.net

Social Security Number: 000-00-0000   Citizenship: U.S.
Veterans' Preference: None
Federal Status: Natural Resource Specialist, GS-0401-09, 7/97 to Present

OBJECTIVE

Natural Resource Specialist/Terrestrial Habitat GS-0401-09
Vacancy Announcement Number: SA-02-11CVA

PROFILE

Natural Resource Specialist with 24 years of extensive Bureau of Land Management ecosystem-based management experience. Valued by managers for expertise in completing innovative and challenging special projects. Strong skills in coordinating interagency partnerships and interdisciplinary team efforts. Specialize in public speaking, timber project layout leadership, wildlife surveys, habitat restoration, cooperative agreements, public outreach to school groups, and representing BLM goals to outside interest groups. Experience in successful resolution of multiple-use conflicts involving wildlife, forest, and botanical resources. Excellent communication, supervision, and negotiation skills.

EMPLOYMENT HISTORY

Natural Resource Specialist, GS-0401-09 (40 hrs/wk)   July 1997–Present
Bureau of Land Management
Tillamook Resource Area
4610 3rd St., Tillamook, OR 97141
Supervisor: Rick Smith, 555-555-5555; may be contacted

As a Natural Resource Specialist, complete difficult and innovative assignments including unparalleled watershed analysis partnerships and a unique outreach partnership with Nestucca High School. Provide effective liaison to the public in wildlife and forest conservation issues. Fulfill a variety of roles centered on team leadership, fostering partnerships, providing expertise and advice on animal populations, performing wildlife surveys, and supervising summer crews for timber sale layout.
- Layout lead exercising professional judgment, interdisciplinary team coordination, and layout crew supervision to implement silvicultural prescription to develop late successional forest habitat for Adaptive Management Area resource project.
- Wildlife biologist involved with planning and implementing monitoring programs, surveys of sensitive species according to protocol, habitat evaluations, and resource-improvement projects.
- Project layout specialist for numerous timber sales.

(continues)

(continued)

- Interdisciplinary Team Leader performing NEPA portion of Resource Area projects.
- Designer and project coordinator of unique, award-winning interagency cooperative agreement and partnership for multiple watershed analyses.
- Service contract writer and project inspector of terrestrial habitat improvement projects.
- Outreach specialist to local school districts for Nestucca Connections Program and other outdoor-education programs.
- Watershed analysis partnership project coordinator at GS-11 rate for four months.
- Human Resources Development Committee representative for two years.

Wildlife Biologist, GS-0486-09 (40 hrs/wk)   August 1996–June 1997
Bureau of Land Management
Tillamook Resource Area
4610 3rd St., Tillamook, OR 97141
Supervisor: Rick Kneeland, 503-815-1100; may be contacted

This employment period was the final 11 months of a 48-month term position that began on the Prineville District BLM. The purpose of this Wildlife Biologist position was to help implement the Northwest Forest Plan. Used knowledge of Resource Management Plans, laws, regulations, and coordination skills to accomplish ecosystem-based management.

- Interdisciplinary Team Leader on two controversial timber projects.
- Project layout team member on numerous timber projects.
- Wildlife biologist for special-status species surveys and bald eagle roost observations.
- Cultural resource survey assistant.
- Public outreach specialist for local high school Career Days presentations.

Wildlife Biologist, GS-0486-09 (40 hrs/wk)   July 1993–July 1996
Bureau of Land Management
Princeville District, P.O. Box 550, Princeville, OR 97754
Supervisor: Dan Tippy, 541-416-6700; may be contacted

As a Wildlife Biologist, practiced ecosystem-based management in a self-directed work team atmosphere. Wildlife Biologist on the Lower Deschutes eco-team assigned to evaluate and improve wildlife and fish habitat. The last four months of this employment period were spent detailed to the wildlife staff of the Lakeview District BLM, Klamath Falls Resource Area.

Princeville Accomplishments:
Wildlife biologist with numerous successes at planning and implementing terrestrial habitat improvement projects for fish and wildlife habitat.

- Coordinator of interagency wildlife survey projects for neotropical bird populations, bighorn sheep releases, raptors, and sage grouse.
- Developer and COR/PI for 25,000-acre wildlife survey contract.
- Lead writer of Environmental Assessments for wildlife habitat improvement projects.
- Negotiator among BLM, Confederated Tribes of the Warm Springs, ODFW, two local power cooperatives, private land owners, and contractor to install osprey nesting platforms.
- BLM liaison at planning sessions with FERC, PAC, watershed councils, state and Federal wildlife agencies, and contractors.
- Surveyor of 150 miles of the Deschutes River and tributaries for Proper Functioning Condition report.
- Human Resources Development Committee Chairperson.

Klamath Falls Accomplishments:
- Coordinator of field studies for habitat conditions and wildlife population status with USFWS, Winema National Forest, and The Nature Conservancy.
- Wildlife Biologist responsible for planning and implementing wildlife surveys according to protocol for northern goshawk, great grey owl, northern spotted owl, and yellow rail.

Wildlife Biologist, GS-0486-07 (40 hrs/wk)   June 1989–June 1993
Bureau of Land Management
Lakeview District
P.O. Box 151, Lakeview, OR 97630
Supervisor: Robert Lund, 541-947-2177; may be contacted

The level of responsibility of this Wildlife Biologist position grew as my skills increased. Began with wildlife and habitat inventory projects and progressed to project coordinator for the 48,000-acre Warner Wetlands Project, environmental assessment writer for various interagency efforts, and public outreach specialist.

- Lead biologist for award-winning study of water-bird inventory at Abert Lake Area of Critical Environmental Concern.
- Coordinator for BLM interests with ODFW, USFWS, and The Nature Conservancy in intensive four-year interagency inventory of snowy plover.
- Interdisciplinary team leader of Environmental Assessments for bighorn sheep releases.
- Habitat improvement specialist for Warner Wetlands Project coordinating waterfowl surveys, planning and installing headgates, managing water levels for desired vegetation communities, and supervising force-account crew in dike construction.
- Lead surveyor of 95-mile detailed stream inventory project.
- Tour coordinator and presenter for college desert-ecology field classes.

(continues)

(continued)

Range Technician (fire), GS-02 to GS-06 (45 hrs/wk)   June 1978–May 1989
Bureau of Land Management
Lakeview District
P.O. Box 151, Lakeview, OR 97630
Supervisor: Dennis Harrington, 541-947-2177

Seasonal firefighter working an average of six months each year on the Lakeview District BLM, with the exception of the 1979 fire season. That season, worked as a firefighter in Cody, WY, on the Worland District BLM.

EDUCATION AND TRAINING

Humboldt State University, Arcata, CA
Wildfire Refresher Course, 2002, Salem District Office
Resource Advisor Training, 2002, Oregon State University
Cable Logging Systems, 2001, Forest Engineering Institute
Level II COR/PI Refresher Training, 2000, Salem District Office
Marbled Murrelet Survey Protocol Training, 1999, Mad River Biologists
Mollusk Survey Protocol Training, 1999, Salem District Office
GPS Field Techniques and File Management Training, 1999, Salem District Office

AWARDS

- Numerous letters of appreciation for instructing interest groups, leading tours on public lands, and participating with Watershed Councils: *1989–2002*
- Star Award for commitment and leadership—Nestucca Connections Partnership: *2001*
- Outstanding Achievement in Safety: *2001*
- Four awards for Group Driving Safety Recognition: *1997–2001*
- Award for leadership role in Watershed Analysis Partnership: *2000*
- Letter of appreciation from Governor Kitzhaber to BLM State Director for recognition of Watershed Analysis Partnership efforts: *1999*
- Washington County Soil and Water Conservation District "Max M. Reeher Award" for Watershed Analysis Partnership: *1999*
- Special Act Service Award—Timber Salvage Project: *1996*
- Salmon Summit Team Award: *1994*
- Superior Accomplishment Award for Survey Technique Development: *1992*
- Award for Warner Wetlands Project achievements: *1992*

Federal Resumes for New Agencies with New Missions

SAMPLE 5: New Agency

Retired Military Officer to Deputy Federal Security Director, SV-340, Transportation Security Administration

This Federal resume is really a combination of a Federal resume and a KSA (Knowledge, Skills, and Abilities) narrative. The knowledge, skills, and abilities that the TSA requires are featured on page 1 of the resume. The TSA does not require separately written KSA statements. This could be a more popular format for Federal agencies in the future because it saves time for both the applicant and human resources professionals.

Howard J. Weaton
2276 Community Dr., Waldorf, MD 20601
Office: (301) 999-9999
Home: (301) 999-9999

Social Security No. 000-00-0000   U.S. Air Force, 5-point Veterans' Preference
Citizenship: U.S.   Highest Federal Civilian Position: NA

Objective: Announcement # TSA-02-1011, Deputy Federal Security Director, SV-340, Job Grade J, US-TN-Lovell Field Airport, CHA, Transportation Security Administration.

Profile: As an Air Force Officer and Federal Law Enforcement Special Agent, 10 years of experience in investigations, aviation security, and counterintelligence. Over 7 years of civilian experience conducting presidential appointment and background investigations for Federal civilian agencies. Expert in physical security assessments and protective service operations. An executive whose hands-on experience enables him to evaluate, guide, and counsel professional staff. An effective communicator with individuals and groups with the interpersonal skills to build relationships with individuals, teams, and cooperating agencies.

Summary of Knowledge, Skills, and Abilities:

- **Knowledge** of law enforcement, aviation security, professional asset/military force protections, and corporate security—gained from a 17-year career including specialized training.
- **Ability** to plan and organize, set priorities, develop schedules and milestones, and formulate and evaluate plans—gained from supervisory assignments at the Air Force Investigative Operations Center in the United Kingdom and Tokyo.
- **Ability** to express ideas and facts in a clear and understandable manner, tailoring communication to the intended audience—gained from experience as a supervisor and by briefing officials at the highest levels of government as well as Air Force top management.
- **Ability** to manage a diverse workforce and lead others, including planning and assigning work, improving and controlling performance, selecting employees, and promoting EEO, human relations, and employee participation—gained from supervisory experience at three major field locations and from headquarters staff duties.

Employment History:

President   7/95 to Present
Weaton Associates, Inc.
2276 Community Dr.   Salary: $87,000 per year
Waldorf, MD 20601   Hours per week: 40
ATF Contract: Bob Smith, (703) 999-9999; may be contacted
Conduct investigations for Federal law enforcement agencies, including the Department of State Diplomatic Security, Federal Bureau of Investigation, Department of Treasury (ATF), and Department of Defense. Run sensitive ambassadorial and other high-level

(continues)

(continued)

presidential appointment investigations in support of the Department of State. Perform or direct over 4,000 background investigations in support of government and nongovernment customers.

Major Accomplishments:
- The highest-producing investigator for the Department of State. At one point, carried over 50 percent of all investigations being done by the department. Known for being professional, timely, and thorough and for producing error-free reports. One report on a presidential appointee was the first to pass the department review process with no corrections.
- Praised for work in a background investigation for uncovering unemployment compensation fraud, resulting in denial of security clearance.

Executive Assistant to the Director   7/94 to 6/95
Air Force Office of Special Investigations (AFOSI)
Investigative Operations Center   Rank: Captain
Bolling Air Force Base   Hours per week: 40
Washington, DC 20332
Supervisor: Colonel Peter Gray (Retired)

Assisted the Director in management of a 150-person organization overseeing all major criminal, fraud, and counterintelligence investigations and critical security matters at Air Force installations and sites worldwide. Applied **knowledge and expertise in law enforcement and aviation security** to guide investigative and law enforcement techniques, including recruiting and utilizing confidential sources, use of behavioral analysis to solve crimes, interview techniques, and physical and technical surveillances. Evaluated and directed productivity, morale, and promotion issues within the organization. Promoted EEO, human relations, and employee participation as the focal point for those issues.

Major Accomplishments:
- Reorganized training program along division lines. Increased by 100 percent opportunities for specialized training. Recognized as model program by senior AFOSI leadership.
- Specially selected to head a unique team evaluating organizational effectiveness and compliance with Federal regulations. Uncovered serious managerial and chain-of-custody problems in weapons and evidence programs.
- Implemented clearer documentation requirements for weapons program and transferred evidence responsibilities to the more appropriate base-level AFOSI unit. Organization received top marks in major inspection.
- Evaluated customer satisfaction and then integrated criminal, fraud, and counterintelligence investigative divisions with their operational counterparts, creating clearer functional lines of responsibility.

Commander/Special Agent In-Charge   7/91 to 7/94
Royal Air Force Base
Upper Heyford   Rank: Captain
United Kingdom
Supervisor: Colonel Mike Lane

Planned, organized, and evaluated the day-to-day operations of an investigative unit conducting major criminal, fraud, and counterintelligence investigations for 10 Air Force installations in England and Wales. Made all decisions regarding allocation of investigative time and resources, and prioritized investigative activity to meet U.S. Air Force commanders' needs. As the top law enforcement officer, was in charge of hiring and firing. Had weekly meetings to discuss progress of investigations. Ensured that agents were following all logical leads and keeping up with the required paperwork. Managed a suspense system for all investigations and other unit duties. Held feedback sessions with all employees, explaining expectations, evaluating individual performance, and giving them the opportunity to respond before I wrote final performance evaluations. Rewarded those employees who excelled by putting them in for awards and decorations.

Oversaw use of confidential informants to collect critical criminal, fraud, and counterintelligence information. Motivated unit investigators; brought them together as a team with a new focus on proactive initiatives. Refocused the detachment by creating a system for measuring agent and unit productivity. Reviewed and finalized Reports of Investigation for dissemination to Air Force installation commanders and senior Air Force leadership. Prepared threat and risk assessments for installation commander. Identified $3.5 million fraud by a British contractor against the Air Force. Managed $150,000 in funds and assets—consistently accomplished mission under budget and on time.

Routinely gave oral presentations and briefed senior military and civilian officials on investigative, security, and counterintelligence matters; identified problems and recommended remedies. Maintained liaison with British police and government officials. Implemented Total Quality Management techniques to more effectively accomplish mission. Resolved hundreds of significant investigations using latest investigative tools and procedures—unit had an unprecedented 99 percent solve rate. Unit awarded highest marks in Europe during major region-wide inspection. Participated as a key player in weekly Law Enforcement meeting with Base and Wing Commanders. Briefed high-ranking commanders on current cases and investigative activity. Reviewed and corrected Reports of Investigation by agents in unit, preparing final reports for publication and distribution. Praised by AFOSI and Pentagon leadership and base-level commanders for clarity of reports.

Major Accomplishments:
- Directed the identification of security vulnerabilities and threats to over 12,000 people and tens of millions of dollars of Air Force resources. Led unit to win "Best in Europe" award.

(continues)

(continued)

- Uncovered and neutralized a terrorist plot to penetrate RAF Upper Heyford and damage F-111 aircraft—increased security, arrested terrorists "in the act" at flight-line perimeter fence.
- Managed a diverse workforce, setting realistic goals for the unit and following through with the agents, which resulted in an increase in productivity of 25 percent and an increase of successful prosecutions of investigations 100 percent despite manpower cuts.

Division Manager for Technology Protection and Operational Security 7/88 to 7/91
Yokota Air Base
Tokyo, Japan   Rank: Captain

Responsible for security of all critical Air Force technologies exported to Japan. Inspected security procedures of Japanese government agencies and civilian corporations possessing sensitive U.S. technologies—ensured technologies were fully protected. Conceived and developed an innovative computer-based initiative to protect critical technologies from foreign intelligence service targeting. Obtained national-level and in-country support and funding. Uncovered targeting of key technologies—program now being implemented worldwide by several Federal agencies. Managed counterintelligence analysis and reporting program and directed Operational Security Assessment Program for all Air Force installations in Japan.

Prepared over 500 sensitive reports responsive to national-level requirements. Briefed high-ranking military and civilian leadership visitors on AFOSI's investigative and counterintelligence mission in Japan. Prepared classified counterintelligence reports for dissemination to a wide audience worldwide. Quality and clarity of reports praised by headquarters leadership and during IG investigation. Prepared, directed, and managed briefing program for the Intermediate-Range Nuclear Forces Inspection Program. Briefed crew and inspectors going to Russia for inspections. Prepared, directed, and managed briefing program for all Intermediate-Range Nuclear Forces treaty personnel flying to the Soviet Union.

Major Accomplishment:
- In charge of the Operational Security Assessment Program and led teams of investigators as we penetrated U.S. Air Force installations surreptitiously, identified security vulnerabilities, and offered remedies to installation commanders and security police officials.

Program Manager for Criminal Investigations   5/85 to 7/87
McGuire Air Force Base
New Jersey   Rank: 2nd Lieutenant
Supervisor: Lt. Colonel Thomas C. Cobb

Prepared numerous reports of investigation on criminal, fraud, and counterintelligence matters distributed to senior Air Force leadership. Implemented initiatives to increase proactive investigative activity. Developed program to interview drug-test positives before formally notified; then recruited them as informants to target dealers. Specially selected to head two major investigative trips to Greenland to conduct security background investigations. Used confidential informants to collect critical criminal, fraud, and counterintelligence information. Worked jointly with FBI, CIA, DEA, and U.S. Customs on matters ranging from espionage and death investigations to sex crimes and counter-narcotics operations. Conducted Protective Service Operations in support of the visiting Egyptian Minister of Defense and President of the United States.

Education:
B.S., 1984, Mathematics, Albright College: Reading, PA
1986 Special Investigator's Academy (AFOSI), Bolling Air Force Base, Washington, DC
1986 Squadron Officer's Leadership School, Maxwell Air Force Base, AL
1988 Defense Language Institute, Japanese—52-week intensive course, Monterey, CA
1989 Systems Protection Security Course, Bolling Air Force Base, Washington, DC
1991 Counterintelligence Collections and Analysis Course, RAF Greenham Common, United Kingdom
1993 Total Quality Management (TQM) Course, RAF Mildenhall, United Kingdom

Honors, Awards, Distinctions & Affiliations:
     Air Force Commendation Medal
     Air Force Achievement Medal

Additional Professional Qualifications:
     Secret SSBI security clearance with the Department of State, Department of Treasury, and FBI.
     Proficient with Microsoft Windows, Word, Outlook Express, and QuickBooks business software.

Other Interests and Activities:
     Hang-Gliding, Hiking, Biking, Golfing

Federal Resumes for Reinstatement

Many former federal employees are returning to government. They are returning out of patriotism, because their private-industry firm has closed or reorganized, because they need to rebuild their retirement funds, or because they want to come back and help their former office manage operations. The challenge of the Reinstatement Federal resume is that the relevant federal experience should be featured, even if it is not the most recent.

SAMPLE 6: Reinstatement

Former Bindery Supervisor and Operator, U.S. House of Representatives Returning Government Applying as Machine Bookbinder, KA-4402, Government Printing Office

---

JAMES E. TAYLOR
7777 Stevens Drive
Annapolis, Maryland 20748
(301) 444-4444

SSN: 000-00-0000   **United States Citizen**
Highest Federal Grade: N/A   Veterans' preference: 5 Points
Certificate of Service, U.S. House of Representatives
Bindery Supervisor and Operator, Acting Mechanic

OBJECTIVE

Machine Bookbinder, KA-4402-00
Government Printing Office, Vacancy Announcement: 01-1113

PROFILE

Bindery manager, supervisor, mechanic and journeyman folder operator with 25+ years experience in the printing and binding industry. Excellent customer service skills. Effective trouble-shooter and problem solver. Motivated self-starter. Work well independently or as a member of team.

EQUIPMENT UTILIZED

Stahl, Bum, Dexter Cleveland and MBO folding machines; McCain 3 knife and 5 knife folder with cover-feeders; automatic and manually fed 16, 32 and 40 box adhesive binders and side-wire adhesive binder combinations; Chandler & Price foil and ink stamping machines; Automated Book flow line with Wohlenberg 3 knife Trimmer; Sheet-fed Casemaker; Nipper and Gluer and Wohlenberg flat-bed cutters; tie jacks; forklifts; power jacks; measuring tools; hand tools.

PROFESSIONAL EXPERIENCE

Folder Operator   *10/1997 to 12/2000*
Enterprise Graphics, Inc.   40+ hours/week
4600 Boston Way, Lanham, MD 20706   Salary: $15.00/hour
Supervisor: Mike Pate, Printer Phone: 301-577-8650, May be contacted.

Examined work orders to determine machine setup. Operated and maintained machines to automatically fold, slit and score printed sheets into signatures for binding. Processed 80,000 to 100,000 printed sheets per day into signatures for binding.

Bindery Supervisor and Operator, Acting Mechanic   08/1971 to 10/1997
U.S. House of Representatives   40+ hours/week
Capitol Hill, Washington, DC 20515   Salary: $41,000/year
Supervisor: George Earley, 202-225-4355

Supervised and coordinated activities of 36 to 52 workers engaged in assembling, forming and finishing products such as pamphlets, periodicals, loose leafs and other printed and published products manually and by machine. Oversaw binding operations to verify conformance with plant standards.

- Supervised workers engaged in forming operations such as folding, cutting, gathering and stapling printed sheets.
- Assembled finished and binding sets, folders and loose-leaf binders.
- Supervised subcontractor workers in setting up and operating machines. Operated machines during absence of folding room machine operators.
- As Acting Maintenance Mechanic, repaired and maintained machinery and mechanical equipment. Advised about and carried tools and equipment to and from storage and working areas. Held and/or tightened bolts to proper torque specifications. Loosened bolts to dismantle machinery. Cleaned machines with sandpaper, solvent and wiping rags to prepare surface for oil and grease.

AWARDS & RECOGNITION

Certificate of Service, U.S. House of Representatives
Numerous letters of recognition, bonuses and awards for outstanding performance and service throughout career

SAMPLE 7: A Private-Industry Resume Converted to a Federal Resume

Many private-industry employees are seeking Federal employment for the first time. There are two challenges to converting a private-industry resume to a Federal resume:

1. Applicants need to add the "compliance details" required by all vacancy announcements (see chapter 8 on work experience for the list of what to include in your Federal resume).

2. The work experience and core competencies/skills section should be written considering the "duties" and skills desired in the government job.

Financial Consultant, Director of Operations/Treasurer/Staff Instructor to Budget Analyst, GS-0560-09, Department of the Treasury, Announcement No. 2002-227BMW

Mark T. Shafter, Jr.
100 East Broadway
Baltimore, Maryland 21021
E-mail: markshafterjr@aol.com
Day/Evening Telephone: 410-555-5555

SSN: 000-00-0000   United States Citizen
Highest Federal Grade Held: N/A   Veterans' Preference: N/A

OBJECTIVE

Budget Analyst, GS-0560-09, Department of the Treasury. Announcement No. 2002-227BMW.

PROFESSIONAL PROFILE

Organized, detail-oriented **finance/accounting professional** with 18+ years' experience in the private and public sectors designing, developing, and managing comprehensive accounting, budgeting, financial, tax, operational, and organizational systems. Extensive staff management and human resources expertise. Multicultural, international business experience and rigorous academic training in taxation, accounting, and business administration. A team player and skilled leader.

CORE COMPETENCIES

- **Budget Analysis:** Strong financial management skills and proven expertise in performance budgeting and budget analysis. Record of success developing and implementing effective business performance outcome measures and strategic business plans. Extensive expertise formulating and tracking annual operating budgets.

- **Planning & Management:** Over 15 years of experience working with senior-level financial managers to plan and implement budgets and long/short range financial plans.

- **Regulatory Knowledge:** A comprehensive knowledge of the principles, concepts, laws, and regulations of performance budgeting for the Federal Government gained through professional experience as a financial consultant, tax accountant, tax auditor, and accounting professor.

- **Research/Data Analysis & Computer Expertise:** Adept at researching, compiling, analyzing, and tracking financial data for object class and line items. Strong database management and statistical analysis skills.

- **Communications Skills:** Excellent oral and written communications skills with strong presentation, negotiation, and client relationship skills. Expertise writing and presenting comprehensive business plans, complex auditing/financial reports, and technical information.

FINANCIAL EXPERIENCE

FINANCIAL CONSULTANT   **1993 to Present**
Director of Operations / Treasurer/ Staff Instructor
Kim's Martial Arts Institute   40 hours per week
5545 Newbury Road, Bel Air, MD 21087   Salary: Volunteer
Supervisor: John Smith, Jr., 410-555-5555. May be contacted.

Financial consultant/advisor with direct responsibility for financial administration, strategic planning, and all state, local, and federal tax matters for this 501(c)(3) nonprofit educational institution. Prepare financial reports and maintain necessary accounting systems to provide effective and efficient accounting controls, including general ledger accounts, accounts payable and receivable, collections, revenue recognition, and budgeting. Report directly to the Institute Director. Serve on Board of Directors as Treasurer.

- Formulate the annual budget and long-term and short-range strategic plan. Coordinate plan with agency director.
- Monitor and track all obligations and expenditures, tabulate cost data, compile data summaries, and prepare annual operating budget. Analyze, verify, and revise budget data.
- Research, compile, and summarize financial data for the formulation of budget estimates. Present all budgets and strategic plans before Board of Directors and Director.
- Seminar coordinator and liaison to Japanese representatives from Martial Arts organizations and international participants. Coordinate and administer all seminar and training venues, travel arrangements, publications and press information, and travel income and expenses.
- Instruct students in the Japanese Martial Art of Aikido, including self-defense and weapons defense.

Key Accomplishments:

- Instrumental in designing and writing a Corporate Business Plan designed to reorganize and return to profitability a small business facing bankruptcy. Wrote, and currently execute, long- and short-term business growth plans designed to transform the organization into a leader in Aiki training in the Baltimore Metropolitan area with the long-term goals for regional expansion. Designed training programs, registration, educational programs, and marketing strategy.
- In 2001, prepared all required IRS documentation to create a 501(c)(3) nonprofit educational institution from a Sub S corporation. Currently direct and oversee all financial operations and serve on Board of Directors as Treasurer.

(continues)

(continued)

PROFESSIONAL DEVELOPMENT

Computer Training Courses:

Microsoft A+ Certification Course, 2002
Windows Operating Systems, 2000, 1998, 1997
Microsoft Office, 2000
Microsoft Word, Excel, and Group Wise 5, 1998

Professional Training Courses:

Basic Auditor Training, Flow Charting, Audit Concepts, Statistics, Sales and Use
Tax, Motor Fuel/Special Fuel Tax, Intangible Personal Property Tax,
and Corporate Income Tax, 1997

Proficient in the use of automated accounting, financial and operational systems,
and desktop computers and related software applications for research, word
processing, spreadsheet analysis, database management, and financial report
generation.

SPECIAL INTERESTS

Instructor/ practitioner of the Japanese Martial art of Aikido since 1998. Hold the
rank of Nidan, 2nd degree Black belt. Instruct students in self-defense, hand-to-hand
combat, and Weapons defense. Conduct self-defense seminars at colleges and
universities throughout the Mid-Atlantic. Volunteer coordinator for seminar
participants from around the world and ambassador to Japanese martial arts
representatives traveling to the U.S.

Summary

One Federal resume format does *not* fit all Federal applicants. It's best if you organize your content based on your most relevant experience. Always focus on the future position and your most impressive information. Your goal is to be "best qualified," to get an interview, and to be hired for your selected new job.

CHAPTER 2

Strategies for Moving Up in Government

The timing for your Federal career advancement couldn't be better. Despite private-sector layoffs and reorganizations over the past decade, job opportunities within the Federal government are on the rise. Why? Three main reasons:

★ The Federal workforce is aging and significant numbers of Federal employees are nearing retirement.

★ Government reductions have forced agencies to restructure their programs and operations.

★ Nearly every agency must now address new demands for technological, information management, and other skills prompted by the creation of the new Homeland Security Department.

First, the retirement dilemma. The statistics are mind-boggling. According to the *Wall Street Journal*, roughly half of all government workers are eligible to retire by 2006, and about one-fifth of those eligible are expected to do so. More Federal workers today are in their 60s than are in their 20s! Agencies that will play key roles in the war on terrorism are among those facing large retirement hits: 30 percent of workers in the Federal Bureau of Investigation and 36 percent of those in the Federal Emergency Management Agency could retire by 2006. Such turnover will cause a growing number of vacancies.

What about earlier government reduction efforts? Doesn't this mean that fewer positions are now available? Ironically, the reduction of nearly 17 percent of government positions during the 1990s created an unexpected shortage in many critical program areas. Often, to reach mandated reduction quotas by the deadlines imposed by Congress, agencies gave $25,000 bonuses to employees who agreed to retire or resign. Although this tactic did cause staffing levels to reach the "magic" number, indiscriminate reductions in some agencies meant that senior employees with corporate knowledge and the most expertise left the Federal workforce. Agencies were forced to reorganize to cope with the reality of having fewer resources to accomplish their missions; and, as a result, many jobs were restructured. Agencies are still scrambling to recruit and/or train employees with a broader experience base who can do a wider range of work than yesterday's specialists. Although there might be fewer actual numbers of positions in the Federal workforce, there are now more opportunities for candidates who are multitalented.

Along with the unique problems caused by government downsizing, the creation of the Department of Homeland Security has created a new demand for special skills government-wide. Federal agencies are now seeking candidates for jobs in law enforcement, intelligence, physical security, cybersecurity, computer technology, and foreign languages. Studies show that the government will need about 16,000 more technology professionals over the next decade, and hundreds of experts in Asian, Middle Eastern, and other languages. These skills will be needed in agencies that handle commerce, transportation, military operations, diplomacy, law enforcement, intelligence, and counterterrorism.

In addition to these three phenomena, the inevitable changes in social values and ideas that occur with each generation could also play a part in causing Federal employment opportunities to rise. Studies show that entrants into today's workforce are less likely to see their career path as consisting of one job or one line of work for their entire lives. Instead, many workers believe that they will change jobs several times or have a series of careers before they retire. Because the Federal Employees' Retirement System (FERS) allows employees who leave government service to convert their retirement accounts to a private plan, this societal shift might very well change the profile of the Federal worker from one who stays employed with the government for life, to one who works for the government for a period of time and then moves on. Although the sociological theories about why this change is occurring are complex and beyond the scope of this book, such changes could signal a trend that a higher and more consistent turnover in Federal jobs could create more employment opportunities for you.

In short, despite the bleak outlook in the private sector, the stars are aligning for those who want to move up in the Federal government. To take advantage of this situation, you need a plan! The rest of this chapter shows you how to formulate one.

Setting Goals Makes the Difference

If you want to position yourself to move into a new job or gain a promotion, you need to do something that makes the difference between staying where you are and moving up. What makes the difference? You must set goals, develop and follow a plan, believe in yourself, and recognize that no one is going to come along and just promote you or hire you away into your dream job.

Your career development strategy needs to be about you: your dreams, your talents, your goals, your needs, and your skills. You must know what you want. If you don't know what you want, who else does? Make a commitment to invest an hour each week in long-term planning and goal-setting for your career development. You could spend the time in self-assessment, rewriting your resume, researching vacancies, or pursuing self-development activities. Whatever you do, the investment in yourself will be like money in the bank, especially if you do land a new job or a promotion. Here are some ideas about how to develop a career strategy.

Step 1: Know Thyself

What are your personal limits? Are you willing to relocate? If you are not willing or able to move to another geographic locale to pursue your Federal career, you will be limited to the Federal job market in your area. There is nothing wrong with staying in your current area; you just need to be realistic about what types and grades of jobs you can expect to land and develop your strategy accordingly.

What about changing agencies? Some individuals are deeply loyal to the agency they work for and wouldn't dream of going to another to pursue their careers. Again, this is fine; just know that you must factor in the turnover rate in your organization and how many people are competing for vacant jobs. For instance, suppose you are not mobile and don't want to switch agencies. You are in your mid-40s and aspire to an SES job, but the supervisors and managers at the top agency levels above you are also in their mid-40s and also aspire to an SES job. Your career strategy will have to be much different than that of the candidate who is willing to relocate and switch agencies.

Step 2: Start with a Statement of Your Dream Job

Don't worry that you probably aren't qualified for your "dream job" right now—that's why you're developing a plan. Don't make your job description too specific. The problem with wanting to be President of the United States is that there's only one job, and it comes available no more often than once every four years. Think about the characteristics of the dream job rather than a specific job title. Do you want a job that uses your communication skills? Provides overseas travel? Helps other people? Doesn't require computer savvy? Try describing what your perfect day on this job consists of—not in terms of the duties, but more in terms of the work situation. Are you working alone or with others? Are you supervising other people? Do you have flex time? Approaching what your dream job looks like from this point of view rather than from a job title will help you see other possibilities besides the ones you already know about.

Step 3: Expand Your Picture

What kinds of jobs would have some, if not all, of the characteristics you like? If you can't get from where you are to your dream job in one leap, what interim jobs or situations would move you in that direction? The best way up is not always straight up—sometimes you have to move sideways first. Factor that into your plan.

Step 4: Consider the Obstacles

What stands in your way? Are you missing certain credentials? Does your experience not fit your goals? Don't be in too big of a hurry to conclude that you need an extra degree. What you might actually need is different skills.

MBA-
LAW

Step 5: Make a Plan for Overcoming Each Obstacle

You must face the obstacles that stand in your way before you can overcome them. If you don't have the right degree or it's not from the right school, how can you get or demonstrate that you have the right skills? If you had a bad experience in a previous job, how can you overcome it, learn from it, put it behind you, or turn it into an asset? If you don't know the right people, how can you meet them? Although a few lucky people are born with the right contacts, most of us have to go out and network to get our foot in the door.

Step 6: Develop a Time Line →

After you identify your goals, the obstacles to those goals, and how you will overcome each obstacle, don't stop there. You need to make a time line for achieving those goals and visualize yourself at the goal line on the due date. How do you do this?

Go back to Step 5, where you described how you will overcome the obstacles to your goal. Break down your plan into phases or steps. For instance, do you need additional education or training? How much time will it take? What is the one thing you can do during your hour of career-strategy planning this week to move yourself toward this goal? Do you need to enroll in a class? If so, what steps do you need to take to line up the enrollment? Do you need to find a source for the training or education? Choose a source? Contact the source? Ask yourself, "what do I need to do first," and then, "what do I need to do before *that*?" Keep going until there is nothing to place in front of the very first task. Then, assign a date and time to each task, and complete the task by the assigned date. Before you know it, you'll have stepped over the obstacle and will be on your way to the next task.

One hour a week doesn't seem like a lot of time, and it isn't. But that's all you need to focus on at this point. In one hour, you could write a draft of the six steps discussed in the preceding sections. In one hour, you could read a couple of chapters in a good career-development book. In one hour, you could meet with a career transition center counselor. In one hour, you could attend an evening lecture by a notable person in your field. In one hour, you could gather all the material you need for your resume. In one hour, you could search the Web for government job announcements. In one hour, you could read your agency's Web site to review new programs and mission statements. In one hour, you could work on a draft of your Federal resume.

Of course, you could put in more than one hour a week, but you don't have to. The advantage of spending one hour a week is that it keeps you from feeling overwhelmed by a long-term project. You will be amazed at how much progress you've made after just a few sessions. Setting up and going through this process gives you a feeling of immense control and personal security. If there's a setback in your agency, you don't have to panic: You're already on your way to something better. If you don't like a particular offer or work situation, you don't have to let desperation drive your decision. You can continue to develop yourself. Invest the time in yourself. It *will* make the difference.

Some Tips on Networking: It Is Who You Know!

Zig Ziglar, in his book *Top Performance,* tells this story: A little boy tried in vain to move a heavy log to clear a path to his favorite hideout. His dad finally asked him why he wasn't using all his strength. The boy explained he was straining as hard as he could. But the father disagreed. "Son, if you were using all your strength, you'd have asked me for help."

We tend to overlook the many sources of help, forgetting that even the legendary self-made people seldom made it on their own. We need others' help to reach our goals. And most people really like to be asked for their help. Besides, most important jobs require teamwork, so now is the time to get started cultivating this skill.

Where to Look for Help

Who can help? Besides the obvious supervisors, mentors, and coworkers, survey your friends and acquaintances. Don't overlook the people you meet at training seminars or those in your social circle outside work. Talk to others about your dreams and goals and ask them what they might be able to contribute. You'll be surprised at the range of contacts and advice you'll get. Here are some more ideas of ways to network and meet people who might be able to help:

★ Attend courses, workshops, and seminars. Use your agency training budget to develop skills that make you upwardly mobile. Ask your supervisor about an agency-sponsored career-development program that could help you advance in government. Take a few minutes to introduce yourself to the leaders or speakers. They always like to hear positive things about their presentation, and most of them are eager to share additional advice and tips with a participant who is willing to listen.

★ Get involved in professional associations and meetings where people in your desired field or industry hang out. Introduce yourself. Most people are happy to share; we all like a receptive audience. Use the "information interviewing" techniques developed by Richard Bolles in his seminal book *What Color Is Your Parachute?*, which is updated annually.

★ Write letters to people who have achieved what you want to achieve. Many will write back, and some will be happy to advise you.

★ Read government news Web sites (such as www.govexec.com and www.federaldiary.com) and pay attention to articles, people, job titles, agencies, missions, and e-mails. If you read an article about new hiring in your career field, write to the author of the article about how you can get more information on these jobs or this executive. People (even executives) can be very helpful if you e-mail them and tell them you are looking for a good government job.

★ Set a goal to meet one person from a different agency or department each week and ask what the person does. The knowledge you gain will help you in your current job, and the networking will help you seek a future job.

Networking Do's and Don'ts: Project the Right Image

As you expand your social circle and range of contacts during your job search, keep the following tips in mind to ensure that your encounters with others are successful:

★ Remember that you are "on" at all times. Be aware that the way you dress, how well you groom yourself, your speech, and your behavior all have an effect on the impression you make on others. Always be courteous. You never know who is watching.

★ Follow up with the people you meet and let them know that you appreciate their help. Written thank-you notes have all but gone the way of the dinosaur. If you want to really stand out, write them.

★ Keep plenty of business cards and a one-page marketing resume on hand. Make sure these items are professional looking, on good stock paper, and are in good condition. They should never be bent, soiled, or have notes written all over them. The information should be current. If your business

address or phone number has changed, have the cards and resume reprinted. If you have to cross out information to update these items, it might make the recipient wonder whether you keep up-to-date on your other business matters as well.

★ As you go about looking for your next job or career-broadening opportunity, never badmouth your current or former employers or coworkers. Even if your current supervisor is Simon Legree and your coworkers have horns, complaining about their shortcomings will only make you look like a whiner and a gossiper. Take the high road. Say that you appreciate the opportunities and experience your current job provides, but that it is time to broaden your skills and meet important career goals.

As you put together your personal long-range career plan, remember that networking is probably the single most important component of that plan, no matter what your goals are. The more people you know, the more likely it is that you will hear about a vacant job through someone else. Use all your strength: Ask for help.

Know Your Agencies

As you go through the exercise of describing your dream job, the characteristics of that job should help you identify specific agencies that have those types of jobs. For example, if you are interested in the environment, the Environmental Protection Agency and Department of Interior both have missions requiring substantial involvement in environmental protection issues. If you do not know which agencies might have the types of jobs you're interested in, you could spend the first few sessions of your weekly career-strategy planning hour browsing the Office of Personnel Management's (OPM) Web site at www.usajobs.opm.gov. You can find all of the agency Web sites at www.firstgov.gov.

Learning about various government agencies and what they do will help you meet new people, pinpoint various agencies' issues, and ask intelligent questions during job interviews. Reading the daily newspaper, the *Wall Street Journal,* and the *Federal Times* will also help keep you up-to-date on current events and might help you spot employment trends. Read the Federal Diary article at www.washingtonpost.com daily for up-to-date news on agencies, people, and change in government.

As you click through the OPM's Web site, you will notice a category called "What's Hot" that highlights specific issues and "pet" concerns of the current administration. Because the sitting President appoints the heads and senior leaders of virtually every Federal agency, the administration's management agenda always drives what these political appointees will do to promote the President's goals. Federal employees who want to move ahead in their agencies can get valuable information from the What's Hot list. For instance, at press time the President's management agenda for Federal agencies was the following:

> Strategic Management of Human Capital
>
> Competitive Sourcing
>
> Improved Financial Performance
>
> Expanded Electronic Government
>
> Budget and Performance Integration

Understanding these goals, which will be the same for every Federal agency, can help you write your resume, cover letter, and KSAs in a way that addresses these current issues and concerns. What are your target agencies doing, specifically, to implement each of the preceding goals? After you figure out what the agencies are doing and what they still need to do to fulfill these goals, you can present your talents and skills as a solution to their specific problems.

Being Proactive: Eliminating the "Wait-and-See" Mentality

By now, you've figured out that you are in a very unique era in the history of Federal career opportunities, and this is the ideal time to plan how to take advantage of it. What else can you do to move things along in your favor?

While you are planning your next career move, remember the following strategies as you look for your chance to make the transition:

★ Do a good job where you are. If you aren't giving your current job 110 percent, prospective employers will assume that you won't give their job your full effort, either.

★ Be willing to do everything. Supervisors cite an employee's attitude as "90 percent of the reason" they select or promote them.

★ Volunteer for details. They not only broaden your experience, but brand you as a "can-do" team player that managers can count on. With reduced staffing levels in virtually all agencies, your value to the organization goes up automatically if you are willing to take on extra tasks.

★ Emphasize your additional strengths. When applying for other jobs, figure out what needs the agency would fulfill by hiring you. Then present your talents as a solution to their problems.

★ Network with everyone. Establish relationships with human resources professionals and other managers, and not just with colleagues in your own office. People in a strategic network will keep you in mind for vacancies and will keep you informed when they hear about one.

★ Try to make an impact on the bottom line. Recall that one of the administration's current agenda items is "budget and performance integration." Coming up with ways to save money or operate more efficiently will identify you as a problem-solver, a role that is in great demand across almost every job series today. Making your employer look good, in addition to doing a good technical job, is a time-honored way to move ahead quickly.

★ If you need to gain experience on an interim job to get to your ultimate goal job, don't get complacent by staying in the interim job too long. Use it to gain valuable experience to build your resume and develop needed relationships. Then continue to carry out your plan to reach your goal.

★ Search out computerized personality tests or arrange to take one of the more well-known self-assessment indicators such as the Myers-Briggs test to identify your strengths and weaknesses. These tests touch on personal behaviors, attitudes, values, and skills and will help you determine where to concentrate your self-development efforts. Do you need to be more flexible or learn to communicate better? Knowing your strong and not-so-strong suits will help you develop career goals in alignment with your natural talents.

★ Arm yourself with the Federal employment facts! Go to the OPM's Web site, www.opm.gov, and find the Fed Fact Federal Employment Statistics (www.opm.gov/feddata/factbook/index.asp). This online publication contains statistics on government-wide and area-specific employee demographics, compensation, payroll, and so on. The site has a special section on employment trends. Current employment information and trends projected for the next 13 months are included in this report. This report is a great resource for proactive job search efforts.

★ What have you done for yourself lately? Your own personal development, continuing education, and technical training are some of the most important career strategy factors over which you have direct control. You cannot afford to sit back and wait for your agency to provide official training opportunities for you. Get busy and take the initiative! Don't have much money to spare? Go to the OPM's Web site and find the Gov Online Learning Center. This government-wide resource is dedicated to developing the Federal workforce. It provides high-quality e-training products and services—free! Everyone can find a way to develop their knowledge and skills, even if money is an object.

Decide to take control of your career. Develop a workable strategy that takes advantage of the current climate. What initiatives will you work on for one hour a week? Be proactive—in the long run, it pays!

The One-Page Resume: A Networking and Self-Marketing Tool

An important component of your career planning strategy is to design a one-page "calling card" resume that you can use while networking. Informing others of your background, interests, and special talents is a smart way to pre-market yourself for task forces, teams, details, and other career opportunities. The one-page resume is not intended to take the place of a job application or other more serious marketing package, but it does help others remember you when they hear about opportunities you might be interested in. The one-page resume can also be used as a biography or to provide information others might use to introduce you for speeches or other award presentations.

ROBERTA E. SPENCER
124 3rd Street, NE
Washington, DC 20002

Home: (202) 567-8910   Work: (202) 267-9976

PROFILE: **Aviation communications professional** with over 15 years' experience demonstrating organizational skills, award-winning media relations, and development and maintenance of positive relationships among government employees, industry representatives, and academia. Recent assignments include special project involving Pacific region air transportation technology and multiple agency missions. Adept at reviewing, analyzing, and maintaining government and private industry programs, budgets, and collateral materials with international effects.

PROFESSIONAL EXPERIENCE:

Federal Aviation Administration, Washington, DC
Deputy Public Affairs Officer, GS-12/4   1995 - Present
♦ Detail, FAA Civil Aviation Security Office (1995)

Public Affairs Specialist, GS-1035-11/12   1993 - 1995
♦ FAA Aviation Education Program Manager

Department of Defense, The Pentagon, Washington, DC
Assistant Command Historian, GS-9   1991 - 1993

EDUCATION & TRAINING:

B.A., Speech & Communications, University of California- Los Angeles

U.S.D.A. Graduate School, Aviation Executive Leadership Program, 1995 - 1996
• Assistant to FAA's International Liaison Officer for 60 days.
• Assisted the Resident Agent-in-Charge with the U.S. Customs Office for 30 days.

PUBLICATIONS:

Co-author, *Women & Minorities in Aviation in Hawaii,* Hawaii Office of Education   1994
"Aviation Progress in the Pacific," *FAA World*   October 1995
"Safety Basics for the Novice Pilot," *Aviation Education News*   Fall 1994
Our Hawaii, marketing book used worldwide by private corporation in Hawaii   1991
The Air War in the Pacific (Honolulu, Air Force Historical Association)   1991

PROFESSIONAL PRESENTATIONS:

Hawaii Conference on Women and Minorities, National Congress on Aviation & Space Education
Civil Air Patrol Commanders' Call Conference, National Association of Travel Agents

HONORS & AWARDS:

Outstanding Performance Ratings seven consecutive years   1995 - 2002
National Award for Excellence in Aerospace Education, Civil Air Patrol (Brewer Award)   1995
Special Recognition Award from Kauai Council of Girl Scouts in Honolulu, Hawaii   1994
FAA Employee of the Year Award (Category III, GS-12 and above)   1993
Chuck Yeager Regional Award for Excellence in Aerospace Education from Civil Air Patrol   1992
Award of Notable Achievement, Dept. of Defense (**for Completion of History Program**)   1991
Public Relations Society Association Award (for **corporate newsletter**)

A sample one-page resume.

Profile

This is where you have the chance to make a good "first impression" by summarizing your experience and strengths. Give the reader a picture of you in as few sentences as possible—ideally, four to five at most. This is not the place to talk about your interest in a career change or advise that you are "willing to learn new skills."

You are using this resume to inform others of your background and strengths, not to apply for a job. Besides, telling others that you are willing to learn new skills is best done verbally. Stating this in writing gives the impression that you do not have anything definite in mind. A good summary profile statement might include something like this:

> 21 years' experience analyzing employees' training needs and recommending to managers optimal ways to meet those needs. Worked with high-level managers and contractors to co-ordinate formal training courses, select and present material, and provide guidance concerning the best candidates to attend the training. Recognized as a highly effective program coordinator with excellent oral and written presentation skills.

You can tweak this statement to incorporate other skills you might want to emphasize, such as budget management, but try to keep the profile statement to no more than five or six lines in length.

Professional Experience

A simple outline will do here. Include current and past job titles, employers, and dates worked on each job. If you have more than 10 years of experience, combine everything over 10 years old into one statement and summarize it. An exception to this rule would be if you accomplished something so spectacular on an old job that you received special recognition for your initiative.

Education and Training

List all college and graduate degrees. Do not list individual training courses unless they provided you with a unique skill or credential.

Publications

This section highlights written communications skills. List all formal publications regardless of how long ago they were published.

Professional Presentations

Oral communication skills are important in every job. List all formal presentations.

Honors and Awards

List special recognition for unusual accomplishments and give a brief statement describing what you did to earn the award. Combine serial performance awards, such as "Seventeen sustained superior performance awards, 1985–2002." Also, list any private-sector honors and awards if they reflect an individual talent and are relevant to a Federal job, such as winning a Toastmasters contest.

Summary

Strategies for moving up in government can be implemented only if you have a great resume. The next chapter will help you get started with writing your new resume.

CHAPTER 3

Federal Resume-Writing Basics: Getting Started

Since 1995, I've been traveling around the U.S. and Europe training Federal employees to write standout Federal resumes. I always start my workshops with this popular question that helps participants get focused on what they need to learn to write an excellent resume:

What do you want to learn today?

Here are a few of the typical answers:

★ I want to learn how to get started. I'm here to see samples and get motivated.

★ I want to learn how to phrase my experience to maximize my points.

★ I want to apply to the Resumix system with a defense agency and I want to learn how to write better KSAs.

★ I want to use a writing style that will set my resume and KSAs apart.

★ I want to learn the best format for a Federal resume for presenting my qualifications and the most readable format for personnel.

This chapter is dedicated to helping current Federal employees and first-time applicants get started on their resumes. There are many Federal resume writing challenges, but these are the most typical writing projects. Which one applies to you?

★ Converting an OF-612 or SF-171 to a Federal resume

★ Rewriting and focusing your current Federal resume draft

★ Converting a private-industry resume into a Federal resume format and developing new language that supports the Federal job

★ Starting to write a Federal resume from scratch

★ Combining KSA answers into a current Federal resume

Getting into the Mindset for Writing a Better Resume

We all know that the Federal resume and application process is complex, but the rewards are great if you can match your experience to the Federal job and make your application stand out from the pile. Let's review your possible Federal job objectives.

Going for Your "High Three"?

Many Federal employees wait until they are near retirement (three to five years) before they seriously start working on a better Federal resume. The Federal government retirement system pays monthly retirement checks based on the job the employee held in his or her last three years in government. So if the Federal employee has been a GS-10 for the last 10 years, he or she would easily qualify for a GS-11 position. The promotion to GS-11 three years before retirement would probably net the employee an additional $100 per month in retirement pay. This is a motivating resume-writing scenario.

Bored, Underemployed?

Tired of doing the same job day in and day out? Tired of asking for new assignments and projects and not getting them? Are you working under your skill level? Then you need a great new resume and KSA statements. You also need to start seriously looking at vacancy announcements and playing the job search game. Chances are, this job is not going to change. You probably won't be able to get the position reclassified (unless you are really lucky and your supervisor will help you), so you should take control and change jobs!

New Challenges?

Want new challenges? Learn new skills? Work with new customers and programs? Then you should be motivated to write your resume to change your work environment, agency, or office so that you can stay challenged every day. If your current job has become dead-end, mundane, routine, and nothing stands out, you need to change your job. If you need additional education to achieve your job-change goals, begin your additional training while you continually study vacancy announcements and write your resume.

Office Being Reorganized?

Look out for yourself! Many government offices are being reorganized. Between the Homeland Security Department shuffle, privatization studies, base realignment and closures, and everyday reorganization, Federal jobs are in flux more than ever. Keep your eyes and ears open and always have a "Plan B" in case you are reorganized along with the office. Be prepared to look for a new job in case your job disappears.

Want a New Agency, Supervisor, or Location?

Bored with your current agency and supervisor; want to work closer to home; relocate? Then you need to write a great resume and take control of the situation. Make a decision to make the change in a reasonable amount of time and continually apply for new jobs.

Setting Goals? Changing Careers?

Do you have new goals for your career? Have you completed new education and courses? Is it time to move on? Write the best resume you can for your new objectives and continually apply for jobs. It's up to you to make it happen.

Trying to Get Back into Government?

Every Federal application changed dramatically in 1995 when the SF-171 was replaced by the Federal resume and another form called the OF-612. The government is hiring returning Federal employees because of the knowledge, skills, and abilities they bring to the agency. You will need to learn how to write a new Federal resume, focus it toward the jobs you are seeking, and write standout KSAs for both your prior Federal experience and your more recent private-industry experience.

Applying for Your First Federal Job?

The application process for government is so different than in private industry. Each announcement has different instructions for How to Apply, and there are at least two resume formats that can be used to apply—paper and

electronic Federal resumes. The process is complex, but the jobs are truly there! The government is hiring 250,000 people in the next two years, so your investment of time can pay off in an excellent, steady, new job.

 Note: Applying for a new Federal job isn't a simple process. In private industry, you update your two-page resume, write a nice cover letter, and respond to ads. Or you might post your resume on www.monster.com and www.hotjobs.com and wait for e-mails to come in. The Federal application process, however, is a "project," not an application. Once you recognize that applying for a Federal job is an investment of time, you can handle the process better. Searching for a Federal job in a concerted way could take 10 to 20 hours per week.

Five Steps to Getting Started on Your Federal Resume

For some people, getting started with writing their Federal resume is the most difficult part. The samples in this book will help you tremendously. But you will need to gather documents and information so that your Federal resume is accurate and complete.

1. Gather Your Information

Pull together all the following sources of information:

* Your current resume, OF-612, or SF-171
* Past KSAs
* Vacancy announcements—current and past
* Supervisory evaluations
* Training certificates
* Position descriptions
* Letters and e-mails of commendation
* Lists of accomplishments, Yearly Annual Reports

2. Go to the Computer and Find Your File

If you have a resume draft that is usable for updating, rewriting, formatting, and focusing, you should use the resume file you have on hand. If you currently have an OF-612, SF-171, or resume that is old and not usable, you should use the resume samples at the end of this book to serve as a template for writing your Federal resume draft. Resume templates and additional samples are available on The Resume Place's CD-ROM, which you can order online (see the back pages of this book).

3. Look at the Samples in the Appendix

The more you look at the samples in the appendix at the back of this book, the better your resume will be. You can choose various sections, formats, writing styles, and language that can improve your draft. Find a format that you like and use it for your own resume.

4. Start Writing

Following the step-by-step guides in chapters 4 through 15, you can begin to write new content for your resume:

* **Chapter 4, "Vacancy Announcement Search":** You will need to find vacancy announcements for your target jobs and use them to extract the "duties" language, skills, and keywords that the jobs require. You will integrate some of this language into your work experience descriptions.

* **Chapter 5, "Researching Your Core Competencies":** You will discover some basic qualities and values that you can

include in your resume so that you will stand out from the competition. Some popular core competencies are customer service, flexibility, teamwork, problem-solving, using initiative, and communications skills.

★ **Chapter 6, "Presenting Your Educational Background and Training":** Organize your education and training so that the human resources professional can clearly see that you are qualified for the job. Impress the decision-maker with your ability to present, compile, and edit your relevant training.

★ **Chapter 7, "Writing About Your Other Qualifications":** The "other" information can make your resume stand out. If you are active in community service, volunteering, or part-time teaching activities, you might demonstrate skills that a competitor does not have.

★ **Chapter 8, "Writing Your Work Experience":** This is the "meat" of your Federal resume. You will need to write about your duties (truthfully) in order to demonstrate your skills at the next level. Writing your work experience descriptions will take at least 60 percent of the total time you will spend working on your Federal resume. Be prepared to write, edit, and then edit again. This is the most important section of your resume.

★ **Chapter 9, "Plain-Language Resumes—Writing Well":** Be sure to convert all of your passive-voice writing style to active voice. Do not use wording such as "responsible for," "duties include," "other tasks include," "additional duties include," "worked with," "assisted with," or other vague and weak wording in your resume.

★ **Chapter 10, "The Magic of Page 1: Focusing Your Resume Toward an Announcement, Promotion, or New Career":** You can focus each version of your printed Federal resume with a Summary of Qualifications or Profile. This "abstract" of your career can impress the human resources professional in seconds and demonstrate how your experience is relevant to the new position.

★ **Chapter 11, "Putting Together Your Federal Resume Application":** If your resume looks great (the typeface is readable, paragraph lengths are succinct, and white space around the text is adequate), your resume will keep the human resources staff's attention a few seconds longer—hopefully impressing them enough to put it in the "best qualified" pile.

★ **Chapter 12, "Electronic Resume Writing":** Learn the format differences and the importance of knowing your skills and the right keywords for your target job.

★ **Chapter 14, "Boosting Your Employment Chances with Great KSAs":** KSA writing will no longer be a mystery after you read this chapter. Look at samples and write about your best examples and projects that demonstrate your knowledge, skills, and abilities.

★ **Chapter 15, "Cover Letters with a Mission":** Summarizing your relevant experience and skills could make your application package stand out to a selecting official.

5. Study Vacancy Announcements

You have to continually research, analyze, and study the vacancy announcements for the jobs, locations, grade level, duties, and deadlines that are right for you. This will take some time, but it is critical to the process. Chapter 4 gives you more insight into the important elements of vacancy announcements so that you can create well-developed resumes that will be successful in the application process.

Information That Must Be Included on Your Federal Resume

Many private-industry applicants submit their private-industry resumes thinking that a "resume" is the same as a "Federal resume." This is not true. It's important to recognize that certain information should be included in your Federal resume that you would not include on a private-sector resume. The human resources professionals need to see certain information as required by the Office of Management and Budget. The Federal resume is a transition from a lengthy, detailed application form and still includes some specific personnel information required on the earlier form.

The list of what to include is simple, but if you do not include information such as your Social Security number, you might not be considered for the job. You can see the list of "what to include" in the following vacancy announcement. Always look for the How to Apply section in the announcement so that you will know exactly what is needed for each application.

Here is an excerpt from a USAJOBS vacancy announcement for the National Archives and Records Administration, which demonstrates the types of extra information you will be required to include on your Federal resume:

Vacancy Announcement Number: CP-03-012B

Opening Date: 12/13/xxxx

Closing Date: 01/17/xxxx

Position: Lead Management and Program Analyst GS-0343-13/14

Salary: $80,690 - $104,900 per year

Promotional Potential: GS-14

Duty Location: 1 vacancy at College Park, MD

HOW TO APPLY: You may apply on

- Resume, Optional Form 612, Optional Application for Federal Employment, or

- Any other written format. (Standard Form 171 is obsolete but is acceptable.)

Your application must include:

Job Information

- Announcement number and position title and grade(s)

Personal Information

- Full name and Social Security number

- Mailing address and day and evening phone numbers

- Country of citizenship (U.S. citizenship is required)

- Veterans' preference

- Highest Federal civilian grade held (also include job series and dates at that grade)

Work Experience

For each period of paid and nonpaid work experiences related to the job you are applying for, provide:

- Job title (include series and grade for Federal jobs)

- Duties and accomplishments

- Employer's name and address

- Supervisor's name and phone number

- Starting and ending dates (month/year)

- Hours per week

- Salary

- Indicate if we may contact your supervisor

Education

- High school (name and address, date of diploma or GED)

- Colleges or universities (name and address, majors, type and year of degree)

- If no degree, show total credits earned and whether semester or quarter hours

Other Qualifications

- Job-related training courses (title and year)

- Job-related skills (language skills, computer skills, tools, machinery, typing speed)

- Job-related honors, awards, special accomplishments (publications, memberships in professional or honor societies, leadership activities)

The First Two Sections of a Federal Resume

The most effective way for you to build your Federal resume is section by section, without consideration for length. Later you will edit, rewrite, focus, and format the material. We'll start with the first two sections, job information and personal information. Later chapters will step you through the other sections of the resume.

Job Information

Recall this text from the preceding vacancy announcement:

Job Information

- Announcement number and position title and grade(s)

Every Federal resume must include information about the job for which you're applying. Use the job title listed in the announcement as your Objective. You should include the vacancy announcement information on every page of your application, which could include the Federal resume, KSAs, supervisory evaluation, and other documents they request.

"Grade" is the job's level of difficulty. If the job announcement specifies several grades (for example, GS-13/14), indicate only the highest grade(s) you are seeking. Read the "Qualifications" section of the announcement to determine the grade for which you best qualify.

If you are not sure and would like to be considered for both grades, send in two separate packages, one for the GS-13 and one for the GS-14.

Thus, your Objective statements will look like this:

Objective: Lead Management and Program Analyst, GS-0343-13
Objective: Lead Management and Program Analyst, GS-0343-14

Personal Information

The vacancy announcement requests the following personal information:

Personal Information

- Full name and Social Security number

- Mailing address and day and evening phone numbers

- Country of citizenship (U.S. citizenship is required)

- Veterans' preference

- Highest Federal civilian grade held (also include job series and dates at that grade)

The preceding personal information is required on all Federal resumes. You will be impressed with how outstanding your personal information can look when you use white space, professional-looking fonts, and headline type size for your name. This is the first impression you will make on the human resources professionals, so select an appealing format.

Private-industry resume writers have always enjoyed the opportunity to create standout resumes, which starts with personal information at the top. Resume experts believe that a resume's appearance can make a difference in hiring and can build your personal confidence about the job search. HR professionals will appreciate your professional presentation.

 Note: If you are a novice Federal applicant, you might be surprised by the additional information required for the Federal resume. You might think that this information will clutter your resume. But you will need to include all of the required information if you want to be a serious candidate for a Federal job.

Contact Information

Include your full name, mailing address, and day and evening phone numbers. You can also include your e-mail address at home or work (preferably at home for Federal employees).

 Note: In some agencies, your office e-mail is considered government property, similar to government postage, letterhead, fax, and envelopes. Do not use government property for job applications, or your resume will be rejected.

Social Security Number

Most vacancy announcements require this. Sometimes, however, it is not required. Read your announcement carefully.

Country of Citizenship

Most Federal jobs require United States citizenship. If you are not a U.S. citizen, give your country of citizenship.

Federal Civilian Status/Reinstatement Eligibility

Were you ever a Federal civilian employee? If yes, write your highest civilian grade and give the job series, the grade level, and the dates you held that grade. Be sure to write the highest grade held, not the current or last grade. Here's an explanation of Federal civilian personnel terms:

★ *Reinstatement eligibility for current and former Federal employees* means that you are eligible for reinstatement based on career or career-conditional Federal status. If you are eligible for reinstatement, attach Standard Form 50 as proof if the announcement requires it.

★ *Status* means that you are currently in a Federal civilian job, or you formerly held a Federal job and you might be reinstated or rehired without competing again.

★ *Career-conditional* is the initial appointment and leads to a permanent or "career" position after three years of satisfactory service.

Read the job announcement carefully to determine whether the position is open to anyone or only to candidates with status. Sometimes the announcement will say "area of consideration" is "nationwide." In this case, the job is open to both status and nonstatus applicants.

For example, if you are a current or former Federal employee, write the following:

Federal Civilian Status: Writer-Editor, GS-301, 11/9, April 1993 to present

If you are not a current Federal employee or are a former Federal employee with no Federal status, write the following:

Federal Civilian Status: N/A

If you are a former Federal employee with reinstatement rights, write the following:

> **Federal Civilian Status:** Program Analyst, GS-301, 12/10, April 1999 to May 2001

Veterans' Preference

Do you claim veterans' preference? If you have never been in the military, write "N/A" and leave the section at the top of the resume, so that Federal HR professionals will not look for military experience. If the answer is yes, write the name of military service, dates, rank, and if you were honorably discharged.

Example if the answer is yes:

> **Veterans' Preference:** 5-point preference, U.S. Army, Sergeant, April 1991–April 1995, Honorably Discharged.

Example if the answer is no:

> **Veterans' Preference:** N/A

Generally, 5 points will be added to your application evaluation rating if you were honorably discharged and served during a war; during the period of April 28, 1952, through July 1, 1955; during the Gulf War from August 2, 1990, through January 2, 1992; or in a campaign or expedition for which a campaign medal was authorized (for example, Lebanon, Kosovo, Somalia, or Haiti). Ten points are added if you have a compensable service-connected disability of at least 10 percent, and in some cases if you are a spouse, widow, widower, or mother of a disabled veteran. If you claim 5 points, attach your DD-214 form or other proof. If you claim 10 points, attach an Application for 10-Point Veterans' Preference (SF-15) and required proof.

Also write one of the following if they are applicable to you:

- ★ 5-point preference based on active duty in the U.S. Armed Forces.
- ★ 10-point preference for noncompensable disability or a Purple Heart.
- ★ 10-point preference based on a compensable service-connected disability of more than 10, but less than 30, percent.
- ★ 10-point preference based on wife, widow, or widower preference.
- ★ 10-point preference based on a compensable service-connected disability of 30 percent or more.

How the Points Help Veterans Get Federal Jobs

Veterans who meet the criteria for preference and who are found eligible (by achieving a score of 70 or higher either by a written examination or an evaluation of their experience and education) will have 5 or 10 points added to their numerical ratings depending on the nature of their preference. For scientific and professional positions in grade GS-9 or higher, names of all eligible candidates are listed in order of ratings, augmented by veterans' preference, if any. For other positions, the names of 10-point-preference–eligible candidates who have a compensable, service-connected disability of 10 percent or more are placed ahead of the names of all other eligible candidates on a given register. The names of other 10-point-preference–eligibles, 5-point-preference–eligibles, and nonveterans are listed in order of their numerical ratings. More information on Veterans' Preference and Employment Programs can be found on the OPM's Web site at www.usajobs.opm.gov/b2a.htm.

You will see examples of how to organize and present your reinstatement eligibility and veterans' preference in the samples that follow. The statements you will write on your resume are much simpler than the explanations just given.

Job and Personal Information Samples

Here are three examples of how to format the job information and personal information sections.

Example 1

RUTH M. MONAHAN

3398 N. Fuller Drive

Eden, UT 84310

Home: (801) 735-1031 Office: (801) 625-5112

rmonahan@fs.fed.us

Social Security No.: 000-00-0000

Veterans' Status: None

Citizenship: United States

Federal Status: District Ranger, Ogden Ranger District, Wasatch-Cache National Forest, GS-0340-13, July 1996 to Present

Example 2

Francis Eugene Johnson

908 Queens Terrace

Fort Washington, MD 20744

Email: francis_joh@msn.com   Cell: 240-381-9227

SSN: 000-00-0000   United States Citizen

Highest Federal Grade: N/A   Veterans' Preference: N/A

Example 3

Meryl A. Sylvester

P.O. Box 270106

West Hartford, Connecticut 06127

Home (860) 561-8966 • Work (860) 713-6199

e-mail: Mlibas@aol.com

Social Security No.: 000-00-0000

Citizenship: United States of America

Veterans' Preference: 10 Points

Federal Status: N/A

Summary

You're off to a good start on your Federal resume. In the next chapter, you will research vacancy announcements so that you can target your resume content and presentation toward particular positions.

CHAPTER 4

Vacancy Announcement Search

Serious Federal job seekers look for great announcements continuously. Using the Internet, you can find Federal jobs within minutes of them being posted from any computer at home, at work, or in a library or career center. To save time, you can sign up for automatic e-mail notifications from some Web sites by setting up a specific Federal job search profile of the job you are seeking. This will save you time. But you might still want to search for your own announcements because job titles don't always reflect the duties of the job. You will become more familiar with the job titles as you read the announcements. A serious job seeker can spend two to five hours per week reading Federal vacancy announcements.

Step 1: Find Vacancy Announcements

You can find most Federal vacancy announcements at the following Web sites. All jobs are posted on these Web sites, including jobs for the Army, Navy and Air Force, which also have their own Web sites and job listings.

www.usajobs.opm.gov—The official Office of Personnel Management Web site

www.fedworld.gov/jobs/jobsearch.html—Federal agency jobs Web site

The following sections detail some of the other places you can find Federal vacancy announcements.

Agency Web Sites

Most agencies list their jobs at their own Web sites, as well as at www.usajobs.opm.gov. If you have targeted a specific agency, such as the Internal Revenue Service, it would be much faster to search for jobs at www.irs.gov than at the OPM's main site. Or if you wanted a job at the National Institutes of Health, you could go directly to www.nih.gov. The agency Web sites are sometimes easier to read, understand, and locate than the main site. If the agency Web site sends you back to the OPM's Web site, that means the agency doesn't post its job listings on its own site.

Private Industry Federal Job Sites

You can find Federal jobs at privately owned and operated databases as well. These cost a few dollars for membership and access, but the databases are nicely managed so that you might be able to find specific jobs faster than on other Web sites:

www.federaljobsearch.com

www.fedjobs.com

Commercial Web Sites

You can find Federal jobs at large database Web sites as well. The www.monster.com Web site lists the Transportation Security Administration jobs for government. Commercial sites will be carrying more Federal vacancy announcements in the coming years. The two best places to look are

> www.monster.com
>
> www.washingtonpost.com

Civilian Job Listings with Defense and Military Agencies

Looking for a job as a civilian on a military base? You don't have to join the military service to work as a civilian in a Department of Defense agency. You can look for job announcements at each of the following Web pages:

> **Navy/Marines:** www.donhr.navy.mil
>
> **Army:** www.cpol.army.mil
>
> **Air Force:** www.afpc.randolph.af.mil/ (click on CIVILIAN, and then scroll down to Job Announcements and Job Kit)
>
> **Department of Defense:** www.defenselink.mil/
>
> **Defense Logistics Agency/Defense Contract Management Agency:** www.dla.mil

Department of Homeland Security

Looking for a job in the new Department of Homeland Security? Look for jobs at www.dhs.gov for the various agencies combined into the new department. Other Homeland Security jobs and information can be found at these Web sites:

> www.whitehouse.org/homeland/index.asp
>
> www.usda.gov/homelandsecurity/ homeland.html
>
> www.homelandsecurity.org/
>
> www.dhs.gov/employees/
>
> www.govexec.com/homeland/

Be sure to read as much as you can about the new and ever-changing Homeland Security Department so that you can write your resume and prepare for an interview based on the latest information.

Other Sources

Other ways to find out about Federal jobs include the following.

Newspaper Ads

In the Washington, D.C., area, the *Washington Post* lists positions almost every Sunday. Major metropolitan papers in other areas of dense Federal employment do, too.

Professional Journals

Jobs that require highly specialized skills such as nursing, banking, data processing, and technical writing can sometimes be found in publications of professional associations.

Job Fairs

Government agencies sometimes hold or send representatives to job fairs. Bring your Federal resume and be prepared to talk about your experiences and skills that could be valuable in a government job.

Your Network

Do you know someone who works in government? What agency does this person work for? What is this person's job? Is this individual's agency growing or downsizing? Is it hiring? What kinds of people does the agency hire? How can you apply? Does the person you know have any clout with hiring managers? These are the questions you should ask your neighbor, golf partner, and fellow churchgoer. This person's agency might be adding a new program where it needs to hire more program managers, contract specialists, and computer specialists. This person might not know that you would like to work for the government and that you have expertise in a particular area. Network. Meet and talk with as many people as you can. You never know where you'll find a good lead.

Federal employees and others will tell you that your network is very important. Think long range. Listen for new programs and initiatives, especially those that will require specialized technical skills.

Reading, Listening to the News, and Keeping Your Eyes Open

Read Federal newspapers, union newsletters, the Federal page in your newspaper if it has one, the Federal pages in the *Washington Post* (available online at www.washingtonpost.com), and *Government Executive Magazine* (also available online at www.govexec.com) to stay on top of what's going on in government. You might see that a Federal agency is relocating to your town or that an agency is taking on new duties. Like private-sector corporations, government organizations relocate, grow, expand, and change functions. By being aware of these changes, you can position yourself to take advantage of job opportunities that the changes might bring about. When an imminent relocation or new program is announced, you might find that you have as much as six months or a year to master or expand technical skills of interest to that potential employer. Find out what skills will be needed. Enroll in a course or technical training to make yourself more attractive. Then, when the job openings are announced, you will be ready.

Step 2: Analyze the Vacancy Announcement

Once you have found a job opportunity that interests you, save or print the vacancy announcement for thorough study. Don't be intimidated by the length and look of the announcement. We'll teach you how to discover the important information in the announcement and what the various sections mean.

Get ready for a challenge. Federal agency human resources offices can choose the announcement format, writing style, instructions on How to Apply, and what to submit as an application. Therefore, most announcements require different application packages. This chapter gives examples of and analyzes five of the most typical announcement formats:

1. A "paper Federal resume and KSA announcement" from an agency that is not automated. Some agencies do not yet have an electronic database; however, more and more agencies are converting to electronic databases. This format might disappear in the next two to five years.

2. A Resumix™ announcement with a supplemental data sheet from the Army. The Army, Navy, Marines, and Air Force use Resumix announcements. NASA and other agencies are also beginning to use Resumix. There are two types of Resumix announcements:

   ☆ OPEN CONTINUOUS
   ☆ SPECIAL HIRING with a specific closing date

3. A Quickhire™ announcement from the Department of the Interior. Quickhire's distinctive format requires the applicant to submit a resume online and answer a 30- to 50-question questionnaire.

4. A USAJOBS announcement that requires a Federal resume submitted by paper (mail), fax, or e-mail. This announcement format also asks for answers to an in-depth questionnaire.

5. Specific agency application process. In this chapter we include a sample of this type that is from the Department of Commerce's COOL Web site. The National Institutes of Health has its own Web site and online resume form (resume builder) as well.

A "Paper Federal Resume and KSA Announcement"

This is a long announcement, but it's well worth reading. This is an Army Fellows announcement (career development opportunity) that requires a paper Federal resume (they will accept an OF-612). This is an excellent opportunity to start with a GS-7 position and grow to a GS-13 position within a specific amount of time after rotational training and mentoring. This is a real announcement opportunity that opens every year. You should write a cover letter with this application as well, stating why you would like to be in this program.

Vacancy Announcement No.: AMC02-01

Opening Date: July 29, 2002

Closing Date: September 30, 2002

Position Title (Pay Plan-Series): AMC FELLOWS (GS-0301)

Grade: 07

Full Performance Grade: 13

Comments   Multiple vacancies will be filled from this vacancy announcement.

THE AMC FELLOWS CHOICE IS:

A CAREER THAT MAKES A DIFFERENCE

The Army Material Command (AMC) is the Army's premier provider of total force materiel readiness technology, acquisition support, materiel development, logistics power projection, and sustainment. As the place in the Army where technology, acquisition, and logistics are integrated to assure readiness for today and tomorrow, AMC is heavily involved in making the Army more responsive, agile, versatile, and sustainable. From beans to bullets, helmets to helicopters, spare parts to spare ribs, AMC does it all.

The AMC Talent Search:

The AMC Fellows Program is looking for at least 50 candidates who possess the competence, motivation, and enthusiasm to participate in a five-year comprehensive management training program focused on the organization's three core competencies: Logistical Power Projection, Acquisition Excellence, and Technology Generation. AMC professionals are dedicated to supporting the mission by delivering world-class business management and technological solutions and services within every aspect of the organizational mission. The five-year Fellows Program starts at the GS-7 level with a target level of GS-13.

Learn While You Earn:

The three pillars of the AMC Fellows Program are: (1) full-time permanent, full salaried, Federal civilian employment, (2) graduate school opportunities, and (3) rotational assignments. The five-year program offers a truly rewarding opportunity through a focused and experiential learning program associated with competency-building development ranging from business systems thinking to management/leadership principles to emerging technologies.

Are you interested? Additional information about the AMC Fellows Program can be found on the following Web site: www.amcareers.army.mil.

*** A RECRUITMENT BONUS IS AUTHORIZED AND MAY BE OFFERED. ***

EARLY SUBMISSION OF APPLICATIONS IS STRONGLY SUGGESTED. IF A SIGNIFICANT NUMBER IS RECEIVED, THIS ANNOUNCEMENT MAY BE AMENDED TO CLOSE EARLIER.

Salary: $30,597 up to $39,779 per Annum (salary includes a 8.64% locality payment)

Region: Northeast

Organization: U.S. ARMY MATERIEL COMMAND

DEPUTY CHIEF OF STAFF, AMC FELLOWS PROGRAM. ALEXANDRIA, VA

Duty Station:

FIRST DUTY STATION LOCATION: AMC LOGISTICS LEADERSHIP CENTER RED RIVER ARMY DEPOT, TEXARKANA, TEXAS

Area of Consideration: OPEN TO ALL US CITIZENS

Duties: Serves as an Army Material Command (AMC) Fellow. The program is a five-year fellowship comprising formal core training, mentoring and leader development, and functional training in two of the following specialty areas: Supply; Contracting; Quality and Reliability Assurance; Engineering and Science (Non-Construction); Materiel Maintenance; and Information Technology.

Qualification Requirements:

OUTSTANDING SCHOLAR PROGRAM:

BASIC REQUIREMENT: Bachelor's degree; a college graduate that has maintained a Grade Point Average (GPA) of 3.45 or better on a 4.0 scale for undergraduate course work completed.

HOW TO APPLY:

Submit the following documents:

1. OF-612, Optional Application for Federal Employment (this form can be found at www.opm.gov/forms/word/of612.doc), or a Resume. The resume may be typed or legibly handwritten and must contain, at a minimum: Announcement Number; Name; Address; Social Security Number; Position Title and Grade of the job you are applying for; Grade Point Average (GPA).

2. College Transcripts.

WHERE TO SUBMIT YOUR PACKAGE:

Please send all required application materials to:

Northeast CPOC, 314 Johnson Street

ATTN: Division 3, Branch J (A. Banks-Jones)

Aberdeen Proving Ground, MD 21005-5283

Applications may be faxed with a cover sheet (to include your name, announcement number, and ATTN: A. BANKS-JONES) to 410 306-0093.

Navy Resumix Open Continuous Announcement

To apply for this job, you would need to submit an electronic resume format into the Navy's Resume Builder (see the How to Apply section for details on how to do this). The closing date is indefinite because the Southeast region is building a database of candidates. You would submit your resume to the Southeast region for this announcement. This is a real announcement. People are hired from the open continuous announcements every day.

Job Opportunity Announcement

Announcement Number: SE1102

Announcement Date: 2/14/2000

Title: CONTRACTING

Pay Plan: GS,DEMO

Series: 1102

Grade: Multiple Grades

Opening Date: 2/14/2000

Closing Date: INDEFINITE

Location: Southeast Geographic Area, Various locations serviced by HRSCSE.

Area of Consideration: The Human Resources Service Center Southeast (HRSCSE) is soliciting resumes to fill current and/or future vacancies in this occupational series. The HRSCSE utilizes an automated inventory referral system that requires the submission of a resume and an Additional Data Sheet in the formats described in the How to Apply section of this announcement. As vacancies occur, resumes will be considered in accordance with the designated recruitment methods, the areas of consideration, and the information provided in the resumes and in the Additional Data Sheets. Who May Apply: Visit www.donhr.navy.mil/Jobs/CategoryDefinitions.asp for a list of definitions on the following hiring categories.

Duties: This series includes positions that manage, supervise, perform, or develop policies and procedures for professional work involving the procurement of supplies, services, construction, or research and development using formal advertising or negotiation procedures; the evaluation of contract price proposals; and the administration or termination and close out of contracts. The work requires knowledge of the legislation, regulations, and methods used in contracting; and knowledge of business and industry practices, sources of supply, cost factor, and requirements characteristics.

How to Apply: PLEASE VISIT OUR WEB PAGE AT www.donhr.navy.mil/HRSC/southeast/localnews.htm for additional information and helpful tips on applying for positions serviced by the Human Resources Service Center SE.

If you have a current up-to-date resume and Additional Data Sheet on file with the Human Resources Service Center Southeast, you may request that it be used to apply for this position by using the APPLICATION EXPRESS button located at the bottom of this announcement. Your most recent resume on record is the resume that will be used for consideration under Application Express.

To prepare your resume, follow the guidelines provided in the Job Application Information for Civilian Positions (Job Kit). To obtain the Job Kit, you may access our Web site at www.donhr.navy.mil/Jobs/JobKit.asp or contact your local personnel office. Faxed resumes will not be accepted. Failure to submit all information and the Additional Data Sheet will result in non-consideration for this vacancy. Resumes will expire one (1) year from the date of receipt in the HRSCSE office.

Evaluation Method: Resumes are evaluated by an automated system (Resumix) that matches the skills extracted from the candidate's resume to the skills identified for the position. In addition, other requirements (i.e., time in grade, education, area of consideration, specialized experience, etc.) must be met to determine the qualified candidates referred to the Selecting Official.

Navy Resumix Announcement for Special Hire (with a Closing Date)

This announcement has a more-detailed "duties" section that reflects this specific job. It also includes the KSAs that should be covered in the resume. You would follow the directions in order to apply online by submitting your resume into the Southeast region database. If your resume is already in the database, you would apply through Application Express.

Announcement Number: SE-03-MKKAP90180-DE

Announcement Date: 12/30/2002

Title: ELECTRICAL ENGINEER, CAREER/CAREER CONDITIONAL

Pay Plan: GS

Series: 0850

Grade: 12, ($56,659 – $72,112 PER ANNUM)

Opening Date: 12/31/2002

Closing Date: 01/07/2003

Location: PARRIS ISLAND, SOUTH CAROLINA

Area of Consideration: Open to all US citizens. Priority consideration will be given to Interagency Career Transition Assistance Plan (ICTAP) applicants who meet advertised requirements.

Relocation expenses will not be paid.

Duties: This position is located at the Installation and Logistics Department, Public Works Division, Design Branch, Marine Corps Recruit Depot, Parris Island, South Carolina. The primary purpose of this position is the performance of electrical engineering services for the direction, control, and appraisal of the planning, design, development, construction, alteration, cost estimates, and inspection of buildings, grounds, and facilities. As the Engineer in Charge (EIC) for design or other engineering services, the employee performs administrative and technical project management. As EIC for projects performed in-house, ensures that the siting and concepts planning are compatible with the activity master plan.

How to Apply: Electronic resumes and additional data sheet must be received no later than midnight Central Standard Time on the closing date of the announcement to receive consideration. Hardcopy resumes submitted in accordance with http://www.donhr.navy.mil/jobs/hardcopyresume.asp must be postmarked by the closing date.

Evaluation Method: Applicants who meet the Office of Personnel Management's basic eligibility requirements will have their resumes further evaluated based on a comparison of the knowledge, skills, and abilities of the position against the quality and extent of the information reflected in their resume. Direct Inquires to: For additional information you may contact Kimberly Perkins at: HRSC SE REGION

Code 52

9110 Leonard Kimble Road

Stennis Space Center, MS 39522

(877) 854-3461/3462

Resumes mailed using government postage and/or internal Federal government mail systems are in violation of agency and postal regulations and will not be accepted.

(continues)

(continued)

Knowledge, Skills, and Abilities: Applicants should include sufficient information in their resume under work experience that demonstrates their experience, knowledge, skill, training, and/or education in the following (ADD KSAPs).

1. Professional knowledge of electrical engineering concepts, principles, and practices applicable to the full range of duties concerned with the design, layout, and construction of facilities structures such as multi-story office buildings, steam plants, hospitals, industrial type shops, and recreation facilities normally found on military installations, and extensive knowledge of high voltage and major commercial renovation projects.

2. Knowledge of practices, policies, and procedures of related functional and administrative activities to include contract administration, engineering, procurement, construction, and skills in effective coordination of plans and programs with these activities.

3. Ability to communicate effectively with individuals and groups representing diverse interests and points of view.

A Quickhire Announcement by the Department of the Interior Minerals Management Service

Quickhire's distinctive format requires the applicant to submit a resume online and answer a 30- to 50-question questionnaire. This announcement was edited for this publication. The information left here pertains to the application instructions and job description. The announcement lists knowledge, skills, and abilities that should be covered in the resume. You would not write separate KSAs. The applicants will self-certify their qualifications to the 23 questions. The applicant will be asked to write one essay within the 23 questions. This essay should be similar to a KSA narrative, only shorter (two or three paragraphs; 500 words).

INFORMATION TECHNOLOGY SPECIALIST (SECURITY) GS-2210-13/14

Salary Range: $66,229.00 — 101,742.00, ANNUAL

Series & Grade: GS-2210-13/14

Closing Date: Jan 15, 2003

Hiring Agency: DEPARTMENT OF THE INTERIOR

Office of the Secretary of the Interior

Minerals Management Service

Who May Apply: Open to Everyone

Position Information: Full Time, Permanent

Duty Locations: 1 vacancy Washington DC Metro, DC

Announcement Number: OS-DA-3-0016

DEU COMPETITIVE EXAMINING VACANCY ANNOUNCEMENT

The Department of the Interior is the Nation's principal conservation agency with responsibility for most of our nationally owned public lands and natural and cultural resources.

MAJOR DUTIES: The U.S. Department of the Interior, Chief Information Officer is responsible for providing direction and leadership for the Interior-wide Information Resources Management (IRM) Program through a highly functioning and customer service–oriented office that supports the mission and goals of the Department in the most secure, effective, and efficient manner. The selectee serves as a member of the Departmental Information Technology Security Staff, Office of the Chief Information Officer.

KNOWLEDGE, SKILLS, AND ABILITIES (KSAs): If you meet the basic eligibility requirements, you will be rated and ranked on the knowledge, skills, and abilities (KSAs) required to perform the duties of the position. The following KSAs have been identified as being important to the performance of this position. The occupational questions shown on the automated application system have been designed to measure your knowledge, skills, and abilities in relation to this position. See How to Apply for further instructions.

1. Knowledge of state-of-the-art ADP/telecommunications and related IRM Technology. (MANDATORY)

(This knowledge is required in order to ensure information systems reliability and accessibility and to prevent and defend against unauthorized access to systems, networks, and data. He/she will also participate in network and systems design to ensure implementation of appropriate systems security policies.)

2. Knowledge of information security standards, principles, and policies. (This knowledge is required in order to ensure that the delivery of all IT services comply with information security policies, principles, and practices. He/she will also be aware of any current developments in information technology security.)

3. Ability to conduct training related to IT security. (The incumbent will conduct security training to foster institutionalized awareness of security programs and accepted security practices.)

4. Ability to resolve IT security problems, analyze alternatives, and recommend solutions. (The incumbent provides technical advice, guidance, and recommendations to management and other technical specialists on critical IT security issues.)

5. Ability to communicate interpersonally (both orally and in writing). (The incumbent has frequent personal contacts with all levels of management in both headquarters and data processing centers in the field. These include information users, computer technicians, contract specialists, and bureau managers.)

BASIS FOR RATING: Ratings will be based on responses to the **occupational questions** listed under How to Apply. Please follow all instructions carefully. Errors or omissions may affect your score. Qualified candidates will be assigned a score between 70 and 100 not including points that may be assigned for veterans' preference.

PLEASE NOTE: Your answers will be **verified against information provided in your application or by reference checks**.

HOW TO APPLY: To apply for this position, click on the link. You must submit your resume and responses to the questionnaire through the automated system.

https://jobs.quickhire.com/scripts/qhwebfed35mms.exe

A Quickhire Announcement by the Department of Interior That Requires an Electronic Resume and Rates Your Skill Level by Asking Task Questions

INFORMATION TECHNOLOGY SPECIALIST (SECURITY) GS-2210-13/14

Salary Range: $66,229.00–101,742.00, ANNUAL

Series & Grade: GS-2210-13/14

Open Period ends: Jan 15, 2003

Hiring Agency: DEPARTMENT OF THE INTERIOR

Office of the Secretary of the Interior

This is a PREVIEW ONLY! To apply for the vacancy you will answer the questions online.

Job Specific Questions

Grade: 14

To qualify for this position you must meet the Qualification Requirements defined on the vacancy announcement.

Select the statement that closely matches your specialized experience for the GS-14 grade.

1. I have at least one year of specialized experience, in a senior level role, performing or advising management of the analysis, evaluation, implementation and modification of Information Technology Security.

2. I have some of the specialized experience stated above but not quite one full year.

3. I have some experience participating in defining IT security requirements, and I have participated in the implementation and support of IT security applications.

4. I do not have specialized experience as defined on the vacancy announcement.

Rate yourself on the following task statements. Please remember that your answers will be verified against information provided in your application or by reference checks. Be sure that your application materials clearly support your responses to the following questions by addressing specific aspects of your experience or education relevant to this position. If you exaggerate or falsify your experience and/or education, you may be removed from employment consideration or your responses may be adjusted to reflect a more accurate description of your qualifications. You should make a fair and accurate assessment of your qualifications.

1. Development of advanced policies relating to IT security. (7)

I have not had education, training, or experience in performing this task.

I have had education or training in performing this task, but have not yet performed it on the job.

I have performed this task on the job at some point in my career.

I currently perform this task on the job, and it has been a regular and recurring duty for at least 12 consecutive months.

I currently perform this task on the job, it has been a regular and recurring duty for at least 12 consecutive months, and I have provided advice or input to other specialists. (If you choose this level, your resume must clearly reflect this level.)

2. Development of advanced procedures relating to IT security.

On the announcement, you would select one of the five selections from above and for each question that follows:

3. Provide technical advice on IT security operations.

4. Ensure the application of information security policies in the delivery of all IT services.

5. Responsible for ensuring the design of network and security systems comply with system security policies.

6. Responsible for the implementation and modification of ADP/telecommunications equipment and systems.

7. Perform troubleshooting on ADP/telecommunications equipment and systems.

8. Conduct system security audits.

9. Conduct security training to foster institutionalized awareness of a security program.

10. Development of procedures related to IT Security training.

11. Responsible for overseeing evaluations on IT Security Training.

A USAJOBS Announcement

The Office of Personnel Management manages some mass recruitments for Federal agencies. The OPM uses its own www.usajobs.opm.gov online Resume Builder plus questionnaire. The questionnaire can consist of up to 148 questions. You will self-certify again, answer Yes and No, and write essays in response to these questions. The Resume Builder on the www.usajobs.opm.gov Web site is not the only resume database for Federal jobs. Each agency maintains its own database. For instance, the Army, Navy, and Air Force have their own separate databases. The USDA hired many of these employees for 141 cities in 2003 because of new Homeland Security inspections.

PLANT PROTECTION AND QUARANTINE OFFICER

Salary Range: $22,737.00 — 36,615.00, ANNUAL

Series & Grade: GS-0436-05/07

Open Period ends: INDEFINITE

Hiring Agency: DEPARTMENT OF AGRICULTURE (USDA)

                    USDA, Animal & Plant Health Inspection Srvc

Who May Apply: Open to Everyone

Position Information: Full Time, Permanent

Duty Locations: MANY vacancies NATIONWIDE, US

Announcement Number: CH-155851-PPQ

CHICAGO SERVICE CENTER

VACANCY ANNOUNCEMENT

VACANCY IDENTIFICATION NUMBER: CH155851

(continues)

(continued)

OPENING DATE: Sep 16, 2002

CLOSING DATE: Indefinite

POSITION: PLANT PROTECTION AND QUARANTINE OFFICER, GS-0436-05 /07

SALARY:

GS-5: $22, 737 — $29,559 per year depending on the location of the position.

GS-7: $28,164 — $36,615 per year depending on the location of the position.

LOCATION(S):

PPQ Officer positions are located in 141 locations throughout the U.S., including Hawaii, Alaska, Guam, Puerto Rico and the U.S. Virgin Islands. For more information on vacancy locations, please see our PPQ recruitment Web site:

www.aphis.usda.gov/ppq/recruitment/openings

DESCRIPTION OF WORK and WORK ENVIRONMENT: Plant Protection and Quarantine Officers work to prevent the entry, establishment and spread of foreign plant pests in the United States and suppress periodic outbreaks of certain native pests. The work involves inspection, survey and detection, regulatory and eradication or control activities. Inspects ships, aircraft, vehicles, cargo, railways cars, mail, baggage, plants, plant products and miscellaneous articles for restricted or prohibited agricultural commodities, animal products and animal byproducts, and pests that may be dangerous to the nation's agriculture.

Plant Protection and Quarantine Canine Officers use detector dogs to inspect ships, aircraft, vehicles, passengers, railway cars, mail, baggage, plants and animal byproducts, etc., for restricted or prohibited agricultural commodities, animal byproducts and pests that may be dangerous to the nation's agriculture.

HOW TO APPLY:

Your application will consist of three components.

STEP ONE:

Complete and submit the Occupational Questionnaire:

To submit your answers online, you may start by clicking on the following link.

Online Application

Instructions for answering the questions in the Occupational Questionnaire:

Please use the following step-by-step instructions as a guide to filling out the required questionnaire. You will need to print the vacancy announcement and refer to it as you answer the questions. You may omit any optional information; however, you must provide responses to all required questions. Be sure to double-check your application before submission.

Social Security Number

Enter your Social Security number in the space indicated. Providing your Social Security number is voluntary; however, we cannot process your application without it.

Vacancy Identification Number

Enter the Vacancy Identification Number: CH155851

1. Title of Job Position Title: PLANT PROTECTION AND QUARANTINE OFFICER

2. Biographic Data

3. Email Address Notify me by Email Would you like to be notified by Email?

4. Work Information

5. Employment Availability

6. Citizenship Are you a citizen of the United States?

7. Background Information

8. Other Information

9. Languages

Occupational Questions

1. Have you completed a 4-year course of study, or do you possess a bachelor's degree in biological science, agriculture, or a closely related field (from an accredited college or university)? This course of study must have included at least 20 semester hours in such course work as agronomy, cell biology, botany, entomology, forestry, horticulture, mycology, nematology, plant pathology, soil science, or other closely related courses (see vacancy announcement).

A. Yes, I have completed (or will complete within 9 months) the education described above.

B. No, I do not possess the education described above.

STEP TWO:

Submit a resume, Optional Application for Federal Employment (OF-612), or other written application format of your choice. Be sure you provide all of the information requested.

STEP THREE:

Submit other application materials, as necessary.

HOW TO SUBMIT OTHER MATERIALS:

U.S. Office of Personnel Management

ATTN: Vacancy Identification Number CH155851

CHICAGO SERVICE CENTER 230 SOUTH DEARBORN STREET, DPN 30-3

CHICAGO, IL 60604

Specific Agency Application Process: Department of Commerce

The Department of Commerce uses the COOL Web-based vacancy announcement and application system. You can apply for a job only through this system, which involves submitting your resume into a database field and then answering questions. When you click the announcement number in the first paragraph, you will see another copy of the announcement with more details. You will have to complete a profile of your information and submit your resume. Then you will be able to view the questions. When your resume is in the database, you can apply for other announcements more easily by going directly to the questions.

> **OPENING DATE: 12/23/2002 CLOSING DATE: 01/10/2003**
> **ANNOUNCEMENT NUMBER: NIST-02-3620-CD**
> **JOB TITLE: Emergency Management Specialist, Series 0080**
> **PAY PLAN: ZA GRADE: 05**
> **DUTY LOCATION: Gaithersburg, MD**
>
> WHAT TO FILE: Applicants should submit the COOL On-Line Application form and any additional supporting documentation specified in the COOL vacancy announcement for this position at the www.jobs.doc.gov web site. To apply for this COOL job, and read the full text vacancy announcement, click on this vacancy announcement number displayed here — NIST-02-3620-CD. DUTIES DESCRIPTION: The incumbent will be responsible for the design, development, and implementation of an emergency preparedness and management program, disaster mitigation, and the security program at NIST, including the NIST Police Force and the Fire Protection Group. The incumbent will be responsible for establishing and managing an emergency planning, response, recovery, and operations mitigation program. Responsibilities include conducting risk assessments and analyses to determine emergency preparedness and security readiness; interacting with local, municipal, state, and Federal agencies involved in emergency planning and response and/or law enforcement; delivering training and presentations to audiences and executive management; acting as liaison on security issues with the Department of Commerce's Office of Security as well as all the Operating Units at NIST; and conducting tests, drills, and exercises. BASIS OF RATING: Applicants who meet the Qualification Requirements described above will be further evaluated based on their knowledge, skills, and abilities as reflected by their responses to the vacancy's job-related questions on the COOL application form. Please follow all application instructions carefully.
>
> CONTACT ADDRESS
>
> NIST, HRMD, 100 Bureau Drive, Gaithersburg, MD 20899
>
> CONTACT NAME: CHRIS DUGGAN
> CONTACT PHONE NUMBER:3019753047

Step 3: Follow the Application Instructions

Chapter 13 reviews the various How to Apply instructions in more detail.

The Importance of the Vacancy Announcements

You can't begin a Federal job search without studying vacancy announcements. This research will give you information about the jobs, duties, salaries, locations, agencies, and what is needed to apply. Continue working on your Federal and electronic resume. In chapter 13, we will come back to the How to Apply instructions. You will be ready to apply by that time and we'll study the various instructions in depth.

Summary

The announcements are difficult to read, but they are important for Federal resume writing. You must study the Duties, Qualifications, and KSA sections in order to find the language for your resume. You also need to include your core competencies that will support a particular agency's mission. You'll learn how to find your Federal core competencies in chapter 5.

CHAPTER 5

Researching Your Core Competencies

Many agency human resources professionals and managers are looking for the important values, soft skills, knowledge, and "core competencies" that an employee or manager can bring to the workplace. Yes, you have to be qualified for the job, but your "value-added" competencies could make a difference and make you stand out. In fact, at some point in the future, the OPM will be combining core competencies with basic qualifications and technical skills in its classification standards. As you will see from the list of core competencies discussed in this chapter, many agencies are analyzing the competencies they seek in the best Federal employees and managers.

What Are Your Core Competencies and How Can You Include Them in Your Resume?

As you read this chapter, underline the competencies that you consider to be your best. For example, I've always thought that my best competencies were flexibility, ability to work hard to complete a project, excellent communications and leadership skills, resourcefulness, initiative, and entrepreneurship. An interviewer might ask you this question: "What are your most notable strengths?" After studying this chapter, you will be ready with an answer.

Dr. Daniel Goleman consulted with the Office of Personnel Management on the development of its core competencies. Dr. Goleman's 1995 book *Emotional Intelligence* (Bantam Doubleday Dell) argues that human competencies such as self-awareness, self-discipline, persistence, and empathy are of greater consequence than IQ in much of life; that we ignore the decline in these competencies at our peril; and that children can—and should—be taught these abilities. His 1998 book *Working With Emotional Intelligence* (Bantam Doubleday Dell) argues that workplace competencies based on emotional intelligence play a far greater role in star performance than do intellect or technical skill, and that both individuals and companies will benefit from cultivating these capabilities.

When including your core competencies in the text of your resume, you should blend it with language from your current and past position descriptions, the vacancy announcement's "duties" section, and your own statements of responsibility. Resume sections that can include core competencies are work experience descriptions, your Profile or Summary of Skills section, or a section near the end of the resume called Other Qualifications.

Using Core Competencies as Transferable Skills When Changing Careers

If you are changing careers, you will want to use this chapter to find your "transferable skills," which can take you from one job series to another. Most jobs require skills in customer service, project management, teamwork, working under pressure, and attention to detail. You can integrate these competencies to match your current skills to the skills that the new job requires.

Every agency has its own list of required competencies and its own interests. If you study the various core competency lists and agency descriptions, you will see that they require diverse values, soft skills, knowledge, and specialized skills for particular occupations. Some of the competencies are similar between agencies, such as customer service, flexibility, decision-making, problem-solving, teamwork, and resourcefulness.

 Note: The OPM's definition of core competencies is the following: "Observable, measurable pattern of skills, knowledge, abilities, behaviors, and other characteristics that an individual needs to perform work roles or occupational functions successfully." (U.S. Office of Personnel Management, Op. Cir., Glossary.)

Many Federal job seekers do not understand or know about the OPM or particular agencies' core competencies. This cutting-edge information can help you build a better resume with more relevant skills, insight, and information about the agency and the job. Knowing the core competencies and mission of an agency can be critical to the success of your interview. If you understand what's really important for an employee at a specific agency, you can speak about your skills in terms of the agency's values and interests instead of just depending on the "duties" listed in the vacancy announcement. The following section shows you how to find these core competencies.

Search for Agency and Company Core Competencies

More and more agencies are developing their own sets of competencies. You can find them by going to www.opm.gov and searching for "core competencies." You can also go to the sites for specific agencies and use their search engines to find "core competencies." Some agencies list them on their sites; others do not. If your favorite Federal agency does not list a set of core competencies, you can also look for private-industry competencies (in the same field or agency mission) by using your favorite search engine. Search for "core competencies" and you will find good skills, descriptions, and competencies for careers and jobs.

The resume samples in chapter 1 and in the appendix include competencies in the work experience descriptions, Profile statements, Summary of Skills section, and the Other Qualifications section. You will integrate the core competencies information into your entire resume. Plus, you should keep a list of your competencies for interview preparation. It's important to know your best skills and competencies so that you can describe them in interviews and even give examples that support your skills.

 Note: Chapter 16, "Applying for the Senior Executive Service," includes samples and descriptions of the OPM's Executive Core Qualifications. These are the core competencies for executives in government.

The following sections include several sets of particular agency core competencies that you can study. They also show you where to go on the Internet to research more information on particular job and agency competencies.

Core Competency Set No. 1: Center for Medicare and Medicaid Services, Managerial Core Competencies

Since 1999, I have been teaching the Managerial Core Competencies to Center for Medicare and Medicaid Services (CMS) employees at GS-13 and above. CMS has decided to change all of its GS-13 and above supervisory KSAs to "theme"

KSAs. Applicants can also use one job-specific technical KSA, but CMS is focusing on leadership competencies for its supervisory managers.

The CMS employees in the class wrote examples and success stories based on these managerial competencies. (In chapter 14, you will learn how to write KSAs based on these examples.) You can incorporate your competencies into your examples. The CMS Managerial Competencies are similar to OPM's Executive Core Qualifications; however, the definitions are slightly different. Management candidates should read the following competencies and incorporate them into their Federal resumes and KSAs.

EXCERPTS FROM STANDARD CREDITING PLAN FOR MANAGERIAL POSITIONS

CORE COMPETENCIES

1. Managing Change

2. Leading People

3. Building Partnerships and Coalitions

4. Producing Results

5. Managing Resources

Theme KSAs for each competency are provided below:

I. MANAGING CHANGE

The ability to articulate and implement an organizational vision which integrates key national and program goals, priorities, and values; continually improve customer service and program performance; create a work environment that encourages creative thinking; and maintain a strategic focus and persistence, even under adversity.

A. Vision—Ability to take a long-term view and act as a catalyst for organizational change, build a shared vision with others, and influence others to translate vision into action.

B. External Awareness—Ability to identify and keep current on key national and international policies and economic, political, and social trends that affect the organization, and determine how to position the organization to achieve its mission in a rapidly changing business environment.

C. Creativity and Innovation—Ability to develop new insights into situations and apply innovative solutions to make organizational improvements, create a work environment that encourages creative thinking and innovation, and design and implement new or cutting-edge programs and processes.

(continues)

(continued)

D. Strategic Thinking—Ability to formulate long-range plans to achieve the strategic aims of the organization, analyze policy issues and proposals with a long-term perspective, determine business objectives and set priorities, and anticipate potential threats or opportunities.

E. Continual Learning—Ability to grasp the essence of new information, master new technical and business knowledge, recognize own strengths and weaknesses, pursue self-development as a leader, and seek feedback from others.

F. Resilience—Ability to deal effectively with pressure, maintain focus, remain optimistic and persistent even under adversity, and recover quickly from setbacks.

G. Service Motivation—Ability to create and sustain an organizational culture that promotes the quality of service essential to high performance, enable others to acquire the tools and support they need to produce exceptional results, show a commitment to principled public service, and influence others to make meaningful contributions to mission accomplishment.

II. LEADING PEOPLE

The ability to design and implement strategies for obtaining the highest return on the organization's human capital investment; establish practices that fully develop and effectively use employees' knowledge and skills; and foster high standards of ethical service in meeting the organization's vision, mission, and goals.

A. Managing Conflict—Ability to identify and take steps to prevent situations that could result in unproductive confrontations, and manage and resolve conflicts and disagreements in a positive and constructive manner.

B. Managing Differences—Ability to initiate and manage cultural change within the organization to improve organizational effectiveness, value and make constructive use of cultural diversity and other individual differences in the workforce, and ensure that all employees are treated in a fair and equitable manner.

C. Interpersonal Skills—Ability to recognize and respond appropriately to the communication styles, feelings, and capabilities of different people in different situations; exhibit tact, patience, and sensitivity; and treat others with respect.

D. Team Building—Ability to inspire, motivate, and guide others toward goal accomplishments; develop and sustain cooperative working relationships; facilitate cooperation within the organization and with customer groups; foster commitment, team cohesiveness, and trust; and develop leadership in others by coaching, mentoring, and rewarding team members.

E. Managing Performance—Ability to evaluate work performance and provide feedback to others on their performance; ensure that staff is properly trained, developed, and coached; recognize and reward positive results; and take corrective actions as appropriate.

III. BUILDING PARTNERSHIPS AND COALITIONS

The ability to explain, advocate, and express facts and ideas in a convincing manner; negotiate with individuals and groups within and external to the organization; develop a network of professional contacts; and recognize the key internal and external political factors that influence the work of the organization.

A. Oral Communication—Skill in making clear and convincing oral presentations to individuals or groups, listening effectively and clarifying information as needed, facilitating an open exchange of ideas; and fostering an atmosphere of open communication.

B. Written Communication—Ability to express facts and ideas in writing in a clear, convincing, and organized manner.

C. Influencing/Negotiating—Ability to persuade others, build consensus through give and take, gain cooperation from others to obtain information and accomplish goals, and facilitate "win-win" solutions.

D. Partnering—Ability to develop networks and build alliances, engage in cross-functional activities, collaborate across boundaries, find common ground with a broad range of stakeholders, and utilize contacts to build and strengthen internal support bases.

E. Political Awareness—Ability to identify internal and external political factors that affect the work of the organization, approach each problem situation with a clear perception of relevant political factors, and anticipate the political impact of alternative courses of action.

F. Organizational Communication—The ability to manage information within an organization to ensure collaboration; provide the level and frequency of communication necessary to successfully support work across organizational boundaries; and provide an accessible record of changing priorities, decisions, and commitments.

IV. PRODUCING RESULTS

The ability to make effective decisions and produce results through the timely implementation of programs and policies, and to hold self and others accountable for achieving results.

A. Accountability—Ability to develop and maintain management controls to ensure the operational integrity of the organization, hold self and others accountable for results and responsibilities, ensure that tasks within areas of responsibility are completed in a timely manner and within budget, and monitor and measure attainment of planned outcomes.

B. Problem Solving—Ability to identify and analyze problems, distinguish between relevant and irrelevant information to make logical decisions, and provide solutions to individual and organizational problems.

C. Decisiveness—Ability to make sound and well-informed decisions; perceive the impact and implications of decisions; and make reasoned and timely decisions, even when data are limited or solutions entail unpleasant consequences.

D. Customer Service—Ability to balance the interests of a variety of customers, adjust priorities to respond to changing client needs, anticipate and meet the needs of clients, produce quality deliverables, and continually improve services.

E. Technical Credibility *(for Group Directors and Deputy Group Directors)*—Ability to understand and apply procedures, requirements, regulations, and policies governing the work of a multifunctional business unit; make sound hiring and capital-resource decisions; integrate the work of the group with that of other organizational components; and achieve results through the direction of management and technical staff.

F. Technical Supervision *(for Division Directors and Deputy Division Directors)*—Ability to provide technical oversight to staff members on complex or unusual duties, and monitor and direct the progress of the work group to ensure that work is completed on time and accurately.

V. MANAGING RESOURCES

The ability to acquire and administer human, financial, material, and information resources in a manner that instills public trust and accomplishes the organization's mission.

A. Financial Management—Ability to understand principles of financial management in government; estimate appropriate funding levels; prepare, justify, and/or administer the budget for a program area; use cost-benefit analyses to set priorities; monitor program expenditures; and identify cost-effective approaches to administration.

(continues)

(continued)

B. Human Resources Management—Ability to apply Merit System principles to ensure staff are appropriately selected, developed, deployed, appraised, rewarded and, if necessary, disciplined.

C. Personal Organization—Ability to manage time, coordinate, and schedule work; and fully utilize staff to accomplish the workload of the organization.

D. Project Management—Ability to use project-management concepts and methods to structure and manage the work of a group to accomplish a complex activity within time and resource constraints.

Here is an example of a CMS announcement that uses the preceding managerial competencies as KSAs:

Supervisory Health Insurance Specialist, GS-107-15

RATING CRITERIA—Knowledge, Skills, and Abilities (KSAs): What are your knowledge, skills, and abilities as they relate to this position? In addition to your resume, please write a 1/2 to 1 page narrative statement explaining the experience you have relating to each KSA listed below. (Instructions for addressing KSAs can be found at www.cms.hhs.gov/careers/apply/ksa.asp.)

1. **Strategic Thinking**—Ability to formulate long-range plans to achieve the strategic aims of the organization, analyze policy issues and proposals with a long-term perspective, determine business objectives and set priorities, and anticipate potential threats or opportunities.

2. **Resilience**—Ability to deal effectively with pressure, maintain focus, remain optimistic and persistent even under adversity, and recover quickly from setbacks.

3. **Influencing/Negotiating**—Ability to persuade others, build consensus through give and take, gain cooperation from others to obtain information and accomplish goals, and facilitate "win-win" solutions.

4. **Organizational Communications**—The ability to manage information within an organization to ensure collaboration; provide the level and frequency of communication necessary to successfully support work across organizational boundaries; and provide an accessible record of changing priorities, decisions, and commitments.

5. **Decisiveness**—Ability to make sound and well-informed decisions; perceive the impact and implications of decisions; and make reasoned and timely decisions, even when data are limited or solutions entail unpleasant consequences.

6. **Financial Management**—Ability to understand principles of financial management in government; estimate appropriate funding levels; prepare, justify, and/or administer the budget for a program area; use cost-benefit analyses to set priorities; monitor program expenditures and identify cost-effective approaches to administration.

Basis of Rating—Applicants meeting the minimum qualification requirements will be rated and ranked on the knowledge, skills, and abilities (KSAs) required to perform the duties of the position. Numerical ratings will be assigned to eligible applicants.

Core Competency Set No. 2: U.S. Marine Corps

The Civilian Marines Web site is https://lnweb1.manpower.usmc.mil/ccld/index.htm. Go to "Training and Education" and then "Leadership Development." The "Competencies" and brief definitions are listed. Civilians with the Marine Corps or other military services should consider these core values when writing an electronic resume and preparing for an interview.

One of the goals of the Civilian Career and Leadership Development Program (CCLD) is to improve leadership skills and competencies of all Civilian Marines. The following are the Civilian Leadership Competencies that are the stepping-stones of every Civilian Marine's career.

Foundation Competencies

Core Values

- Exhibits through personal performance the principles of honor (ethical behavior), courage (mental strength to do what's right), and commitment (technical excellence and quality of work)

Customer Orientation

- Actively seeks customer input
- Ensures customer needs are met
- Continuously seeks to improve quality of services, products, and processes

Decisiveness/Flexibility

- Takes action and risks when needed
- Makes difficult decisions when necessary
- Adapts to change in work environment
- Effectively copes with stress

Diversity Awareness

- Respects and values the differences and perceptions of different groups/individuals

Interpersonal/Team Skills

- Considers and responds appropriately to the needs, feelings, capabilities, and interest of others
- Provides feedback
- Treats others equitably

Mission/Organization Awareness

- Possesses knowledge of the mission and organization of the Marine Corps, including an understanding of how the organization fits into the entire Department of the Navy

---

(continues)

(continued)

Oral Communication

- Listens to others
- Makes clear and effective oral presentations to individuals and groups (NOTE: Use of sign language interpreter may be appropriate for persons who are deaf or hard of hearing)

Problem Solving

- Recognizes and defines problems
- Analyzes relevant information
- Encourages alternative solutions and plans to solve problems

Quality Principles

- Understands and applies quality principles such as teamwork, quantitative decision making, and continuous process improvement to meet or exceed customer expectations

Self-Direction

- Realistically assesses own strengths, weaknesses, and impact on others
- Seeks feedback from others
- Works persistently towards a goal
- Demonstrates self-confidence
- Invests in self-development
- Manages time effectively

Technical Competence

- Demonstrates technical proficiency and an understanding of the impact in areas of responsibility

Written Communication

- Communicates effectively in writing
- Reviews and critiques others' writing

Supervisory Competencies

Change Management

- Serves as a positive agent for changes in the organization's structural alignment, climate, or operational processes

- Learns about and proactively advocates and influences the adoption of promising new ideas, methods, services, and products from knowledge of best practices in government and industry

Coaching/Counseling

- Develops skills in observation, listening, and one–on–one teaching; applies them to assist others to learn to continually improve their performance; and provides effective feedback

Conflict Management

- Anticipates and seeks to resolve confrontations, disagreements, and complaints in a constructive manner

Human Resources Management

- Ensures effective recruitment, selection, training, performance appraisal, recognition, and corrective/disciplinary action

- Promotes affirmative employment, good labor relations, and employee well-being

Influencing/Negotiating

- Networks with, and provides information to, key groups and individuals

- Appropriately uses negotiation, persuasion, and authority in dealing with others to achieve goals

Managing a Diverse Workforce

- Recognizes the values of cultural, ethnic, gender, and other individual differences

- Provides employment and developmental opportunities for a diverse workforce

Situational Leadership

- Demonstrates and encourages high standards of behavior

- Adapts leadership styles to situations and people. Empowers, motivates, and guides others

Team Building

- Fosters cooperation, communication, and consensus among groups

Managerial Competencies

Innovative Thinking
- Develops insights and solutions
- Fosters innovation among others

Mentoring
- Develops the ability to counsel others to help them achieve personal and professional growth

Model/Reinforce Core Values
- Instilling values (honor, courage, commitment) is an integral part of making every Marine and, as a component of readiness, is essential in winning battles

Presentation/Marketing Skills
- Demonstrates the ability to clearly articulate, present, and promote ideas and issues before a wide range of audiences to include senior officials, in such a manner as to ensure program credibility

Process Oversight Management
- Develops/demonstrates the ability to examine systems and workflows within the organization to facilitate process improvement

Program Development/Planning and Evaluating
- Establishes policies, guidelines, plans, and priorities
- Identifies required resources
- Plans and coordinates with others
- Monitors progress and evaluates outcomes
- Improves organizational efficiency and effectiveness

Resource Management
- Prepares and justifies budget
- Monitors expenses
- Manages procurement and contracting

Risk Management
- Identifies potential risks to product/program/processes early and implements effective abatement and control measures
- Defines evaluation criteria early and continuously collects, assesses, shares, and responds to data appropriately

Technology Management

- Encourages staff to stay informed about new technology

- Applies new technologies to organizational needs

- Ensures staff are trained and capable

Executive Competencies

External Awareness

- Stays informed on laws, policies, politics, administration priorities, trends, special interest, and other issues

- Considers external impact of statements or actions

- Uses information in decision making

Joint Service Perspective

- Demonstrates an understanding of the role of the Department of Defense and the importance of the support roles and missions of all the Military Departments and Defense Agencies and how they contribute to the success of the DoD overall

Organizational Representation and Liaison

- Establishes and maintains relationships with key individuals/groups outside immediate work unit and serves as spokesperson for the organization

Strategic Vision

- Creates a shared vision of the organization

- Promotes wide ownership

- Champions organizational change

Core Competency Set No. 3: Veterans Administration

Read the entire descriptions of these core competencies at the Department of Veterans Affairs Web site at www.va.gov/visns/visn02/emp/learning/index.html. If you are applying for jobs at the Veterans Administration or other Federal agencies, you can include some of this language in your Federal resume and KSAs.

Interpersonal Effectiveness	Creative Thinking
Customer Service	Organizational Stewardship
Systems Thinking	Personal Mastery
Flexibility/Adaptability	Technical Competency

Core Competency Set No. 4: Department of the Interior, National Park Service, Universal Competencies

These competencies are a combination of employee competencies/values and specific knowledge of the agency policies, legislation, and programs. You can read more about this agency at the National Park Service Web site: www.nps.gov/training/uc/home.htm.

Mission Comprehension—This competency requires a thorough background and understanding of the 1916 NPS Organic Act and its many ramifications and the additional responsibilities that have been added to the NPS throughout its history; and a perspective of how the National Park System began as a part of the Conservation Movement that continues today.

Agency Orientation—This competency requires a basic comprehension of the structure and organization of the NPS at the park, cluster, field area, and Washington Office levels; an understanding of the structure and organization of the Department of the Interior and its place in the Federal Government; and the development of an insight into an individual employee's role in the NPS in particular, and in the Federal Government in general.

Resource Stewardship—This competency requires an overall understanding of the spectrum of resources protected by the NPS, the range of NPS responsibilities in managing these resources, the individual's role in resource stewardship, the planning process and its purpose in the NPS, and working with partners outside the agency to promote resource stewardship.

NPS Operations—This competency encompasses a general comprehension of the basic operations of the NPS, especially at the park level; how these operations interact to fulfill the Mission of the NPS; and why visitors come to parks and how the NPS "manages" them.

Fundamental Values—This competency focuses on an employee's ability to exhibit certain attitudes and behaviors to accomplish an assigned job and to contribute to the overall health of the organization. These include leadership and teamwork behaviors, ethical behavior towards people and the organization, support of cultural diversity and fairness issues in the workplace, support of accessible parks and workplaces, an attitude towards safe behavior for one's self and for others, and mental and physical fitness.

Communications Skills—This competency encompasses the ability to communicate effectively with the public and employees in writing and speech, use interpersonal skills to be an effective employee, and exhibit basic computer abilities.

Problem-Solving Skills—This competency deals with the ability to analyze a problem, build consensus, make decisions, and practice innovation in various aspects of one's job.

Individual Development and Planning—This competency considers an individual's being able to work with one's supervisor and agency to plan a course of action for one's performance, career, and, ultimately, retirement.

Other Core Competencies

The Office of Personnel Management Web site (www.opm.gov/hrd/lead/trnginfo/trnginfo.htm#core) offers core competency resources for many other Federal agencies. We've included a sampling of them in the following sections.

Oregon Department of Fish and Wildlife
www.dfw.state.or.us/core.html

This Web site provides a core competency ladder and core competency list for management people with the State of Oregon Department of Fish and Wildlife.

Joint Financial Management Improvement Program

www.jfmip.gov/jfmip/corecomp.htm

This site includes core competencies for accountants, budget analysts, financial managers, financial systems analysts, financial management for IT professionals, financial management analysts, and project managers implementing financial systems.

Information Technology Core Competencies

www.cio.gov/Documents/ lo%5Ffinal%5F2001%2Ehtml

This CIO Council Web site contains the Clinger-Cohen competencies for people in the IT workforce.

Summary

Knowing your strengths and core competencies can help your resume stand out and impress an interviewer. You can also impress the interviewer with your education and training that is relevant to your objective, which is covered in the next chapter.

Part 2

Writing Your Federal Resume

CHAPTER 6

Presenting Your Educational Background and Training

Your educational background is an important part of your Federal resume. The amount of information you provide, the way you present the information, and the organization of this section can impress HR professionals and hiring managers. HR professionals are looking for specific degrees, majors, courses, and specialized training to determine whether you are qualified for the position. Some Federal jobs require degrees; other Federal positions will accept specialized or generalized experience in place of college degrees. The Federal job announcement is clear about the qualifications for the position. Read the "Specialized or Generalized Qualifications" section of the vacancy announcement to see whether you have the necessary educational qualifications for the position. If the qualifications require that you have 25 credits in accounting for a Staff Accountant position, you *must* have these credits. List them in your resume and add up the credits.

Here is the education information that *must* be on your Federal resume, according to OPM brochure OF-510:

★ High school (name and address, date of diploma or GED)

★ College or universities (name and address, majors, type and year of degree; if no degree, show total credits earned and whether semester or quarter hours)

Considerations for Organizing Your Educational Background

The personnel staff will appreciate reviewing your entire educational background in a concise, organized format. One of the best features of a Federal resume is its formatting flexibility. If you want to highlight a recent degree or course work, you can do so by the way you position it. Recent and returned college graduates can include with each college listing their educational honors, awards, scholarships, grade-point average, activities, significant courses, major papers or thesis, and assistantships.

Education is usually a separate category from Training. In the Education category, you will list your high school and college education and degrees. Your Training, Professional Development, or Continuing Education (three suggested headings for this section, all with similar meanings) can be listed separately. You can combine the Education and Training sections to improve their presentation if you want. If you possess extensive job-related training, you can create functional headings for the training. Many Federal employees receive considerable training in computers, management, leadership, supervision, accounting, budget, contracts, and project management, and they can group their training under subheadings that indicate their areas of focus.

The vacancy announcement might mandate the inclusion of classroom hours. Read the announcement to determine the information required, or include the hours just in case. Some announcements require you to provide transcripts; others don't. You can attach a course list if you feel that your courses are significant in showing your qualifications and performance for a particular Federal job. (See Example 5 later in this chapter for a sample course list.)

Education Section Samples

Here are 12 examples of how to organize, present, and highlight your Education and Training sections. The samples are arranged by the following Federal applicant groups:

★ No college degree

★ Recent college graduates or those with new degrees

★ GS-9 through GS-14 (current Federal employees and first-time Federal applicants)

★ GS-15 through Senior Executive Service

No College Degree

According to Dennis Damp in *The Book of U.S. Government Jobs* (Bookhaven Press), 63 percent of all Federal workers do not have a college degree. The required education level depends on the position. In many cases for general administrative and management positions, you can replace a college degree with a certain number of years of specialized or generalized experience. You can read the education qualifications for each position in the vacancy announcement.

Example 1: Applicant for GS-5 Border Patrol Agent

This high school graduate worked as a border patrol agent on a contract basis in his senior year of high school and is seeking a permanent position with the Immigration and Naturalization Service. This resume uses a combined Education and Training section. You can simply write the year you completed the training (represented here by xxxx).

EDUCATION AND TRAINING

USDA Work Conference, xxxx

USDA APHIS VS Tick Identification and Awareness, xxxx, 4 hours

Federal Law Enforcement Firearms Training, xxxx. Qualified to carry firearms.

Pesticide School, xxxx

Graduated Carrizo Springs High School, Carrizo Springs, TX 78834, xxxx

---

Example 2: GS-8 Information Technologist with Special Training

This current Federal employee does not have a bachelor's degree but has completed extensive specialized professional training.

EDUCATION

B.S., Information Systems, Northern Virginia Community College, xxxx

University of Maryland, College Park, Maryland, 20 semester hours, Information Systems, xxxx

Montgomery Community College, Rockville, Maryland, 20 semester hours, Information Systems, xxxx

United Association of Mechanical Trades School, Journeyman Steamfitter Diploma, xxxx

H.S. Degree, Garfield Senior High School, Woodbridge, Virginia, xxxx

PROFESSIONAL CERTIFICATES & LICENSES

Microsoft Certified Systems Engineer, xxxx, MCP ID# 2073283

Microsoft Certified Professional + Internet, xxxx

Certified Netmaster (Internet Security), xxxx

Certified Netguard (Internet Firewall Administrator), xxxx

Certified Novell NetWare Engineer, xxxx, Certificate #6006032

PROFESSIONAL COURSES & SEMINARS

UNIX Systems:

- SCO UNIX OpenServer Rel 5 Administration I & II, Introduction to SCO UNIX Systems, xxxx

Web Site Design:

- Mastering Web Site Fundamentals, xxxx

Windows Networking:

- Windows NT MCSE Boot Camp, Introduction to Windows 2000, xxxx

- Administering Windows NT Workstation, xxxx

- Performing an Audit of the Year 2000 Project, Raptor Firewall NetGuard & NetMaster Training, xxxx

- Advanced Data Communications, xxxx

(continues)

(continued)

Novell NetWare:

- Novell 5.1 Adv. System Administrator & Novell 5.1 System Administrator, xxxx

- Novell 4.0 Systems Administrator, xxxx

- Novell Network Adv. System Administrator & Novell Network System Administrator 3.11, Introduction to the Internet, xxxx

- Networking Technologies, NetWare OS Features & Revue, NetWare Advanced System Manager, Advanced DOS, xxxx

- NetWare Services and Support, NetWare 386 System Manager, xxxx

Mainframe Applications:

- Introduction to Data Communications, xxxx

- MVS Structure and Logic, MVS Job Control Language, MVS TSO/JCL Introduction, xxxx

Building Designs and Installation Planning:

- Air Conditioning/Electrical Requirements for Computer Rooms, Drafting/Blueprint Designs, xxxx

Recent College Graduates and Those with New Degrees

Recent college graduates and people who have recently earned a new degree should list the Education section before the employment history in order to emphasize their most important qualification.

Example 3: New College Graduate and First-Time Federal Applicant

This college graduate is pursuing a position as Information Technology Specialist (Application Software) with the U.S. Farm Service Agency.

EDUCATION

BS, Computer Science/Math, Drexel University, Philadelphia, PA 19104, xxxx

AA, Chemical Technology, Community College of Philadelphia, Philadelphia, PA 19130, 118 Semester Hours, xxxx, GPA: 3.5

HS (GED), Community College of Philadelphia, Philadelphia, PA 19130, xxxx

ACADEMIC AWARDS AND HONORS

Drexel Anthony Scholarship, xxxx–xxxx

Community College of Philadelphia, Dean's Honor List, xxxx–xxxx

---

Example 4: New College Graduate and First-Time Federal Applicant

This new graduate may be seeking a Federal career internship or a position as writer-editor, public affairs specialist, or researcher. The applicant included an extensive list of relevant internships and workshops.

EDUCATION

B.S., Human Ecology, College of the Atlantic, Bar Harbor, ME, May xxxx
Course Concentration: Creative Writing and Poetry; 3.9 GPA
Honors and Activities:

- OUTSTANDING SCHOLAR
- Writing Tutor for Freshmen.
- One-Act Theater—Producer, Writer, Actor.
- Editor, *COA News* newspaper (two years).
- Wrote and produced 30-minute audio tour for ocean-wide campus.
- Produced Web-based interactive curriculum for science course.
- Designed and wrote multimedia Web site using Dreamweaver.
- Produced books and wrote more than 30 poems and major papers.

Catonsville Senior High School, Catonsville, MD, May xxxx
Honors and Activities:

- Honor Roll, average GPA: 3.8/4.0.
- Departmental Honors—English, Creative Writing, and Theater Arts.
- Awarded the Presidential Award for Academic Excellence.
- Honored for perfect attendance, senior year.
- Awarded William E. Brock Scholarship—full college scholarship.
- Advanced Placement U.S. History (4) and English coursework.
- First-place competitor, Lincoln-Douglas Debate, Junior year.

Internships:
Archivist, Copper Canyon Press, Port Townsend, WA, Sept.–Nov. xxxx.

- Archivist for Publisher Sam Hamill's correspondence, unpublished manuscripts, and materials. Established organizational format for 20 years of materials. Established database in Excel for future purchase and use by research university. (40 hours per week)
- Co-teacher, Creative Writing, Catonsville High School, Spring xxxx.
- Co-teacher, Introductory Theater Arts, Catonsville High School, Spring xxxx.
- Interpreter, Department of the Interior, Haleakala National Park, Maui, HI, Sept.–Dec. xxxx.

Workshops:

- Hawaiian Language and Culture, Maui Community College, Kahului, Fall xxxx.
- Writing and Thinking, Lewis & Clark University, Summer xxxx.
- National Outdoor Leadership School, Lander, WY, Summer xxxx.
- Baltimore Area Writer's Forum, Essex Community College, Spring xxxx.
- Andre Braugher ("Homicide") Shakespeare Workshop, Winter xxxx.
- Selected for highly competitive theater workshop based on audition.
- Writer's Workshop, Susquehanna University, Summer xxxx.
- Women in the Workplace, Park School, Baltimore, MD, Spring xxxx.

Example 5: Recent College Graduate and First-Time Federal Applicant

This applicant is seeking a GS-7 Criminal Investigator position with the Drug Enforcement Administration.

EDUCATION:

B.A.S. Degree, May xxxx, University of Delaware, Newark, DE 19711

Dual Major: Criminal Justice and Psychology

GPA: Criminal Justice: 3.53 Psychology: 3.63

University of Scholchere, Fort De France, Martinique

French Studies, Winter Session xxxx

Academic Honors:

OUTSTANDING SCHOLAR

Dean's List for Academic Excellence, University of Delaware

Golden Key National Honor Society, University of Delaware Chapter, xxxx

National Psychology Honor Society, Psi Chi, xxxx

Graduate, Catonsville High School, Baltimore, MD, xxxx

Papers and Presentations:

AD/HD: The Current Epidemic. Research paper undermining the application of the biomedical model to the construction of Attention-Deficit/Hyperactivity Disorder and its treatment. March xxxx.

The Myth of Emotional Venting. Discussion paper summarizing Moore and Watson's research on the ill-effects of uncontrolled anger expression and possible coping strategies to combat emotional flooding. Presented to a select inmate population at Baylor Women's Correctional Institution in Delaware on April 11, xxxx.

Example 6: GS-12 Current Federal Employee Completing a Master's Degree and Special Training

This Federal employee is working on a master's degree and a DAWIA Certificate in Procurement and Acquisitions as part of a Career Track Program in Procurement with grade-level potential to GS-15.

EDUCATION

Master of Arts in Procurement and Acquisitions Management, xxxx; GPA: 3.8
WEBSTER UNIVERSITY, Bolling AFB, Washington, DC
Honors:
- Distinguished Graduate
- Thesis: Alternative Dispute Resolution

Defense Acquisition Workforce Improvement Act (DAWIA)—level I and level II certified
DEFENSE ACQUISITION UNIVERSITY, xxxx; GPA: 4.0
Honors:
- Distinguished Graduate for Automated Information Systems
- Honor Graduate for Government Contract Law
- Distinguished Graduate for Intermediate Contracting

Bachelor of Science Degree in Political Science, xxxx; GPA: 3.5
BALL STATE UNIVERSITY, Muncie, Indiana
Minor in Military Science
Honors:
- Dean's List
- G.T.E. Academic All-American and scholar athlete award in college football

Relevant Coursework:
Information Technology Contracting, Information Systems Security, Computer Resources and Information Management, Contracting Fundamentals, Contract Pricing, Government Contract Law, Intermediate Contracting, Intermediate Contract Pricing, Congressional Research Training, Library of Congress Training, Negotiations, Logistics, Pricing, Operations Management, Security Management, Analysis of Management Systems, Proposal Preparation
Specialized Training:
In addition to the skills I have learned as a contract specialist, I have also taken the following specialized training: Defense Acquisition University, Small Business Contracting, Commerce Business Daily Transmissions Using the Internet, Service Contract Act, Trade Agreements Act, HTML/Internet Programming and Usage, Defense Acquisition Workforce Improvement Act, Government Ethics, Security in the Workplace, Procurement Integrity Act, Blanket Purchase Agreements, Privacy Act and Freedom of Information Act, Communications with Congress and Department of Defense Heads.
(All of the above training took place from xxxx to xxxx and lasted from 2 hours to 4 weeks).

GS-9 Through GS-14

Example 7: Private-Industry Professional Pursuing First Position in Government

This individual is applying for a position as a GS-9 Training Specialist with the Oregon Military Department (HR Office). Notice that he lists his graduate school hours because he has not yet completed the degree.

EDUCATION

Masters Degree in Secondary Education from National University, San Diego, CA
In progress—completed 70 quarter hours. GPA: 3.608. Expect to complete degree May xxxx.

Significant courses include

Educational Foundations	Competency-Based Technology
The Diverse Classroom	Health Ed/Across Curriculum
Curriculum/Procedures	Psychology App Teach
Instructional Technique	Exceptional Children in Class
Early Field Experience	Curriculum Design and Research

B.A., History, California Polytechnic State University, San Luis Obispo, CA, xxxx

---

Example 8: Private-Industry Applicant Applying for First Federal Job

The following applicant is seeking a Health Insurance Specialist position with the Centers for Medicare and Medicaid Services.

EDUCATION

M.S., Business Management, Johns Hopkins University, Baltimore, MD, xxxx

B.A., Health Science and Policy, University of Maryland, Baltimore County, Baltimore, MD, xxxx

A.A., Nursing, Catonsville Community College, Catonsville, MD, xxxx

HS, Deptford High School, Deptford, NJ, xxxx

PROFESSIONAL TRAINING

Integrating People, Process, and Technology in Search of Excellent Quality, Starbase Learning Institute, 16 hours, xxxx.

Teaming for Excellence, Computer Sciences Corp., 40 hours, xxxx.

1999 AMIA (American Medical Informatics Association) Annual Symposium, xxxx.

Example 9: GS-12 Public Affairs Specialist at FAA Seeking Career Change

This employee is seeking a career change toward aviation operations management with the Federal Aviation Administration. The Professional Training section of his resume is categorized into major areas of training: aviation technical, management, and communications.

The USDA Career Development Program, which is part of the Executive Potential Program (EPP), provided him with aviation operations experience. This program offers motivated Federal employees classroom training, rotations, mentors, and specialized training in a new career area. In this case, the applicant sought and received aviation operations experience.

EDUCATION & TRAINING:

Bachelor of Arts (Speech & Communications)	University of California–Los Angeles Los Angeles, CA 95701	June xxxx
Associate of Arts	Simi Valley Community College Los Angeles, CA 95701	June xxxx
Diploma	Robert Fulton High School Queens, NY 10065	June xxxx

PROFESSIONAL DEVELOPMENT/TRAINING:

U.S.D.A. Graduate School, Career Development Program   **xxxx–xxxx**
Aviation Executive Potential Program (EPP)
Mentor: Charlene Perry, (707) 554-0900

Successfully completed developmental assignments emphasizing leadership and management potential. Formalized classroom training included leadership styles, managing conflict, empowerment, stress, and cultural diversity management. Cluster group assignments focused on improving performance management in a team environment.

Assistant to FAA's International Liaison Officer for 60 days in planning and performance of multinational meetings developing protocols to shift air traffic control technology over Pacific Ocean routes. Coordinated media presence in three-day international meetings, securing substantial favorable coverage for the U.S. government and the agency. (40 hours per week, April–May, 1998)

Assisted the Resident Agent-in-Charge with the U.S. Customs Office for 30 days. Managed public affairs for international smuggling conference, providing important coverage for new international law enforcement protocols governing movement of passengers and freight. Supported operation through media expertise and technical familiarity with airspace system operations. (40 hours per week, February, 1998)

Other Professional Courses

Aviation Technical Courses:

　　　Detail, FAA Civil Aviation Security Office (xxxx)

　　　Introduction to Emergency Readiness (xxxx)

　　　Air Traffic Control History (xxxx)

　　　Managing Public Communication, FAA Center for Management Development (xxxx)

(continues)

(continued)

> Management Development Courses (All in xxxx):
>
> | | |
> |---|---|
> | Seven Habits of Highly Effective People | The Quality Advantage |
> | Management Skills for Non-Supervisors | Investment in Excellence |
> | Discovering Diversity/Valuing the Diverse Workforce | Thinking Beyond the Boundaries |
>
> Communications Training:
>
> Public Involvement Training (xxxx)
>
> Collateral Duty Recruiter Training (xxxx)
>
> Constructive Communications (xxxx)
>
> Communications Training Workshop (xxxx)

GS-15 Through Senior Executive Service

Example 10: GS-15 Special Assistant Pursuing SES Position

This applicant's Professional Training section emphasizes leadership and management training.

> ### EDUCATION HISTORY
>
> MAS, Management, Johns Hopkins University, Baltimore, MD 21229, xxxx
>
> BA, History, University of Maryland, College Park, MD 21229, xxxx
>
> ### PROFESSIONAL TRAINING
>
> Team Building and Coaching Skills for Managers, xxxx
>
> Certified Trainer, William Bridge's Seminars on Managing Organizational Transitions, xxxx
>
> Appearing at Your Public Best, Georgetown University, xxxx
>
> Certified Trainer for Pritchett & Associates, Business as Unusual, xxxx
>
> Seven Management and Planning Tools, Goal/QPC, xxxx
>
> Workshop for Team Leaders & Team, OPM, xxxx
>
> Management Effectiveness Seminar, Career Track, xxxx
>
> Front Line Leadership, Zenger-Miller, xxxx
>
> Training prior to xxxx available upon request

Example 11: GS-15 Division Director Applying for Assistant Regional Administrator (Executive Service)

PROFESSIONAL TRAINING AND EDUCATION:

Federal Executive Institute, Leadership for a Democratic Society   xxxx
General Services Administration, Trail Boss Contracting   xxxx
General Services Administration, Quality Management Master Trainer Program   xxxx
Office of Personnel Management, Management Development Seminar   xxxx
Georgia State University, Atlanta, GA, B.B.A.—Management   xxxx
Colonial Hills High School, East Point, GA   xxxx

Example 12: GS-14 General Engineer Seeking Promotion

This candidate wants to move to a GS-15 position.

EDUCATION

Certificate, *Program Management,* USDOE/OPM, Washington, DC, xxxx

Executive Training Program, USDA Graduate School, Washington, DC, xxxx

Certificate, *Civil Engineer, Industrial Engineer,* USAF Academy, Wright/Patterson AFB, xxxx

BSME, *Fluid Mechanics & Thermodynamics,* Johns Hopkins University, Baltimore, MD, xxxx

Diploma, Kenwood Senior High, Baltimore, MD, xxxx

CHAPTER 7

Writing About Your Other Qualifications

Outside of your 9 to 5 position, you might have another life. That's what "Other Qualifications" is about: the experience and qualifications you've gathered outside of work and formal education. Among the many possibilities are specialized skills, other languages, honors and awards, accomplishments, publications, professional memberships, community involvement or leadership, and public speaking. HR professionals might be impressed or interested in what you do above your job description. There's no guarantee that this information will qualify you for a position; however, many outside activities demonstrate leadership, communications skills, planning, and the ability to manage time and resources. It is important to present the whole picture!

Be sure to notice, however, the number of times the phrase "job-related" is repeated in government requirements. Your Federal resume should emphasize recent and job-related information. Federal HR professionals are looking for skills, accomplishments, and professional involvement that qualify you for a specific Federal position.

A Federal vacancy announcement might ask for "Other Qualifications" in the following way:

Other Qualifications

Job-related training courses (title and year)

Job-related skills (language skills, computer skills, tools, machinery, typing speed)

Job-related honors, awards, special accomplishments (publications, memberships in professional or honor societies, leadership activities)

 Note: Individuals applying for the first time to the Federal government have an advantage: The "Other Qualifications" section is typical and might already be included in your current private-industry resume. You can copy and paste this information from your private-industry resume into your Federal version.

Other qualifications might also include the following:

★ **Job-related skills:** You can demonstrate job-related skills through a list of training courses and certifications. Some examples in this chapter show separate Skills sections; others use training and certification lists that demonstrate specialized skills.

If you are writing an electronic resume, your job-related skills list will be one of the most important parts of your resume. In certain automated resume systems, the human resources recruiter will search for qualified candidates by certain skills. These can be included in the "Other Information" section of an electronic resume. Electronic resumes are discussed in chapter 12.

★ **Job-related certificates and licenses:** Only certain positions require specific certificates or licenses, so not every resume will list them.

★ **Job-related honors, awards, and special accomplishments:** These might include publications, memberships in professional or honor societies, and leadership activities.

Examples of "Other Qualifications" Sections

The following examples show the kinds of "other qualifications" information you can provide in your Federal resume.

Example 1: GS-7 Computer Specialist Seeking a GS-8 Position Using Novell Training

This applicant is seeking a position as an IT Specialist.

COMPUTER SKILLS

Office Products: Microsoft Office Suite (Word, Excel, PowerPoint), WordPerfect, PageMaker

Database/Financial: Oracle, MS Access, Quicken, Membership Plus

Groupware: Novell NetWare, MS Access

Systems: Windows 98/2000/XP

Example 2: GS-7 Computer Specialist Using a Combination Section of Skills, Training, and Certification

The diversity of this FEMA Computer Specialist's certifications, training, and skills is amazing. This Federal employee has extensive training and uses it every day.

COMPUTER SKILLS

Architectures: Intel 80x86, Pentium, Pentium Pro, Pentium II/III, XEON.

Operating Systems: UNIX BSD, MS-DOS, PC-MOS, VMS, CP/M, Windows, Windows for Workgroups, Windows NT 3.1–5.0, Windows 95/98. Windows 2000 Server, Workstation, and Advanced; Windows XP.

Network: Novell NetWare 3.11/12–4.10-5.1, UNIX, Linux, Windows for Workgroups, Windows 95/98, Microsoft Networking, Windows NT 3.1–5.0, TCP/IP, FTP, Telnet, UDP, DNS, NNTP, IRC, SMTP, FDDI, SSL, RAS, Token Ring, Wireless LAN Topology.

Databases: Proficient in SQL and Relational Database Management Systems, Access, Quattro, Paradox, FoxPro, dBASE III/IV, Btrieve.

Languages: UNIX—C, C Shell, Bourne Shell, Korn Shell; Microsoft Visual C++; Microsoft Backoffice (Internet Information Server and SNA Server); ODBC; OLE DB.

Internet: Perl and Java application development. CGI, HTML 1.0–3.0, Visual J++, Java, JavaScript, VBScript, Visual Basic Control Creation Edition, COM/DCOM, ActiveX. Internet mail, FTP, Usenet news groups, gopher, Archie, veronica, World Wide Web, Netscape Navigator, Netscape Navigator Gold, Microsoft FrontPage, HTML Assistant Pro, Hot Dog HTML, Microsoft Internet Explorer, Office Internet Assistant (Word, Excel, PowerPoint).

Graphics Design: Adobe Photoshop, Kai's Power Tools, CorelDRAW, QuarkXPress, Corel PHOTO-PAINT, Corel Xara, LView Pro, Paint Shop Pro, Asymetrix Web 3D, Hijaak, extensive image scanning and editing experience.

Education & Professional Training

BSBA, Management Information Systems, Thomas Edison State College, Trenton, NJ, December xxxx

Diploma, Hawthorne Academy, Hawthorne, NJ, xxxx

Certificate, *NT Course,* 4.0 GPA, County College of Morris, Randolph, NJ, xxxx

EM Police Officer, New Jersey State Police Academy, Paterson, NJ, xxxx

Certificate, New Jersey State Hazardous Materials Level I, xxxx

Certificate, Customer Service Training, xxxx

Certificate, Government Ethics Training, xxxx

MCSE, *MCSE Training Course,* New Horizons, Iselin, NJ, xxxx

Microsoft & Novell Official Curriculum, July–August xxxx, 120 hours

---

- Implementing and Supporting Microsoft Exchange Server 5.5

- Implementing and Supporting Microsoft Internet Information Server 4.0

- Internetworking with Microsoft TCP/IP on Microsoft Windows NT 4.0

- Networking Essentials

- Implementing and Supporting Microsoft Systems Management Server 2.0

- Implementing and Supporting Microsoft Systems Management Server 1.2

- Internetworking with Microsoft TCP/IP on Microsoft Windows NT 4.0

- Implementing and Supporting Microsoft Windows 95 and 98

- Novell 3.12/5.0, Certification Course for Administration and Engineering

Other Certifications

Certificate, IT Enterprise System, xxxx

Certificate, COMSEC Custodian, xxxx

Certificate, Exchange FEMA Administrator, xxxx

Certificate, Federal Communications Commission Technician Amateur Operator, xxxx

Certificate, Department of Defense United States Army MARS License, xxxx

Example 3: Electronic Resume Skills Summary for an Equal Employment Opportunity Specialist

This employee is with a Department of Defense agency. The Skills Summary contains many keywords and phrases found in the vacancy announcement and in her position description. Some electronic resumes should include certain keywords that will be critical for a human resources professional to "find you" through a database query. Knowing the keywords for your career is very important. See chapter 12 for more information on this.

Skills Summary

EEO/Affirmative Action and discrimination complaint processing, writing, analytical skills, fact-finding, case management, oral communications, negotiations, stress management, community liaison, public affairs, Corps of Engineers Early Resolution Program, EEO program evaluation, reports, EEO Executive Orders, Public Laws and Civil Rights Act, AR 690-600, CEERP, Career Program-28.

HQ, U.S. Army Corps of Engineers; Office of Public Affairs Representative and Recorder; Special Emphasis Program Committee; Member, Office Managers Advisory Committee; Recorder, Special Emphasis Training Committee.

(continues)

(continued)

Office management, organization, efficient systems, files management, systems design: Exceptional Performance Rating and cash award (xxxx)

Town Planning Commission Chair, Middletown, VA (xxxx–xxxx). Sensitive rezoning hearings, presentations, fact-finding, negotiations, mediations, hearings, reports, leadership.

Example 4: New College Graduate Applying for Law Enforcement Positions

Licenses & Certifications:

NREMT-P, Nationally Registered Paramedic, Registry 4PO00000

ACLS—Advanced Cardiac Life Support

PALS—Pediatric Advanced Life Support

CPR—Cardiopulmonary Resuscitation and Emergency Cardiac Care, American Heart Association

EMT—Emergency Medical Technician, certified in the state of MD

Nationally Registered Paramedic, Registry 4PO855719

Firefighter II, National Professional Qualifications Board

Example 5: GS-12 Contract Specialist with the DAWIA Certification

Certification:

Defense Acquisition Workforce Improvement Act level I and level II certified, xxxx

Example 6: Applicant for FAA Aviation Operations Position

LICENSES & CERTIFICATIONS:

Private Pilot, Instrument Rating

COMPUTER SKILLS:

ATP, AIRPAC, FLIESOFT, A/P DIRECTORY, SOURCE BOOK, AVITAT, INM, SIMMOD, Word, Excel, PowerPoint. Awarded for developing a new system database.

Example 7: Private-Industry Applicant for GS-13 Sanctuary Manager

The position this candidate seeks is with the National Oceanic and Atmospheric Administration (NOAA).

LICENSES:

U.S. Coast Guard Licensed Master, 100 Gross Tons

Professional Association of Dive Instructors: SCUBA Instructor

---

Example 8: GS-10–12 Operating Accountant, NIH

The candidate has included the CPA certification after her name at the top of the resume. The Professional Development section includes a listing of specialized accounting knowledge and skills.

Carolyn Harvey, CPA

EDUCATION

BS, Marketing, *Summa Cum Laude,* California State University, Fresno, CA, xxxx

Diploma, Riverdale High School, Riverdale, CA, xxxx

PROFESSIONAL DEVELOPMENT

Continuing Professional Education:

Financial Statement Preparation using QuickBooks, 8 hours, xxxx; Income Tax Considerations in Financial Planning, 8 hours, xxxx; New Time Mastery for the Accounting Professional, 8 hours, xxxx; Tax Traps for C Corporations, 8 hours, xxxx; When Clients Die—Post-Mortem Tax Returns and Tax Planning, 8 hours, xxxx; Excel for CPAs, 8 hours, xxxx.

Post-Graduate Accounting Classes:

Cost Accounting, 3 credits, xxxx; Advanced Accounting, 3 credits, xxxx; Tax Accounting—Partnerships and Corporations, 3 credits, xxxx; Intermediate Accounting (IRS in-house), 3 credits, xxxx; Auditing, 3 credits, xxxx; Tax Accounting—Individuals, 3 credits, xxxx; Intermediate Accounting I, 3 credits, xxxx.

Honors & Recognition:

Passed CPA exam (at first sitting)

Internal Revenue Service Enrolled Agent designation

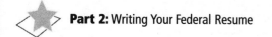

Example 9: Registered Nurse and Federal Applicant

This nurse is applying for the position of Health Insurance Specialist with the Centers for Medicare and Medicaid. Her clinical experience, case management, and certifications will be desirable for this medical insurance provision agency.

CERTIFICATIONS

Licensed Registered Nurse, Maryland and Washington, DC, current.

Critical Care Registered Nurse (CCRN), American Association of Critical Care Nurses (AACN), xxxx–xxxx.

Certified Case Manager (CCM), Commission for Case Manager Certification.

Professional, Academy for Healthcare Management Certification (PAHM).

PowerMHS Certified

Example 10: New College Graduate with an Economics Degree

This person is an applicant for a Labor Economist position with the U.S. Department of Labor.

Summary of Skills Developed from B.S. Degree Program in Economics:

Economics

Utilize knowledge of economic relationships to advise senior researchers.

Apply money, banking, and foreign-exchange principles to current research.

Econometrics

Prepare economic and governmental forecasts.

Provide information to support policy decision-making.

Computers

Mini-tab and SAS statistical software.

Data compilation, statistical analysis.

Spreadsheet and report production.

Internet and Microsoft Suite for research and report production.

Written Language

Construct clear, concise, audience-specific reports.

Conduct extensive research to support team-oriented work projects.

Public Speaking

Design and present informative, demonstrative, and persuasive speeches.

Deliver animated conference-level presentations with visual aids.

Interview specialized professionals and executives on economic research.

Example 11: Consular Assistant, Department of State, Moscow, Russia

Language Proficiency

Russian: 3/3 Level. Moderate speaking and writing. Able to interpret and translate adoption and legal documents and correspondence for both Americans and Russians.

International Travel

Extensive travel in over 50 countries. Lived in Australia for the entire year of xxxx. Lived in Italy for 3 months in xxxx. Lived in Russia for 2 years from xxxx to present. Traveled more than 2 months in over 10 countries.

Example 12: GS-7 Secretary/Office Automation with the Immigration and Naturalization Service

Languages

Bilingual, English and Spanish; reading, speaking, and typing

Example 13: GS-9 Secretary/Office Automation, NIH

Web Development Skills: Trained and experienced in HTML and Adobe Acrobat for programming and posting office travel schedule, program information, and mission statement to office Web site. Self-taught in both programs with experience for the past 10 months in compiling data, editing, programming, and posting more than 300 pages of documents viewed by internal and external customers. Skilled in Internet research, e-mail management, and creating links from other Web sites of interest to our customers.

Example 14: GS-11 Computer Specialist

EXPERTISE

Networks: Novell, Windows NT, Ethernet, TCP/IP (DHCP/WINS, DNS), NetWare, Token Ring, ARCNET, FDDI, and Remote Access Service (RAS)

Systems: UNIX; Windows NT, 95, 98, 2000; MS/DOS

Software: MS Exchange Server; MS Office Suite 95/97/2000—Word, Excel, Access, FrontPage, PowerPoint, Outlook; MS Visual Studio 6.0 w/Visual Basic & Visual Interdev; Telnet; WS_FTP; HTML; Norton Utilities and AntiVirus; Oracle Designer 2000; ILSMIS; SACONS; Simplified Procurement System (SPS); Contract Management System (CMS); and Quality Assurance Data Report (QADR)

CERTIFICATES & LICENSES

Microsoft Certified Solutions Developer, xxxx

Microsoft Certified Professional, xxxx
DAWIA Level III, xxxx

Example 15: GS-13 Information Technology Specialist

SUMMARY OF RELEVANT SKILLS:

Program Design: Skilled in programming and design including Object-Oriented design techniques.

Data Analysis and Graphics: Experienced with the management, analysis, and visualization of statistical data.

Web and Database Development: Knowledgeable in Web-based development using JavaScript and HTML. Database expertise with Microsoft Access, Oracle, and SQL.

Technical Support: Provided one-on-one tutoring and student/user assistance in a technical setting.

Project Support: Completed, tracked, and reported on technical projects.

Customer Service: Worked with end customers in a municipal environment.

COMPUTER SKILLS:

Languages: C/C++, HTML, JavaScript, SQL, Microsoft Visual Basic/J++, and VBScript

Software: Borland C++ 5.01, JDK 1.3, Microsoft Visual Studio, Microsoft Office, Oracle

Operating Systems: Windows 95/98/2000/NT

> **PROFESSIONAL TRAINING:**
>
> Public Speaking, Community College of Philadelphia (xxxx)
>
> WebMaster Training, Neumann Institute of Technology (xxxx)

Job-Related Honors, Awards, or Special Accomplishments

Your honors, awards, and special accomplishments might be important in qualifying you for certain positions. This section on your resume can include such items as publications, memberships in professional or honor societies, leadership activities, public speaking, and performance awards, as well as the dates you received them. Here is an overview of the items you might list and describe in this section on your Federal resume:

★ **Honors and awards** demonstrate career or educational excellence and recognition.

★ **Professional memberships** demonstrate involvement, motivation to learn about specific industries, and knowledge of state-of-the-art industry information through reading newsletters and attending conferences and meetings.

★ **Public speaking and presentations** show communications skills before groups and the ability to write and present information orally.

★ **Publication lists or written works** illustrate your ability to research, write, edit, use computers, and study a specific topic area.

★ **Collateral duties** in your Federal job can be listed in this section. These additional responsibilities might lead to new careers and positions. The responsibilities you carry out 5 to 20 hours per week can provide the skills you need to make a career change.

★ **Community or civic activities** demonstrate personal interest, dedication, and time committed to helping others. Involvement in community activities might give you valuable responsibilities such as leading groups, planning, promoting and coordinating events, managing budgets, negotiating contracts, directing volunteers, and achieving organizational goals.

The following sections contain examples of various resume sections for your honors, awards, memberships, public speaking, and publications. You can follow these examples when you write your own Federal resume.

Example 16: GS-14 Senior Budget Analyst, FDA

HONORS/AWARDS

FDA Group Recognition Award (Honor), two in xxxx

Quality Service Cash Award, xxxx–xxxx

Award for Patriotic Service, Department of the Treasury, xxxx, xxxx

Special Service Award, xxxx

Special Act Cash Award, xxxx

FDA Commendable Service Award (Honor), xxxx, xxxx

Certificate of Appreciation, District of Columbia Public Schools, xxxx

Certificate of Appreciation for work with FDA Career Development Forum, xxxx

Presidential Outstanding Scholastic Achievement Citation, xxxx

Outstanding Employee Performance Management System (EPMS) Rating, xxxx, xxxx

Numerous performance awards and letters of appreciation

COMMUNITY SERVICE

Coach, State Champion Odyssey of the Mind Team, Urbana High School, Ijamsville, MD

Administrative Board Member, Youth Group Leader, Finance Committee Member, Education Committee Member: Providence United Methodist Church, Kemptown, MD

Example 17: GS-12 Procurement Specialist

AWARDS:

Outstanding Performance Appraisal Review System Award, xxxx, xxxx

Quality Salary (Grade) increase, xxxx, xxxx, xxxx

Tac-4 Contract Recognition Award from Vice Admiral

Tac-4 Protest Recognition Award from Rear Admiral

Outstanding Achievement Award for xxxx Navy Contracting Intern Training Conference

Navy Intern Conference Letter of Commendation from Assistant Secretary of the Navy

Distinguished graduate for Contracting 201, 211, and 241 courses

United States Government Outstanding Scholar Program recipient

Letter of Commendation from FISC executive officer for outstanding customer support

G.T.E. Academic All-American, all-conference academic team in college football

College Scholars of America

Letter of appreciation from U.S. Senator Carl Levin for outstanding constituent support

LEADERSHIP AND ACTIVITIES:

Civilian Leadership Development Program, College Football team captain for over 100 players, National Contract Management Association, Ice Hockey team captain responsible for organization of 20 teammates, Benevolent and Protective Order of Elks, Friends of the National Zoo, Sons of the American Revolution, NISMC blood drive coordinator, Soil and Water Conservation Society, Government Ethics Representative, High School class president responsible for class reunion of over 300 people, Ball State University Alumni Association and Varsity Club

Example 18: GS-12 Computer Specialist, U.S. Customs Service

HONORS & AWARDS:

Dinner for Two Award for the upgrade of the NLECC Network wiring system, xxxx

Certificate of Meritorious Service for support of administrative and program management missions, xxxx

Letter of Appreciation for communications support provided to the EEO Conference, xxxx

Letter of Appreciation from Deputy Director, EEO, for the setup and monitoring of the telecommunications center for the National EEO Training conference, Orlando, FL, xxxx

Certificate of Appreciation for U.S. Customs TECS I to TECS II data center conversion from San Diego, CA, to the Newington Data Center, xxxx

Letter of Appreciation, U.S. Customs Service Assistant Commissioner, Office of Investigations Executive and International Association of Police Conferences, xxxx

Certificate of Award, Director of NLECC, for research, testing, and implementation of the Motorola Centracom Series II Traffic Logger configuration and successful installation, xxxx

Time-Off Award, North Florida CMC, for keeping the networks functioning at peak efficiency, xxxx

Certificate of Award, North Florida CMC Director, Excellent performance of duties, xxxx

Superior Performance Award, Office of Information and Technology, xxxx

Employee of the Month Award, U.S. Customs Service, xxxx

Certificate of Appreciation, TECS II Law Enforcement Computer Systems Conversion, xxxx

Example 19: GS-13 Logistics Section Chief and Paramedic, Disaster Medical Assistance Team

LICENSES/CERTIFICATIONS:

National & Massachusetts Registered Emergency Medical Technician—Paramedic

Advanced Cardiac Life Support

Pediatric Advanced Life Support

Advanced Basic Trauma Life Support

Certified to the expanded scope of practice for interfacility transfer of critically ill patients

HONORS AND AWARDS:

Military decorations include the Air Force Commendation Medal w/oak leaf cluster and the Air Medal

Personally and individually thanked by former First Lady Hillary Clinton on behalf of the President for disaster-response work on St. Thomas after Hurricane Marilyn in xxxx

Outstanding Member of the Year, Metro-Boston DMAT, xxxx

MEMBERSHIPS AND AFFILIATIONS:

Massachusetts Firefighters Association

International Association of Firefighters

International Association of EMTs and Paramedics

Massachusetts EMT Association

Ancient Free and Accepted Masons

Lions Club

MENSA

Example 20: Advertising Executive Applying for GS-12 Public Affairs Specialist, USDA

HONORS & AWARDS

Gamma Beta Phi Honor Society

2001 Champions Away, Open Class Skydiving

PROFESSIONAL MEMBERSHIPS

National Association of Broadcasters & American Advertising Federation

COMMUNITY SERVICE

Public Relations Director, Organization Originator, Carolina Skydiving League, Raleigh, NC, 1999 to Present: Originated and organized professional formation skydiving team from the ground up. Developed key sponsorship to offset team training, pay league and travel expenses, and fund competitive events. Organized and implemented public-relations events to garner support for, promote, and inform the public about skydiving. Developed league logo and informational and promotional materials, including photography. Gained national recognition through several published articles in *Parachutist Magazine.* Received local TV and newspaper coverage throughout the 2001 season.

Example 21: GS-9 Aviation Operations

Specialized Knowledge:
- Corporate Aviation: 91 vs. 135
- Aircraft Valuations
- Aviation Regulations: 61, 91, 135 121
- Advisory Circulars
- Insurance: Aircraft Pilots
- Legal Assistance: Accidents/incidents
- FAA Orders
- Corporate Status; Legal Research
- Taxes: Sales/Use, Income
- Aviation Sales
- FAA Enforcement Actions
- Title/Escrows and Liens
- Airman Certification
- Marketing Surveys
- Maintenance: ADs, MPRMs

Professional Affiliations:
National Business Aviation Association
American Association of Airport Executives
Aircraft Owners and Pilots Association
Florida Institute of Technology School of Aeronautics Alumni Association

Example 22: GS-12 Nurse Consultant Seeking Public Health Advisor, Centers for Disease Control

Accomplishments

- Plan and direct analysis of long-term health care institutions; provide technical assistance and consultation to health care providers in identifying issues, developing performance measures and benchmarks, and evaluating program performance.

- Exercise oversight of Kansas State Agency surveyors in carrying out Medicaid and Medicare guidelines and policy as outlined in the *State Operations Manual*.

- As a nurse consultant, assist long-term health care institutions in compliance with Medicaid and Medicare beneficiary requirements.

- Adjunct Clinical Instructor, Sanford Brown College, North Kansas City, MO.

- Nominated as an instructor in HCFA's 2000 Presidential Classroom Volunteer Instructor Program because of "ability to work effectively with persons of various backgrounds and strong personalities," and because "he brings a new pinnacle of energy and vigor into his nurse consultant role at HCFA."

Languages

Spanish as a Second Language—Intermediate Level

Licenses & Certificates

Registered Professional Nurse, Missouri

Certificate: Federal and State Surveyor

Certificate: Emergency CPR

Certificate: Instructor Candidate Training

Computer Skills

Microsoft Word, PowerPoint, Excel, Mail, Windows; database applications, COBRA, Internet research

Honors & Recognition

Numerous Letters of Commendation and Certificates of Appreciation throughout career

Successful Performance Evaluations, HCFA, 1999 to Present

Example 23: Performance Monitoring Team Senior Enlisted Advisor Seeking GS-12 Training Instructor

QUALIFICATIONS:

Experienced in course development: Trained and supervised instructors in course development, presentation, testing, and evaluation skills. Certified as Navy Master Training Specialist and Curriculum Developer. Researched, developed, and beta-tested courses. Knowledgeable and experienced in design, development, and coordination of both basic and highly specialized training programs for personnel.

Skilled instructor: 15 years of experience training diverse student body of adult learners. Experienced in evaluating student progress. Proficient in training large or small groups: trained groups of 1 to 1,600 students.

Accomplished presenter: Experienced in conducting workshops, courses, and seminars to highly diverse groups of individuals. Presented wide range of technical and security-related materials to skilled personnel.

Expertise in security education: Proven record of training personnel in all aspects of technical and security issues. Direct experience in security and safety-related activities including information-based security and physical law enforcement.

JOB-RELATED SKILLS:
Proficient with Microsoft Office including Word, Outlook, and Excel.
Experienced curriculum developer using Microsoft PowerPoint software.
Instructional skills evaluator for a major Navy training facility.
Qualified in CPR and basic First Aid.
Math teacher at Sylvan Learning Center; high school math tutor with Navy Personal Excellence Program.
Teach math and science as well as test-taking skills and calculator use.
Adult Education Literacy instructor at the Camden County Adult Literacy Center.
Assisted 33 adults in earning their GEDs.
Volunteer facilities aid at a local family abuse shelter.
Subase Kings Liaison with the Camden County School Board.

CERTIFICATES and LICENSES:
Top Secret Security Clearance
Certified Navy Master Training Specialist
Scholastic Aptitude Test (SAT) Preparatory Course Facilitator

HONORS, AWARDS, and MEMBERSHIPS:
Navy Commendation Medal
Navy Achievement Medal
Good Conduct Medals
Letters of Commendation
Navy Pistol Expert Marksman: xxxx to Present
Meritorious Unit Commendations

Example 24: GS-8 Secretary, FDA, Seeking GS-9 Paralegal Specialist, Department of Justice

Professional Development

MS Outlook, 8 hours, 2003; Customer Service, 4 hours, 2003; Time Management, 8 hours, 2003; Workplace Security Procedures, 4 hours, 2003

Computer Skills

Westlaw, Lexis/Nexis, Microsoft Windows, Help Desk operations, Lotus 1-2-3, SPPS, Corel Office, Microsoft Office (including Word, Excel, Outlook, PowerPoint, Access), WordPerfect, GroupWise, Internet research, Harvard Graphics, various off-the-shelf and proprietary databases, OCR applications, automated document-management applications. Type: 65 wpm

Awards & Recognition

Performance Awards, last five consecutive years—xxxx–xxxx
Cash awards—xxxx, xxxx
Time-Off awards—xxxx, xxxx, xxxx
President's Grant (University of Maryland)—xxxx
Numerous Letters and Certificates of Recommendation throughout career

Community Service

Key Worker, Combined Federal Campaign, DHHS, xxxx
Chairperson, Savings Bond Campaign, DHHS, xxxx
Volunteer Tutor, Reading and Math, grades 1–6, xxxx–Present
Volunteer, Immanuel's Church Dinner Ministry, xxxx
Volunteer, Teen Mania Ministries, Teen Summer Missions, xxxx–xxxx

Sports, Activities, and Special Interests

You might wonder why this information should go on your Federal resume. This information will not help you qualify for the position. However, if the hiring manager is an avid golfer, sailor, or Orioles fan, you'll give him or her a short vacation from the serious side of candidate reviews. These outside activities usually show leadership, communications ability, organizational skills, creativity, entrepreneurial spirit, planning, management, budgeting, mentoring, counseling, teamwork, and interpersonal-relations skills. Outside activities also show energy, interest, enthusiasm, community spirit, involvement, caring, giving of time, the ability to manage multiple functions, and commitment and service to others. That's a lot. If this information makes your resume stand out, you should include it, just in case.

This resume section could be titled *Personal Interests* or *Personal Information* and be listed at the end of the resume.

Example 25: GS-12, Program Analyst, Department of Commerce, Seeking GS-13 Program Manager Position, U.S. Army Corps of Engineers

> **Avid youth softball league coach, volunteer, and fan** with 2 children, ages 12 and 14, active in the community league; schedule practices and more than 25 games per season. Supervise, train, and coach a team of 18 middle-school youths in softball skills and team spirit.
>
> **Member of Getaway Sailing Club Race Team** sailing J-23s on a weekly basis in the Baltimore Harbor. Successfully won 3 out of 3 races as Captain. Train team and manage practices.
>
> **Member of Semi-Pro Men's Tennis League,** Capital Hills, Washington, DC (xxxx–present). Active player of Men's Singles and Doubles, achieving a regional championship out of 5 states.

Media, Quotes, Articles, and Public Speaking

If you've been quoted in a newspaper, spoken before a class or association on your area of expertise, been interviewed on the radio, or done something brave or incredible, write it in your resume and include it again in your KSA statement. The popular KSA statement, "Ability to communicate orally and in writing" can be answered with detailed statements regarding your public speaking and articles.

The following examples show how to feature this kind of information on your Federal resume. You can list this information under the category of *Published Works*, *Articles Written*, or *Media Reviews*.

Example 26: Various Applicants

> **Quoted and featured in newspapers** on the subject of resume writing, small business management, and politically related career-change processes in *The Washington Post*, *The Baltimore Sun*, *Warfield's Business Weekly*, *Patent Publishing Co.*, and *FEW News & Views*.
>
> **Community leader.** Subsequent to a terrorist bomb attack on our office building in Riyadh, Saudi Arabia, November 13, xxxx, recognized as the community leader for the organization of family support efforts, casualty visitation, donations, and counseling services.
>
> **Publications, speeches, articles.** Frequent guest speaker/trainer at numerous state and local CSE conferences and workshops. "Improving Program Performance Through Management Information," DHHS, xxxx.

Travel Experience

If you travel extensively through your work or on your own, it might interest the hiring manager. Many job applicants travel so much in their work that they forget to mention it. If you travel extensively in your work, tell the reader where you travel and for what reasons. The Travel Experience section goes at the end of the resume, along with any personal information you choose to add.

Example 27: Various Applicants—International Travel

If you are an international traveler, be sure to add this to your resume. The government is a global employer and you might find a position that requires international or domestic travel.

International Travel:

Extensive travel in over 50 countries. Lived in Australia for the entire year of xxxx. Lived in Italy for 3 months in xxxx. Lived in Russia for 2 years from xxxx to present. Traveled more than 2 months in over 10 countries.

International Travel:

Traveled extensively as Project Manager and Technical Support since xxxx to more than 100 customers in Europe, The People's Republic of China, and throughout Asia.

Summary

The Other Information section can add to your "likeability factor." But the next chapter, "Writing Your Work Experience," can actually get you ranked "best qualified," and even hired. Keep reading and soon you will have your Federal resume completed.

CHAPTER 8

Writing Your Work Experience

Now you are ready to start writing the most important and difficult part of the Federal resume—your Work Experience section. This chapter covers writing about work experience for the Federal resume based on the following: your current resume, OF-612, or SF-171; your private-industry resume; part-time and small-business positions; and unpaid experience. All of the sample resume excerpts include "duties" and "accomplishments" so that you can remember to cover both types of information in your most relevant positions.

You will also be introduced to the "writing partner" concept. Brainstorming with a colleague or friend can help you talk about your work in more detail and with more enthusiasm than you would write. You'll learn how to get feedback and expand your job experiences to include specifics, accomplishments, and a more clear description. Finally, this chapter will teach you how to make your job descriptions follow the HR professional's Factor Evaluation System (FES), ensuring you have covered all important elements for the human resource professional's review.

Since the 1999 edition of the *Federal Resume Guidebook,* there has been one major change in writing the Work Experience section. In 1999 most Federal resume writers were converting their long, detailed work experience sections into more succinct, shorter descriptions. Recently, resume writers have gone to the other extreme. The descriptions are usually too short and do not include all of the job elements, FES factors, and accomplishments that can get applicants selected as "best qualified" for a specific job.

This chapter is dedicated to helping you write just the right amount of copy for your work experience descriptions—not too short, not too long. We'll help you recognize important details and specifics about diverse experiences and spell out accomplishments that will "sell" you to the decision-maker. You'll also learn the right keywords to include for your particular occupational series.

Allow plenty of time to write your Work Experience section. This one section could take you 5 to 10 hours to write, edit, and rewrite.

Why is the Work Experience section so important? Steve McGarry, an official with the OPM, says that the first goal of the Federal resume is simply to show that the candidate meets the basic qualifications for the vacancy announcement (for example, academic degrees, years of experience, areas of expertise, and technical capabilities). The KSAs tell whether a candidate is qualified to perform the specific position (see chapter 14 for more on writing KSAs). HR professionals want the hard facts—not a life story—that allow them to screen the resume quickly and see basic qualifications.

What the Work Experience Section Should Include

Here is the Federally required information for the Work Experience section, taken from OPM brochure OF-510:

WORK EXPERIENCE

Give the following information for your paid and nonpaid work experience related to the job you are applying for (do not send job descriptions):

Job title (include series and grade if Federal job)

Duties and accomplishments

Employer's name and address

Supervisor's name and phone number

Check out the OPM's only official instruction on how to write the Work Experience: "duties and accomplishments." Those three words translate into hours of thinking and writing, and pages of text. Those three words are what you do at work and are a major part of your resume.

As you think about and possibly get overwhelmed with writing your work history, you're probably wondering how much you have to write, how many years you have to go back, and how many jobs you should include. Here are quick answers to a few typical questions and a review of what's most important to include in your Federal resume:

★ **How much should I include in a description of a job?** Now that the long "life-history" descriptions that people had to include for the SF-171 have pretty much disappeared, applicants have gone to the other extreme, writing very short job descriptions. After the HR person reads them, he or she really has no idea what the applicant does. Some job applicants write work experience descriptions that focus only on achievements, giving the reader no clear idea of what the applicant's job was, and others do not include achievements

at all. The best way is to include a clear, point-by-point description of what you do and a separate section that identifies several accomplishments.

★ **How far back should I go?** Focus on the last 10 years. You will need to cover 10 years of work experience and include all compliance details. Positions you held 15 to 20 years ago will not be of interest to the busy readers.

★ **Should each description be the same length?** Summarize or write shorter descriptions of jobs prior to the last 10 years. You can include these jobs if they are relevant to your objective; otherwise, leave them out. Gaps in dates are okay. The HR professionals want to read the relevant and recent positions.

★ **What if the most important job I held in relation to my current objective was 10 years ago?** If you are returning to a job/career you held 10 years ago, emphasize that job, even though it was 10 years ago. Many people return to previous careers. Develop that job as though it were your current position. Play down the other jobs that are not as relevant to your current objective.

★ **How long should my current job description be?** Most of your time and energy will be spent writing this description (if it is your highest level and is most closely related to your objective). You could budget one to five hours for writing it. The description will be from three paragraphs to several pages long. If you have been in your current position for five years, most of the difficult, important writing will be over when you finish this description.

★ **Is the Work Experience section the most important section?** Yes, this is the section that will get you rated as qualified or best qualified for the job (in addition to your KSAs). You generally can use the following list, but you won't necessarily use all of the headings. You can adapt this list for writing about your major and most recent positions.

  ✰ Job Information and Compliance Details (title of job, agency, office, address, supervisor, supervisor's phone, salary, hours per week)

  ✰ Introduction (overview of the office's mission and service)

  ✰ Duties & Responsibilities

  ✰ Accomplishments/Projects

  ✰ Teams/Collateral Duties

★ **How long should my second job description be?** This description will be approximately half as long as the first position, unless it is your most job-related position.

★ **Can I include community service and volunteer positions or unpaid experience?** Remember to include both paid and unpaid work experience related to the job for which you are applying, for positions within the last 10 years. You can include the following: community and civic leadership positions, association or nonprofit leadership positions, teaching, consulting, and small-business experiences. Don't

follow the format of the preceding list for these positions—just give compliance details and a few descriptive lines. At the end of the chapter, you'll see examples of how to format these types of work experiences.

★ **What about jobs I held prior to the last 10 years?** It's your choice whether to show a short chronology of your early career. If this experience is job related, you need to describe the positions in detail so that you will qualify for the position.

Know Your Audience: Who's Going to Read Your Resume?

In the private sector, the audience of a resume is the hiring official. Personnel staff might do some preliminary screening, but that's all. The hiring official hires whomever she or he wants, and the personnel staff simply process the paperwork. In the Federal government, the personnel function is much more important.

HR Professionals

There are at least two audiences for your resume. First the HR professional will review your resume to determine whether you are qualified for the job. Since the founding of the Civil Service and the overturning of the "spoils system," a goal of the Federal personnel process is to ensure that the most qualified candidate is selected and that political and personal influences on the process are minimized, at least for so-called "statutory" positions. You must take seriously the role of personnel staff in the process and realize that your Federal resume must meet this audience's needs.

The HR professionals will determine whether your stated qualifications fit the formal requirements of the position and, if so, will classify you as "qualified." Depending on the number of qualified applicants, they usually perform a deeper evaluation to select the "best qualified" candidates. Only the best-qualified candidates are forwarded to the selecting official (your potential supervisor).

Do not assume that the staffing specialist is an expert in your career field, although many are quite knowledgeable. Help the specialist understand and interpret your qualifications by writing your work experience descriptions in language they can understand. If you make the specialist's job easier, you will get more benefit of the doubt. Confuse or obscure your qualifications and you will earn a lower score than your experience merits.

The Selecting Official

The second reader will be the selecting official, who has some discretion in choosing the candidate she or he likes best from among the best qualified.

When the hiring official sees your Federal resume, it is in a folder along with resumes from other highly qualified candidates (your competition). The hiring official does not normally have to interview all highly qualified candidates. Who gets interviewed? Qualifications are important, of course. But so is the "feel" the hiring official gets from the resume. Is there a "likeability factor" in your resume? Does your resume appeal to the hiring official in terms of your experience, expertise, accomplishments, and writing style?

The official might also be asking him- or herself such questions as "Is the applicant a positive person?" "Is he hard working?" "Will I like him?" "Will she fit my team?" "Is she going to be a threat to my job?" You can deal with these issues in a resume by watching your writing's tone. Show your final version to friends and ask how they feel about the person on that piece of paper. Read your resume out loud to see whether it seems positive and interesting.

Do Your Research

Before you can start writing, it is vital that you do your research, both on your own work experience and on the agency that you are targeting.

Researching Your Work Experience

Go to your computer, your files, your bookcases, and your briefcase and gather your latest resume, KSAs, SF-171, OF-612, and any other agency employment form. This will be helpful information for the chronology, overview, and compliance details. Also look for the following information:

★ **Position descriptions (PD) for your last two positions.** Beware of depending on the PD for the duties and responsibilities of your job. Is the PD up-to-date? Does it really say what you do? You should not write directly from the PD—this could result in a 171 life-history document. Use the PD to ensure you include the most important aspects of your jobs.

★ **Supervisory evaluations.** Look for the text and keywords used in the evaluations. Read the evaluations to find out where your strengths are. If your evaluations are "pass/fail," look at the key elements of the evaluation—these probably reflect your major duties.

★ **Independent Development Plans.** Many critical skills, keywords, and accomplishments included in IDPs can be used in your resume.

★ **Annual Achievements List or Yearly Annual Reports** (if you write one). This is great information for the accomplishments portion of your job description and also for KSA statements.

★ **Agency brochures and mission statements** (from the Web site or your office). This description can give you insight into customers, services, programs, and future plans that you can use in your work experience writeup.

★ **Letters of commendation and appreciation awards.** Hopefully you saved these letters and awards to remind yourself of your value as an employee. The awards and letters are written by others about you and your accomplishments. These descriptions can be great resume and KSA material. Remember that you are trying to "sell" yourself. If you have received recognition for outstanding service, this is a demonstration of your work excellence!

★ **Vacancy announcements.** The announcements include keywords, skills, and information that you can use to build your Federal resume and KSAs.

★ **Transcripts of college courses and college course catalog descriptions.** If you are a recent college graduate or a returned college graduate, you might need to describe your courses. You can find wonderful keywords and language in the course descriptions that might help you write your critical skills.

Researching Federal Agencies

Know your agencies before you apply. Check out the following resources so that you can target your Federal resume and KSAs, and prepare for an interview.

Background information on your potential employer can be very helpful. Information about Federal agencies will help you write your Work Experience section with more confidence, and your interviews will go much more smoothly. If you are seeking your first government job, read the *U.S. Government Manual* (available online at www.access.gpo.gov), agency Web sites, and the Federal budget to get a good perspective on departments, agencies, and programs. If you are

a current Federal employee, read your job description in the Qualifications Standards and your agency's Web site to review its mission.

Here are more details on where to find information on Federal government jobs and agencies:

★ **Qualifications Standards.** A list of the classification standards for each occupational series is online at www.opm.gov. Or if you have time or access to your local Federal Agency Personnel Office or Federal Job Information Center, you can find *The Qualifications Standards Operating Manual* (formerly called the X-118). This lists basic descriptions of each major government position, which can help you write your Work Experience section and KSAs. Another reason to check the official standards is for keywords and skills. If you use the same language as the official standards for your series, it's easier for the staffing specialist to determine that you possess the needed experience.

★ **Classification Standards.** Also available on www.opm.gov is the *Introduction to the Handbook of Occupational Groups & Families*. You can find your occupational series in this file.

★ **Agency Web sites.** At agency Web sites, you can read and print the mission statement to gain an understanding of the organization. You can find information about agency programs, services, and customers so that you can focus your Federal resume and KSAs toward meeting the agency's goals. Read recent press releases and any "what's new" items so that you can be prepared for an interview as well.

★ **Other Web sites.** Search other sites such as www.washingtonpost.com and www.govexec.com for articles and information on specific agencies. Sometimes you can read about customers, problems, challenges, and success stories of agencies that can give you insight for writing your package and preparing for an interview.

★ *The United States Government Manual.* This is a giant guideline and resource for agencies and programs. It is available from the Government Printing Office (GPO; www.access.gpo.gov to download a PDF version).

★ **The Federal budget.** If you are willing to work harder than the average person and really want an edge, get a copy of the Federal budget (available online at http://w3.access.gpo.gov/usbudget/fy2002/ fy2002_srch.html). This hefty tome is packed with information, although it's hard to extract. Among the information in the budget is a table of expected employment levels in agencies and programs. You can discover which agencies are getting more people and which are scheduled for major shrinking.

What if you're just answering a specific announcement or two? Try to research the agencies so that you can integrate specific terminology into your package. You will be far more impressive on paper and in an interview if you have done your homework on an agency's mission, programs, and future.

More Preparation Before Writing

You've done your homework and now you're almost ready to write. But first you should get in the right frame of mind for writing by looking at your reasons for writing your resume. You might also enlist the help of a writing partner to help you brainstorm for your resume content.

Getting Psyched to Write
Writing a great resume for yourself requires determination, motivation, and positive thinking.

You have reasons why you are writing a new Federal resume. Check off the motivating factors from the following list that will inspire you to write your new resume in the best possible way:

❑ My job series is being discontinued, so I *have* to change series.

❑ My agency is relocating, so I *have* to find another job so that I can stay in this geographic area.

❑ My office just won a privatization contract, but my job will be downgraded in one year, eventually resulting in less pay and no advancement opportunities.

❑ I need to make more money. I want a promotion.

❑ I am bored and I want new challenges.

❑ I'm getting nowhere; I need to change jobs/agencies/offices…something.

If any of these motivating factors works for you, it could drive you to get this resume rewritten, work with your "writing partner" (see the next section), research jobs (see chapter 4), and *get hired!*

When you write the descriptions of your positions, think about impressing the HR professional and the decision-maker. Be positive, upbeat, and enthusiastic and sell your accomplishments. If you need help getting motivated and inspired, enlist a writing partner to get you moving.

Getting Help from a Writing Partner
Recruit a friend to help you brainstorm about your work experience write-ups. Most people have trouble remembering everything they do. Or they just can't stand to think about all of their work—"since they do so much." I use the "writing partner" approach in my office and workshops. I have found that people talk about their work duties much better than they write

about them. The feedback you will receive from your writing partner will be empowering and will help you build confidence. PLUS, this is great interview practice!

Find someone who will interview you about your job. It would be better if this person were *not* a coworker. A coworker will know the job too well and might overlook important duties that they assume are there. Your writing partner can interview you about your job and write the answers on a separate sheet. Soon you will start talking about your job's challenges and problems (that you fix—potential KSA material), the new programs, the customers, meeting the organization's mission, and so on. If you get excited about your job and recognize that your work is important and valuable, you will write an interesting description of your work.

Here are some suggested interview questions that you and your writing partner can ask one another:

★ What does your organization do? (What is its mission?)

★ What do you do all day long? (This information is for the Duties and Responsibilities section. An example is, "Talk to customers, use the computer, travel, and write." Write percentages following the major areas of their work; for example, "telephones 20%; administrative 50%; writing and e-mail 30%.")

★ Are you really busy? (The answer to this implies the level of work you handle. Can you quantify this in any way?)

★ Who are your major customers? (The answer should be titles rather than people's names and descriptions of who they are. Include both internal and external customers.)

★ How do you communicate with others? (By telephone, e-mail, fax, in person, travel.)

★ Do you use a computer to do your work? (List specific software programs that you use.)

★ What is the hardest part of your job? (You know this one.)

★ What kind of challenges do you face at work?

★ What do you like the most about your job? (Think hard about this.)

★ Have you done anything at work this past year that makes you really proud? (**Important:** This is the accomplishments question for your resume now and for your KSAs later.)

Converting Your SF-171, OF-612, or Private-Sector Resume into a Better, Expanded Federal Resume

You've gathered your information, reviewed it for relevancy, and been interviewed by your writing partner. It's time for you to start writing. The first step in writing should be to get everything on paper. A famous newspaper editor told a young reporter, "Don't put more fire into your work. Put more of your work into the fire." Write it all, go into excruciating depth, and cut from there. Your first draft should be a life-story approach, which you will edit profusely. Write everything, but be sure not to send it yet. Here is an example of how to start.

What the Job Was or Is

Write like you speak, at least in this draft. You might write something like this:

> I am responsible for the shop repair and modification of heavy mobile equipment, as well as represervation of Principal End items for weapons systems for the Marines.

Add Detail

Imagine your daily routine and write it all down (you'll edit later). Explain this as if you were writing for a stranger who knows nothing about what you do:

> I oversee a warehouse and parts facility for the repair and assembly of heavy mobile equipment and weapons systems. I plan the work schedule for the repair team. I monitor work processes, train the staff, ensure safe work practices, and implement efficiency measures to improve performance. I also write reports and order parts as needed for the field customers. I am an engineering advisor, as well. I analyze sketches and blueprints to determine the best methods of repair and retrofit of complex heavy mobile equipment, some of which were originally manufactured in the 1940s but are still servicing the Marine Corps in land operations and training exercises. I participate in budget planning for the shop operations.

Did you leave out any steps? Reread your draft and add to it if necessary.

Next, Quantify Everything

Put in numbers that help flesh out the picture. Tell the reader how many, how big, how much, and so on.

> The warehouse and parts facility that I manage is 100,000 square feet with more than 10,000 items. I supervise, plan projects for, and train 10 skilled tradesmen, including heavy mobile equipment repairers, preservation servicers, tire repairers, material handlers, and a tool and parts attendant. We generate $1.5 million in billings per year for Marine Corps repair services. Our customers are located throughout the world, some in preparation for war, others in training exercises and bases. I keep track of time for chargeable billings to the various base functions. I have improved efficiency and time for completion of major projects by 30% by improving reports, the availability of parts, and the management of inventory and the warehouse. Our safety has improved by 70%.

Organize and Add Accomplishments

Now that you have a good general description, organize your content into the major functions of your job. Add accomplishments separately so that they stand out. Have you received awards or recognition?

> 12-2002 to present; 40 hours per week; Heavy Mobile Equipment Repairer Supervisor 1, WS-5803-08; Temporary Promotion. Preservation and Maintenance Section, Fleet Support Center, Marine Corps Logistics Base, Barstow, CA 92311; MSgt. John Stein, 666 666-6666; may contact.
>
> FIRST LINE SUPERVISOR for Yermo Preservation and Maintenance Section. Plan, schedule, direct, and control the repair, modification, depreservation operational check, and represervation of all Principle End Items—PEIs—tactical or nontactical heavy mobile equipment, weapon systems, engineering, and commercial equipment, including sub-assembly or accessory components. ACCOMPLISHMENT: Devised more efficient and economical work processes in support of new and rollback receipts, care-in-storage programs, Preposition War Reserve requirements, Repair and Evaluate, and initial issues of PEI.

PLANNING: Evaluate work requirements, deadlines, available manpower, and equipment; plan sequence of work operations; interpret instruction, sketches, drawings, specifications, standards, and other written criteria. Plan, prioritize, and assign daily work to subordinates to meet operational needs and completion dates. Make adjustments in assignments when required to address unforeseen circumstances. Coordinate with other units on layout and execution of special projects. Provide input on annual budget and long-range plans for the shop's operation. ACCOMPLISHMENT: Improved production by 35% through planning and communication with other units for project completion. Saved an average of 20 hours per 100-hour project.

PRODUCTION MANAGEMENT: Coordinate flow of material into and out of shop with other divisions, branches, and sections base-wide. Evaluate manpower resources, material, and equipment needed; determine technical skills of employees, and assign and control workflow, assuring completed work meets established production and quality standards. Keep superiors informed of jobs in progress, material and equipment, and the need for adjustments in schedules and materials. ACCOMPLISHMENT: Reviewed work in progress for efficiency and safety of operations; resolved work production problems; took action to prevent delays caused by bottlenecks, equipment breakdowns, or material and employee shortages. These actions resulted in improved production by an overall 25% in the shop.

EMPLOYEE TRAINING and SAFETY: Instruct and train employees on proper work methods and techniques; establish and maintain employee safety program through meetings, inspections, training, written guidelines, and policies. ACCOMPLISHMENT: Developed regular safety training and communications program. Managed continuous maintenance program to eliminate unsafe working conditions and assure proper upkeep of tools, machinery, and equipment.

ADMINISTRATION: Prepare management reports on production, safety, work improvement, work stoppages, or problem areas. Maintain records of time chargeable to various functions; provide information to higher authority on production, accidents, and cost estimates. Order and maintain technical data, current specifications, and standards for vehicle rebuild, repair, and preservations. Submit reports on attendance, vehicle utilization, training, fire and security checks, equipment, accidents, manpower utilization, and other special reports. ACCOMPLISHMENT: Improved consistent reports, orders, and records of time chargeable to functions, which impressed senior leadership with accountability and production output. Received a Superior Evaluation and Recognition for Outstanding Service to Customers.

The Factor Evaluation System (FES)

Human Resources Professionals use the FES to evaluate work and to determine its proper level of monetary compensation—in other words, its proper title, series, and grade level. The nine FES factors are useful to you because they form a handy and logical checklist to ensure that your job descriptions are effective, persuasive, and written with the mindset of the reviewer in mind. When you have written a draft of your Federal resume job descriptions, you can review them against the FES factors to ensure that certain key elements are covered. Although you might not need to cover all nine of the FES factors, it is a good idea to include small elements of several of these factors in each of your job descriptions.

The key to using the FES factors as a guide in writing the job description portions of your resume is that human resources professionals in

Federal agencies are sensitive to these factors as methods of "sizing up" the importance of your job experience. Although you should not use the FES factors to aid you in exaggerating the importance of your experience, you should *definitely* use them as a means of helping HR officials give you full credit for the "grade level" of the work you accomplished in each of your jobs.

The FES Criteria

The FES criteria for each position are the following:

1. **Knowledge required for the position** (the specific knowledges you applied to do your work)

2. **Supervisory controls** (the level of supervision you received while doing your work; for instance, "Performed the duties of Administrative Assistant with a high degree of independence, and sought the advice of my supervisor only on rare occasions...")

3. **Guidelines** (the written guidelines you followed in doing your work, particularly if they were complicated and required a great deal of independent interpretation on your part)

4. **Complexity** (the level of complexity that best describes the work that you accomplished)

5. **Scope and effect** (the scope and impact of your work on the agency, particularly if your work impacted the expenditure of dollars or influenced the use of resources across your organization or agency)

6. **Personal contacts** (the kind of contacts and the purpose of the contacts you made on a regular basis; for instance, "regularly had contact with members of Congressional offices staff")

7. **Purpose of contacts** (the reason for the contact; i.e., "for purposes of clarifying or exchanging information, scheduling and arranging meetings, and making travel arrangements")

8. **Physical demands** (the physical requirements of the position; for instance, "PHYSICAL EFFORT: Required to climb, bend, stoop, and work in strained and cramped positions. Subject to prolonged standing, walking, and kneeling and must be physically fit to perform daily duties.")

9. **Work environment** (where work is performed; for example, "WORKING CONDITIONS: Works inside and outside in inclement weather. Work areas may be drafty, noisy, and have toxic fumes present. Exposed to danger of cuts, burns, shock, strains, and broken bones.")

Analyzing Your Work Experience Section to Make Sure It Covers All FES Components

Compare each of your position descriptions against the following criteria.

Knowledge required for the position. What level of knowledge is required? Knowledge can be general ("Respond to and assist dire-need and hardship inquiries by underserved Medicare/ Medicaid beneficiaries referred by the office of the Administrator and CBC front office. Act as an advocate for beneficiaries by accessing Medicare and other health care benefits, obtaining pro-bono work, and rectifying insurance issues") or specific ("Translate broad agency policy, legislation, regulations, and directives into new policies or methodologies. Serve as subject matter expert in program and operational areas."). This is a powerful factor. It explains, for example, why a Health Insurance Specialist (or other Federal employee) should receive a promotion because of subject-matter expertise.

Supervisory controls. If you perform your work independently, lead teams, use judgment, make decisions, use initiative, or plan and execute, it will be clear that you work independently to perform your job.

Guidelines. What guidelines are there for you to use? Are there general agency guidelines, detailed technical manuals, or vendor instructions? Are the guidelines current, or are they inadequate and frequently inapplicable? Do you need to apply independent judgment and make difficult decisions?

Complexity. What factors make this work complex, or is it really a simple job? Remember, simple and complex are in the eyes of the beholder. If you have 15 years' experience in highly technical work, hold a Ph.D., and are generally considered a national expert, you might think the problems and situations in your work are simple. An outsider, comparing your work to that of other people, would conclude that your job was highly complex. Do not sell yourself short. You will deal with some of your complexity issues in the knowledge and guidelines criteria. Specific complexity issues include having to make decisions with insufficient data, dealing with competing interests and demands, changing of basic systems, and responding to congressional or public controversy or pressure. Complexity can relate to office politics, but you have to be careful in choosing your words when you write about complexity arising out of office politics.

Scope and effect. Scope and effect tell the reader how vast the work is. Do you support a local office, regional offices, global customers, government, industry, or academia? Give a good description of the scope and effect of your work.

Personal contacts/purpose of contacts. This is the "customer service" factor. Write about your internal and external customers. Who do you talk with on the phone and receive e-mail from? Congress? The Office of the Secretary of Defense? The Office of the Department Secretary? Regional Directors? The American public? Ph.D. professors? Other agencies? Why do they call or write to you?

Physical demands and work environment. Do you travel? Do you work in the field and in the office? Do you lift lots of boxes? The HR professionals need to know about your work environment so that they can understand and envision you at your work.

Congratulations! You have now completed a first draft. It's probably too long and not written powerfully, but it's the first step. Take the rest of the day off and start again after your draft has had a chance to cool down. Believe it or not, you can make it better!

The Rewriting Stage

James Michener once said, "There are no great writers—only great rewriters." Use a small paragraph format for rewriting the material you have gathered so far. Begin your job description with a general overview paragraph (one to two sentences) to describe the work and follow it with small paragraphs, each helping to make the case for your qualifications. Remember to address the components of the FES in your copy. You don't have to address each FES factor—only those that are key to your goals.

A Before-and-After Example

Here's a before-and-after example of a rewritten position description.

BEFORE

1989 to present: CONTRACT SPECIALIST, ACQUISITION PROFESSIONAL, Certified Level III; Robert Morris Acquisition Center, Aberdeen Proving Ground (APG), Aberdeen, MD 20001; GS-1101-12; Current salary: $64,975 per year; 40 hours per week. Supervisor: Edward Waters, 410-222-2222.

Manage and administer all contractual actions from pre-award to post-award, including initial planning, contract award, and administration. Contracts include firm-fixed price, fixed-price incentive, fixed-price economic price adjustments, cost plus fixed fee, cost plus award fee, and cost plus incentive fee. Analyze all procurement requests to determine requirements, contracting method and type, and procurement plan. Conduct cost and price analyses, determine incremental funding, and determine rate and cost adjustments. Coordinate time extensions, coordinate issue and document contract modifications, and justify emergency procurements as needed. Perform stop-work orders, cure notices, show cause letters, and terminations for default and/or convenience. Also monitor quality-control performance and government property reporting, approve progress payments, and ensure timely closeout of delivery orders and contracts.

This is a Contract Specialist "Generalist" description that sounds like hundreds of other Contract Specialist descriptions. It doesn't tell what's special, unique, unusual, or outstanding about this person. Read the following impressive rewrite. The accomplishments, numbers, contracts, and problems solved are impressive and will result in interviews and discussions with selecting officials.

AFTER

WORK EXPERIENCE:

1989 to present: CONTRACT SPECIALIST, ACQUISITION PROFESSIONAL, Certified Level III; Robert Morris Acquisition Center, Aberdeen Proving Ground (APG), Aberdeen, MD 20001; GS-1101-12; Current salary: $64,975 per year; 40 hours per week. Supervisor: Edward Waters, 410-222-2222

Certified Level III Contract Specialist and Acquisition Professional for specialized procurements for the Aberdeen Proving Ground (APG). Provide contractual support for 54 tenants and 5 depots throughout the Western region of the United States. Manage and administer all contractual actions from pre-award to post-award, including initial planning, contract award, and administration. Contracts include firm-fixed price, fixed-price incentive, fixed-price economic price adjustments, cost plus fixed fee, cost plus award fee, and cost plus incentive fee.

Analyze all procurement requests to determine requirements, contracting method and type, and procurement plan. Conduct cost and price analyses, determine incremental funding, and determine rate and cost adjustments. Coordinate time extensions, coordinate issue and document contract modifications, and justify emergency procurements as needed. Write stop-work orders, cure notices, show cause letters, and terminations for default and/or convenience. Also monitor quality-control performance and government property reporting, approve progress payments, and ensure timely closeout of delivery orders and contracts.

PRIMARY INTERFACE with Commanders, Tenant Facility Managers, Government Engineers, Small Business Administration, and contractors at the APG and other installations, under the Soldier Biological Chemical Command (SBCCOM). Recommend procurements to program officials using best value basis.

LEAD NEGOTIATOR: Lead contract negotiations on price and technical requirements, as well as actions to determine contract terms and conditions. Assist with statements of work and perform detailed cost analysis of contractor proposals in order to determine competitive range. Develop negotiation strategies, lead pre-bid proposal conferences, and negotiate fair contract price and contract modifications with contractors. Interpret and provide advice on contractual provisions. Analyze bids for compliance with established guidelines.

POINT OF CONTACT for Reverse Auctioning Procurements. Member of the marketing team for the Robert Morris Acquisition Center.

KEY CONTRACTS: 1990 to present: Key advisor for procurement planning and coordination for maintenance, repair, and new construction Base Operation Support Task Order Contracts (TOC) totaling $75 million, customized to a 10-year master plan, for APG, Maryland; Dugway Proving Ground (DPG), Utah; Umatilla Proving Ground (UPG), Oregon; Desert Chemical Depot (DCD), Utah; and Pueblo Chemical Depot (PCD), Colorado. Administer over 300 individual delivery order contracts in excess of $30 million. Monitor compliance with contract terms, including use of government property, performance criteria, and delivery timetables. Ensure financial and accounting reports are submitted and complete, as applicable. Update management regarding potential controversial or problematic issues when appropriate.

ACCOMPLISHMENTS: Initiated, and continue to promote, partnering sessions between government agencies and contractors for all specialized procurement contracts. The sessions include preplanning and followup meetings with government Contracting Officer Representatives (CORs) and contractors to identify potential problems and evaluate contractor performance, as well as the use of Alternative Disputes Resolution (ADR) to resolve problems. *Result:* No government claims have been paid on any of the multiyear contracts I have managed.

Because of my facilities-management expertise, I was detailed for 7 months, 12/1999 to 6/2000, to the Soldier Biological Chemical Command (SBCCOM) facility office to accomplish two key assignments: Identify excess space and establish a space utilization policy; and develop and prepare a 1391 for an estimated $40 million state-of-the-art Chemical Research Laboratory requiring congressional funding. *Result:* Both tasks were accomplished: The 1391 was forwarded to the Army Material Command (AMC) for prioritization and has received DA sponsorship. The space-utilization policy and findings resulted in an estimated overall savings in excess of $1 million. Received performance and special act awards for my accomplishments.

A good Federal resume can be three to five pages in length, as opposed to a traditional private-sector resume, which seldom exceeds two pages. Remember that you should describe previous positions in progressively less detail.

Examples of Work Experience Sections Rewritten from Previous Federal Resumes and OF-612s

Here are some examples of Work Experience sections that you can follow as you rewrite your Federal resume experiences.

Example 1: Occupational Health Nurse (Contractor) Seeking Conversion to Full-Time Permanent Occupational Health and Safety Officer, GS-0018-13/13

BEFORE

Scope of Responsibility

Inspected environment and occupational health in a research laboratory facility where employees had potential exposure to biological agents, hazardous chemicals, radioactive material, and research animals. Active member of Safety and Health Committee at Research Lab Facility.

Specific Duties and Accomplishments

Identified degrees of control over hazard risk; hazard and time-duration of exposure to chemicals or biological agents; or risks in lab, office, or environmental surrounding. Utilized Material Safety Data Sheet information to ascertain exposure to potential hazards at the workplace. Identified incidents that occurred during performance of specific tasks by employees or machinery in occupational environment. Identified abatement measures to control hazards and prevent future incidents. Coordinated and worked with Industrial Hygienist to assess water and indoor air quality and employee concerns; made recommendations and implemented policy in accordance with OSHA and other applicable Federal regulations. Assessed and evaluated employee safety and health concerns in a research laboratory and office environment. Communicated with the Health and Safety Officer to coordinate corrective action. Coordinated the implementation of the Respiratory Protection Program. Performed Spirometry testing on employees. Evaluated results and made recommendations. Established and maintained statistical data on a number of significant findings.

Coordinated and administered special immunization programs for employees with biological agents. Coordinated research program at lab facility with Centers for Disease Control on biological agent, Botulinum toxin. Maintained statistical data and reports on project. Established and implemented record-keeping tools for a number of adverse effects and titers. Implemented Occupational Health Surveillance Program. Performed medical surveillance screening for 250 employees per year. Assessed and compiled statistical data on results of Occupational Surveillance exams for work-related significant findings. Trained in ergonomics. Conducted ergonomic evaluations at employee workstations. Provided recommendations to improve workplace setup or body posture. Provided technical advice and recommendations to improve procedures and personnel protective equipment to managers, supervisors, and employees (e.g., safety glasses, respirators).

AFTER: New Federal Resume

Occupational Health Nurse   7/98 to Present
Department of Health and Human Services
National Institutes of Health, 9000 Rockville Pike, Bethesda, MD 20892
Salary: $45,000 annually; Hours worked: 40/week
Supervisor: Sheila Oppenheimer, R.N., 301-987-1234

Directed the Safety and Health Committee at Research Lab Facility. Inspected environment and occupational health in research laboratory facility where employees had potential exposure to biological agents, hazardous chemicals, radioactive material, and research animals. Identified degrees of control over hazard risk; hazard and time-duration of exposure to chemicals and/or biological agents; or risks in lab, office, or environmental surroundings.

Specific responsibilities:

- Utilized Material Safety Data Sheet information to collect information and determine degree of exposure to potential hazards in workplace.

- Documented incidents that occurred during performance of specific tasks by employees or operation of equipment in occupational environment.

- Identified abatement measures to control hazards and prevent potential future incidents.

- Developed plan and worked with Industrial Hygienist to assess water quality, indoor air quality, and employee concerns; made recommendations and implemented policy in accordance with OSHA and other applicable Federal regulations.

- Collected data and evaluated employee safety and health concerns in research laboratory and office environment; collaborated with Health and Safety Officer to develop and implement corrective actions.

- Implemented Occupational Health Surveillance Program. Executed medical surveillance screening for 100 employees per year.

- Analyzed statistical data on results of Occupational Surveillance exams for work-related significant findings and generated formal reports for distribution to key staff and decision-makers.

- As trained specialist, conducted ergonomic evaluations at employee workstations and made recommendations for improvements for arrangement or body posture.

- Provided technical expertise and made recommendations to managers, supervisors, and employees concerning how to improve procedures and personnel protective equipment (e.g., safety glasses, respirators).

(continues)

(continued)

Accomplishments:

- Served as a member of NIH, Division of Federal Occupational Health (FOH) Task Force, responsible for establishing updated guidelines for Wellness Physical Examinations; guidelines were implemented in Federal Occupational Health Units throughout the continental United States and are currently in use today.

- Implemented new Respiratory Protection Program; performed Spirometry testing on employees, evaluated results, and made recommendations. Also generated and maintained statistical data on a number of significant findings.

- Developed plan; directed and administered special immunization programs for employees working with toxic chemicals and biological agents.

- Developed and managed research program at lab facility studying extremely dangerous biological agent; maintained statistical data, generated reports on project, and developed new, more efficient record-keeping tools for a number of adverse effects and titers.

Example 2: Trainer and Program Retention Specialist Seeking Federal Position in Training, Human Resources Recruitment, and Management Assistant

BEFORE

RETENTION SPECIALIST & CUSTOMIZED TRAINING ADVISOR
Empower Baltimore Management Corporation
3 South Frederick Street, Suite 801
Baltimore, MD 21202
November 1998–Present

Planned and implemented the Retention Pilot Program with Johns Hopkins Hospital. Coordinated and implemented first job fair, which resulted in the participation of more than 50 employers and more than 1,100 job seekers. Establish partnerships with employers and educational institutions to help identify and resolve hiring and staffing needs by providing workforce-development services. Develop and coordinate customized training programs. Conduct job-site analysis and job-task assessments. Assist employers with completing customized training applications. Evaluate customized training applications. Analyze, calculate, and negotiate customized training budgets. Develop job specifications that include defining core basic skills and educational requirements. Develop and implement recruiting and preemployment screening process, which includes, but is not limited to, administering and interpreting aptitude tests. Monitor training programs to determine/document contract compliance. Contact training team weekly to assess and discuss issues related to implementation of the training. Arrange meetings or conference calls with employer and/or employee to address any issues regarding the training. Conduct monthly post-employment followup, for 90 days, to ensure job retention. Provide vocational and career development. Maintain appropriate documentation. Provide weekly and monthly reports to Customized Training Supervisor.

AFTER: Army Resumix Resume

Work Experience

May we contact your current supervisor? Yes

11/1998 to present. Hrs per week: 40. Customized Training and Retention Specialist; Customized Training Advisor, 11/1998 to 2/2000; Empower Baltimore Management Corporation, EBMC, 3 South Frederick St., Baltimore, MD 21202. Supervisor: Janet Jones, 410-555-5555.

MONITOR and MANAGE general-education and training programs. ESTABLISH partnerships with executive, educational, and business leaders to identify and resolve staffing needs. Create, plan, and organize vocational training opportunities through workforce-development programs.

Manage and monitor customized training programs from concept to completion including curriculum and vocational training development, administration, compliance monitoring, and post-employment followup. ANALYZE PROBLEMS, identify significant factors, and recognize and develop solutions to improve education and vocational training programs. Conduct job site analyses. Evaluate job tasks and skills requirements. Promote career development and educational and training programs.

ACCOMPLISHMENTS: Helped over 150 candidates find employment. Convinced a large bank to change hiring policies that eliminated potential employees from qualifying for entry-level job openings. As a result, 40 new employees were hired and trained.

Planned, developed, and coordinated first EMBC Job Fair. Successful event attracted 50 employers and over 1,100 attendees. Conducted oral interviews to screen and select over 100 candidates for customized vocational training program. Wrote promotional communications. Over 75 percent successfully completed the program and obtained jobs.

Developed partnerships with educational institutions to establish ongoing customized education and training programs. Key advisor for curriculum development. Spearheaded successful pilot program to improve long-term, entry-level employee retention.

Example 3: Receptionist and Executive Assistant, GS-0303, Seeking Records Management Assistant, GS-04/05

BEFORE

WORK EXPERIENCE

Back-up Receptionist/Assistant to COO November 1999–Present

Empower Baltimore Management Corporation, Baltimore, MD 21231

At Empower Baltimore, I am responsible for being the backup receptionist, making copies, faxing, scheduling appointments, giving directions, serving as assistant to the COO, updating databases, checking addresses, and sorting the mail.

AFTER

WORK EXPERIENCE

October 2001 to present; 40 hours per week; ADMINISTRATIVE ASSISTANT, $14,586 per year, Empower Baltimore Management Corporation, EBMC, 3 South Frederick Street, Suite 800, Baltimore, MD 21202; Supervisor: Tisha Edwards, Chief Operating Officer, (410) 783-4400; may contact.

Executive Administrator for the Chief Operating Officer (COO). Provide comprehensive, direct executive-level administrative support to the COO. Coordinate administrative functions to ensure smooth and efficient operation of the office and its programs. Work independently to accomplish administrative tasks. Organize, collect, analyze, and distribute information related to EBMC programs and projects.

DATABASE MANAGEMENT: Utilize office automation, database management, word processing, and financial software programs. Establish and maintain electronic and paper files. Enter and retrieve data files. Use manual and automated filing systems to establish and maintain administrative files.

COMMUNICATIONS: Create and distribute correspondence and reports using office automation tools. Perform various clerical duties. Answer recurring questions and resolve administrative and clerical problems. Provide backup front-desk support on multiline telephone system. Receive and refer visitors. Greet customers. Answer, screen, and route as many as 100 daily telephone calls. Disseminate customer information. Distribute mail and messages.

TRAVEL AND SCHEDULE MANAGEMENT: Manage executive schedules and appointment calendars. Schedule reservations and travel arrangements.

ACCOMPLISHMENT: Instrumental in the creation and organization of the first EBMC Policy Database, a historical database created in Access summarizing six years of funding history, board actions, and policy changes. Created the database and researched, analyzed, categorized, summarized, and consolidated hundreds of pages of written source documents to create automated records and summary data for use as a historical reference.

Expanding Your Job Descriptions and Converting Your Private-Industry Resume

People working in private industry and seeking Federal jobs might think that their current resumes will be effective as a Federal resume format. This is not true. As you can see from the samples in this book, the Federal resume is more detailed and longer than the typical one- to two-page private-industry resume. Private-industry resumes do not cover all of the FES factors. And they certainly don't cover all of the elements in the vacancy announcement. Because government is accustomed to receiving longer resume versions

with details that describe a position thoroughly, you will have to expand your descriptions for your Federal resume. You will also need to cover all of the duties, responsibilities, and KSAs listed in the Federal job announcement. The Federal resume might serve as an application and an interview because you might not meet the hiring manager in person. And keep in mind that the Federal human resources specialist or hiring manager might not understand your private-industry job and how it relates to government. *You* have to interpret these responsibilities and skills and explain your job in terms of the needs of the Federal agency. That's the challenge!

Example 4: Deployment Consultant Seeking Emergency Management Program Manager Position with Homeland Security Agency

BEFORE: Private-Industry Resume Position Description

Employment History:

Zerone, Inc.   10/97–08/02

Deployment Consultant. Managed the joint deployment of a sophisticated retail point-of-service system with IBM, NCR, and MCI for the U.S. Postal Service (USPS).

- Supervised and coordinated the operational activities of 45 USPS regional and state coordinators in 26 states with IBM and MCI multifunctional field teams utilizing an Internet-accessible application.

- Met all deployment schedule deadlines during five-year period in face of repeated major schedule changes, database support issues, and a changing deployment criteria baseline.

- Developed and managed the hardware acquisition and deployment schedule for 22,000 computer terminals valued at $150 million to 6,300 USPS high-revenue-generating retail facilities.

- Saved USPS $7.5 million by managing a hardware recycling program.

- Operated a Visual Basic, MS Access, and browser-based front-end deployment management system connected to an Oracle and MS Access back-end tool for generating EDI contractual orders for IBM hardware and installation services, and telecommunications orders to MCI for establishing network connectivity to USPS facilities.

- Wrote a training manual and implemented a nationwide training course for 96 USPS regional and state coordinators and 344 maintenance and contract personnel.

AFTER: Federal Resume Position Description

PROFESSIONAL EXPERIENCE:

Deployment Consultant	**10/97–8/02**
USPS POS ONE Program Office	40+ hours/week
475 L'Enfant Plaza, SW, N. Bldg.	Ending Salary: $80,537/year
Room 5322, Washington, DC 20260	Beginning Salary: $71,350/year

Supervisor: David Sossamon, contact can be made, (202) 363-1360.

Managed the joint nationwide web-enabled deployment of a sophisticated retail point-of-service system with IBM, NCR, and MCI for U.S. Postal Service (USPS). As the single point of contact and key advisor, communicated and coordinated daily operational activities of 45 USPS regional and state coordinators nationwide with IBM and MCI multifunctional field teams and senior USPS program managers, utilizing an online status-management system. Provided liaison with internal, external, and senior-level coordinators, managers, and outside companies.

Developed and managed hardware acquisition and deployment schedule with a 120-day site preparation cycle for the installation of 22,000 computer terminals valued at $150 million to 6,300 facilities affecting over 40,000 USPS retail personnel.

Operated Visual Basic, MS Access, and browser-based front-end deployment management system connected to Oracle and MS Access back-end tool to generate EDI contractual orders for IBM hardware and installation services, and telecommunications orders to MCI to establish network connectivity to over 10,000 USPS facilities.

Key Accomplishments:
- Met all deployment schedule deadlines during five-year period in face of repeated major schedule changes, database support issues, and a changing deployment criteria baseline.
- On-time installation success rate in excess of 99%.
- Saved USPS $7.5 million by managing a hardware-recycling program.
- Wrote training manual and implemented nationwide training course for 96 USPS regional and state coordinators and 344 maintenance and contract personnel.

Example 5: Business Process Analyst Seeking Management Assistant, GS-0344-07

BEFORE

Business Process Analyst, 2002–Present:

Provide required resources and expertise to support the planning and execution of events; conduct AGC events and presentations and provide facilitation and process support in diverse areas to ensure smooth and successful execution. Determine the purpose and requirements of the customer to include, but not be limited to, identification of the participants and any unique support required, and appropriate technology systems. Prepare an activity security plan and a plan outlining the resources and staffing required to meet customer requirements/objectives.

AFTER

Professional Experience

Business Process Analyst
Computer Science Corporation (csc.com)   May 2002 to Present
1201 M Street, Washington, DC 20376   40 hours per week
Supervisor: Erin Gantt, (202) 675-4993, may be contacted.   Current Salary: $47,000
(A Federal contractor providing conference/special events services)

As Administrative Assistant and Events Representative, provide comprehensive administrative, clerical, and technical support for Admiral Gooding Center, Command Events Planning Branch of the Naval Sea Systems Command (NAVSEA). Manage and coordinate administrative functions to ensure the smooth and efficient operation of conference facilities and services. Report to the Director of Events Planning.

- Organize and coordinate logistics and provide administrative and technical support for special events, meetings, conferences, and seminars at the Center. Maximize use of software applications to create project correspondence and support materials and record program documentation.
- As Events Assistant, serve as key client interface and on-site technical representative from pre-event planning to post-event followup. Use state-of-the-art computer technology, Graphic User Interface (GUI), to hyperlink client information to PowerPoint and other software to create multimedia presentations. Play integral role in planning meetings. Key contact for high-ranking military personnel.
- Assist with basic accounting/finance functions. Track bank card transactions and purchase orders. Review financial reports to ensure accuracy.
- Answer and screen telephone calls, greet and register incoming visitors, and disseminate information to customers, the public, and staff. Conduct facility tours.
- Administer workflow, and establish and maintain subject-matter files. Provide secretarial/clerical support. Track and document project status using spreadsheet applications.

Key Accomplishments:
- Improved data collection, documentation, and access, and reduced errors by consolidating six spreadsheets into one. Also created pivot tables to extract requested data more efficiently.
- Utilized Word and Excel to create and implement a more efficient system for tracking and documenting conference/meeting project status and followup.
- Assisted with financial report review and uncovered a $30,000 calculation error. Revised and improved the report implementing Excel software.
- Consistently exceed performance standards. Valued by management and staff for increasing internal efficiencies and cutting administrative costs by creating new ways to automate office procedures and duties.

Questions and Answers About the Work Experience Section

The following sections answer common questions about writing the Work Experience section.

What if My Best Job Is Not My Most Recent Job?

If your second or third position is more relevant to your objective than your current position, you should emphasize the second and third over the first. In fact, if you are an accountant who wants to return to contracts work, you could even list your jobs out of chronology. You could create subheadings such as these:

CONTRACTS EXPERIENCE

List your second job here.

List your third job here.

ACCOUNTING EXPERIENCE

List your first job here that is not as relevant as the contracting positions.

What if I Am Applying for Jobs in Lots of Different Series? Do I Need to Rewrite My Federal Resume Each Time?

In general, one properly thought-out Federal resume will work for just about every job for which you apply. I once had a client who had two career ideas: a spy for the CIA or a career in military music. If your career goals are that diverse, write two (or more) Federal resumes, each with the appropriate focus (see chapter 10). For most people, however, one resume is sufficient. Remember, the KSAs are your primary opportunity to tailor your background to the specific position.

With the ease of PCs, you can use a few different approaches for your most recent or relevant jobs and copy and paste one of them into your resume each time for different announcements. However, don't do this unless you see a strong need. You can spend your job-hunting time better by using it to uncover more job leads.

What About Really Old Jobs?

As you move back in your career, write less and less about each position. Jobs more than 10 years old can be summarized as is done in the following three examples:

"Previous experience includes computer programming, administration, and part-time teaching positions."

"Prior 10 years' experience included writing, editing, and research with academic, industry, and research institutions."

Prior Positions

Social Insurance Specialist (GS-105-09), Social Insurance Claims Examiner (GS-993-07 through GS-993-09) as Retirement Specialist and Disability Specialist with the Social Security Administration.

Writing Your Part-Time and Small-Business Job Descriptions

If you have part-time or paid small-business experience that is relevant to your objective, you can list this experience as a complete job entry—with the compliance details—or you can mention your experience under "Other Qualifications" (see chapter 7). Just remember that the announcements state that you should include only "job-related" positions and experience in your resume. If this part-time work demonstrates skills that are relevant to your career, you should include the job and a short description.

FINANCIAL EXPERIENCE

FINANCIAL CONSULTANT   1993 to Present
Director of Operations / Treasurer / Staff Instructor
Aiki Martial Arts Institute   20 hours per week
12301 Belair Road, Kingsville, MD 21087   Salary: $25,000/year
Supervisor: Mark Hiemmer, 410-592-5233, may be contacted.

Financial consultant / advisor with direct responsibility for financial administration, strategic planning, and all state, local, and Federal tax matters for this 501(c)(3) nonprofit educational institution. Prepare financial reports and maintain necessary accounting systems to provide effective and efficient accounting controls, including general ledger accounts, accounts payable and receivable, collections, revenue recognition, and budgeting. Report directly to the Institute Director. Serve on Board of Directors as Treasurer.

- Formulate the annual budget and long-term and short-range strategic plan. Coordinate plan with agency director.
- Monitor and track all obligations and expenditures, tabulate cost data, compile data summaries, and prepare annual operating budget. Analyze, verify, and revise budget data.
- Research, compile, and summarize financial data for the formulation of budget estimates. Present all budgets and strategic plans before Board of Directors and Director.
- Seminar coordinator and liaison to Japanese representatives from martial-arts organizations and international participants. Coordinate and administer all seminar and training venues, travel arrangements, publications and press information, and travel income and expenses.
- Instruct students in the Japanese martial art of Aikido, including self-defense and weapons defense.

Key Accomplishments:
- Instrumental in designing and writing a corporate business plan designed to reorganize and return to profitability a small business facing bankruptcy. Wrote and currently execute long- and short-term business growth plans designed to transform the organization into a leader in Aikido training in the Baltimore metropolitan area with long-term goals for regional expansion. Designed training programs, registration, educational programs, and marketing strategy.
- In 2001, prepared all required IRS documentation to create a 501(c)(3) nonprofit educational institution from a Sub S corporation. Currently direct and oversee all financial operations and serve on Board of Directors as Treasurer.

Writing About Unpaid Work Experiences

The Federal job announcement instructions give you the opportunity to describe paid and unpaid work experiences that are related to the position for which you are applying. In some cases you will want to include the number of hours you worked in these unpaid positions and activities. If you would like to include a supervisor's name and telephone with the activity, you can do so. You might use these other work experiences as statements for KSAs as well. Examples of unpaid work you might list include volunteer teaching, community service, and other volunteer work.

Volunteer Teaching

Many people are invited to teach a high school or college class. You could be an adjunct professor, presenter, guest speaker, or panelist. This experience demonstrates expertise, communications skills, visibility, and the ability to be professional in representing a group or field. Here's an example:

Guest Speaker, Baltimore, and Howard County Public Schools. Recruited by Career Development Program Directors to teach resume writing, cover letter writing, and job search strategies to 10th- through 12th-grade students. Developed successful curriculum that became the classroom text published by JIST Publishing, Inc., Indianapolis, IN. *Creating Your High School Resume* will be published in a second edition in 2003.

Community Service and Other Volunteer Positions

Being an active member or leader of a community, town, school, or nonprofit organization can set you apart from your competition. The resume reader might remember you specifically because of your unique "outside interests."

Community service examples are great for use in KSA statements. You can demonstrate your "ability to communicate orally," or "ability to plan and coordinate projects," or "ability to negotiate and resolve problems" through outside activities, skills, and accomplishments as an organizational leader. The following are some examples of how to list this information on your Federal resume.

Example 6: IT Specialist with Volunteer Experience

OBJECTIVE: IT Specialist (Customer Service), GS-2200-GS-7

VOLUNTEER AND OTHER EXPERIENCE

- Trinity United Methodist Church

  1205 Dolly Madison Blvd., McLean, VA 22101, 9/97–10/99, 15 hours/week, $7.00/hour. Supervisor's Name: Pastor James Marks. Phone: 703-333-3333

  Provided administrative support for a church office: developed an Excel database to track church visitors; maintained Automated Church System (ACS) database; exported and published reports used for the church phonebook, Rolodex records, and correspondence. Edited, published, and supervised bulk mailing of the monthly newsletter (1,000 copies) and coordinated other church correspondence. Trained 25 volunteers to assist with the weekly newsletter mailings.

- Little Rocky Run Architectural Review Board

  Clifton, VA, 5/94–6/96, 5 hours/week, Volunteer.

  As Vice President for the Architectural Review Board, chaired monthly meetings, reviewed requests for architectural variances, inspected architectural applications, made decisions based on LLR Homeowner's Manual, recommended solutions for controversial board decisions, attended homeowners meetings to support board decisions on appealed applications, and presented recommendations to the homeowners association regarding changes to the manual.

Example 7: Social Science Research Analyst with Volunteer Experience

OBJECTIVE

Social Science Research Analyst, GS-101-13, Department of Health & Human Services, Centers for Medicare & Medicaid Services

COMMUNITY SERVICE

Created a screening process and developed referral policies and procedures to help the front-line office staff at the McLean Baptist Church to process a high volume of social-services requests.

Worked as a consultant to help establish Birthmothers, Inc., a nonprofit adoption organization for pregnant, unwed adolescents and women in Fairfax County, Virginia.

On behalf of the Frank Foundation, a DC nonprofit child-placement agency, provided counseling and information services regarding local adoption initiatives, court processes, and problems to Russian officials. Served as liaison to Russian officials for child-placement facility tours and provided information regarding substitute care for foster-care children.

As part of Master of Social Work:

- Conducted research for U.S. Census Bureau grant project: Evaluated methodology for counting the homeless.

- Led committee of private and public agencies to expand services for the homebound elderly.

- Led committee to develop comprehensive policy and procedures manual for continuing-education programs for 21 senior centers.

Example 8: Using Volunteer Experience to Demonstrate Leadership

This applicant is seeking a supervisory position and is using volunteer work to demonstrate leadership.

COMMUNITY LEADERSHIP:

1997–Present; **EXECUTIVE DIRECTOR,** 6th District Leadership Council.

Write and disseminate press releases to area organizations to gather support for the improvement of living conditions in the 6th District of Baltimore County. Facilitate cooperation between 186 community organizations and 200 businesses and places of worship. Organize annual neighborhood events to build connections between neighbors and Federal, state, and local officials. Recruit, organize, and establish volunteer committees to build and strengthen communities and to address area family and youth needs. Coordinate crime-prevention efforts with neighborhoods. Coordinate efforts to solve problem properties throughout the district.

- Experience with grant writing and articles of incorporation to form a 501(c)(3).

- Knowledge and skill creating a public-media targeted communications strategy.

- Capability to identify communications needs and develop informational materials to further the organization's goals.

1995–Present; **PRESIDENT,** Uplands Homeowners Improvement Association.

Direct board and monthly community meetings. Represent the community on neighborhood issues. Identify community needs and execute a plan of action to resolve issues and concerns. Plan and coordinate guest speakers, programs, and activities for the community. Write and edit community newsletter.

- Instrumental in reversing proposal to house 51 violent sex offenders in our community through written and oral communications with government leaders and the formation of a partnership between the treatment center and government representatives.

- Negotiated on behalf of 5,000 community members regarding construction of a new worship facility. Served as project leader to coordinate efforts, resolve differences, and address concerns throughout a 3-year process.

- Coordinated efforts between residents and city and state government officials, including clergy and staff, Mayor Schmoke of Baltimore City, and the Bureau Heads of the Department of Public Works, Department of Transportation, Department of Water and Waste Water, Department of Planning, and the Board of Municipal Zoning.

- Received Mayor's Citation for my contribution to the civic welfare of our municipality, as well as other letters of commendation from clergy and community residents.

Example 9: Volunteer Historian

This avid volunteer historian and interpreter seeks a permanent position as a park ranger.

Objective:
Park Ranger, GS-0025-09, Interior-NPS C&O CANAL NHP

Qualifications Summary:
Historian/Historical Interpreter with rigorous academic training and over nine years of diverse business experience. Background includes extensive experience as a historical consultant, researcher, archivist, educator, and "Living History" presenter. Active member of Civil War and Revolutionary War reenactment organizations. PC proficient.

- Education: M.A. and B.A., American/European history. Graduate thesis, "The Battle of Williamsburg: Premonitions of Greatness," requested for inclusion in the Colonial Williamsburg Foundation Library.

- Accomplished writer and presenter: Strong public speaking and writing skills. Presenter of polished oral and multimedia historical presentations at National and State parks and museums, conferences, schools, and special events. Expertise writing guidebooks, handouts, and text for historical displays.

- Meticulous Researcher/Archivist: Expertise researching cultural, archeological, and historical landmarks and analyzing, cataloging, photo indexing, and referencing artifacts for museum collections and other presentations.

- Acknowledged historian for the following: *We Came to Fight: The History of the 5th New York Veteran Infantry,* a book by Patrick Schroeder; and *The Battle of Guilford Courthouse: Turning Point in the South,* a new tactical game.

- Historical Consultant/Subject Matter Expert for the following projects:
  Consultant for the National Park Service file, "Another Such Victory," about the Battle of Guilford Courthouse during the Revolutionary War.
  Consultant for the National Park Service educational film, *Antietam: A Documentary.*
  Respected authority on key Civil War battles on the 9th NYSV.
  Contract Historical Interpreter and Consultant at Antietam National Battlefield Park.
  Interpreter/Living History presenter, Colonial Williamsburg.

What Have You Accomplished? The Importance of Your Career and Volunteer Accomplishments

What is the one question a prospective employer is most interested in when interviewing you for a job—the question that comes up in every job interview you will ever have? You guessed it: It's the "What have you accomplished recently," or "What have you done in the past year or so"

inquiry that every employer wants to know about—and for a good reason.

From an employer's point of view, accomplishments, unlike the duties and responsibilities outlined in every job description and resume ever submitted (which an applicant might or might not have done well), show what you have actually done. And it is only by your actions and your accomplishments that an employer can make an educated guess as to whether you can actually do the job for which you are applying.

This cannot be overstated. Your accomplishments and the way you present them are the keys to securing employment and then to advancing your career.

What Are Accomplishments?

Your accomplishments

★ Are what set you apart from all other candidates.

★ Show the hiring authorities that you are the most qualified applicant for the job.

★ Form the foundation of your "skill sets" and your "Knowledge, Skills, and Abilities" responses (see chapter 14).

Accomplishments are the "headlines" of your career experience and the measure of how well your current skills and abilities will fit the requirements of the job you are applying for. They are anything you have done or are doing: work, projects you have completed, classes you have finished, or volunteer programs you are involved with. In short, accomplishments are descriptions of anything you have done and the results of those actions.

Here are some accomplishments from five paid and two volunteer jobs that seven applicants used to successfully apply for Federal employment:

Volunteer Accountant

Managed all bookkeeping and accounting functions for this small nonprofit organization. Prepared financial statements. Prepared and filed all required tax and reporting forms. Planned and coordinated fund-raising events that yielded up to $20,000 each in small donations. Singlehandedly conducted a targeted solicitation mailing to 200+ potential donors.

Secretary, GS-0318-8

- Served as core member of the Communication Work Group that analyzed and improved workplace productivity and environment.
- Formed and chaired the Secretarial Work Group to optimize office functioning and productivity.
- Trained and supervised summer office clerks.

Supervisory FOIA/PA Specialist, GS-0301-13

- Developed and implemented agreements between multiple INS FOIA (Freedom of Information Act) Units and the National Records Center FOIA Division that has "significantly" reduced the number of backlogged FOIA/PA cases nationwide.
- Recommended the centralization of all INS FOIA operations at the National Records Center, which has been approved by INS Headquarters and is currently awaiting implementation.

Military Personnel Clerk (Typing); GS-0204-5

- Received Certificate of Completion for acquiring knowledge of personal computers and their function within a LAN and other aspects of the Squadron's computer systems.
- Served as Squadron security representative. As such, completed and taught co-workers Operation Security processes and advised Squadron staff on all security measures regarding subversive or terrorist activity.

(continues)

(continued)

Chief Planning Branch, GS-0401-14/3

- Conceived, planned, and developed policy, criteria, and standards for forecasting, assessing, protecting, enhancing, and mitigating impacts of Air Force operations on both natural and cultural resources to include 44 listed threatened and endangered species, wetlands, 2,500 archeological sites, a 214-building National Historic Landmark, and the Man in Space National Historic Landmark at Cape Canaveral Air Station, FL.
- Developed, advocated for, and managed annual $5.2 million operating budget.

Photographer, GS-1060-09

- Input scanned data into the Slide Librarian Pro database according to title, keyword(s), date of the slide, priority, quality, author, and whether the slide may or may not be published.
- Reorganized and cataloged the slide collection database to make the collection user-friendly and easier to maintain.

Volunteer Fund Raiser

- Organized, coordinated, and planned a 3-day weekend running/camping event for 250 Leukemia Society Team In Training participants in 1999, 2000, and 2001; oversaw the entire registration process.

How to Write About Your Accomplishments

As you can see from the preceding samples, the best accomplishments are *specific* descriptions. In every case, they describe a specific action or steps you have taken to resolve a problem or to do your job. You will also note that the applicants used numbers, dollars, and percentages to describe what they had accomplished. This is important because, by describing your accomplishments and projects in *measurable and quantifiable terms,* you give prospective employers the tools they need to figure out the scale and scope of your accomplishments and see how your accomplishments relate to the job they want to fill. For example, in the preceding Chief Planning Branch example, how much of a difference would it make in your mind if the operating budget the applicant had been responsible for was only $5,200 per year instead of $5.2 million? Would you be more or less impressed with the applicant's ability and experience?

Would you imagine there was a different order of skill involved between managing a $5,200 budget and a $5.2 million budget? If you were looking for someone to manage a large branch, would the numbers count in your hiring decision?

The easiest way to write about your accomplishments is to make a list of projects and tasks that you have worked on and completed over the past few years. Begin with an outline like this:

1. Project or task—what problem did the project or task solve?
2. What you did (the steps you took to solve the problem).
3. The results (what happened as a result of the steps you took).

Make a list of 5 to 10 projects or tasks you have worked on over the past few years. Then write and apply three-to-four-line accomplishment statements to your resume and KSAs (see chapter 14).

Guidelines for Writing Job-Winning Accomplishments

There are three major things to keep in mind when you are writing about your accomplishments:

1. Be specific. For example:

> *Supervisory Contract Specialist, GM-1102-14:* Nominated for the Secretary of the Army Award for Excellence in Contracting for developing and implementing the Acquisition Development Assistance Team (ADAT) concept and for developing the Customer, Contracting, and Commerce (C3) industry partnership initiative.
>
> *Secretary, GS-0318-7:* Managed a staff of 5 secretaries. Provided administrative and secretarial support to the Director and Assistant Director, Intermediate Office of Taxpayer Service and Compliance.
>
> *Personnel Management Specialist, GS-0201-9:* Developed and implemented a comprehensive psychiatric occupational management program with instruction manuals, client worksheets, and documentation notes; <u>a first for the unit</u>. The program is now being exported to other military bases.

2. Describe your accomplishments in measurable and quantifiable terms whenever possible. For example:

> *Tax Consultant/Owner (private sector):* Increased gross revenues 22% and filed 1,300 individual tax returns in two tax seasons of ownership.
>
> *Public Affairs Specialist, GS-1035-12:* Write and produce 5 to 7 live television newscasts per week, primarily for a 90-minute morning show, "Wake Up Baltimore," and two 30-minute weekend shows, "2 News at 6:30" and "2 News at 11."
>
> *Construction Analyst, GS-828-9/11:* Conducted over 1,500 damage assessments for residential and business properties including multistory office buildings and residential projects valued at over $20 million dollars.

3. Target the vacancy you are applying for.

In chapters 4 and 5, you learned how to analyze vacancy announcements and how to research your core competencies and keywords. That work now becomes the "blueprint" for writing about your accomplishments (and later, your electronic resume or KSA responses).

Keep the keyword list you developed in your vacancy analysis close to your monitor. As you turn your project and task outline into narrative statements, make sure you include some of that language in your accomplishments. This strategy will pay big dividends when your application package is being read and scored later in the application process.

Project Lists

In some professions, such as engineering, architecture, and computers, applicants have long used "project lists" as part of their application packages. Project lists are just collected accomplishments, but they can be very effective if used judiciously as an addendum to your resume and as the basis for KSA responses.

Partial project lists for an architect, auditor, computer specialist, and social services executive follow.

Architect

Completed projects include:

- *Theodore Roosevelt Federal Building:* $25 million—program development study.

- *OPM Headquarters Office:* $270 million—planning, design, budget, and group personnel interviews for the consolidation for new facility.

- *Theodore Roosevelt Building Cafeteria:* $300,000—program study and budget formulation.

- *Avondale Executive Training and Conference Center:* $20 million—program development study.

- *Theodore Roosevelt Building Fitness Center:* $200,000—program development, design and space-management planning, and budget proposal.

Auditor

General Accounting Office

- Project manager for the preparation of diagnostic analyses of the internal control environment within the payroll, procurement, and budget cycles. The analyses prepared consisted of systems internal control flowcharts and narrative summaries of controls. In addition, these analyses were designed to help members of the Steering Committee understand, interpret, and make recommendations for improvements in the overall evaluation process.

General Service Administration, Audit Plans and Procedures for FTS2000

- Developed strategic and detailed audit plans to support GSA's oversight of a new digital telecommunications network providing voice, data, video, and integrated telecommunication services to over 1,500 locations throughout the United States, Puerto Rico, Guam, and the U.S. Virgin Islands.

- Defined the AT&T billing system audit objectives; conducted a preliminary review and identified risks for each audit sub-area; made preliminary risk assessments.

- Selected audit procedures to be used within each audit sub-area based on an assessment of the functionality, the control environment and techniques, and the perceived risks.

Computer Specialist

Business Strategy & Support

- Instrumental in supporting rapid growth of the business to $90 million in revenue and 800 employees located at client sites and in remote offices across the U.S.

- Led corporate-wide business automation, introduced electronic information and integrated messaging services, and instituted applied process and applied technology to create a sophisticated IT infrastructure.

IT Organization Development & Team Building

- Substantiated cost, benefit, make/buy, and outsourcing decisions as a means to effectively allocate IT investments and intellectual assets.

- Implemented end-to-end IT project-management methods with clear parameters for direction, timelines, accountability, and quality control. Cut system/application development time by as much as 30%.

- Upgraded information security and systems integrity to protect mission-critical systems and information from unauthorized access. Instituted all policies and guidelines to move away from open-access environment.

Enterprise Technology Solutions

- Migrated five different systems used in Human Resources, Finance, and Procurement into a fully integrated technology architecture that provided real-time access to key information for planning and decision-making.

- Saved up to 30% in time and labor costs by shifting the entire payroll function to an electronic timecard system and paperless processing of 800+ employee biweekly paychecks with weekly time collection.

Social Service Executive

Community Service (Volunteer Work)

- **Member,** Planning Committee, Community-Oriented Policing (COPS).

- Developed and implemented the Community Youth Centers for the COPS program in Baltimore City.

- **Facilitator,** Baraka School Program. Facilitated a joint venture among the Abel Foundation, Baltimore City Public Schools, and the Kenyan government that provides African American males aged 12 to 14 with a boarding-school experience in Kenya. Recognized by Maryland's Lt. Governor, Kathleen Kennedy Townsend.

- **Participant,** White House Meeting on Comprehensive Strategies for Children and Families. One of 25 people invited to a 3-day meeting to discuss provision of community-based services to children and families through Federal, state, and local collaborations.

- **Member,** Department of Juvenile Justice Speakers Bureau. Delivered speeches to requesting organizations on children's and family issues.

As you can see from these project examples, the form the lists take can vary considerably because they are targeted to specific audiences. What makes sense for a senior IT person might not make sense for an auditor, architect, or social services executive.

As with your accomplishments, make sure your project statements relate directly to the vacancy you are applying for and that you use words you identified in the vacancy analysis.

Summary

If you:

1. Outline the projects and tasks you have worked on over the past few years;

2. Follow the strategies outlined in this chapter;

3. Use your vacancy announcement analysis and the list of keywords and skills as a "blueprint" to guide you;

You will find that

★ Writing about your accomplishments can be more of a "filling in the blanks" exercise than trying to write the great American novel; and

★ Your application package will score better in the review process.

The next chapter teaches you how to polish your whole resume by writing in plain language. You will never write "responsible for" again! You will learn how to use more verbs and nouns in an active-voice writing style.

CHAPTER 9

Plain-Language Resumes: Writing Well

How do you look on paper? It's high time for civilians and current Federal employees to learn to write about their career accomplishments in a concise, clear, and nonbureaucratic writing style. You need to communicate your skills and accomplishments, and even brag a little, but a three- to five-page resume does not allow the space to write every little detail of your work. Now you have to select the most important experiences and write the resume in a new style, which I call plain language.

This chapter might be one of the most important in this book. Following the 10 resume-writing principles spelled out in this chapter will result in a well-written, easy-to-read, likable, factual, concise, and marketable resume. And a well-written resume will help you get selected for a promotion, increase your salary, and add to your retirement fund. All of the writing and editing effort will pay off!

Most of us don't give ourselves enough credit in our resumes. Sometimes this is due to misplaced modesty. Sometimes it's because of the "I can't take full credit for that because we do this work as a team" attitude. More often, though, it's either a failure to recognize the significance of our performance or an inability to articulate our performance in a way that sounds meaningful.

Fortunately, writing a good resume can be manageable, simple, and even easy, if you follow a few guidelines. Although there's no substitute for experience, even a first-time resume writer can produce a perfectly fine resume. And the more you practice, the better you will become.

To write a good resume, you have to be able to do three things:

★ Write well. Face it: you can't make a good resume out of poor sentences. You will learn how to write well by following the principles in this chapter. If you work at it, you can do it.

★ Perceive your abilities and accomplishments clearly and objectively, neither diminished through false modesty nor exaggerated through undue pride.

★ Assemble the well-written and accurate description of your qualifications into a compact, focused package.

Many people feel that their writing is not good. Even famous writers struggle with this feeling. And many people who need to put together a resume don't do much writing and have had little practice. At the same time, however, most people are good at telling a story to a friend—perhaps a funny thing that happened at the market, or an interesting program they saw on television. This ability is all you need to write a good resume! Your resume is really just a story about you.

You start with good content. If you are a poor worker and have accomplished little, your resume will not be impressive. But the fact that you are reading this book means that you are dedicated to improving your situation, and that's a sign of a good worker. If you have been reading and working with the chapters in Part II of this book, you have some good content by now. Now let's make it work for you.

I have identified 10 principles of good writing. They are neither hard nor complicated to learn and follow, and they work. Apply them yourself and see!

First Principle: Use Plain Words

The purpose of a resume is to impress the reviewer with your qualifications for the job. Many people think fancy writing is impressive. There are three problems with this. First, such writing is usually a turn-off. (Are you impressed by someone who uses a lot of flowery words? Or do you just think he or she is pompous?) Second, your resume should demonstrate how impressive YOU are—not your resume. Third, if you use boastful words incorrectly, not only do you fail to seem impressive; you seem downright dumb.

Here's an example of some overblown writing:

> My current employment situation encompasses the deployment of a duly licensed motorized vehicular conveyance in furtherance of conducting various personnel via local service routes from their place of location to their intended destinations.

This atrocious sentence means: "I drive a taxi."

 Tip: Here's a simple way to test whether your resume contains any bad, overblown writing. Read it aloud to a friend. Can you keep a straight face? Or are you embarrassed? Plain language is the single most important key to good resume writing. But if your resume does not pass the "straight face" test, how do you go about making it simple? You must look critically at *every single word* in your resume. Every word must pull its weight. You must mercilessly chop out every word that does not pack a punch. Use the fewest words possible to say the most.

Second Principle: Use Short Sentences

Long sentences are confusing and boring. They do not belong in your resume. Short sentences crackle with excitement! Abraham Lincoln once made the statement, "If you need me to give a long speech, I am ready now. If you want me to give a short speech, it will take me some time to prepare." No wonder the Gettysburg Address consists of just 10 short sentences. What is true of speeches is even more true of resumes. The last thing you need in your resume is a string of long sentences that take the reviewer a lot of time and effort to figure out.

Ideally, a sentence conveys only one clear thought. It flows logically from the preceding sentence and leads into the next sentence. There is no magically prescribed length for a good sentence. Good writing generally alternates between sentences of medium length and sentences that are much shorter. This creates variety and can set up a rhythm that keeps the reader's attention. See?

If your sentences have grown too long, you can break them into smaller sentences. Each small sentence can convey one piece of the full thought. Don't put a "laundry list" of ideas into one sentence. Here's an example:

BEFORE

> Coordinated review of specification, acquisition, statement of work, test plans, and procedures documents to ensure that all written test processes are in accordance with the Acquisition Management System (AMS), Test and Evaluation guidelines, and WJHTC System Test and Evaluation Process documents.

AFTER

> Coordinated review of all written test processes. Ensured compliance with Acquisition Management System (AMS), Test and Evaluation guidelines, and WJHTC System Test and Evaluation Process documents. Reviewed specification, acquisition, statement of work, test plans, and procedures documents.

Third Principle: Do Not Use "I"

There is no *I* in *resume*. Avoid writing your resume with the personal pronoun "I." Resumes are a unique breed of writing in which sentence fragments are preferred, as long as their meaning is clear. Omit the first-person pronoun and most other pronouns and articles whenever possible. Doing so will keep all your descriptions from starting with the same word and will keep it from looking like you are overly focused on yourself.

The following before-and-after examples demonstrate using a strong verb instead of "I am responsible for, I performed, I am the…." Your resume will be a more active document when you replace the "I" with a solid verb.

BEFORE

> I am responsible for the Strategic Information Resources Management (IRM) Plan, all automated system projects from formulation through implementation to include the development of "Automated Information Systems Proposals," the annual funding plan, and the allocation of funding among all the IRM projects.

AFTER

> Manage the implementation of the first Strategic Information Resources Management Plan, as well as all automated system projects. Direct projects from formulation through implementation. Coordinate development of "Automated Information Systems Proposals," the annual funding plan, and the allocation of funding among all the IRM projects.

Fourth Principle: Use Powerful Words

If you use plain language in short sentences, how is your resume going to impress anyone? Through the use of powerful words! Powerful words convey strong and unambiguous meaning. You should use a thesaurus to find stronger substitutes for weak words in your resume. But this won't take you all the way. To clear away the debris of weak words, you need to think about writing in a new way. For example, consider the following statement:

> Serve as point of contact for all matters pertaining to personnel.

Serve as is not impressive. It does not tell the reader anything. Chop it. *Point of contact* is good, but *chief liaison* is better. *Sole liaison* is better still (if true). *Pertaining to* adds nothing, so eliminate it. Just say, *all personnel matters.* Thus, the following statement is a good phrase:

> Sole liaison on all personnel matters.

Every single word in it contributes significantly to the idea.

To get more power out of words, convert verbose phrases into economical nouns. *Tasks include administrative aspects of office management* becomes *Office manager* or *Administrator of 25 staff office.* Include more nouns in your resume wherever you can.

Fifth Principle: Beware of Acronyms

There are several reasons why you should not depend on acronyms to describe your job. Many people might not recognize what the acronyms stand for. Describe your experience with both acronyms and descriptions to be safe.

Sixth Principle: No Bureaucratese, Colloquialisms, or Technobabble

If you are converting from an OF-612 or SF-171 to a Federal resume, you can write in a more clear and meaningful style without the bureaucratese. You should also be careful not to be too chatty in your resume by using colloquialisms from your field of work. Technical writers should beware of technobabble that the human resources staff might not understand.

No Bureaucratese

Bureaucratese is a style of language characterized by jargon and euphemism that is used especially by bureaucrats. This is the language bureaucrats speak, and it is often a confusing, cold, and cloudy one. All of us, but particularly those of us who work for the public, have a responsibility to handle language with care. We need to be accessible and clear. We need to avoid jargon

and bureaucratese. Examples of jargon include the following:

★ Overuse of the passive voice (see the tenth principle for more on this)

★ Using Federal and state program names without explaining what the programs are

★ Using and misusing words such as impact, interface, prioritize, modality, and ascertain

★ Using phony words and phrases such as analyzation, conduit, augment, and determine the nature of

BEFORE: Bureaucratic Writing Style

> Security Manager: Closely monitored Sentinel Key (a computerized system developed to track security clearances to see when upgrades, downgrades, or re-accomplishments were required per regulation on military and civilian personnel) for 512 personnel. Utilized extensively and instructed use on the Electronic Personnel Security Questionnaire (EPSQ) system supplying pertinent information routing through USAF Security Forces to the Department of Defense (DoD) Security Clearance Investigation Service and (OPM) Office of Personnel Management. Tracked the process insuring clearances were current in a timely manner and correcting any problems within the paperwork. Accompanied senior management to Air Force Security Forces or Navy Brig debriefing individuals that lost their clearances due to felony actions, etc.

AFTER: Active Writing Style That Is More Friendly and Direct

> Security Manager: Closely monitored the computerized Personnel Security system (Sentinel Key System) tracking security clearances. Managed system upgrades and downgrades based on changing emergency alert personnel regulations. Instructed employees in the use of the Electronic Personnel Security Questionnaire system. Facilitated security clearance services through USAF Security Forces to the Department of Defense, Security Clearance Investigation Service and Office of Personnel Management. Ensured that clearances were issued in a timely manner and resolved problems with documentation. Accompanied senior management to Air Force Security Forces or Navy Brig debriefing employees who had lost their clearances due to felony actions, etc.

No Colloquialisms

Resumes simply cannot be colloquial, chatty, cute, clever, or otherwise casual—especially in the civilian DoD agency environment. They must be purely professional. This does not mean that they should be stiff or overly formal—just

professional. Where do you draw the line? You must know the audience. If you are applying for a position in finance or other fields that demand precision and accountability, casual language can easily disqualify you. If your goal is a job doing puppet shows for children in hospitals, some flexibility in the direction of the casual might not hurt. The bottom line: Better to be too professional than too colloquial, no matter what the position is.

No Technobabble

Computer professionals are a good example of resume writers who typically write either too much or too little. Either way, it is a challenge for them to write a full, clear sentence that a non-technical person can understand. An Information Technology (IT) professional in today's working world must be able to communicate verbally and in writing with customers who are struggling to use information technology systems efficiently.

I met an IT entrepreneur on an airplane who told me that he never hires a computer person who does not include the word "customer" in his or her resume. In fact, he says he hires IT professionals for their ability to communicate

and provide customer service. The technical skills are expected, but the service side is the real challenge. In your resume, you should consider technical expertise and communications skills equally. Remember who is reading the resume: human resources, customers, administrators, and technology managers. The complex, long, multiple-thought sentences won't impress readers if they can't understand the meaning.

Seventh Principle: Tell a Story or Describe a Project

The best resumes flow with well-written, interesting prose—almost like a story. Many Federal employees are involved in major projects in their work. Their entire resumes can be composed of descriptions of projects.

On a resume, you can tell a story this way:

Director: Special Backlog Reduction Project, May–June, xxxx

Appointed by Office Manager to lead special project to reduce chronic filing backlog. Devised innovative cross-reference filing system that significantly reduced file retrieval time. Reported to work one hour early each day for one month to remedy backlog, while still performing all regular duties. Successfully eliminated 13-month backlog within 30 days. Office Manager commended me in writing for this achievement and mandated adoption of my new system department-wide.

This story shows that you are hard-working and conscientious, punctual (even coming in one hour early), organized, and more—all of the qualities you wanted to convey. You can also use a special title for this position. The title sounds important and says exactly what you did. You can use such a title to good effect, even if the Office Manager never officially bestowed it, as long as it is true. Speaking of which….

Eighth Principle: Tell the Truth and Don't Exaggerate

An attorney once served on a committee to assess the qualifications of applicants for an elite unit. Each applicant submitted a resume and a writing sample. As he was reading one of the writing samples, it struck him as being well written, but familiar. This is no surprise because it turned out that the attorney had written it himself! The applicant had plagiarized his work for her writing sample (probably not realizing he would be reviewing it). Needless to say, this individual did not get the job. If you exaggerate your accomplishments to the extent of being misleading, you are hurting yourself.

In the same category, avoid superlatives as a general rule. Phrases such as *all, very, every, the greatest, the only,* and so forth raise a red flag. Use superlatives only for objectively quantifiable accomplishments or when reciting the opinion of

a knowledgeable person. Example: "My supervisor has praised me as being the most efficient office manager he has ever known." Though subjective, the opinion of a supervisor is meaningful.

Ninth Principle: Be Consistent with Verb Tenses

The rule about tense in resumes is to use the present tense for all present responsibilities and skills and the past tense for all past responsibilities. Here are a few samples:

ELECTRONICS TECHNICIAN (September xxxx to present)

Field installer. Ensure security and protection of University property and individuals through electronic systems. Install, test, maintain, and repair electronic security systems throughout the campus. Troubleshoot systems and communicate with contractors concerning warranty and specialized repairs. *(Present tense.)*

SENIOR STAFF ATTORNEY (August xxxx to December xxxx)

Handled over 75 complex litigations from start to finish. Promoted from Attorney Level II to Attorney Level III in record time. Carried caseload 42% above office-wide average. Consistently rated "outstanding," highest possible rating. Won annual award for "Top-Performing Staff Attorney" three years in a row. *(Past tense.)*

Tenth Principle: Avoid the Passive Voice

Human resources professionals write vacancy announcements in the passive voice. Many civilians became accustomed to writing their SF-171s in the passive voice. Now, however, you should avoid doing so. Use the active voice whenever possible. This means that your sentence has a subject and a verb, and the subject is performing the action indicated by the verb.

A sentence written in the passive voice has a subject and a verb, but the subject is not doing the action of the verb. Rather, the subject is having the action of the verb done to it by someone or something else; for example, *The sentence is being written.* "Sentence" is the subject. "To

write" is the verb, but it is passive rather than active. Who is writing the sentence? We don't know. The passive voice is vague and elusive because it raises a question (who is writing?) but does not supply an answer, which is annoying.

Identifying passive sentences is sometimes confusing in resumes because the subject is often "I," and is often omitted from the sentence; for example, *I handled over 75 complex litigations.* "I" is the subject and "handled" is the verb. Remember from the Third Principle earlier in this chapter that you should not use "I" in your descriptions. Therefore, the sentence is written like this: *Handled over 75 complex litigations.* All of the sentences here could start with "I," but we have deleted "I" so that the sentences emphasize the action rather than the subject.

Here are a few examples of passive voice followed by the versions rewritten in active voice. The passive voice examples don't say that the person really DID anything. Someone else did the work, or the statement is simply a statement without action.

BEFORE

> Other duties: classroom control (25 to 30 students in each class), student discipline, and student grading and evaluations—much the same as a supervisor but with more bodies. Work entails handling multiple tasks in the classroom; flexibility, discipline, alertness a requirement in this job. Must also be a good listener at all times.

AFTER

> Managed classroom control (25 to 30 students in each class), student discipline, and student grading and evaluations. Demonstrated classroom flexibility, discipline, listening skills, and alertness in meeting student needs.

BEFORE

> When the property management program began coordinating the property acquisition, job responsibilities were aligned more closely with the procurement process. This job assisted offices in acquiring necessary equipment and services. The Data Systems Division continued to improve and enhance the property management application.

AFTER

> Established a property management program for the Data Systems Division. Procured equipment and services and advised staff in purchasing processes.

Summary

Because your resume reflects who you are, you should feel comfortable with it. Can you speak it out loud without embarrassment? If not, you could end up being embarrassed if the interviewer asks you about your accomplishments as recorded on the resume.

Resumes should be written in a way that allows you to read them aloud in a natural and comfortable fashion. What works for one person might not work for another. How would you speak about your experience to a friend? Look at the passive voice examples in the Tenth Principle section. Do you see the difference in readability between the passive voice and the active voice?

The new writing style is more personal without being too casual, the flow of the prose tells a story, and the sentences are complete and written in active voice. These paragraphs are written as you would speak them.

The Magic of Page 1: Focusing Your Resume Toward an Announcement, Promotion, or New Career

When job seekers ask me or my resume-writing staff whether they should have more than one resume, we always say, "Most likely you can have just one resume, as long as you focus it toward your career objective on page 1." Because writing a resume takes many hours, it helps Federal job seekers to know that one good Federal resume is really the best approach. You can focus your resume toward your objective using the various special "focusing" sections illustrated in this chapter:

★ Profile statement (or Summary of Skills)

★ Critical Skills List

★ Accomplishments List

You can write a new Profile or Summary of Skills in about one hour and then have time to work on writing your knowledge, skills, and abilities narratives (see chapter 14) and finding more vacancy announcements (see chapter 4). You place these focusing sections on page 1 of your resume—the most important "real estate" on the page. The busy human resources representative will look at the first page of your resume hoping to see some of the skills and keywords from the vacancy announcement.

You can choose to write one or all three of these focusing sections. They are challenging to write, especially the Profile statement. If you are on a tight deadline and cannot take the time to write the focusing sections, they are not mandatory. You can come back and write these sections when you have time to focus your application and objectives. Even though you place these three sections on the first page of your resume, you write them last because they summarize your skills and experience in relation to the vacancy announcement.

Later in this chapter you will see examples of Profile statements, Skills Summaries, and Accomplishments Lists. I've also included a writing strategy for each focusing section.

Overview of the Three Types of Focusing Sections

Here is a brief description of each of the three focusing sections that I recommend for your resume. You can choose to use one or all of the focusing techniques.

Profile Statement

The Profile statement is an abstract of your career. It addresses the interviewer's inevitable statement, "Tell me about yourself." The Federal resume format allows you to strengthen your application by summarizing your qualifications in an opening Profile statement, an option that the OF-612 did not give you. You can use this profile of your career to feature your experience and skills, as well as keywords directly from the vacancy announcement. Private-industry resumes almost always include a Profile statement to introduce the reader to the applicant's qualifications and background. This section can save the human resources professional's time. Do you want the reader to be interested in you and keep reading your resume? Then you need a Profile statement on your resume.

Here is an impressive Profile for a GS-5 Accounting Aide who is emphasizing administrative and professional support skills rather than accounting and clerical work. She wants to change her job series so that she can be promoted to a GS-7 position.

> Secretary/Administrative Assistant/Accounting Aide with seven years' solid experience in Federal government offices. Experienced in Taxpayer Services, Quality Assurance, and Planning and Special Programs Departments. Able to effectively support 5 to 15 professionals with projects, word processing, correspondence, and schedule and telephone management. Completed 10 months of professional secretarial training.

Critical Skills List

The Critical Skills list is easier to write than the Profile statement. This is a list of skills that you have that are also in the vacancy announcement. This simple list of skills should be easy to read. The Critical Skills section is especially useful for technical positions where certain skills are mandatory. Do you have specific expertise that is required for your desired position? Make a list and place it on page 1.

The following is a Critical Skills list that supports the Profile statement for the GS-5 Accounting Aide that you saw in the preceding section. From this list, she looks very qualified for a GS-6 or -7 position as an administrative assistant or secretary. Because the candidate is determined to leave the accounting field, she has left out the basic accounting skills.

> **Critical Administrative Skills:**
>
> - Providing programmatic and technical support.
> - Producing accounting and budget reviews and reports.
> - Utilizing computerized data management system for input, research, and updating.
> - Tracking information to support programs.
> - Monitoring and maintaining client files.
> - Solving administrative and computer problems; researching discrepancies.
> - Editing, formatting, and proofreading written documents in WordPerfect and Word.
> - Coordinating projects; monitoring deadlines.
> - Handling multiple projects.
> - Detail oriented, efficient, able to design administrative systems to improve location of information and accessibility.
> - Word processing with WordPerfect 8.0, Windows, Lotus 1-2-3, keyboard 70 wpm.

Accomplishments List

Accomplishments can be included in two places in your Federal resume. They can be included in your "Work Experience" section, as we discussed in chapter 8, or they can be featured at the top of your resume to emphasize significant accomplishments.

Do you have an accomplishment that demonstrates you are an excellent and valuable employee to your office? Was this project challenging, interesting, and successful? Did it result in new methods or processes in your agency? Would you like this accomplishment to stand out? Do you want to impress someone with your abilities and experience in a particular area? Then you can write a three-to-five-line statement focusing on the results of your accomplishment. You can include between three and five statements before the list becomes too long.

Here are two examples of accomplishments that could be featured on page 1 of the resume so that the resume will stand out:

Saved the agency $50,000 in printing fees by recommending and coordinating in-house printing of large biannual publication. Received a Superior Performance Award and $250 cash bonus for recommendation. *(Position: Records Management Technician)*

In just 90 days, negotiated and managed a sole-source multimillion-dollar contract using new Acquisition Reform practices. Received Letters of Appreciation from my supervisor and the vendor for streamlining the process and meeting the acquisition and budget deadline. *(Position: Procurement Specialist)*

Your resume accomplishments can be the same as your KSA accomplishments, except that your accomplishments will be longer and more detailed in your KSAs. As you are writing accomplishments, be aware that your resume's Accomplishments section must be brief and written differently than the same examples in your KSAs. Chapter 14 on KSA writing gives examples of the narrative writing style of a KSA.

The resume Accomplishment section should include the following for each accomplishment:

★ Description of the situation or project

★ Result

The Accomplishment section could also include a significant award or recognition that would be impressive.

The KSA includes the following:

★ Situation/project

★ Methods or solutions

★ Challenge

★ Result

Targeting Your Resume to Each Announcement

You should target each announcement by changing your Profile statement. It takes only about an hour or so to customize each Federal resume for each vacancy announcement.

Reading, understanding, and valuing the information in the announcement are important when you are focusing your resume. Read and analyze the Duties and Responsibilities section of the announcement. Read between the lines, too! If you don't understand the position description, go to the agency's Web site and find out the agency's functions and programs. Think about the agency's and the hiring manager's needs. You are applying for this job—you will be the person who will perform this job. Whatever problems or special situations exist in this office, you will be person who will solve them. Chapter 4 reviews how to analyze the announcement in more detail.

Vacancy announcements are difficult to read most of the time. You should analyze the "duties" carefully. You could copy and paste the "duties" section from the online vacancy announcement into a Word file. Then you can enlarge the type, find the keywords and skills, and consider using the keywords in your Work Experience section or Profile statement.

The following is a vacancy announcement for an Aviation Operations Specialist and the Profile of an FAA Public Affairs Specialist who wants to move into aviation operations. Her Profile highlights her job-related responsibilities and skills.

VACANCY ANNOUNCEMENT LANGUAGE

Responsible for <u>planning</u> and <u>developing policies and activities</u> related to the <u>FAA's international program</u>; <u>analyzing data</u>; <u>conducting studies</u> that support those policies and activities; <u>organizing, executing, and managing</u> activities; implementing the FAA's international policies and programs; and <u>supporting the overall activities</u> of the Division and office.

FEDERAL RESUME PROFILE STATEMENT TARGETING THE DUTIES OF THIS POSITION

Aviation communications professional with over 15 years' experience demonstrating planning and organizational skills and analysis of international programs. Award-winning media relations and development and maintenance of positive relationships among government employees, industry representatives, and academia. Recent assignments include special project involving Pacific region air transportation technology and multiple agency missions. Adept at organizing, executing, and managing information on programs and budgets for international programs.

By rewriting the Profile, you can have more than one version of your Federal resume. You can save your various versions on your computer and have them ready to paste into applications. You can change your Profile for each field of work. For instance, one Federal applicant would be qualified for and interested in the following positions: training director, educational specialist, and human resources specialist. Each Profile would be slightly different, highlighting the specific language of the announcement. It's possible that one person can apply for jobs as Training Specialist, Webmaster, Human Resources Professional, and Writer-Editor. The Profile statement and Summary of Skills would certainly be different for each of these career objectives.

The Profile sets the tone of the resume, so you do not have to rewrite the entire resume.

Changing Careers Using the Focusing Sections

Changing careers calls for a different resume strategy. What if the job you held two jobs previous is the most relevant to your new objective? Would you like to highlight skills and experience you gained *before* your current position? Would you like to *play down* your current job title and responsibilities? Would you like to highlight a new degree or training you've received? You can use the focusing sections to do all this and more.

Highlighting Skills from Prior Jobs

It's easy to emphasize the skills from the second job on your resume by using the Profile statement and Summary of Skills. Using this more creative presentation, you can list the relevant skills on page 1. One Federal job seeker wanted to return to Contract Specialist work, which she performed for 10 years before her current job. In her Profile statement she featured her contracting skills rather than her accounting skills so that she could be deemed "best qualified" for jobs in her former series.

Another example is the following Security Technician. Her job is being contracted out to private industry and she needs to change occupational series. Before taking her DoD job, she had extensive accounting and administrative experience. I have highlighted her accounting and administrative skills in this electronic DoD resume format. This skills-based resume was successful; a database query picked up 120 accounting-related skills. You'll learn more about electronic resume writing in chapter 12.

PROFILE
Accounting and Administrative operations expertise in systems and organization, accounting, and security.

CRITICAL SKILLS
ADMINISTRATION: office operation and management, personnel training and supervision, human resources, and personnel records management.

BOOKKEEPING AND ACCOUNTING: error and discrepancy identification, account reconciliation and analysis, payroll preparation, report preparation.

SECURITY ASSISTANT: data collection and audits, reviews, processing, disbursement of personnel security investigation in strict compliance with Department of Defense guidelines, technical guidance, policy and procedure interpretation, direction of a team of Security Clerks, regulatory compliance, and achievement of time and quality of work objectives.

Personal qualities include being able to research and resolve problems, demonstrate interpersonal skills, and handle multiple projects effectively. Also can work independently or as an effective team leader.

COMPUTER SKILLS: Microsoft Word, Microsoft Excel, keyboard 50 wpm.

Highlighting a Recent Degree

Many professionals are returning to college so that they can advance in a certain job series or change careers. Maybe you would like to highlight your recent degree before you start describing your work history. This applicant returned to school after years as a credit and collections

specialist in private industry. She is now qualified for an economist or international trade specialist position in government. Her Critical Skills section describes skills she gained in the graduate program. Because she does not have work experience as an economist, her education and skills are critical.

Critical Skills:
>   Analyze international development economics
>   Understand international economic relationships
>   Apply money, banking, and foreign-exchange principles to economic analysis
>   Compile data and write clear, concise reports
>   Statistical analysis and spreadsheet and report production
>   Perform research to support team-oriented work projects
>   Budget management, forecasting, and cost analysis

Education:
George Mason University, Fairfax, VA
M.A., International Transactions, Concentration in Developmental Economics, January 2003
GPA 3.75/4.00
Courses included Economic Analysis (macroeconomic theory and policies); International Finance and the Global Economy; Approaches to International Transactions encompassing accounting for investments and foreign exchange; and Data Identification Analysis (quantitative methods).
(See attached course descriptions.)

Howard University, Washington, DC
B.A., Accounting, May 2000
G.P.A. 3.56/4.00; National Dean's List, 1998–2000

More Profile Statement Examples

The following sample Profile statements will give you some ideas about what yours should contain. There are examples for people seeking promotions as well as those seeking to change careers.

Applicants Seeking Promotions

These Profile statements were written for applicants seeking a promotion in the same field.

Biochemical Research Director

Biochemical research director with extensive experience in the oversight and development of national research programs. Effective record establishing and nurturing research teams of national prominence to promote scientific and technological progress. Strong commitment to developing new instrumentation technologies. Solid record in applied research. More than 85 publications in leading refereed journals. Seeking to build on experiences managing research-grant programs in biomedical or biophysical sciences.

Geochemical Engineer and Financial Analyst

Experienced geochemical engineer and financial analyst with extensive environmental research skills. Broad experience includes seismic, geochemical, and business assessments of mineral development and agricultural properties, natural resource evaluations, oceanic and watershed research, and missile research abatement. Technological consulting includes innovative special effects for futuristic movies. Advanced law student seeking opportunities to apply scientific and business experiences in a position involving natural-resource-management responsibilities.

(continues)

(continued)

Business and Marketing Executive

Senior marketing executive with background in information technology solutions and services for both commercial and government sectors. Central to success in both arenas is the proven ability to communicate clearly and concisely the issues, challenges, and technical substance associated with the integration of complex information-technology solutions. Skilled in planning, organizing, implementing, and monitoring of Integrated Logistics Support (ILS) of major systems acquisitions, including operational and training systems. Experience includes effective participation in Logistics Reinvention and Modernization (LR&M) Industry Steering Group and Joint DoD Industry Digital Information Interchange Task Group. Seeking opportunity to build upon knowledge of emerging technology requirements in defense-contracting arena.

FBI Agent

Experienced investigator with extensive record coordinating successful operations with Federal, state, and local law-enforcement organizations. Extensive record of organizing and presenting evidence to prosecutors in concise formats, supported by detailed background and written analyses. Consistent and reliable witness in numerous cases, including Federal (civil and military), state, and local prosecutions. Active in community organizations promoting sporting and athletic competitions. Seeking opportunities to continue conducting background investigations on a contract basis.

Environmental Expert

National Expert in Environmental Management Systems—voluntary programs and U.S. regulatory systems. Seven years' experience as Counsel to the U.S. Environmental Protection Agency, Office of Enforcement and Compliance Assurance. Experienced in designing performance measures, directing audits, writing national policies, advising on cost-devising strategies for compliance, and interpreting enforcement policies. Principal advisor to the EPA Administrator; member of U.S. delegation on international environmental commissions and technical advisory groups. Law degree and ISO 14000 lead Auditor Candidate.

Information Systems Specialist

Experienced information systems professional with solid record as a team leader and contracting officer's technical representative on major information systems design and development projects. Consistent record of effective support for major Department of Education programs and excellent customer service optimally to process and support department-wide information systems. Background includes frequent interaction with executive branch IRM policy officials to facilitate development and modification of data systems to support Department of Education's mission.

Career Changers

The next set of Profile statements is for applicants who desire a career change.

Executive Transitioning to Market Research

This executive has experience doing business with the government. He is emphasizing marketing research and program management rather than general management.

> Highly accomplished professional with over 20 years of experience in marketing research, strategic planning, project management, contract negotiations, and product development. Special expertise in applying marketing techniques to reduce social problems. Clients are Federal agencies such as the Environmental Protection Agency, the Food and Drug Administration, and the Equal Employment Opportunity Commission; nonprofit organizations; and corporations.

Teacher Transitioning to Educational Program Management

This classroom teacher wants to leave the classroom and focus her career toward educational program management in government.

> Accomplished professional with 11 years of experience as an elementary school special-education teacher. Achievements include serving as chair of current school's Local Screening Committee; initiating, planning, and coordinating programs such as a support group for parents of students with Learning Disabilities and Attention-Deficit Disorder; serving as current school's "designated administrator"; teaching preschool hearing-impaired students; and developing and implementing technology-based learning programs. Strong management, public relations, leadership, presentation, and writing skills.

J.D. Candidate Interested in Legislative Work

This dual-career professional is offering legal, political, legislative, speaking, and advocacy skills for a Policy Analyst, Writer-Editor, or Congressional Committee position.

> Successful political campaigner with expertise as an analyst, fund-raiser, and events planner/coordinator for local, statewide, and national races.
>
> Juris Doctor Candidate with experience as a Legislative Coordinator for the Senate of Maryland; as a Law Clerk for Patrick A. O'Doherty, Esq., of Baltimore; and as a Judicial Intern for the Honorable Christian M. Kahl, Circuit Court of Maryland, Baltimore County.
>
> Accomplished Legislative Coordinator for the State of Maryland Senate, Select Committee 11 (Baltimore City Senate Delegation—1998 session).
>
> Outstanding leader and public speaker. Strong advocate and appointed leader for higher education issues.

Federal Resume Case Studies with Page 1 Focusing Sections

The applicants in the seven resume case studies that follow focused their resumes toward a specific position by using the Profile statement, Critical Skills section, or Accomplishments section. The primary objective of a resume's first page is to target your area of interest and keep the reader's eyes on the page. Just like a Dean Koontz thriller, keep them turning the pages of your resume.

Case Study 1: Profile with Summary of Positions and Qualifications

Program Manager, GS-13: Mark was recently promoted to a GS-14 by using this Objective and Profile statement. He emphasized the skills desired at the GS-14 level, including project management, improving efficiency and effectiveness of public programs, Team Leader, Supervisor, and Mentor.

Program Management position where I can apply my outstanding managerial and supervisory experience, as well as analytical, project-management, and writing skills to achieve mission objectives. Broad knowledge of human resources programs and policies, and operations to improve the efficiency and effectiveness of public service.

PROFILE:

- Program manager and senior advisor to agency officials at all levels.

- Assistant project manager for complex headquarters-level projects on program structure and effectiveness, far-reaching in impact and multi-year in scope.

- Team leader; creative problem-solver.

- Supervisor of headquarters and field professional and administrative support staff.

- Skilled in communicating orally to groups/individuals with diverse responsibilities and backgrounds.

- Professional writer-editor and credentialed as Certified Professional Resume Writer.

- Coach, mentor, and developer for subordinate staff, employees with disabilities, and motivated career aspirants inside and outside the agency.

- Effective mediator of disputes and facilitator of problem-solving teams.

- Experienced negotiator and agency representative in third-party procedures.

- Recognized with awards for proactive leadership in Equal Opportunity/Civil Rights.

Case Study 2: Profile Highlighting Education, Travel, and Languages

Consular assistant, Department of State: John summarized his entire professional career in the first paragraph. He covered his language skills, his international experience, his private-industry background, and his broad program background. His objective is to stay in the international field and stay overseas but change his position.

John T. Phillips
Permanent Address: P.O. Box 1111, Savannah, GA 22209

Work Telephone: 011-7-096-909-8989
Fax: 011-7-096-565-7878

Permanent U.S. Telephone: (708) 900-0999
e-mail: john.phillips@dos.us-state.gov

Social Security No: 444-44-4444
Veteran's Status: N/A
Federal Status:
Consular Assistant—Immigration Unit, Department of State, U.S. Embassy, Moscow, Russia

Citizenship: U.S.

Objective: Federal Law Enforcement Agencies

Profile: Recent college graduate with 18 months' Department of State experience at the American Embassy in Moscow, requiring almost-fluent Russian-language skills. Skills include database, international services, and case management; writing and editing; excellent communications and interpersonal skills; and problem-solving abilities. Adept at learning complex U.S. and foreign government regulations, interpreting and conveying laws and processes to customers, and ensuring compliance with procedures. Recognize the importance of quality, efficiency, and service in customer-oriented government agency that involves international travel, substantial constituent financial investment, and highly sensitive personal/family/emotional (and sometimes political) issues.

Education:

University of Tennessee, Knoxville, TN 37996
B.A., Russian   December xxxx
Dean's List   GPA: 3.2/4.0

Gornyii Institute, St. Petersburg, Russia   Summer xxxx
Intensive Russian Language Program, 40 hours per week, 12 weeks

English Valley High School, N. English, IA 52316
Graduated xxxx

Language Proficiency:

Russian: 3/3 Level. Moderate speaking and writing. Able to interpret and translate adoption and legal documents and correspondence for both Americans and Russians.

International Travel:

Extensive travel in over 50 countries. Lived in Australia for the entire year of xxxx. Lived in Italy for 3 months in 1990. Lived in Russia for 2 years from 1/xx to present. Traveled more than 2 months in over 10 countries.

Case Study 3: Summary of Qualifications and Education for Career Change

Special Agent seeking a career change to Analyst, Policy Analyst, and Program Analyst positions based on recent education and competencies: The Qualifications Summary emphasizes national security programs with a focus on analytical, program, and team work with other agencies. The candidate seeks new opportunities that will involve negotiations, communications, and managing relationships with other agencies.

QUALIFICATIONS SUMMARY

- Proven analytical, investigative, and problem-solving skills including criminal/terrorist/national security program development, planning, and management.

- Creative thinker and high-energy professional with demonstrated success making accurate risk assessments and employing nontraditional problem-solving methods.

- Proven ability to manage and direct obscure and/or complicated research, projects, and criminal investigations (including elements of proof required for successful prosecution). Experienced with classified programs with far-reaching national and international implications.

- Proficient at developing/nurturing working relationships with numerous local, state, and Federal agencies, and coordinating or leading efforts to implement strategic plans.

- Master's degree and specific training and in-depth work history in Clinical Psychology provide basis for expertise as "psychological profiler" and investigative advisor to groups such as Special Agents for FBI Field Offices nationwide.

- Comprehensive understanding of, and experience in, the psychology of strategic negotiations.

- Keen propensity for quickly analyzing critical situations precisely and for making swift and appropriate decisions regarding the correct action to take.

EDUCATION

M.S. in Health Promotion Management/Health Care Management
Marymount University, Arlington, VA—Degree expected xxxx

M.A. in Clinical Psychology
George Mason University, Fairfax, VA—Degree awarded with Highest Distinction xxxx

B.A. in Developmental Psychology
George Mason University, Fairfax, VA—xxxx

Case Study 4: Quoting a Supervisor in a Profile

Department of the Interior Park Ranger: Carolyn's Profile is directed toward quality, experience, and knowledge of the National Park Service. Her Profile is impressive and interesting to read because it was actually written by a supervisor.

CAROLYN D. O'CONNOR

Permanent Address: P.O. Box 310 Kula, HI 96790

Local Address: National Park Service, Haleakala National Park
P.O. Box 369, Makawao, HI 96768
Email: Carolyn_oconnor@yahoo.com
Evening: (808) 744-4324 ◦ Daytime: (808) 572-9306 (ext. 5510)

Social Security No.: 000-00-0000   Citizenship: United States
Federal Status: Park Ranger, GS-025-07/01, 8/20/xx   Veteran's Preference: N/A

PROFILE: More than five years of experience in four different National Parks. Highly qualified in a wide range of skills from those involved in creating original interpretation programs to radio dispatch, emergency medical service, firefighting, and administrative support using various computer software applications. Effective supervisor and trainer. Energetic, creative, and eager to learn about and participate in all aspects of work at our National Parks. A former supervisor writes: "*Carolyn's performance has been outstanding. She learned the park operations and resources quickly and is able to execute her duties independently without close supervision. She consistently exceeds expectations and does more than is required for the job.… Her motivation, initiative, proactivity, and reliability have been truly exemplary. She is an employee of high caliber and dedication.*"

Case Study 5: Qualifications and Skills Summary–Returning to Government Management Position

U.S. Army Reserves officer and former WorldCom employee: John is seeking to return to a civilian position in government and is focusing on his leadership, international, economic, and telecommunications experience gained from the Army Reserves as a Major rather than his commercial experience. He emphasizes his competencies and transferable skills that are applicable to positions in information technology and telecommunications systems.

QUALIFICATIONS & SKILLS SUMMARY

Offer 15+ years of in-depth and far-reaching experience in areas of economic development, advanced information technology, and telecommunications systems. Diverse and proven management and leadership abilities based on intrinsic and exceptional interpersonal skills, developed through increasingly responsible military and private-sector professional history. Demonstrated talent for innovative and practical problem solving of complex issues. Expertise in this problem-solving capacity involves international, cultural, and economic concerns, as well as corporate matters related to fiscal, management, and technology development. Established reputation for exhibiting excellent communication and organizational skills, and for working well with people in executive management and all levels of support staff. Strategic planner adept at understanding, conceptualizing, and successfully implementing change. Consistently recognized by superiors for outstanding capabilities, professionalism, and dedication.

Case Study 6: Demonstrating Expertise for an Executive Promotion

Health Insurance Specialist, GS-107-14, seeking a GS-14 supervisory position: This senior executive is a subject-matter expert and supervisor who demonstrates many of the Managerial Core Competencies listed in chapter 5. Competencies include leading teams, motivating staff, negotiation skills, decision-making, political savvy, problem-solving, and building coalitions. These are featured on page 1 of the resume, as well as in KSA narratives.

QUALIFICATIONS SUMMARY: Offers 20+ years as healthcare professional with far-reaching and in-depth experience in private-sector and government settings and organizations. Possess comprehensive understanding of administration and operation of national health insurance programs such as Medicare and Medicaid, from both government and private healthcare perspectives. Extensive expertise in the development, implementation, and evaluation of healthcare quality-improvement projects with special interest in disparities. Professional history ranges from establishing/operating healthcare company to serving as Government Task Leader within the Centers for Medicare and Medicaid Services. Management experience includes first-line and staff responsibility.

Skills/Expertise Highlights

- Knowledge of and extensive experience in dealing with health issues related to disadvantaged populations, with particular emphasis on Medicare and Medicaid.

- Proven ability to successfully develop measurement tools and strategies such as quality indicators, data-collection methods, and baseline data analysis for Quality Improvement Organizations (QIO) projects.

- All-inclusive skills in leading teams and building relationships/coalitions—practical experience (e.g., developing, guiding, and motivating teams who provided therapeutic drug monitoring [including 150 professional staff] over large geographic region), as well as specialized training in formal graduate-education program.

- Outstanding track record for successfully managing numerous quality-improvement projects related to Medicare and Medicaid Programs for QIOs.

- Excellent verbal and written communication skills with established reputation for delivering effective presentations to small and large groups of professionals, as well as to other diverse populations concerned with Medicare and Medicaid issues.

Case Study 7: Profile and Accomplishments

Information Technology Specialist (Web Development), GS-2210-7: This resume targets positions in Web site design, development, and computer programming. Jonathan graduated with his B.S. in 2000 but had worked in programming since 1998. Now he wants a steady IT position in government.

SUMMARY OF QUALIFICATIONS

Excellent Web design skills: Creative and meticulous Web designer. Developed Web-based "Information Center" for Drew University. Won 2nd place for computer graphics in a statewide art competition in xxxx; honorable mention in xxxx. Web designs and programs frequently used by instructor to demonstrate to class members examples of unique solutions to particularly difficult technical situations.

Superior programming skills: Logically minded programmer with project-management experience in database development. Programming skills enhanced by motivation, diligence, and reliability.

TECHNICAL SKILLS

Languages: C, C++, Visual Basic, Turbo Pascal, JavaScript, VBScript, ASP, HTML, DHTML

OS: Windows 98/NT/2000

Applications: Visual InterDev 6, FrontPage 2000, Dreamweaver 3, Flash 4, Photoshop 5.5, MS SQL Server 7/2000, MS Office 97/2000, MS Exchange 2000 Server, MS IIS 4.0/5.0

Summary

Congratulations! You have just finished focusing your resume toward the position you are seeking next. You can refocus your resume for each announcement that you find by selecting and using some of the skills, competencies, and keywords you find in the announcements.

This is the final resume-writing chapter and the end of part 2. The next step, in part 3, is to package your Federal resume, proofread it, edit it, improve the format, and make sure that the final presentation is impressive and perfect. Chapter 11 discusses type fonts, sizes, and spacing, as well as options for organizing sections of your resume. You're almost finished with an outstanding Federal resume that will get results!

Electronic Resumes, Cover Letters, KSAs, and Applications

CHAPTER 11

Putting Together Your Federal Resume Application

You will need to package your Federal resume in two ways: as a "paper" Federal resume and as an electronic resume. Each resume type has a distinctive look. Paper resumes are formatted with embellishments such as bold type, bullets, indentations, and borders. Electronic resumes, which are covered in more detail in chapter 12, are flush left and ragged right with no bold type or bullets. Both of your resume versions need to be readable and impressive. With all of the competition and the piles of Federal resumes human resources professionals receive, your resume needs to look good to stand out.

So get ready to make your Federal resume package look like a million dollars! Now that you have written your Personal and Job Information (chapter 3), Education and Training (chapter 6), Other Qualifications (chapter 7), Work Experience (chapter 8), and focusing sections (chapter 10) and learned how to word them clearly (chapter 9), you need to put it all together and make it look great. This chapter gives you suggestions for organizing your resume sections and designing your resume for maximum effect.

There is always a debate about what is more important in a resume—content or presentation. For government jobs, the content has to be more important. But if the content is excellent and the presentation is terrible (as it was on the old SF-171 application), the package might not be successful. The presentation of your total document is what impresses your audience and sells your skills.

Be sure to refer to the samples in the appendix. You can follow them as a formatting guideline for your own Federal resume. There are samples of both paper Federal resumes and electronic resumes.

Organizing Your Resume Sections

Federal resumes are chronological resumes, with the most recent information listed first in all sections. Here are two suggestions for the order in which to present your resume sections:

Resume organization for technical applicants, where the emphasis is on licenses, certifications, and educational training:

- ★ Personal and Job Information
- ★ Profile
- ★ Critical Skills and/or Accomplishments
- ★ Licenses and Certifications

★ Education and Training (this can move after Professional Experience if experience is more important than education)

★ Professional Experience

★ Other Qualifications (memberships, publications, presentations, community associations, special interests, travel, and so on)

Resume organization for a position that does not require specific education or licenses (Professional Experience is listed before Education):

★ Personal and Job Information

★ Profile

★ Critical Skills and/or Accomplishments

★ Professional Experience

★ Education

★ Training

★ Other Qualifications

Professional Experience versus Education— which section is your best seller? If your education is outstanding or recent and can be written in a small amount of space, you might want to list it first. The Experience section still starts on page 1. If your education is not recent and your experience is more impressive and relevant, put the Experience section first. You will have to look at the two sections and your job objective to decide which section you will list first.

Formatting Your Federal Resume

An attractive yet readable resume is an important part of your Federal job search. The following sections outline the main points to consider as you design and format your resume.

Type Font and Size

The most popular resume type fonts are Times New Roman and Arial. However, if you have access to or prefer another type font (such as Bookman, Souvenir, or Century Gothic), you can use it to make your resume distinctive. You should create your entire package in the same type font.

The following two examples show how different a resume can look depending on which type font is used. The first example is in Times; the second is in Arial.

SUSAN C. DOBSON
1390 Florence Road
Mount Airy, MD 21771

Home: (301) 888-9090
E-mail: susancdobson@yahoo.com

Work: (301) 888-8888

SS#: 000-00-0000
Federal Status: Waste Management Scientist, GS-1301-14
3/22/95 to present

U.S. Citizen
Veterans' Preference: N/A

Objective: Program Analyst, GS-0343-15/15
Announcement #WA-GS-8-0769

A resume written in Times New Roman font.

SUSAN C. DOBSON
1390 Florence Road
Mount Airy, MD 21771

Home: (301) 888-9090
E-mail: susancdobson@yahoo.com

Work: (301) 888-8888

SS#: 000-00-0000
Federal Status: Waste Management Scientist, GS-1301-14
3/22/95 to present

U.S. Citizen
Veterans' Preference: N/A

Objective: Program Analyst, GS-0343-15/15
Announcement #WA-GS-8-0769

The same resume written in Arial.

Text should be in 11-point type. Use 10-point type only if you are trying to tighten up the copy and allow nice page breaks. Section headings can be in 12- or 13-point type. Your name can be in bold 14- to 18-point type, in all caps, uppercase and lowercase letters, or small caps.

Joe Friday
2500 Rolling Road
Baltimore, MD 21228
Home: (410) 555-1212 ♦ Office: (410) 844-1212
jfriday@aol.com

Social Security Number: 000-00-0000
Veterans' Preference and Federal Civilian Status: N/A
Country of Citizenship: USA
Vacancy Announcement Number: 898-99-999
Job Title: Law Enforcement Officer

EDUCATION
  University of Maryland—Baltimore County, Baltimore, MD 21228
  B.S. degree, *Magna Cum Laude,* May 1994

Resume header using different type sizes.

Be consistent with your resume headings and sections. Your major resume section headings should be in bold all caps or bold uppercase and lowercase letters. Be consistent with every heading.

BOLD CAPS	**Bold Upper- and Lowercase**
PROFILE	Profile
CRITICAL SKILLS	Critical Skills
ACCOMPLISHMENTS	Accomplishments
PROFESSIONAL EXPERIENCE	Professional Experience
EDUCATION	Education
TRAINING	Training

BOLD CAPS stand out more than bold upper- and lowercase letters.

Employers, Job Titles, College Names, and Degrees

The type style you use for employers' names should be different than the one you use for your job titles. Along the same lines, the type style for your college name should be different than the type style you use to list your degree. For example, you could set off your job titles and college names in boldface or a bigger point size to make them stand out.

EDUCATION
University of Maryland—Baltimore County, Baltimore, MD 21228
B.S. degree, *Magna Cum Laude,* May 1994

PROFESSIONAL EXPERIENCE
Rehoboth Beach Police Department   5/96–8/96
6501 Coastal Highway, Rehoboth Beach, MD 21842
Sgt. John W. Kraemer, Supervisor; Telephone: (410) 555-1212
Salary: $8.28/hour
Hours: 40+ hours/week

Probationary Police Officer
- Enforce laws pertinent to the Maryland Annotated Code, Maryland Motor Vehicle Law, and local ordinances.

Making colleges and job titles stand out with boldface and larger type.

Margins and Tabs

The ideal amount of white space around the resume is 1 to 1.25 inches. You can start your resume with a 1.25-inch margin all the way around (at the top, bottom, left, and right). If you need more space, you can reduce the margins on the left and right sides to 1 inch. If absolutely necessary, you can make the top and bottom margins .75 inches.

Tab settings must be consistent throughout the resume. Two or three tabs are acceptable, but more than that will make the resume look disorganized to the reader. Indenting the text from the left margin makes the resume easier to read and makes it easy to see at a glance the number of employers you've had.

The following resume is formatted with these four tab settings:

- ★ Left margin: major headings
- ★ Tab 1: names of employers and job titles
- ★ Tab 2: bulleted text
- ★ Tab 3: flush-right "compliance details"

PROFESSIONAL EXPERIENCE:

DEPARTMENT OF THE NAVY, Washington, DC 20350   9/80 to present
Secretary of the Navy (Administration Office)

CORRESPONDENCE ANALYST/EXPEDITER (GS-8)   2/92 to present
Allan Grisolm, Supervisor (703) 744-4324   40 hours/week
Supervisor may be contacted

Responsible for analyzing, prioritizing, and making decisions for the appropriate handling of correspondence for professional staff within the Administrative Office of the Secretary of the Navy, the Department of Defense, and other agencies.

- Maintain awareness of events, programs, priorities, and issues in order to perform responsibilities.

A sample Federal resume that uses four tab settings.

Headers, Footers, and Page Numbers

Your entire Federal application should look like one package. Many Federal announcements ask that you put the vacancy number on each page of your application. You can add a header or footer on the second and following pages of your resume with the following information:

John T. Smith, SS# 222-22-2222

Candidate for Program Analyst, Vacancy Annct: 98-88-8888

Or, to save room, put it all on one line:

John T. Smith, SS# 222-22-2222, Vacancy Annct: 98-88-8888

Be sure to include page numbers on every page of your word-processed application package except page 1, which should not include a page number.

Line Breaks and Page Breaks

Use Word's Print Preview feature to see how the pages will look before you print your resume. Try not to leave any "widows"—a single word on a line by itself. This takes up valuable space and does not look good. Here's an example:

Support two agents in the Planning Programs Department with special audits.

Edit this line by taking out one word equal in size to the word *audits*. This will make your resume look tighter. Just eliminate the word "Department" so that the sentence does not take up an entire extra line.

Support two agents in the Planning Programs with special audits.

Also be careful that one, two, or three lines don't hang over to the next page from the preceding paragraph. There are many things you can do to the resume to edit one or two lines:

★ Check for and fix widows.

★ Delete white spaces (but be consistent throughout the resume).

★ Consolidate two lines if they can be combined.

★ Change the page margins to expand the line length. (If you have the right and left margins set to 1.25 inches, change them to 1 inch.)

Length

Federal job announcements don't give a specific maximum length for paper resumes. Your Federal resume will average two to five pages. Some Federal resumes for professionals and senior executives can be longer than five pages. You might need to add a list of publications, speaking engagements, projects, and other professional information to demonstrate capabilities for a senior executive or technical position. Even if your Federal resume is seven or eight pages, that is still much shorter than if you used the old application format, which could have made your application package 30 pages or more.

Justified Versus Flush-Left Text

Whether to format your text as justified or flush-left is a matter of personal preference. Justified means that the text is even on both the right and left sides. Flush left means that the text is flush on the left side and uneven on the right. Here are the pros and cons of each:

★ Justified text is neat in appearance but can leave large white spaces between words if you are not using hyphenations.

★ Flush-left text does not have the large white spaces between words, but you will not have the neat appearance of justified paragraphs.

Here is an example of justified text:

Duties & Responsibilities:

♦ Demonstrated thorough knowledge of National Housing Act, D.C. Relocation Act, and DHCD policies and procedures.

♦ Identified needs of individuals and families based on legal, economic, and social basis and recommended many practical solutions through reports, meetings, and periodic updates.

♦ Conducted home visits to obtain relocation assistance information; demonstrated thorough knowledge of program assistance available from multiple public and private agencies; discussed socioeconomic factors; and obtained data relating to family composition, age, living conditions, size, income, employment, and related problems.

Justified text.

Here is an example of flush-left text:

Duties & Responsibilities:
- ♦ Demonstrated thorough knowledge of National Housing Act, D.C. Relocation Act, and DHCD policies and procedures.
- ♦ Identified needs of individuals and families based on legal, economic, and social basis and recommended many practical solutions through reports, meetings, and periodic updates.
- ♦ Conducted home visits to obtain relocation assistance information; demonstrated thorough knowledge of program assistance available from multiple public and private agencies; discussed socioeconomic factors; obtained data relating to family composition, age, living conditions, size, income, employment, and related problems.

Flush-left text.

Grammar, Consistency, and Proofreading Tips

Proper grammar and spelling are just as important as your resume's look. Keep in mind the pointers in the following sections.

Avoid Mixing Verb Tenses

Make sure that your verb tenses are the same throughout each section of the resume. You will encounter one of the biggest challenges of verb tenses when writing your current position. If you have both present and past responsibilities that are part of your current position, how can you have both present and past tense in the same description and have consistent tenses? Here are some suggestions.

★ Separate the present tense from the past tense with a separating phrase, as in the following example:

Maintain awareness of events, programs, priorities, and issues in order to perform responsibilities.

Create abstract of the correspondence using keywords, cross-references, and relationships to other correspondence and programs.

Track documents and maintain information concerning action items and deadlines.

Review and ensure quality control of documents for the Secretary of the Navy's signature.

Previously until 10/02:

Representative for an Information Systems Group. Advised users concerning system and application updates.

Wrote and edited correspondence to congressional offices and Department of Navy heads concerning programs and initiatives.

★ Even though this drives English-grammar experts crazy, list all current responsibilities first; then list the past responsibilities. If you have held a position for a lengthy period, it is not unusual that certain responsibilities will have ended, but you certainly cannot leave them off the resume.

★ If previous responsibilities could be considered accomplishments, you can pull these statements out of the duties description and highlight them in an Accomplishments section.

If you can't figure out how to handle this verb-tense dilemma, find an English-grammar expert to help you fix the verbs so that they are both accurate and correct.

Proofreading

Of course, use your spellchecker. But beware—the spellchecker will not find every error, and it can even introduce new ones. Simple errors that can be missed include *lien* and *line, Bethesda* and *Beheads, golf* and *gold,* and *trial* and *trail.* You know the words that your spellchecker refuses to check. I learned the *golf* and *gold* error because of a client's Special Interests section, which included tennis, gold, travel, and gardening. Watch *trial* and *trail* carefully in legal resumes.

Read the resume for context line by line with a ruler to review the spelling of your name, addresses, ZIP codes, telephone numbers, proper names, and supervisor's name; and to find inappropriate words and inconsistencies with grammar and punctuation.

If you are not a good proofreader or editor, find a person who can do this for you. Even if you are a good proofreader, it is helpful and valuable if someone else can read the resume, too. Finish your package a day ahead of your mailing deadline so that someone else can read it and you can still make corrections.

Packaging Your Application

Your resume, cover letter, and supporting material should be packaged in this order:

★ Cover letter (see chapter 15)

★ Resume

★ Executive Core Qualifications (for SES packages; see chapter 16)

★ KSAs (see chapter 14)

★ Last supervisor's evaluation

★ SF-50, DD-215, Form 15, and other required forms

★ Course list (if needed)

The best resume paper is a 20- or 24-pound-weight paper. Use a good-quality paper that is 100 percent recycled or 25 percent cotton bond. A light ivory or bright white makes the best presentation. Grays, blues, and speckled sheets will not fax, scan, or copy well. The color names to look for include Colonial White, Ivory, White Wove, and many others.

The best styles of paper are called linen, wove, laid, and so on. Linen has a nice linen-textured effect. Wove is usually very flat and type prints very clearly on it. A laid finish has lines in it that create a unique look. You can examine each style and decide which you like the best.

Use envelopes measuring 9 × 12 inches so that you don't have to fold the contents. Any color of envelope will work. It is not necessary to purchase colorful envelopes. They will not be seen by any decision maker. **Important:** Type or neatly print the vacancy announcement at the bottom-left corner of the envelope so that your application can be routed properly.

Use the following checklist as you assemble your resume package to be sure you've included everything correctly.

Checklist for Your Resume Application Package

Personal Information and Job Information Section:

❑ Check your name, address, phone numbers, e-mail address, Social Security number, job title, and announcement number.

Education Section:

❑ Check college names, degrees, majors, dates, cities, states, and ZIP codes.

❑ Check high school name, address, ZIP code, and dates.

Training Section:

❑ Check course titles and dates.

Work Experience Section:

❑ Check the compliance details for each job in the last 10 years: street addresses, ZIP codes, supervisors' names, telephone numbers, hours worked per week, salaries, and permission to contact your present supervisor.

Format and Type Font:

❑ All margins and tabs are consistent.

❑ All type fonts, sizes, and styles are consistent.

❑ All lines have periods or not.

❑ Page breaks are okay.

❑ Line breaks are okay.

❑ All major headings have colons or not.

Proofreading:

❑ Spell-check the entire document.

❑ Proofread the entire document.

❑ Have another person proofread the entire document.

The Total Application—Are All the Following Pieces There?

❑ Cover letter

❑ Federal resume

❑ ECQs and/or KSAs

❑ Other documents as required by the announcement; read How to Apply in the announcement to ensure that you have included all required documents.

❑ Sign the resume if the announcement asks for an original signature.

❑ Make sure unnecessary attachments are not included.

Duplicating:

❑ Quality is perfect—either laser or high-quality photocopy.

(continues)

(continued)

Envelope:

❑ Neatly typed and includes the vacancy number on the outside of the envelope.

❑ All elements are unfolded in the envelope and are not stapled (in case the agency electronically scans the resumes it receives).

❑ Federal employees: Do not use government postage or paper for your application.

❑ If you are mailing an application, use a service where you can receive a receipt. If you are faxing, do not wait until the last hour; the fax could be busy. If you are e-mailing, don't wait either because the security firewalls could take time to get the file into the office.

❑ Envelope includes enough postage for the weight.

❑ Application is postmarked by the deadline on the announcement.

Disk:

❑ Save your application on your hard drive and/or disk so that you can easily edit it for the next application.

❑ Save a copy on a disk as a backup.

If you've worked hard to create a great-looking "paper" federal resume, and you come across electronic resume builders and Internet templates, don't think you have wasted your time. Just copy and paste your resume content into a resume builder. You will be able to use your paper resume version at an interview, or at personal meetings.

Summary

I am sure that your Federal resume looks outstanding and that you are proud of your work. It's possible that you are so impressed that you are thinking, "Is this really me?" That's the reaction I've seen many times when a Federal job applicant dedicates time and effort to writing a Federal resume. If you're not impressed yet, find an editor, designer, or writer to help until you are impressed with your resume presentation. My company, The Resume Place, provides consultation, editing, design, and review services for Federal job seekers who have written their federal resumes the best that they can but need help to complete the final package. See a description at www.resume-place.com.

CHAPTER 12

Electronic Resume Writing

Government agencies used to receive stacks and stacks of thick paper applications every day that had to be stored in physical file cabinets. Today, Federal human resources professionals are reviewing resumes and searching for best-qualified candidates in databases at their computers. The resumes are printed for the selecting officials to review actual paper versions for interview and hiring decisions.

More than 70 percent of all Federal vacancy announcements request applicants to submit an electronic resume format through an online resume builder. This chapter will help you write an effective electronic resume that you can submit online into a database instead of mailing it to the human resources office.

In general, an outstanding resume has always been synonymous with a good resume design that is visually appealing and beautiful. With electronic resumes, you have little control over the presentation or look of the resume because you will copy and paste your resume text from your file into an online resume builder or template.

The final resume output (which a human selecting official will eventually read) will be in a strictly text format (flush left, ragged right), or in a format designed by the automated HR system. You won't be able to impress personnel or the selecting official with a beautiful resume presentation with varying type fonts, indentations, bullets, shading, or other stylizing of presentation. So, with electronic resume submission, the actual words, skills, and organization of information are critical for a successful electronic resume. This is true of both government and private-industry electronic resume applications.

The words and writing in an electronic resume are the only way you can present your career experience to the hiring official. This creates a more level playing field because a person cannot be persuaded with presentation—only writing style, experience, and skills. Writing is difficult for most people, so the electronic resume is more difficult to write successfully.

In this chapter, you will learn how to write and format an easy-to-read electronic resume without special formatting and stylized type, but with the right skills, impressive content, and accomplishments. You will also learn how computers process resumes, which Federal agencies are using computers to process resumes, and the differences between a resume builder and an online form for submitting your resume.

The Major Differences Between Electronic Resumes and "Paper" Federal Resumes

Three basic rules make electronic resumes different from regular resumes:

★ You must format your resume so that the QuickHire, Resumix, USAJOBS, or other online resume-collection system can easily read it.

★ For Resumix systems, you must use keywords and phrases when you write your resume to maximize the number of items the software matches (hits) during a hiring search. For QuickHire, USAJOBS, COOL (Commerce), and others, your resume must contain sufficient detail so that your answers to the questions on the vacancy announcement correlate with the content of the resume. QuickHire Applicant Questions may involve multiple-choice, yes-or-no, and essay answers to job-related questions.

★ You must follow to the letter specific instructions in agencies' job kits or in the How to Apply sections of vacancy announcements.

The following table identifies just a few of the most important differences between the traditional "paper" Federal resumes and electronic resumes.

Major Differences	Paper Federal Resume	Electronic Resume
HR processing time	Time-consuming, often two to three months for evaluation and preparation of certificate of eligible candidates sent to hiring manager.	Time-saving, often two to three weeks for HR to read the highest-ranked resumes and prepare a certificate; sometimes less time.
Obtaining information on status of app	Call or e-mail HR designated contact. Most HR offices are responsive, but service is based on staffing of HR office.	Immediate e-mail, plus various methods listed on vacancy announcement, sometimes including instant online means to verify status.
Applicant's time to prepare and submit application	After the Federal resume is prepared, frequently it takes several hours to tailor it and prepare KSA replies to a single vacancy. Also, it takes time to make copies of required supplementary materials and prepare the package for mailing.	Once the resume is in the database, very little time is needed to submit the application (frequently called the "self-nomination" process), unless narrative replies are requested (QuickHire).

Major Differences	Paper Federal Resume	Electronic Resume
Format	Presentation is important. Designed with various type fonts, styles.	Flush left, ragged right, no type font changes. QuickHire allows organizational flexibility.
Content—general	Comprehensive, yet the objective is to be concise. No page limit, but average is three to five pages. Must contain all required "compliance" information (veterans' status, highest grade held, last promotion date, and so on).	Page limits force applicant to focus on describing work experience most relevant to target position. "Compliance" information is included in supplemental data.
Content—Profile or Summary	Yes; a Profile or Summary is an essential introductory personal statement.	Resumix has no section for Profile or Summary. Such information could be incorporated into Other Information. QuickHire allows for a Profile.
Content— work experience	No limit as to what you can include.	Some Resumix systems limit the number of work experiences you can describe (for example, the Navy limit is six). No limitations in QuickHire, except for total character limit.
Content—education	Education can be highlighted.	In Resumix, education must be precisely described in a speci-fied format, with no flexibility. QuickHire allows flexibility in how education is presented.

As you can see, the paper Federal resume offers the greatest opportunity for the applicant to make a personal statement because of format and length flexibilities. However, applicants must recognize the reality that the trend is clear-ly toward requiring electronic submissions in as many cases as possible, as HR offices continue to seek ways to improve the accuracy and effi-ciency of these systems. In order to remain competitive, applicants must be familiar with both resume formats.

Ten Steps for Preparing and Writing a Successful Electronic Resume

It takes research for keywords, concise writing, impressive accomplishments, and the right format to stand out in a database. Learn how to write the best possible electronic resume by following these steps.

1. Use the Proper Format for an Electronic Resume

Read the announcement instructions of the agency's job kit if there is one available. In most cases, however, you can follow these general guidelines:

★ Use a minimum margin of one inch on all sides of your printed resume.

★ Use any font at 10 or 12 points. You will copy and paste the text into the online form, so the type style will become text when it goes into the database.

★ Use CAPITAL LETTERS for section headings and major functional skill areas.

★ Do not use any of the following highlighting features: vertical or horizontal lines; graphics; boxes; two-column format; or fancy treatments such as italics, underlining, shadows, or bullets.

★ Avoid acronyms or abbreviations. Use only acronyms that are well established and commonly understood. If you use an acronym, spell it out completely the first time. Because you should avoid parentheses in most resume builders, you can "set off" the acronym with commas or hyphens (for example, "the Americans with Disabilities Act, ADA, was enacted…").

★ Unless otherwise required by a job kit, list dates using the format mm-yyyy.

★ Avoid symbols and certain punctuation marks such as *, #, %, &, /, <, >, and ^.

★ Use white space and line breaks between sections or topics. For eventual readability by the human eye, keep paragraphs to a limit of eight lines.

★ For resume builders, you can present some information in paragraph format if necessary to meet character length limits (for example, awards, training, and so on). However, you can also list entries in a "left-justified" format with a carriage return between lines.

★ List all multiple entries in reverse-chronological order for consistency: work experience, education, training, licenses and certificates, awards, honors, recognitions, publications, military service, and other information. However, if your early experience is more relevant to your current career objective, you can list information in straight chronology (earliest entry first).

2. Include Your Most Relevant Work Experiences

Concentrate on your most recent and relevant work experiences that have occurred in the past 10 years. The exception to this is if you have experience that is particularly relevant to the target position that occurred prior to that (such as earlier supervisory experience when lately you have occupied a nonsupervisory senior specialist position).

In some cases, you might find it appropriate to combine related work experiences, particularly if there has been an agency reorganization, you transferred with the function, and the responsibilities of your job are substantially the same. In such a case, you would list the current or most recent organizational information for prior work experiences.

Similarly, if you performed similar positions at different grade levels, you can combine the positions into one job description.

3. Remember That You Have Two (Maybe Three) Readers: The Computer Database, the HR Staffing Specialist, and the Selecting Official

Strike a balance between writing for the *computer,* writing for the *personnelist* who reviews the resume, and writing for the *selecting official* who will decide who to interview. Although you are trying to maximize the success with database searches, keep in mind that eventually human eyes will be laid on your resume. Don't write

> Responsible for interpreting personnel policies and regulations, and developing recommendations.

Be more specific and positive by writing

> Developed and recommended improved personnel policies and procedures to streamline automated resume submissions…

All the keywords are there for the computer and the sentence is interesting and impressive for a person. That's why it's important for you to think carefully about every word you write on an electronic resume. You want to maximize space, include the right words, and make the resume readable and interesting.

4. Describe Your Marketable Skills Clearly in a Summary or Work Experience Section

Make it easy for the computer database or human resources reviewer to see your skills. Over the span of your career, you've learned how to do many things. You can include a summary in your resume in different ways, depending on

the automated system and resume builder the agency uses:

★ A **QuickHire electronic resume** can include a Summary of Skills section at the top of the resume.

★ The **Resumix resume builder** provides space for skills in "Other Information" at the end of the resume.

★ The **USAJOBS Resume Builder** has space for a Career Objective at the top, where you can write a summary of your objectives and qualifications.

Here's an example of a Summary of Skills section for a QuickHire electronic resume for an Administrative Officer:

> Experienced administrative officer and database manager. Knowledgeable in collection management, auditing, and staff advising concerning personnel security investigation information management. Expert in DOD guidelines for military, industrial, and civilian personnel investigative requests. Experienced analyst. Able to manage multiple projects and perform effectively under pressure of deadlines.

Here's an example of a Resumix Other Qualifications Summary that includes skills and core competencies:

> SUMMARY OF SKILLS: Experienced supervisor and trainer. Background in program management, including contract planning, acquisition planning, forecasting requirements, milestones achievement. Recognized for success with program integrity and effectiveness through self-evaluation, ethical standards, program accomplishment reporting. Experienced Program Analyst. Able to identify and analyze problems, conduct research, evaluate findings, and prepare summaries of results. Effective speaker and writer of reports, briefings, and presentations. Effective in customer service, customer education, and management advisory services.

The following Other Information section is for a Project Manager who is moving away from Information Technology and focusing more on Program Analyst projects (GS 13/14 level):

> ## OTHER INFORMATION
>
> Executive Profile: Hands-on, results-oriented program administrator. Highly analytical. Able to comprehend complex theory to resolve problems and develop a practical strategic plan. Organize and plan, with focus on best practices and providing quality deliverables.
>
> Leadership Results: Cultivate respect of clients and co-workers. Mentor others and motivate team members to deliver desired results. Respect and recognize that diversity in professional and personal backgrounds adds to the value of the organization's products and services.
>
> Communications: Proficient in oral and written communications. Direct, assertive, positive, and persuasive. Create collaborative relationships; facilitate discussions with colleagues, clients, executive leadership, and staff members. Demonstrate professionalism, courtesy, and tact in dealings at all levels from line staff to executive management.
>
> Practical Experience: Over 16 years of broad-based experience encompassing project management, leadership motivation, supervision and performance management, human resources management, business liaison relations, systems analysis conversions, budgeting negotiations, policies and procedures, problem solving, and change management.
>
> Computer Proficiencies: Wrote business specifications—including design, testing, and approval—used by Wells Fargo Mortgage Division, for Productivity On-Line Worksheet—POW—to track employees' time and production and determine staffing needs; PATSY to complete variety of stages of loan payoff to recording deed; and RATS. Utilize MS Word, Excel, Access, PowerPoint, and Visio; Planview; FileNet Optical Imaging System; and Internet.

The following is for an Acting Chief, Safety and Occupational Health, GM-018-14—Department of Defense.

> Environmental safety, occupational health, and industrial hygiene. Program Manager. Technical expert. Safety: safety engineering surveys, risk assessments. Occupational health: medical surveillance, fitness for duty, radiation health. Environmental health: IH, air quality, environmental engineering. Environmental exposure assessments and abatement. Hazardous, toxic, and radiological waste control. Health physics. Personal protective equipment. Chemical weapons. Emergency response. OSHA and NRC Regulations, and compliance inspection procedures. Graduate studies in industrial engineering, with emphasis on safety, product safety, acoustics, fire protection, and photogrammetric engineering/remote sensing. Proficient in written and oral communications.

The following Profile statement is for the electronic resume for a business professional seeking an Administrative Officer/Program Analyst position, GS-301 series.

> Successful government contractor with annual revenues to $1.255 million. Experienced in writing contract proposals, negotiating and managing performance contracts, and ensuring quality control and customer satisfaction. Team leader in all aspects of business development and growth: start-up and project management; product marketing; human resources management; financial planning, analysis, and control; accounting data management; risk and change management; determining and exceeding customer expectations. Experienced in private, public, and nonprofit sectors: fund-raising, wholesale and retail, manufacturing and distribution, consumer products, food products, and commercial and residential real estate. Internet and e-commerce: product marketing and sales, and customer service.

5. Review the Vacancy Announcement—Include Specifics and Keywords from Your Occupational Series

If you're tailoring your resume to a specific job vacancy, make sure you use the key phrases and words from the "Duties and Responsibilities" section of the vacancy announcement. Of course, you must actually be doing this work in order to make these claims on the resume because all entries on your application are subject to verification.

In this example, although the applicant did not have experience in sports programming, she clearly offers superior experience and qualifications in health-care management, covering all other aspects in the vacancy announcement and making her a highly competitive candidate.

Vacancy Announcement Language

> APPLICATION DEVELOPMENT: Performs IT application development encompassing the design, creation, and/or modification of applications. Tasks may involve software and interface coding in current languages (e.g., SQL, Oracle, JAM, Access, C, Visual Basic, Delphi, FoxPro, and HTML); configuration design of supporting hardware/networks; development of procurement specifications, and testing during development.
>
> SOFTWARE TESTING: Performs formal "proof" or other testing on applications/software by validating proper functionality and system performance. Identifies discrepancies and provides recommendations for improvements and problem resolution. Prepares test plans identifying milestones, resources, training, and test scenarios/scripts.
>
> APPLICATION PROJECT MANAGER: Functions as software project manager. This includes gathering and analyzing data and preparing synopses that compare alternatives in terms of cost, time, equipment, and staff. Coordinates interfaces, priorities, methods, procedures, testing and implementation plans, and system documentation. Serves as an application expert. Provides consultation to functional area users and works closely with application managers.

Experience and Qualifications Described in the Resume

WORK EXPERIENCE DESCRIPTION: INFORMATION TECHNOLOGY SPECIALIST, GS-2210-12

PROJECT MANAGEMENT: Provide technical leadership and direction, and assign priorities to teams to plan and complete complex project assignments that involve determination of user requirements and analysis of complex systems. Complete Plans of Action and Milestones, and other schedules for the project. Assure conformity to project specifications, application software, and security requirements; design innovative and cost-effective processes, methods, and procedures to enhance, consolidate, or replace existing procedures. Prepare estimates in resources including personnel staffing requirements, budget needs, and time frames required to complete project tasks. Special Recognition: Selected to be a member of the Project Management Standards Team.

SUBJECT MATTER EXPERT: Develop, interpret, and define policies, procedures, and strategies; provide technical expert advice on complex projects. Prepare new releases for applications and draft official release notices. Compile written reports, such as project status reports, for managers, users, and customers. Provide "hands-on" training classes to users and prepare standard operating procedures—SOPs—for technical personnel, and coordinate turnover to production units.

During Cost Workshops, defined new system requirements, studied functional user requirements, and reviewed current system documentation and 30-year-old programs to respond to changing requirements by creating new design documents. Designed database relationships, tables, indices, and sizing. Created spreadsheets for calculating required database space and modified spreadsheets to resize according to customers' needs. Designed, developed, and documented the system programs. Analyzed and designed file layouts, data flow, output design, and program and module designs. At implementation, executed the necessary conversions, imported data into the databases, completed parallel processing, and verified results.

---

6. Use Industry Jargon and Keywords from the Position Description—Use More Nouns and Proper Names

When managers are looking for prime candidates, they search for keywords in their areas of expertise. If you know these keywords, put them in your resume. As noted in the preceding section, the vacancy announcement usually contains these terms, unless the announcement is a short, generic, database-building announcement that does not have specifics of a job. Additionally, your position description, assuming it is current, is potentially a rich source of keywords that you can use in your resume.

Here is a description of specific work performed by a contract employee, equivalent to a WG-3546-08 Railroad Repairer, that was written in a position description:

Switch and Track Maintenance: Conduct inspections, such as checking tracks for obvious defects—loose spikes, rotted ties, broken rail, uneven joints, washed-out ballast, and clogged drainage systems. Carry out preventive maintenance, involving minor and major repairs of all on-base railroads; assure operative condition of track switches. Repair or replace switches, switch points, switch bars, switch targets, switch latches, frongs, derails, guardrails, rail anchors, angle bars, rail selections, rail joints, joint bolts, cross ties, cross-tie plugs, spikes, lates, gauge rods, shims, etc. Skeletonize track sections and prepare for ballasting; hand place ballast along track beds, jack track section, and space cross ties; line and level track sections.

You should also include detailed information about specific projects, including title, budget, and scope.

> **Department of Defense, U.S. Marine Corps Client-Server Information System—initiative:** Provided leadership, program and project management, staff supervision, planning, procurement, administration, and software engineering supervision. Managed seven teams of over 40 individuals involved in software reengineering, hardware and software integration, system rollout, help-desk, and end-user support. Planned and executed program operating budget that ranged from $5 to $20 million annually. This UNIX–Windows NT system also included Lotus Notes, Netscape, Global Command and Control System, TCO, and IAS, and was implemented across seven sites worldwide in one year.

7. Use More Action Verbs

Pronouns are not necessary in any resume. Start each sentence with an action verb. This presents your work experience in an active voice rather than a passive voice, and will capture the attention of the human reader. The following is an example from the resume of an individual with private-sector experience in safety and occupational health. This demonstrates use of active voice for his experience in handling workers' compensation cases:

> **SAFETY, OCCUPATIONAL HEALTH AND INJURY COMPENSATION, SEEKING MID-LEVEL SAFETY AND OCCUPATIONAL HEALTH POSITION.**
>
> CLAIMS MANAGEMENT AND ADJUSTMENT: Managed workers' compensation claims. Reviewed and processed claims for liability relative to injury claims. Assisted field personnel in resolving minor claims; advised the insurer and assisted the adjuster in settling claims consistent with corporate policy. Participated in accident investigations and arbitration hearings. Administered return-to-work program.
>
> COST CONTAINMENT: Monitored claims cost and developed strategies to improve corporate risk performance. Conducted retrospective and account analysis. Maintained necessary documentation related to claims review and management. Provided Risk Management with current claims information and additional assignments per Risk Manager.

8. Use a Concise Writing Style

Labels and keywords are the most direct method of communication. In traditional resumes and SF-171s, bureaucratic and long-winded explanations were used to describe a job. But in an electronic resume, you need to include as many skills as you can, and describe them briefly and clearly.

The following example describes the work of a GS-2010-11 Inventory Management Specialist:

BEFORE

> Duties require my effective material support by the integrated management and control characterized by a high degree of equipment complexity that requires a thorough knowledge of practices and functions of the various readiness support elements at a national inventory control point. My acquired knowledge and skills include the ability to make decisions on supply-management processes for system-wide supply operations from initial planning, the acquisition stage, storage, and the issue stages, as well as the proper disposal requirements.

AFTER

> MATERIEL SUPPORT: Support logistics operations and procedures for electronics communications equipment—both major and secondary items. Integrate logistical requirements into a comprehensive plan for management and control. Conduct analytical studies for quantitative and budgetary forecasts, procurement authorization, funds management, and decisions for distribution or redistribution of materiel. Ensure efficient movement of equipment between points of manufacture, depots, or customer activities. Manage logistical plan from initial planning to acquisition, storage, issue, and disposal.

9. Write About Accomplishments and Special Projects

The way your resume can stand out from a stack on the selecting official's desk is to include accomplishments. Your accomplishments, projects, and *results* will help the hiring official select your resume for an interview or job offer. If the manager sees that you have accomplished impressive things in your last job, he or she will envision your quality performance in the organization. You can use the word "ACCOMPLISHMENTS" in the Work Experience write-ups and lead the reader's eye to your best stories.

For the most effective presentation of an accomplishment or special project, consider following the CCAR format:

★ **Context:** Describe the situation.

★ **Challenge:** Describe what needed to be done.

★ **Action:** Describe specifically what you did—your role.

★ **Results:** Describe the outcome in concrete, verifiable terms.

By following this formula, your example will demonstrate specifically what you have achieved. The challenge and results will be interesting and tangible evidence that you can perform your job.

Consider this brief example from the resume of an IT specialist that follows the CCAR formula. You do not need to use the words "context, challenge, and results" in the example. But you should keep the word *results*.

> ACCOMPLISHMENT: [Context] Installed and tested Computer Aided Dispatching on Windows 2000 utilized by 200 users in 12 police and fire departments throughout the U.S. [Challenge] CAD initially failed to run properly. [Action] Successfully identified and solved operating problems. RESULTS: Debugged and fixed over 300 bugs for CAD systems with high and low priorities to support important emergency management dispatch services in the State of Maryland.

Many applicants sell themselves short in this area, perhaps thinking "I was just doing my job." However, you might be doing some remarkable things that make a difference. You can review your past performance reviews, customer satisfaction letters, and e-mails concerning projects and special work efforts.

Another good source for ideas of accomplishments and special projects is in the justification for a performance award. These frequently are concisely written—usually 25 words or less—and can be the basis for a powerful entry on the resume.

Finally, you should note any special assignments in the Work Experience section. These can be the result of a temporary detail to different duties, or if you assumed additional duties during a period of short staffing until the vacancy could be filled. A formal detail that was documented, particularly if it involved a promotion to a higher-level position, could appear as a separate work experience. Additional duties for a short duration due to "doubling" an assignment could be captured as a "special assignment" paragraph in the corresponding Work Experience section.

10. Follow Job Kit Instructions

Because the application and resume-building instructions are different for each agency, it is important to follow vacancy announcement or job kit instructions. For example, the Army allows 2,000 characters for each job description and three pages total for your resume, plus the additional Supplemental Data Sheet. The Navy allows 6,000 characters per work experience block and five pages. You may not include any more than six work experiences for any DoD Resume Builder. The QuickHire online submission provides space for 16,000 characters with complete flexibility on organization of resume sections.

The Bottom Line: Read the Directions Carefully

There are two resume formats for Federal applications: the "paper" Federal resume and the electronic resume for online submissions. Read the vacancy announcement directions carefully.

At the writing of this book, there are multiple resume builders and online forms available for submitting resumes to Federal agencies for jobs. You will read in chapter 13, "Applying for a Federal Job," about the online resume systems that the Office of Personnel Management and Federal agencies use. At some point in the future, all agencies could be using only one resume builder—the one at www.usajobs.opm.gov. "Recruitment One Stop" is a planned electronic initiative that will make it easier to apply for Federal jobs.

For an up-to-date report on Recruitment One Stop (ROS), visit www.resume-place.com/USABJOBS.ROS for the latest information on applying for Federal jobs online.

Ten Steps for Preparing and Writing a Successful Electronic Resume

1. Use the proper format for an electronic resume.
2. Include your most relevant work experiences.
3. Remember that you have two (maybe three) readers: the computer database, the HR staffing specialist, and the selecting official.
4. Describe your marketable skills clearly in a Summary or Work Experience section.
5. Review the vacancy announcement—include specifics and keywords from your occupational series.
6. Use industry jargon and keywords from your position description—use more nouns and proper names.
7. Use more action verbs.
8. Use a concise writing style.
9. Write about accomplishments and special projects.
10. Follow job kit instructions.

CHAPTER 13

Applying for a Federal Job

Now that your Federal and electronic resumes are drafted (with great effort), you are ready to apply for many Federal jobs. The approach that most determined Federal job seekers take to the Federal job application process is to apply to many positions—not just one or two, but more like 20 to 30 positions. Because the application review process is fairly long, it is better to submit your application to many agencies and databases, and basically "play the numbers."

You've already been reading vacancy announcements, so you know that the How to Apply instructions are different for each announcement. Now that you are ready to start applying for the jobs, it's time to learn how all of the agencies are receiving resumes, as well as a few details about the selection process.

When you get to the How to Apply section of the vacancy announcements, you will see brand names of automated human resources systems such as QuickHire, Resumix, Avue, PeopleSoft, COOL, and EZ-Hire. You will be curious about how these different systems will handle the application process and resume submission. You'll also see that some agencies and announcements are still asking for paper Federal resumes and Knowledge, Skills, and Abilities statements to be mailed or faxed. This chapter reviews the various methods of submitting your resume to Federal agencies so that you can apply correctly.

USAJOBS and Recruitment One-Stop—The Near Future

Before reviewing the various agency HR automated systems, however, here's big news about improvement in the future of Federal application processes through www.usajobs.opm.gov, the official Office of Personnel Management Jobs Web site. In the near future, applying for Federal jobs will be much easier and less time-consuming.

An outside vendor has been contracted to design and manage an improved USAJOBS Web site with better search capabilities and nicer-looking and shorter vacancy announcements. The Office of Personnel Management's *Recruitment One-Stop* e-Gov initiative is a collaborative effort among the outside vendor, Office of Personnel Management (OPM), and Federal agencies to design an improved USAJOBS Web site to simplify Federal job search and application systems.

Current features of this site include the following:

★ One portal advertising thousands of Federal government job opportunities across the nation and around the world.

★ One job search engine that allows you to search for jobs by job family, job location, salary, or level of experience.

★ One standard display for all vacancy announcements.

★ One site to build and store an online resume.

In the future, job seekers looking for a job with the Federal government can look forward to the following key features on the *Recruitment One-Stop* site:

★ One method of applying for positions that provides immediate feedback on basic eligibility.

★ One site to build and store an online resume (for multiple agency submissions).

★ One place to check on the status of your application.

★ Seamless movement of job applicants' resumes from USAJOBS to the agency databases and assessment systems. Your resume will be forwarded to all (or most) of the agencies that are of interest to you. When your resume arrives at the selected agency, the agency's selected automated human resources systems (QuickHire, Resumix, Avue, PeopleSoft, or other proprietary systems) will manage the resume selection and database processes.

The Present Situation: Several Different Automated HR Systems Manage Resumes for Federal Agencies

The Defense Department's Civilian Personnel Offices for Army, Navy, Marines, and Air Force (home to half of the Federal government's civilian employees) started using an automated human resources management system called **Resumix** to manage resumes in 1997. They have made significant strides in simplifying and centralizing their processes and achieving uniformity. The vast majority of these civilian

personnel announcement instructions state that they prefer electronic submissions. Occasionally, a Resumix announcement requests a paper submission with Federal resume and KSAs for a special job announcement.

Federal agencies have quickly jumped on the bandwagon, recognizing that automation could offer significant efficiencies to this labor-intensive process. Many have opted for the **QuickHire** system. A recent statistic developed by Monster Government Solutions states that 67 percent of Federal vacancy announcements and instructions are QuickHire customers.

Most of the automated resume-collection systems will not accept SF-171s or OF-612s. The www.usajobs.opm.gov announcements state that you can submit any application format, but a resume is preferred because the content will have to be manually input into the database by administrative staff. This could be a problem with tight announcement deadlines. Technically, the government has a policy that any of those formats should be acceptable; but if the agency is an automated agency, it can request only electronic resumes.

Some agencies are still requesting and accepting paper applications, which include a Federal resume and Knowledge, Skills, and Abilities statements, but the paper application agencies are becoming fewer. However, the "paper" Federal resume with formatting will still be an important resume format for job seekers for interviews, faxing, networking, mailing, and other people-related job search activities.

Here is a list of agency names and Web sites where you can find employment information and vacancy announcements. These Web pages could change from time to time with reorganizations (especially Homeland Security agencies). For an up-to-date list of Federal agency vacancy announcements and electronic submission instructions, go to www.resume-place.com/info/links.html.

Agency Employment Information and Vacancy Announcements

Agency	Web Address(es)
U.S. Government Official Jobs Web site	www.usajobs.opm.gov
Air Force Personnel Center	https://ww2.afpc.randolph.af.mil/resweb/
APHIS—Animal Plant Health Inspection Service	www.aphis.usda.gov
Army Civilian Jobs	www.cpol.army.mil Centralized Job Kit: www.cpol.army.mil/employ/jobkit/
BCBP—Bureau of Customs and Border Protection (formerly known as Border Patrol)	ww.immigration.gov/graphics/workfor/index.htm#bcbp
BCIS—Bureau of Citizenship and Immigration Services (formerly known as INS—Immigration and Naturalization Service)	www.immigration.gov/graphics/index.htm Jobs with Immigration Programs: www.immigration.gov/graphics/workfor/index.htm
BICE—Bureau of Immigration and Customs Enforcement (formerly known as INS—Immigration and Naturalization Service)	www.immigration.gov/graphics/workfor/index.htm#ice
CDC—Centers for Disease Control and Prevention	Training and Employment Opportunities: www.cdc.gov/train.htm
CIA—Central Intelligence Agency	Analyst and Clandestine Jobs: www.cia.gov/employment/
Coast Guard's Civilian job site	http://dothr.ost.dot.gov/Employment_Opportunities/employment_opportunities.html
Customs and Border Protection	www.customs.gov/xp/cgov/careers/customs_careers
Defense Department	http://persec.whs.mil/hrsc/index.html
DHS—Department of Homeland Security	www.dhs.gov/dhspublic/index.jsp www.usajobs.opm.gov/homeland.htm
DISA—Defense Investigative Service Agency	Job Openings: http://jobopps.disa.mil

Agency	Web Address(es)
DLA/DCMA—Defense Logistics Agency—Defense Contract Management Agency	www.hr.dla.mil/onjams/searchform.asp
DoJ—Department of Justice	www.justice.gov/06employment/index.html Justice Job Openings: www.justice.gov/06employment/06_1.html Online Application: www.avuedigitalservices.com/dojjmd/applicant.html
DoN—U.S. Navy	www.donhr.navy.mil
DoT—Department of Transportation	Security Screening Personnel—new ruling: http://jobs.faa.gov Security Screener Qualifications: http://jobs.faa.gov/SecurityScreeningRequirements.htm Federal Aviation Administration—Federal Air Marshal Jobs: http://jobs.faa.gov/
DTRA—Defense Threat Reduction Agency	www.dtra.mil Civilian Openings: www.dtra.mil/jb/jb_civilian.html
EPA—U.S. Environmental Protection Agency	www.epa.gov/
FAA—Federal Aviation Administration	www1.faa.gov/careers/employment/jobinfo.htm
FBI—Federal Bureau of Investigation	https://www.fbijobs.com Contract Linguist: https://www.fbijobs.com/jobdesc.asp?requisitionid=25 FBI Non-Paid Academy: www.fbi.gov/employment/academy.htm
FEMA—Federal Emergency Management Agency	Emergency Management and Disaster Jobs: www.fema.gov/career/index.jsp
HHS—Department of Health and Human Services	www.hhs.gov/jobs/
Human Resource Services, National Capital Region	http://persec.whs.mil/hrsc/index.html

(continues)

(continued)

Agency	Web Address(es)
Justice Dept. Jobs Overview Immigration and Naturalization Service (many Border Patrol Agents are being recruited for U.S. borders)	www.justice.gov/06employment/index.html FBI, DEA, Border Patrol Agents, U.S. Marshal, Federal Bureau of Prisons
NASA—National Aeronautics and Space Administration	www.nasajobs.nasa.gov/
NIH—National Institutes of Health	www.jobs.nih.gov/
NIST—National Institute of Standards and Technology	www.nist.gov/public_affairs/employment.htm
NRC—Nuclear Regulatory Commission	Career Paths: www.nrc.gov/who-we-are/employment/careers.html www.nrc.gov/who-we-are/employment.html
NSA—National Security Agency	www.nsa.gov/programs/employ/index.html
PHS—U.S. Public Health Service	www.usphs.gov/html/jobs.html
Secret Service	Careers: www.secretservice.gov/opportunities.shtml USAJOBS: www.usajobs.opm.gov/a9usss.htm
TSA—Transportation Security Administration	www.tsa.gov/public/theme_home2.jsp USAJOBS: www.usajobs.opm.gov/a9tsa.htm
USACE—U.S. Army Corps of Engineers	www.usace.army.mil Employment Page: www.usace.army.mil/working.html Careers with USACE: www.hq.usace.army.mil/cehr/e/recruit/career.pdf
USGS—U.S. Geological Survey	http://www.usgs.gov/ohr/oars/index.html Student Jobs: http://www.usgs.gov/ohr/student/

How Automated Human Resources Systems Manage Resumes

As stated in the preceding section, the Office of Personnel Management, Federal departments, and civilian agencies have chosen different automated human resources systems for receiving, storing, and rating resumes. Be ready to apply a variety of ways as you study the instructions under How to Apply in the vacancy announcement. This section discusses four major automated and nonautomated resume application systems: the USAJOBS, QuickHire, Resumix, and paper Federal resume and KSA narratives application processes.

USAJOBS

The Office of Personnel Management provides a recruitment, selection, and resume review service for some Federal agencies that are customers. To apply for an Office of Personnel Manage-ment, USA Staffing announcement, here's what you have to do:

1. Fill out the Occupational Questionnaire.

   Complete answers to the Occupational Questionnaire or Form C.

   Answer up to 151 multiple-choice, yes-or-no, and essay questions about your skills and qualifications.

2. Copy and paste your resume into the Resume Builder. Or you can fax, e-mail, or mail it.

3. You should also include other application materials as appropriate. Examples of these other materials include your college transcripts (if required) and documentation of veterans' status (if applicable).

When managers are looking to fill a position, the USA Staffing HR recruiters post an announcement, receive the resume through the Resume Builder, review your answers to the online questionnaire, receive your faxed or mailed supplemental information (transcripts, performance reviews, DD-214s), and review and select the best-qualified candidates for the agency customer. A "certified list" of candidates is sent along with the applicants' resumes to the agency hiring manager for interviewing and hiring decisions.

QuickHire

Many agencies use QuickHire. To apply for a QuickHire announcement, here's what you have to do:

1. On the "Personal Profile" page:

   Copy and paste your resume. Scroll down to the online template or field where you can copy and paste your entire resume in one block.

 Note: It takes just a minute or two to copy and paste your entire electronic resume into one field.

---

2. On the "Application Questions" page(s):

   You will respond to 15 to 50 application questions with multiple-choice, yes-or-no, and narrative examples in some cases. The questions are similar to interview questions and help the human resources and selecting officials "rate and rank" your application.

The resume will determine whether you are qualified for the job, but the questions are important to determine your ability to perform the job. You will need to make sure your resume reflects the skills covered in the questions.

When managers are looking to fill a position, the QuickHire HR recruiters post a vacancy announcement and write a list of applicant questions. The HR professionals find the resumes that are submitted for this announcement and review the answers to the applicant questions. The HR staff develops a "certified list" of best-qualified candidates to forward to the selecting official for interviewing and hiring considerations. They send print copies of your electronic resume along with the "cert."

You can easily edit and update your resume in the QuickHire systems so that the resume reflects the duties in each announcement and the questions in the online application.

At this point, you will need to copy and paste your resume into each agency's database for consideration for that agency's jobs. QuickHire services approximately 60 Federal agencies at this point.

The QuickHire application management system is *not* a "keyword system" as is Resumix (see the next section). In QuickHire, your resume is simply stored in a database and retrieved by applicant name, target job announcement, and other data rather than by keywords and skills.

Resumix

The Department of Defense agencies are using the Resumix automated human resources staffing system, which is now owned by HotJobs and Yahoo!. The Resumix system is used by Disney, MCI, other corporations, and municipalities to manage and retrieve resumes in databases. The Resumix system is a "keyword/skill" system where the HR recruiter searches for the best-qualified candidates with a short list of keywords and skills that are identified by managers.

Here's how to submit your resume with Resumix:

1. Use the Resume Builder:

    First you submit your resume by copying and pasting your text into the Resume

Builder (this is the preferred submission method).

You can also submit your resume to the database by e-mail or regular mail. Follow the announcement directions for regular mail submission.

2. Fill out the Supplemental Data Sheet:

    You will answer personal profile information in the supplemental data section (located at the beginning or end of the Resume Builder). The supplemental questions (up to 20 questions) involve selection of particular occupational series (possibly two or three series), grades and geographic locations, military status, and past Federal positions.

    Be sure that your information matches the series requirements.

3. For particular occupational series or specialized jobs, you will need to "self nominate."

When managers are looking to fill a position, the HR recruiters perform a database query in the specific occupational series database. The system then ranks applicants based on how well their resumes match the manager's requirements. The more matches (or "hits") a manager's search makes with your resume, the higher you appear on the manager's list. If you've written your electronic resume following chapter 12's instructions, you will have a better chance of coming up at the top of the manager's search results.

You can find a more detailed explanation of the Resumix system in the *Electronic Federal Resume Guidebook,* by Kathryn Kraemer Troutman.

Paper Federal Resume and KSA Applications

Some Federal agencies are still accepting only paper applications, which usually involve a Federal resume that is formatted for human review, as well as Knowledge, Skills, and Abilities statements.

These vacancy announcements give you a street address, mailing address, fax, and sometimes e-mail address so that you can send the package by e-mail. Carefully read the announcement instructions on how to apply. The closing date can mean the package must be postmarked by the closing date, or the instructions might state that the package has to be at the office by close of business on the closing date.

The paper application package is usually comprised of the following:

★ A cover letter

★ Your Federal resume

★ Your KSA narratives

★ Your most recent supervisory evaluation

★ Transcripts, DD-214, and other information that might be requested in the announcement

To submit your package, mail the package flat in a 10 × 13 envelope. Write the vacancy announcement number and job title on the front of the envelope. Be sure to send the package with a return receipt so that you can track the acceptance of the package.

 Note: Fewer and fewer agencies are accepting paper applications.

When managers are looking to fill a position with paper applications to review, the HR recruiters will review the Federal resume first to determine whether you are basically qualified for the job based on education and generalized and/or specialized experience. If you are qualified, they will read your Knowledge, Skills, and Abilities statements. The KSAs are rated and ranked based on a personnel standard. The scores are reviewed and the highest-scoring/best-qualified candidates are forwarded to the selecting official or hiring panel. You will receive excellent scores if you write KSAs based on the instructions in chapter 14.

Two Typical Kinds of Vacancy Announcements—Open Inventory Announcements and Current Job Announcements

With different automated resume systems, the vacancy announcement instructions also are different. There are basically two different kinds of announcements: Open inventory announcements and current job announcements.

Database-Building/Open-Inventory/Open-Continuous Announcements

These announcements work like large resume-collection job sites. These announcements are posted so that you can submit your resume to a specific occupational series announcement and database. For instance, for the Navy Northeast Region (www.donhr.navy.mil), the Engineer, Interdisciplinary vacancy announcement is open for the following job series: 0801, 0806, 0819, 0830, 0850, 0854, 0855, 0893, 1310, and 0894 for the following locations: Vacancies at Naval Surface Warfare Center, Carderock Division, Philadelphia, PA; Bath, ME; Arlington, VA; and Washington, DC.

The Human Resources Service Center—Northeast (HRSC-NE) is soliciting resumes to fill current and/or future vacancies in this occupational series. Resumes accepted will receive consideration as vacancies occur within geographical areas identified by applicants on the Additional Data Sheet (ADS) form available on the Resume Builder.

HR personnel are building an "inventory" of candidate resumes for future searches when positions are open. Federal job seekers sometimes think that these are not "real" job announcements where people can really be hired, but they are real. HR recruiters search these databases everyday on behalf of managers who are looking for qualified candidates.

Open-inventory or database-building vacancy announcements can save HR departments significant time and costs by avoiding the expense and time lag associated with advertising an opening. These vacancy announcements could have a closing date of 2099 or some other far-off date. If you are a serious job candidate, you should submit your resume to a database-building announcement so that your resume will be waiting when a search is performed.

If you see a specific new job with a closing date, you would follow a two-step process. For step one, your resume must be in the database. If you submitted it previously for an Open Continuous announcement, step two will be to self-nominate for the position. For most announcements, you will scroll to the bottom of the page and then click on "Application Express" or "Self-Nominate." A short form will appear and you can just fill in basic information about the announcement. That's it. You have applied for the job! You will receive an e-mail back stating that the database has received your self-nomination.

Specific Job Openings

Many people think of these as "real job openings." Many agencies post specific vacancy announcements written for particular positions. These announcements have a closing date that is one to three weeks in the future. A job applicant applies to each position as it is posted and follows the application directions in the announcement. The application instructions vary for each agency, depending on their automated HR processes.

Summary

At this writing, there are multiple resume builders, online forms, databases, and other methods of applying for Federal jobs. Read the How to Apply directions in the vacancy announcement. Read any job kit, if one is available at the agency's Web site, for more instructions. When you are familiar with the various automated systems, you will be able to apply for many positions correctly and successfully. Initially, there is a learning curve to becoming familiar with the application systems.

At some point in the future, you might be able to submit one resume through the resume builder found at www.usajobs.opm.gov and apply for all Federal jobs through that site. For an up-to-date report on the Recruitment One Stop (ROS) initiative, you can visit www.resume-place.com/USABJOBS.ROS for the latest information on applying for Federal jobs online.

Boosting Your Employment Chances with Great KSAs

The best part of putting together a Federal resume is doing your KSAs! Most people dread even the thought of having to write four to six one-page essays, but the truth is that this is the part of the Federal application process that gives you a really unique opportunity to reach out in a personal way to your "interviewer." Think of the KSAs as being your first interview; only in this case, you aren't put on the spot and required to answer the questions without preparation. You actually get to think them through thoroughly and in advance. For this "interview," you can entirely avoid the regret of "I wish I had thought about telling them that!"

What Is a KSA?

KSA stands for *Knowledge, Skills,* and *Abilities.* KSA statements form the second part of most applications for a Federal job or promotion. In the resume, you tell about your specific job history and skills and how they relate to the position you are seeking. In the KSAs, you tell *why* you can do the job! In devising which KSA statements it asks for, the government takes the time to analyze each position and pull out the essential elements needed to succeed in the job. In most cases, they are not the straightforward and obvious skills, such as "Can you program in C?", "What are your computer skills?", or "Can you put together a project plan?" The KSAs usually touch on the more intangible, complex abilities that the position requires. They require you to answer questions such as "Can you get disparate groups of people to work together?", "Can you handle multitasking?", "Can you thrive in a stressful environment?", or "Can you solve complicated, multifaceted problems?" Good interviewers know that past performance is the best indicator of future behavior. The KSAs are your opportunity to show that you have what it takes to succeed in the job!

You might have heard rumors about KSAs: what they are, how human resources people "grade" them, and how to write them. In this chapter, I'll give you the real heads-up on KSAs; show you how to identify requests for KSA statements in job vacancy announcements; explain how to write KSA statements with basic rules, helpful tips, and examples; and show you how to format your KSAs. Remember that an excellent set of KSAs puts you in the final heat of the job race. No KSAs, or poorly written KSA statements, mean you won't even be on the starting block!

An In-Depth Look at KSAs

KSAs are supplemental statements to your application that give specific examples of paid and nonpaid work experience, education, training, awards, and honors that support each major work area of an announced position. There are usually four to six KSAs listed in each announcement. KSAs are written in the first person (_I did this and that_), and are typically one-half to one full page each. In one sense, the KSAs are a selection tool, and often an elimination tool. KSAs are initially graded, or "rated," by first-level personnel reviewers. You have to pass this first level for your application to go on to the hiring panel or hiring manager.

You can also think of your KSAs as a writing test. They require you to interpret the details of the announcement, research the agency's mission and purpose, organize and relate your experience to the special needs of the hiring organization, follow directions closely, and apply good computer and writing skills to develop a document that clearly articulates your job knowledge, skills, and abilities.

As it is for any author, your goal is to engage your reader. The successful KSA not only presents a good account of how your experience closely matches what the hiring agency is looking for; it also tells a "good story." Put yourself for a moment in the rater's shoes, with possibly hundreds of applications to evaluate. After reading KSA after KSA comprised of laundry lists of "I did this" and "I did that," how refreshing to happen upon one that tells an interesting, maybe even thought-provoking tale. Would your reaction be to slow down for just a minute, wonder about the individual who is telling the story, maybe even think about following up to learn more about this person? That is exactly what you are hoping for. The reader should enjoy reading your KSAs. A good set of KSAs sets you apart from your competition and showcases the unique qualities you bring to any job.

The Office of Personnel Management's (OPM's) Definition of Knowledge, Skills, and Abilities

Here's how the government defines knowledge, skills, and abilities:

★ **Knowledge.** An organized body of information, usually of a factual or procedural nature, which, if applied, makes adequate performance on the job possible.

★ **Skills.** The proficient manual, verbal, or mental manipulation of data, people, or things. Observable, quantifiable, and measurable.

★ **Abilities.** The power to perform an activity at the present time. Implied is a lack of discernible barriers, either physical or mental, to performing the activity.

Sometimes announcements request _KSAOs,_ which means "Other" Personal Characteristics. According to the government, the _O_ stands for a special, specific personality factor or aptitude, or a physical or mental trait needed to do the work, which appears either in addition to, or to a greater extent than, what is generally expected of all employees in all jobs.

How Agencies Grade KSAs

Federal personnel staffing specialists have a "rating and ranking" system for each KSA statement, called a _crediting plan._ The crediting plans vary from job opening to job opening and are used by the reviewer as an objective tool to rate your submission. Your statements will be rated from "Superior" to "Not Acceptable." By writing your statements with sufficient detail so that the reviewer can determine the level of your knowledge, skill, or ability, plus using an effective presentation, you can convince the hiring staff to rank you as "Superior." Here is an example of what a crediting plan might look like for a GS-7 secretary position. The points can range from 5 to 25, depending on the importance of the desired skill.

1. Ability to maintain and plan schedules, respond to changes in scheduling in order to maintain supervisor's calendar, and assure smooth flow of office operation. _____ **points**

2. Skill in utilizing word-processing programs and other automated programs in order to prepare correspondence and reports and to track the status of such documents. _____ **points**

3. Ability to communicate orally in order to receive and direct calls and to give technical assistance. _____ **points**

4. Ability to independently plan and carry out multiple assignments under short deadlines and to provide substantive support on special projects. _____ **points**

5. Ability to acquire and apply knowledge of the responsibility of various administrative and program offices in order to refer calls and correspondence to appropriate offices and to coordinate and review the format, grammar, and organization of various work products from these offices. _____ **points**

Because the crediting plans are a personnel tool, they are not public information. So you probably won't know which KSAs the hiring managers consider to be the most important. Just remember when you're writing the KSAs that you are being graded and that you want to achieve maximum points for each KSA.

A KSA by Any Other Name Is Still the Same

Deep in the text of the dense Federal vacancy announcement, you will find instructions for writing additional statements that will further describe your ability to perform the job. You already know what they're called: KSAs.

Agencies don't always call these statements "Knowledge, Skills, and Abilities." Sometimes agencies refer to them as "Quality Ranking Factors," "Narrative Factors," "Supplemental Statements," and so on. Announcements might ask for a separate sheet of paper with a response

to three to five elements; factors; or knowledge, skills, and abilities statements.

Each announcement will be different in content, instruction, detail, format, and font type. Look carefully for any KSA requirements. Look particularly at any length restrictions, format requirements, or other instructions detailing how you should present this information. Even if the announcement indicates that the KSAs are optional, you should consider them mandatory.

Federal Job Announcement Examples with KSA Requirements

Here are parts of three Federal job announcements that give requirements for KSA statements. I have placed footnotes in each announcement where I want you to notice particular instructions and information. Analyzing the instructions and responding correctly can make a difference in your candidacy for the position.

Job Announcement Example 1

Position: AGRICULTURAL PROGRAM SPECIALIST, GS-1145-09/12

DEPARTMENT OF AGRICULTURE (USDA)

USDA, Farm Service Agency

SPECIALIZED EXPERIENCE

Specialized experience is experience that demonstrated the following:

Knowledge[1] of the laws and regulations governing agricultural stabilization and conservation programs and of the particular application of national policies and objectives at the State level; Understanding of farming practices and customs in the United States, and of the economic needs of farm communities at the State level; Knowledge of current State and Federal agricultural trends; and Ability to establish and maintain effective relationships with representatives of public and private organizations, farmers' associations, and others, and to interpret regulations, programs, and policies affecting them.

Examples of qualifying specialized experience include:[2] Agricultural extension work as a subject-matter specialist, county agent, or assistant or associate county agent. Teacher of vocational agriculture. District Director, State program specialist, or county office employee performing duties in the operational phases of farm programs such as production adjustment, price support, and conservation. Experience at the county, district, or State government levels in the operational phases of farm programs of the type carried out through such agencies as the Soil Conservation Service, Farmers Home Administration, or related programs.

Knowledge, Skills, and Abilities Required (Mandatory):[3]

For each of the criteria listed below, describe specifically and accurately the relevance of each of the following: experience, training, education, and awards.

You should include specific tasks performed,[4] the dates you performed them, and where you were working at the time.

Knowledge of FSA farm programs and operations.

Knowledge of the FSA county office workload and work measurement system.

Ability to analyze and interpret written material.

Ability to communicate in writing.

Ability to communicate orally.

Notes:[5] There are no special forms for these statements. They may be submitted on plain paper with your name and the announcement number at the top. Candidates who do not submit the supplemental statement will not be considered.

Supplement on plain paper, in narrative format, information that concisely addresses each of the knowledge, skills, and abilities listed under Ranking Factors. Include work experience, education, and training that clearly demonstrates how well you possess each element. Current Federal employees applying for promotion under this announcement will not receive further consideration if KSA narrative is not submitted.

Please submit the following:

- Application

- Performance Appraisal

- Supplemental KSA (knowledge, skills, and abilities) Statements[6]

Author's Comments

1. This announcement is very specific; it tells you the required knowledge very clearly.

2. Tasks—very unusual, but the announcement gives you examples of tasks to support the KSAs.

3. For Knowledge, Skills, and Abilities, notice the word *mandatory*. That means include them or don't apply.

4. Again, the announcement tells you to write about specific tasks.

5. Very detailed instructions about how to write the KSAs/Ranking Factors.

6. KSAs are referred to here as "Supplemental Statements."

Job Announcement Example 2

Legal Secretary, GS-7

FDIC

JOB INFORMATION CENTER

WASHINGTON, DC 20429-9990

QUALITY RANKING FACTORS (DESIRABLE KNOWLEDGE, SKILLS, AND ABILITIES):[1]

1. Knowledge of administrative policies, procedures, and requirements of a legal office.

2. Skill in controlling correspondence, maintaining a suspense system, and following up on assignments.

3. Skill in locating, analyzing, and summarizing information from files and documents in order to respond to correspondence or telephone calls.

4. Skill in composing and preparing routine correspondence.

5. Ability to establish and maintain a filing system.

EVALUATION METHODS:[2] Applicants will be evaluated on the basis of information provided in their application package as to their experience, training, self-development, and awards; knowledge, skills, and abilities; and performance appraisals. Failure to provide specific information as to your qualifications for the position to be filled (including any selective and/or quality ranking factors described in this vacancy announcement) could result in disqualification.[3]

Author's Comments

1. These KSAs are called "Quality Ranking Factors."

2. Evaluation methods are provided.

3. These KSAs are mandatory.

Job Announcement Example 3

TYPE OF POSITION: COMPUTER ASSISTANT, GS-0335-7

SALARY: $26,075-$33,893 PER ANNUM

LOCATION: Information Technology Division, VAMC, CHARLESTON, SC

RATING AND RANKING:[1] The following KSAOs[2] (Knowledge, Skills, Abilities, and Other Characteristics) will be used to further evaluate applicants who meet the qualification requirements described by determining the extent to which their work or related experience, education,

(continues)

(continued)

training, awards, and outside activities, etc., indicate they possess the knowledge, skills, and abilities described below. All applicants should address each KSAO listed, providing clear, concise, accurate, detailed information that shows level of accomplishment or degree to which they possess the knowledge, skills, and abilities.[3] KSAOs (job elements for wage grade jobs) can work to your advantage. It is important that you put time and effort into developing responses to these evaluation factors that are relevant only to this job vacancy.[4] Qualified promotion candidates will be evaluated using a rating guide developed on the KSAO concept (job element for wage grade jobs). All relevant information available on each qualified candidate, taken as a whole, will be evaluated against each rating factor or job element, as appropriate, to determine the amount of credit to be granted. Information on how to respond to KSAOs is available from the Human Resources Management Service.[5]

- Knowledge of electronic principles and mechanics of the computer, related components, and auxiliary and peripheral equipment.

- Ability to apply computer logic and communication protocols.

- Knowledge of operating systems such as Windows 95, Windows NT, and application packages, etc. Consideration is given to scope of knowledge of these systems and application packages.

- Ability to train others in computer applications.

- Ability to problem solve, evaluate, and analyze problems and propose and implement working solutions in Local Area Network environment.

- Skill in the installation, repair, and maintenance of electronic digital computer systems, auxiliary, or peripheral equipment. Please provide examples.

Author's Comments

1. This announcement gives many details of rating and ranking for your information.

2. The KSAs are referred to as KSAOs. "Other characteristics" represents the fourth letter here.

3. Detailed instructions on the importance of showing the level of accomplishment.

4. Emphasis on the importance of these "evaluation factors" and that they should be relevant to this position.

5. A KSAO rating guide is available from the Human Resources Management Service (HRMS). You can call this office and get a copy of the crediting plan on these KSAOs. The name of the HRMS staff and phone was in the announcement.

How to Write Great KSAs

Remember that your KSAs have two goals. First, you want to present convincing evidence that your knowledge, skills, and abilities are a close match to those that the advertised position requires. Second, you want to tell an engaging story, one that rings true to the reader and presents you as a person of depth and character.

Therefore, your KSA should include the elements of a good story: It should grab your attention right away, flow smoothly, have a logical progression, keep your interest, have a point, and then draw a conclusion. Now you might say, "I haven't lived that interesting of a life!" But you have, if you frame it properly. Even a very simple experience can be made interesting to the reader—and it doesn't take exceptional writing skills and creativity to make that happen. In a sense, this is formula writing. And I am going to give you the formula.

The basic outline for any KSA is as follows:

1. A good opening that makes some general statement about you, your experience, your opinions, or what you think is important about this KSA.

2. Two strong examples that follow the CCAR (Context, Challenge, Actions, Result—*hold on, I'll get to that in a moment*) format. One good example could also be effective, if the example is excellent and demonstrates the KSA.

3. A closing that draws it all together.

Let's take a look at a very short example to make this point. You are asked to write a KSA about your verbal communications skills (a very common KSA). You could write something like this:

My job requires me to communicate a lot. On a daily basis, I answer the phone and deal with a variety of questions from individuals inside and external to my Division. I also receive visitors to the office and refer them to whoever can resolve their query or problem. I have also volunteered on several occasions to provide training for other administrators in our group. I carefully planned my presentation, used my excellent verbal skills to present the training, and was complimented by my supervisor for a very effective training course.

Now ask yourself, does this grab you as the reader? Does this convey anything about your personality? How can we take this same simple scenario and make it more interesting?

The keys to making this a better KSA: Add details! Put it in the context of a challenge! Make a general observation that is reflective of your general philosophy or approach. Be honest—tell how you really felt about this experience. Make sure it comes from the heart. Make sure it uses common language and reaches your listener on a human level. Forget about striving for beautiful, impressive prose. Work instead for clarity and simple language. Make sure it is logical and that it "flows." Here's the revised version:

Secretary, GS-301-7 KSA, Ability to Communicate Orally My job as the administrative lead for our office requires top-notch communications skills on a daily basis. A significant part of my day involves greeting office visitors either in person or on the phone. Although most callers present matter-of-fact queries, I have also been in the position to handle difficult situations and upset individuals. I have learned that many tense situations in the office can be defused by imagining myself on the side of the irritated party.

On one occasion, a very senior manager called our office several times but had not been able to reach a particular staff member. When I answered, I could feel the irritation on the other end. My tactic was to recognize how important the caller's issue was to him and to relay what I could do to ensure that the message got to the intended staff member. I provided the specifics of what I would do—leave both a phone and written message for the individual and follow up personally when the individual was available. In addition, I provided the caller with my name in case he did not hear back by the end of the day.

This same tactic worked well for me in a training class that I presented for my fellow administrators on the use of a new payroll program. I could tell that one participant was getting frustrated with the computer exercise we were following. Working individually with the person, I commiserated that I had personally found that aspect of the program challenging as well but had learned a few tricks that might help out. My supervisor observed the class and complimented me on my sensitive handling of the incident.

What's different in this example? First of all, it includes details—what your job is, what class you taught, and the details of a problem or two that you had to deal with. It still lists essentially the same elements as the first example but portrays you as an individual. It also recognizes that the workplace does present problems and that you are up to solving them! Best of all, it provides some insight into the type of person you are—what you think, how you handle challenges, and how you deal with other people. This is exactly what the hiring manager is looking for.

The first example is too short and generic, but this second example could work as a KSA statement. Now let's study the CCAR formula and expand this KSA even further.

Driving Your KSAs with the CCAR Format

OPM recommends that if you are writing an accomplishment-based KSA (which we recommend that all KSAs should be), you should include the *Context,* the *Challenge,* your *Actions,* and the *Result* (CCAR) for each example that you cite. Here are more details on each of these elements:

★ **Context:** What was the specific circumstance that led to the task or challenge you are going to describe? Where were you working? Had you just started the job, or had you been there for quite a while? Were you assigned the task, or did you show initiative by identifying a problem yourself

that you felt needed resolution? What was the situation that made this issue critical to the organization?

★ **Challenge:** What was the specific task you had to resolve? What obstacles did you have to overcome? What made completing this example a challenge? Short timeframe? Gaining cooperation from others? First-time project? The challenge(s) of your project can earn more points because it shows "why" you were working on the project.

★ **Actions:** What were the detailed steps that you took to resolve the challenge? These do not have to be earth-shaking. The fact that you met with your team or management, pulled together a plan, and then executed it is just fine. By providing details, you bring the situation to life and set yourself apart from the competition. The reader will know that you really were there and lived through this—that you are not just recounting a general circumstance that anyone might conjure up.

★ **Result:** What happened? In some cases, you might be able to provide quantitative results (for example, your actions resulted in saving significant costs or time for the government). In other cases, you might have received an award or at least a personal thank-you from your supervisor or another party. You might even be able to use an example in which the resolution was not ideal, but in which you made the best decision in a difficult scenario and at least mitigated the outcome.

 Note: You can use this same CCAR model for writing SES Executive Core Qualifications (see chapter 16 for more on applying for SES positions).

Ten Steps to Writing Really Effective KSAs

Now you are ready to start writing. Here are the 10 steps I recommend to build truly effective KSAs.

1. Pick Your Announcement Wisely

If you are truly qualified for a position, you should be able to come up with good examples for all, or almost all, of the KSAs. If you find that you really do not have good examples for many of the KSAs in an announcement, you should honestly question whether you are qualified for the position.

2. Read the KSAs and Associated Instructions Very Carefully

How long should the statements be? Exactly what is the announcement asking for? Refer back to the full description in the job announcement and relate the KSAs to what is in the job announcement. This should give you some idea of what the agency is looking for and why these particular factors are important.

3. Brainstorm Several Detailed Examples for Each KSA

You might have some examples that work for more than one KSA. List the examples by each KSA they apply to and come back later and determine which you will use for each KSA. Avoid repeating any example. The only exception, and *only* if you cannot think of a separate example, is that you can use a different aspect of the same situation for two different KSAs. For example, you could emphasize the written documentation that you did for a task for one KSA, and more of the organizational or people interactions of that same example in a different KSA. Remember, your examples do not have to be Nobel Prize–winning examples; they just have to be related to the required job knowledge, skill, or ability, and you have to have really done what you say you have done. The details will show

that you truly accomplished what you are recounting.

Of course, the level should be appropriate to the level of the position you are applying for. KSAs for senior-level positions should use examples that illustrate division- or agency-wide initiatives. It is good to think of recent examples. You can include some that are ongoing—the problem might not yet be resolved fully, but at least you have a course of action defined. It is even alright to select an example that did not have a positive outcome, as long as you impose the right slant, illustrating that sometimes getting 100 percent consensus is not possible and that you took the necessary steps or made the appropriate decision given the difficult circumstances.

How do you decide which examples to use? If you have a choice, select those in which you truly had a problem or a challenge to resolve, you showed initiative, you had to take multiple steps to complete the task, and you can show some measurable results.

4. Select Two Examples for Each KSA and Work on the CCAR Details

Now you need to plan out the CCAR details you will include for the two best examples you have for each KSA. At this point, you *still* should not have written anything. So far you are just outlining! For each example, follow the CCAR format: Context, Challenge, Actions, and Result. Consider each of these and jot down anything that comes to mind. Don't be judgmental—just put it down and decide later whether you will use it.

- ★ **Context:** What was the situation when you received this task? Where were you working? What group were you participating in? Did you just start a new job?

- ★ **Challenge:** How did you receive this task? Was it assigned, did you walk into it, or did you see a problem and take the initiative to resolve it?

★ **Actions:** What steps did you take to research, prepare, resolve, and/or report on the task? Again, these don't have to be award-winning—just walk through the step-by-step actions you took. For example, you might have read the existing documentation, interviewed people, set up a meeting, put together an action plan, built consensus, gained approval, ordered supplies, reported on the milestones, celebrated at the end, and so on.

★ **Result:** Now try, if possible, to quantify the result. You saved $30 million, you reduced the time to implement by six weeks, you pumped out 50,000 widgets in record time, you identified 25 improvements in your office that were implemented, you completed the budget on time despite setbacks, you received an award, you got a pat on the back, and so on.

5. Start Writing the Opening

Now you are finally ready to write. I find it helpful to go ahead and write the opening as opposed to doing the examples first because I want to make sure it all flows together. My best advice is to remember that writing and editing are two separate activities. *Don't* try to get each sentence perfect before you go on to the next sentence—that is your editing job, which you will do in a later step. Sit down and just write. Write it like you would say it out loud to a friend or family member: Ramble, put something down, and make no corrections! You will come back later to organize and edit. Start with a short paragraph that leads into your theme, such as "Here is what I think is my special skill or approach in this area." Here are some good examples of opening lines that you can customize to the theme that you have selected:

★ I am the kind of person who does what it takes to get the job done.

★ I have often heard it said that….

★ My core job function is….

★ My personal heroes growing up were….

★ One of the things that I truly enjoy about….

★ I have been actively involved in….

★ Budgeting is not simply about putting numbers to paper….

★ For me, …is about….

★ If it has to do with…, I have probably done it!

★ With all the many…I have performed, the most satisfying experience was….

★ I genuinely enjoy working with people from all backgrounds, and in my job I frequently….

★ The challenges in my positions over the past several years in the…are also what I have enjoyed most in each job.

★ I consider myself to be a very accurate person. This is a strength that is invaluable in my daily work.

★ No matter what job I tackle, big or small, it always ends up requiring me to….

★ I like to consider myself a…as opposed to a…because….

★ I have been in a unique position at the center of….

★ I first learned about….

★ The mark of a good leader is….

★ At the center of working…is managing….

★ One of the aspects that I really enjoy about my role as…is….

★ My goals in managing…are….

★ The amount of data required to track and forecast…are….

★ I've always been a computer enthusiast, so….

6. Write the Two Examples

Now, do the same in writing your two examples—just write! Keep in mind the CCAR approach, but look at your notes only in passing. Mainly just tell the story. Think about a good transition between the two examples. How would you do this in conversation at a party? You wouldn't just stop one example and start the next; you would lead from one to the other example to keep your fellow partygoers interested. Here are a few sample transition lines to get your creative juices flowing:

★ On another occasion, I was faced with a very different [or similar] challenge....

★ Many of the projects I led have involved....

★ Frequently during budget cycles, I have had to....

★ One of the more interesting experiences I had was....

★ Very recently, I have been involved with....

★ I have also authored a wide range of....

★ I am also frequently called on to....

★ The other major...that I have worked with is....

★ A good example of...is....

★ I have also been the prime investigator for....

★ Sometimes avoiding...can be a challenge....

★ I also have a continuing role....

★ Earlier that year, I also supported....

7. Write the Ending

Now you might think that you are done with your initial brainstorming draft, but I purposely left out a very important part of the outline: the ending. The best time to compose this is *after* you have written your first rough draft for your opening and two examples. The full outline is really this:

I. An Opening

II. Example One

III. A transition to Example Two

IV. A closing that brings it all together

I don't recommend that you summarize everything you've said so far. Quite the contrary—this is where you provide a thoughtful comment that provides closure or insight for the "story." Do not think of this as the "moral" of the story. It can be, but it can also provide a "twist" that might be even more effective. Read what you have thus far and summarize it as concisely as you possibly can in your head. Ask yourself: What is the point of all of this, or what have I really learned from all of this?

8. Include Keywords

With the number of applications that are initially reviewed electronically, it is important to include keywords in your KSAs. The computer will scan your document and search for words that coincide with what is being sought after for the position. When the raters review KSAs, they also look for keywords that will jump out to them and demonstrate that you are familiar with the terminology and job-related lingo. Are you using words that are job-related and position-specific (without being overly technical)? Have you included well-known acronyms? Do you have phrases that are associated with the position? Have you listed specific technical skills that would be expected of someone applying for the position you are interested in? A good test is to once again scan the announcement, and position description if you have it, and make sure you have similar words listed within your KSA.

The effective use of keywords can also result in a higher grade on your application. The verbs, nouns, and proper names that you select to describe your knowledge, skills, and abilities can demonstrate your level of expertise. Look at a few ways to describe your responsibilities, skills, and abilities, and the ratings that will result from each:

KSA statement: Ability to use regulatory material.

- ★ Superior: Interpret regulatory material.
- ★ Good: Research regulatory material.
- ★ Satisfactory: Apply regulatory material.
- ★ Barely acceptable: Recognize regulatory material.

KSA statement: Ability to schedule work.

- ★ Superior: Schedule work to accomplish agency mission.
- ★ Good: Schedule work to accomplish project goals.
- ★ Satisfactory: Schedule work to accomplish unit objectives.
- ★ Barely acceptable: Schedule work to accomplish own work.

KSA statement: Ability to communicate in writing.

- ★ Superior: Write technical reports.
- ★ Good: Write critiques.
- ★ Satisfactory: Write letters.
- ★ Barely acceptable: Write internal communications.

KSA statement: Ability to plan, organize, and schedule work.

- ★ Superior: Process action to meet project goals.
- ★ Good: Process action to meet given objectives.

- ★ Satisfactory: Process action using established precedent.
- ★ Barely acceptable: Process action using procedural instructions.

9. Edit Your Writing

Are you done yet? No, but hopefully it hasn't been too painful so far. Remember that we have purposely avoided working for beautiful prose. You should have been concentrating on just getting something down on the paper in plain, simple, everyday language that tells your story. That's the key of just typing—your personality *will* come out if you don't bottle it in by trying to make each sentence perfect.

But alas, now the time has come to edit. Leave your work, hopefully for a day, and then come back and read what you have and start the editing. You will find that having a brainstormed document actually removes the stress. You should be able to edit what you have to make it sound better and flow more clearly. Feel free to—in fact you should—move whole segments around to make the statement flow better. Maybe that second example makes more sense first.

Edit as well to shorten your document down to the required length, or to around one page if you are not given a specific required length. Force yourself to do this. If you make yourself get this down to one page, you will get rid of the fluff and verbiage that really add nothing to the overall value of the story.

10. Proofread Carefully

Well, we have to have 10 steps! The last step is a careful, close proofreading. Look for spelling and grammatical errors that your spell-checker might have missed. Have a friend, colleague, or relative read your KSAs and consider their suggestions and corrections.

A Few Extra Pointers

★ **Write in the first person** ("I"). This is one of the few occasions where using "I" in a formal document is appropriate. Your resume and your KSAs are about you and your experience. Personalize them by writing in the first person. You should even avoid referring to your group ("we") excessively. The reviewer wants to know what "you" did!

★ **What if you really do not understand what the KSA is asking for—or what if it looks identical to another KSA?** Go back to the job announcement and read it carefully. Are there any hints there? Get another individual to read the KSA description and brainstorm on the meaning and possible approaches. Look at the Web site for the agency or organization. Are there any clues there? Should you call—probably not; it's doubtful that you will get in touch with the person who wrote the KSA. Just try to come up with good examples that are along the lines of what the announcement is asking for and that show off your skill set.

★ **What if you really do not have any background or an example that fits this KSA?** If it is just one KSA, the best advice is to read up on the topic. Go out to the agency's Web site and read everything you can find on this question. Then build a KSA that truthfully indicates that you have studied up on the topic, points out a few interesting challenges that apply to this position, and relates any similar experience you can think of in your background. If it is reasonable that you would not have the required experience (in other words, only someone in government would, and you are coming from industry), it is okay to mention that specifically and again relate something in the corporate world that is a similar challenge. If there are multiple KSAs that do not ring true with your experience, you should seriously reconsider whether this job is a good match for you.

★ **It is okay (and desirable) to show a little flair, pizzazz, and zing!** Remember, the point is that you want to illustrate that you are not only qualified for the position, you are the *best* person for the job! You want to come across as friendly, down-to-earth, thoughtful, interesting, energetic— someone they want to have on their team and definitely want to interview! Big, erudite words don't convey this. Standard, plain English that clearly demonstrates your point does convey the right impression. (There might be some exceptions—if you are applying for a nuclear physicist or other highly technical or scientific position, a little erudition is a good thing. See chapter 18 for more on applying for technical jobs.)

★ **It's good to brag, but do so tactfully.** Avoid terms such as "my vast knowledge," "my exceptional communication skills," "my excellent facilitation skills," and so on. Let your actions speak for themselves. Put self-compliments in impersonal terms. Here are some examples:

  • "My job frequently requires the ability to think on my feet."

  • "Managing multiple priorities is a core requirement of my job."

  • "Communicating effectively in a variety of situations is essential in my position as the…."

Another way to brag smartly is to provide statistics—to quantify the results of your actions in dollars and time saved, projects delivered on time, quantifications of output, or even the size and scope of the operation you support.

You can also quote supervisors, customers, or team members who have written you complimentary awards, faxes, e-mails, or letters regarding your performance. Let them brag about your strengths and value to the mission.

★ **Use their lingo, but don't copy verbatim.** Religiously avoid talking "down" to your reviewer! Merely copying the announcement verbatim might not convey the impression that you want. Definitely use many of the technical words and phrases in the job announcement, but don't overdo it.

Include Job-Related Education, Courses, Training, and Awards

In addition to writing paid and nonpaid work examples for your KSAs, you should also include job-related training, educational courses, awards, and memberships. Overall, you need to look like you can perform well in the specific KSA area.

Five Approaches to KSA Statements

Here are some of the best ways to approach KSA statements:

★ Describe a specific *situation*.

★ Give an *overview* of your experience.

★ Give an example of relevant *education* or *training*.

★ Describe an *award* given for specific accomplishments.

★ Describe an experience in your previous jobs in the *history* format.

Don't feel tied to one approach. Feel free to combine different types in a single statement. Each KSA statement, for example, can be made up of paragraphs that give an overview, describe a situation (one or two of these), discuss relevant education, and describe an award or recognition. The following sections show examples of the five types of KSA statements.

Situation KSA

A situation KSA is a specific example that demonstrates your knowledge, skill, or ability in a certain area. The following is an example of a nonpaid work experience KSA statement for a Budget Analyst, GS-9:

ABILITY TO PERFORM EFFECTIVELY AND MAINTAIN COMPOSURE IN TENSION-FILLED SITUATIONS:

As a member and Chairman of the Middletown, Virginia, Town Planning Commission, I directed sometimes tension-filled Rezoning Meetings that affected the commercial activity of the town, but would also affect the residential character of the town. I was successful in mediating controversial rezoning issues concerning Main Street. I also chaired many sensitive hearings, acting as sounding board for longtime residents. The rezoning activities involved local media coverage and required skills in problem-solving and public relations.

Overview KSA

The following overview KSA is an introductory, summary KSA statement for a Secretary, GS-7.

SKILL IN EXPRESSING IDEAS CLEARLY, LOGICALLY, AND GRAMMATICALLY CORRECTLY, BOTH ORALLY AND IN WRITING:

As a Secretary to three senior government executives, I have developed a clear, logical, and grammatically correct writing style my supervisors trust. I am skilled in communicating clearly both orally and in writing. My supervisors depend on me to communicate priorities and significant information to department heads, congressional offices, and the public. I am sensitive to public-affairs issues, politically accurate responses, and tense situations. I speak and write with excellent grammar.

The next KSA was written by a Security Specialist, GS-12:

KNOWLEDGE OF THE THEORIES, PRINCIPLES, PRACTICES, AND TECHNIQUES OF AUTOMATED INFORMATION SYSTEMS (AID) SECURITY FOR U.S. GOVERNMENT COMPUTER SYSTEMS AND INSTALLATION:

As a result of experience in both Army and Navy operations, in overseas as well as with U.S.–wide computer systems, I have maintained extensive knowledge of U.S. government computer systems. In addition, due to widely varied experience, I have cultivated a network of top computer experts in the U.S. and abroad who regularly inform one another about the latest updates and developments in sophisticated systems.

Education/Training KSA

The following is a statement of related education and training that supports the KSA. The employee is Chief of Medical Technical Equipment, GS-12.

A GENERAL KNOWLEDGE OF THE MISSION, ORGANIZATION, AND ACTIVITIES OF A HEALTH CARE FACILITY:

Education and Specialized Training:

Currently enrolled (with 42 hours earned) in dual-degree Bachelor's program at Howard University, Washington, D.C., in Business Management and Computer Sciences.

Earned well over 1,500 hours' training with advanced medical technology and equipment (see complete listing attached to Federal resume).

In earlier career, completed over 400 hours as firefighter in fire safety, prevention, and emergency medical care.

Award/Recognition KSA

An award or recognition indicates the quality of your performance and usually contains a short statement, which can be the basis for a KSA narrative. The record of the award must contain sufficient information about relevant behaviors or activities to show that the KSA was demonstrated at some level. The following KSA excerpt was written by an Environmental Specialist, GS-13.

KNOWLEDGE OF FEDERAL HAZARDOUS MATERIALS TRANSPORTATION REGULATIONS:

At the conclusion of a recent Safety Review by the Office of Motor Carriers, I was commended for knowledge of regulations and programs developed for the company. In addition, on my most recent performance evaluation I was cited for having "excelled at meeting new challenges and improving the performance of the Fleet Safety Programs."

The next example was for a Foreign Affairs Officer, GS-13.

ABILITY TO PLAN AND DIRECT PROGRAM ACTIVITIES:

Commended on most recent performance review for being "only division officer who planned and managed two town meetings, one month apart, in St. Louis and San Francisco. The results were outstanding. The St. Louis event drew over 350 citizens (despite the floods) and great media coverage. The San Francisco meeting, with a record-breaking attendance of 1,300, was the first such meeting in over 13 years. Both the Secretary and the spokesperson commented publicly on their tremendous success."

Historic KSA

This is a summary of past experience that supports the KSA for a Vocational Rehabilitation Specialist, GS-12.

ABILITY TO PROMOTE THE REHABILITATION PROGRAM AND TO NEGOTIATE CONTRACTS AND AGREEMENTS WITH PROSPECTIVE EMPLOYERS AND TRAINING FACILITIES:

My work in vocational rehabilitation for the department has spanned over 20 years, and, through regular positions and special assignments, I have gained a broad understanding of the department's mission, goals, and programs. As a result, for the past three years I have been selected to speak on panel presentations regarding "Effective Client Strategies" at the annual National Rehabilitation Hospital Conference.

Here is another historic KSA example, this one for an Inspector General, GS-12.

SKILL IN THE ANALYSIS OF COMPLEX MULTIMILLION-DOLLAR FINANCIAL TRANSACTIONS:

For the past 10 years, I have managed cases that involve individuals charged with economic crimes, as well as local and national businesses charged with such offenses as money laundering and procurement fraud. For example, I serve on task force investigations in complex....

Recommended KSA Format

Each of the sample KSAs shown here include The Resume Place's recommended "proposal-style" heading for the most impressive KSA presentation. Follow this format when you write your own KSAs. The fonts and paper you use should match your resume.

Department of Health and Human Services

Program Support Center

Division of Supply Management, Quality Assurance Branch

Perry Point, MD

Announcement Number: 98P-01
Title of position: Project Coordinator, GS-301-12

Candidate: Thomas Richard Smith, SSN: 000-00-0000

KNOWLEDGE, SKILLS, AND ABILITIES

Examples of Good KSAs

To help you get started with your own KSAs, carefully read the three KSA examples that follow. What approaches do they take? Are all the basic elements there?

Position Applied for: Logistics Management Specialist, SV-0346-00/00, with Proposal-Style Heading

Current Position: Avionics Technician, Private Industry

Transportation Security Administration

Title of Position: Logistics Management Specialist, SV-0346-00/00
Announcement Number: TSA-003-123

Candidate:
P. Alexander Butler
SSN: 000-00-0000

Ability to learn specialized job procedures and related computer skills. Include examples of your experience in this area.

For over 17 years, in the military and private industry, I have consistently sought more efficient ways of doing business by learning specialized job procedures and becoming proficient in numerous computer software programs. In addition to position-specific computer programs, I have experience with Windows NT, 95, 98, and 2000; Microsoft Office Professional; and the Internet.

While assigned to the Marine Fighter Attack Squadron 321 at Andrews Air Force Base, I became aware of a new computer program, Survival Equipment Asset Tracking System/Increased Capability Program (SEATS/ICAPS), designed to enhance the ability to track time-sensitive components and explosive devices used in aircraft. The program had not yet been distributed throughout the Navy and Marine Corps. Recognizing the benefits of SEATS/ICAPS, I contacted a representative at the Indian Head Naval Weapons Center and arranged to have a copy sent to my squadron. After installing the program on the department's computers, I trained work center personnel on its uses. Once implemented, the program permitted the user to calculate and track life expectancies of survival gear and cartridge actuated devices electronically, rather than manually through the use of paper records. The program also allowed the user to print data concerning explosive devices installed in aircraft and to install data directly into the aircraft's permanent logbook. The installation of SEATS/ICAPS on department computers reduced the staff-hours necessary in maintaining survival equipment records by as much as 75%.

At American Airlines, I learned to use the Sabre reservation system. Once assigned an aircraft to work on, I would first go into Sabre and search the aircraft's history, going back at least 30 days to identify whether there were any related discrepancies. If there were, I would make note of all maintenance actions and the outcomes. This additional information reduced my troubleshooting time by telling me what had been previously attempted. After finding a solution to the aircraft discrepancy, I would return to Sabre to cross-reference part numbers, check availability, and determine the location of parts needed to correct the aircraft discrepancy. As a follow-up, I always used Sabre to check the status of the aircraft after its next flight to ensure there were no repeat faults in any system I had signed off on.

My interest in, and dedication to, continuously learning new job procedures and computer skills has enabled me to remain on the cutting edge of technology. I have brought new computer programs to my departments, and have created opportunities for staff to learn the new programs and acquire additional skills. I am always looking for ways to save time and money, and I have received awards and recognition for positively impacting the bottom line through my professional pursuit of improved programs and procedures for accomplishing tasks and departmental goals.

Position Applied for: Special Project Officer (Public/Private Ventures), GS-0301-13

Current Position: Director of Finance, Private Industry

Ability to Analyze Problems and Develop Solutions.

My formal education and career are in two problem-solving disciplines: engineering and operations research. I have developed solutions to extremely complex and complicated problems by developing case studies and using analytical tools. And I have solved urgent and high-visibility problems that required the simultaneous application of communication, negotiation, and people skills. When appropriate, I can use quantitative problem-solving methods, such as decision trees, statistical studies, case studies, and mathematical models. Frequently these are more useful in obtaining the necessary support than in initially deciding what to do.

I was managing partner of two real estate partnerships that owned office condominiums. We had purchased the condominiums at fire-sale prices in the early 1990s, primarily because the common area needed a lot of work. The objective was to keep the condominiums rented, while increasing the value by fixing the common area defects. As managing partner, I had three challenges:

- Work with the condominium association to get the improvements made within the original budget.
- Maintain positive cash flow from rental income.
- Sell the properties at market or near-market, not fire-sale, prices.

By applying negotiation and relationship skills, I was able to

- Build cooperative relationships with other owners and work with the construction oversight committee to get the modifications completed with no new assessments.
- Train small-business renters to pay their rent every month and not consider the security deposit as a form of prepaid rent.
- Agree with a few other owners to turn down offers at fire-sale prices for long enough that the real estate agents would stop encouraging potential buyers to present low offers.
- Sell the condominiums at over 40% higher than the purchase price.

In another job as an engineering project manager, I was very successful at managing projects for Japanese clients (who were thought to be the most difficult and demanding). Over several years, I was able to complete all the engineering projects for Japanese clients successfully and within the contract budget. I did this by learning Japanese attitudes about client-customer relations and then developing management principles consistent with the expectations of the Japanese engineering companies. As a result, all the new Japanese projects were assigned to me.

People consider me an excellent problem solver and frequently ask for my assistance or advice. I approach problems with a logical methodology to define the problem, identify any root causes, identify constraints, develop a solution that removes the root cause whenever possible, obtain resources, and implement the solution. I believe the reason that I have been very successful, not only in solving problems, but also in reducing the number and severity of self-inflicted problems, is that I work well both within the organization and with stakeholders to create solutions that fit into the culture and don't "make people wrong."

Position Applied for: Program Manager (Museum Management), GS-0340-14

Current Position: Museum Curator (Supervisory), GS-1015-13

Ability to manage a program.

Some of my greatest successes over the past 25 years with the National Park Service's cultural resource and museum programs are a direct result of my extensive experience in program management.
While at the Southeast Regional Office:

- I was responsible for the development and implementation of the region's curatorial program. This program included historical and scientific research for cultural and natural resources, and the planning, development, budgeting, management, and supervision of all curatorial activities in the 64 National Parks that comprise the Southeast Region. In addition, I had curatorial oversight responsibility for curatorial operations at the Southeast Archeological Center and the 21 university repositories that hold archeological collections from the region's parks.

- I developed a Regional Computer program for use in the cataloging and accountability requirements for museum property. This program was adopted by the NPS National Catalog as the servicewide Automated National Catalog System (ANCS) computer program. Several private, state, and local museums adopted the program as their basic format for museum record-keeping requirements. I also modified the program for use as the Southeast Archeological Center's program for inventorying, categorizing, and monitoring its archeological site inventories and cataloging artifacts.

- I created and implemented a Curatorial Assessment and Evaluation Program for the region. To do this, I evaluated curatorial operations in the parks, the Southeast Archeological Center, and repositories for compliance with NPS and professional curatorial standards. I then developed both short- and long-range plans to be used to meet these standards. Finally, I made comprehensive recommendations to the Regional Directorate, Park, and Center management concerning the management, preservation, maintenance, exhibition, use, security, and storage of museum collections in their care.

At Harpers Ferry Center, I was responsible for developing the servicewide curatorial support program. This was accomplished through the creation and management of the NPS Clearinghouse of excess museum objects, the development of a centralized curatorial supply operation, and the implementation of servicewide curatorial training.

- I effectively managed the NPS Clearinghouse by evaluating park museum collections, determining artifacts in excess of park needs, preparing lists for servicewide distribution, coordinating placement of selected artifacts, and disposing of unwanted artifacts utilizing appropriate procedures. I maintained a collection of over 3,000 artifacts at the center for possible placement in parks.

- I managed the servicewide program of purchasing and distributing curatorial supplies and equipment to 337 national parks. This program entailed working with curatorial supply and equipment companies to develop supplies and equipment needed to properly manage and store the diverse museum collections held by the National Park Service. As a result, the service negotiated with storage cabinet manufacturers to design an NPS Standard Cabinet and "modular" storage concept. This centralized curatorial supply program allowed for volume buying and contract negotiations, resulting in savings of over $50K/year.

- I developed and presented the servicewide "Curatorial Methods" training courses. I designed specific criteria to present the training in three phases: Curatorial Methods I, II, and III. I was responsible for all course content, objectives, and scheduling. Each year, I consistently improved the course content to address current needs and management thrusts. As a result of my program-management skills, curatorial training was increased by three classes per year.

My successes in program management are the direct result of my ability to effectively set goals, supervise staff, familiarize myself with the ins and outs of each program, and develop a strong working relationship with the various groups and individuals involved in the positive outcome of each program. Based on my accomplishments, I have been consistently sought after to lead and manage numerous service programs.

Summary

Now you have a firm grasp on what a KSA statement is, how to locate requests for KSAs in a vacancy announcement, what hiring managers are looking for in KSAs, the basic elements of great KSAs, and five ways to approach writing them. It's time for you to practice writing your own. Be sure to refer to the examples in this chapter as you draft, rewrite, and perfect your KSAs. You can also find more examples on this book's companion CD-ROM (see the back of the book for ordering instructions).

CHAPTER 15

Cover Letters with a Mission

Should you include a cover letter with a public service application? Yes, if you can. Any vacancy announcement that tells you to send a resume, KSAs, and other paperwork to the agency implies that you can send a cover letter as well. You might also be able to include a cover letter when you apply for Federal jobs online. There are basically two types of resume builders, one of which allows you to include a short cover letter and one of which doesn't:

★ The Defense Department's Resume Builder has specific fields for every piece of resume information. There is no place to write a cover letter, however.

★ The EPA, USGS, Department of Commerce, and other agencies use the QuickHire system for automated selection and management of candidates. This builder has one field where you can copy and paste your entire resume and a short introductory letter. Be aware, however, of the limit on the number of characters allowed in the field: 3,000 characters without spaces. The cover letter will have to be very short.

Sending a cover letter gives you the opportunity to

★ Introduce yourself informally and summarize the best you have to offer.

★ Write about your interests or passions in a certain field or job.

★ Highlight your expertise and qualifications that fit the job.

★ Mention your knowledge of the agency's mission.

★ Top off your application package with a few of your best qualities and your value as an employee.

★ Create a compelling rationale for why you are an outstanding candidate.

All this in one page! A well-written cover letter can help your application stand apart from the others.

Why Should You Include a Cover Letter?

There are many special reasons for including a cover letter with your application. It's an important part of your sales pitch. It can also help you get across your sincere interest in the position, which is very important to hiring personnel. A cover letter can also be considered your "proposal" for doing the advertised job. If necessary, you can use it to explain your special situation or any accommodations necessitated by a disability.

To Strengthen Your Sales Pitch

Remember that in your application package, you are selling yourself to the potential hiring manager. Sales guru Tom Hopkins advises people on mastering the art of selling. "You don't sell something by telling your customer what the features and benefits are *one time.* You repeat these items of interest several times in your sales pitch by introducing the product, reviewing the features and benefits, giving a demonstration, and telling the customer how the product will help achieve their business goals."

The same goes for you when you are selling yourself to a public-service personnelist, hiring manager, or panel:

1. In your cover letter or letter of interest, tell them what you are going to tell them in the rest of your hiring package.

2. Tell them again with facts and information (features and benefits) in your Federal resume.

3. Tell them again in a different way by including your knowledge, skills, and abilities in your KSA statements (see chapter 14) or with accomplishments and examples in your resume.

To Express Your Interest in the Job

A cover letter or "letter of interest" is not mandatory for a Federal or private-industry application. However, this is a meaningful letter because it truly needs to convey your interest in the job. If you can't demonstrate your interest in the job in a one-page letter, you won't be considered for it. You must demonstrate interest in the company, agency, mission, organization, or office.

To Propose Your Services

Your letter and application package is your "Services Proposal" to the organization. If you earn $40,000 per year and you hope to be employed at least five years, this proposal is worth at least $200,000 to you, plus benefits. This is a serious proposal and investment of time and resources for both you and the employer.

To Explain Special Circumstances

Hiring managers want to understand your application. People have special situations and interests that should be explained early in the application process. Comfort the readers by telling them certain things that will help your application make sense. If you are in Baltimore and the job you are seeking requires a complete career change, decrease in salary, and a move to Seattle, the entire application will not make sense without an explanation. They will not take the time to figure it out, call you and ask for your rationale, or try to use intuition to understand. You must explain what you are doing in a reasonable way. For example:

★ If you are relocating to be near family, it's good to say so.

★ If you have purchased a second home in a beautiful region of Tennessee and hope to move there and eventually retire in this area, tell them what your goals are.

★ If you want to leave the Washington, D.C., metro area and live and work in the West because it has been a dream of your life, say so.

★ If you are currently in a job making $27,000 and you were making $35,000 in your previous job, explain in the letter what happened.

★ If your current job is outside your career path because of a corporate reorganization rather than your own choice, explain this change.

If it isn't obvious, tell the personnelists and managers why you are seeking the job you are seeking. Do not wait for the interview to explain the situation because you might not even get an interview if your application is not clear.

To Explain Special Accommodations Needed for Disabilities

If you are a person with a disability, focus first on the skills, interests, objectives, and services you can provide to this organization. Then in a third section of the letter, write about the special accommodations you will need to perform at the highest level of your capability. For instance:

I would be an asset to your organization because:
[insert text here]

My relevant qualifications include:
[insert text here]

Special Accommodations:
I am a person with a 90-percent visual disability. In order to perform effectively in my position, I would simply need special software on the computer so that I could listen to my e-mail and other data. I have excellent health and hearing capabilities, so I am a high-performing employee with the exception of sight capability. I travel easily with a cane and learn quickly new physical environments. I have a positive attitude and am willing to work hard and learn new policies, procedures, and programs.

It is a personal decision whether to write about your disability in your initial application. But the hiring person and agency will need to make special accommodations to provide a position for you. The agencies do have resources to help them with special software, hardware, and physical accommodations so that you can be productive in a meaningful, well-paid position. You should talk with your State Rehabilitation Specialist and your family to decide how you should market your strengths and your special needs.

Public-service agencies have excellent job opportunities for all people—those with and without disabilities. But the hiring managers and personnel staff need to know your needed special accommodations to determine whether the job will work for your skills and abilities. I believe that if you are forthright, positive, informative, and honest about your capabilities, the agency will work with you to achieve a win-win job situation for you and them.

Draft Your Cover Letter

Your cover letter should start with an introductory paragraph stating your reason for writing the letter. For example:

I am submitting the enclosed resume as application for the position of Public Health Advisor with the National Safety Council.

This paragraph should be followed by two main sections. The first section starts with a phrase like this:

My relevant qualifications include:

In this section, you should highlight your relevant experience and education in a bulleted list. Make sure that you pay attention to the vacancy announcement. If you have the required qualifications as stated in the advertisement, repeat these qualifications here. Here's an example of this section:

My relevant qualifications include:

- Public Health Advisor at the National Institutes of Health, Centers for Disease Control and Prevention for 12 years, where I managed projects and provided consultation to private organizations and educational institutions; and through the media improved information on physical activity and nutrition.

- Expert in physical activity and nutrition issues including authoring curriculum, classroom text chapters, press releases, newsletters, grants, and training materials; as well as consulting with government, education, and nonprofit organizations.

- Successfully directed the first public-policy conference for public health graduate students and national forums on the importance of physical education to health and well-being.

- My education includes an M.S. in Health Promotion and Wellness from American University and a B.S. in Exercise Science with a concentration in Health Education from the University of Virginia.

The second section begins like this:

I would be an asset to your organization because:

Be persuasive here. You want to present a strong case that results in you getting a phone call inviting you for an interview. You want to make it to the "best qualified" list. Tell the reader why you would be very well qualified to work in this organization. Tell them what you know that will be useful to them. Here's an example of this section:

I would be an asset to your organization because:

- I am seeking new opportunities where I can use my knowledge of physical activity and nutrition issues gained from my years at the National Institutes of Health. I know that disseminating environmental and health information into the school systems is vital and challenging.
- I would like to get closer to the students and teachers in schools by writing, creating, and managing educational programs that will have an impact on environmental health through education.
- I believe that, with my research and government program knowledge, I can contribute extensively to the mission of the National Safety Council and the Council's focus on public-education programs and environmental health.

You then close with a short paragraph that provides a "call to action"—in this case, asking the reader to call you for an interview. Then you finish off the letter with your signature and an enclosure line.

I am available to meet with you to discuss your objectives and my background. You can contact me at either telephone number above. Thank you for your time and consideration. I look forward to your response.

Sincerely,

Helen R. Waters
Enclosures: Resume, Letter of Reference

Sample Cover Letters

This section provides several examples of full cover letters to accompany Federal resumes.

Law Enforcement Officer, GS-1811-9

Johnson Q. McKittrick
354 Hyattstown Boulevard
St. Louis, MO 63105
(314) 655-5578

February 27, XXXX

Director of Personnel
United States Secret Service
Law Enforcement Training Academy
Quantico, VA 22594

Dear Personnel Director:

This letter transmits my completed federal resume in response to your announcement of law enforcement officer positions, TREA/SS/1811/7-9, 98-345X. Thank you for your consideration of this application. I have dedicated my career preparation to law enforcement professions, and I am eager to build upon my military experience in your organization.

Let me direct your attention to my basic qualifications. After completing a bachelor's degree in the criminal justice program at the University of Missouri—St. Louis, I entered the U.S. Air Force and served a four-year enlistment as an Air Police Officer. I rose to the rank of sergeant (E-5) during those years and gained valuable street-level experience in law enforcement. I am fully dedicated to this profession.

In addition to the descriptions of my employment, I have included the following for your evaluation:

- A copy of my DD-214, indicating my service with the U.S. Air Force, and an honorable discharge, effective July 27, 1997. Part of this service included support of the U.S. Forces in Bosnia, which qualifies me for a five-point veterans' preference.

- A copy of the completion certificate from the Air Police Academy, reflecting previous training related to the position advertised.

- Five one-page statements responding to the knowledge, skills, abilities, and other factors identified on the job announcement.

Thank you for your consideration. I look forward to hearing from you.

Sincerely,

Johnson Q. McKittrick

Program Specialist, GS-343-12/13

MARISUE M. SWEETWATER

776 Horizon Terrace ▪ Lincoln, NE 67798 ▪ 555-555-5555 ▪ mmsweetwater@hotmail.com

May 22, XXXX
Federal Emergency Management Agency
500 C Street, SW, Room 1125
Washington, DC 20909
ATTN: Florence N. Smithson

Dear Ms. Smithson:

I am submitting this application for the position as a program specialist advertised in your announcement, FEMA-98-47326-MAJ. This announcement indicates that several positions will be filled in the GS-11-12-13 range. I would appreciate your consideration and believe that my education and experience make me qualified at the highest level.

This packet contains all information requested in the position announcement. I have included a complete Federal resume as requested in the announcement. Allow me to elaborate upon the knowledge, skills, and abilities identified there.

My knowledge of Federal, state, and local government operations has developed through both my education (a political science minor) and seven years of progressively responsible work for state and Federal agencies with interwoven responsibilities.

My knowledge of program analysis and evaluation also developed through college courses in business and economic analysis, policy evaluation, and mathematics. These skills were required in previous experiences at the GS-7 and GS-9 levels.

My ability to conduct research and develop reports is reflected in both a senior thesis, "The Legacy of Failure in Educational Policy," and in reports prepared in junior positions at the Department of Housing and Urban Development. One of these was cited by my current supervisor in proposing me for the Secretary's Award, which I won this year.

My recent responsibilities included service on an interagency task force that required evaluation of national security contingency plans. Members of the working group included representatives of state and local governments. My college studies included courses in American history, constitutional politics and law, and American politics (including a section on national security policy).

Thank you for your consideration, and I am eager to provide any additional information that you might need to evaluate this application.

Sincerely,

Marisue M. Sweetwater

Associate Director for Research, Applied Sciences, ES-1301

JOSEPH T. JOHNSON
147 Seven Locks Court ▪ Raleigh, North Carolina 28509
(919) 549-9876 ▪ jtjohnson@msn.com

April 10, XXXX

Office of Executive and Technical Resources
U.S. Department of Energy
ATTN: Robert W. Sherman
1000 Independence Avenue, SW
Washington, DC 20585

Dear Mr. Sherman:

Enclosed is my application responding to announcement #ERD-98-79, Associate Director for Research, Applied Sciences (ES-1301). This application contains the following:

A Federal resume highlighting my accomplishments in a Federal career that now spans more than 22 years. My current position, Director of Waste Disposal Technology Research for the Environmental Protection Agency's Air and Radiation Research Laboratory, demonstrates my ability to design and manage a program of the scope and complexity of the one envisioned in your announcement. In addition, my third previous position as Deputy Director of EPA's Office of Federal Facility Compliance required regular review of waste disposal plans developed by Department of Energy personnel. In that capacity, I assisted the approval process for several Environmental Impact Statements that would be relevant to the advertised position.

A summary of additional professional training relevant to this position. I earned my Ph.D. in mechanical engineering at Michigan State University and have more than ten years' experience directing major engineering research and development programs. These records also document my presentation of more than 50 technical papers at professional conferences including the American Physical Society, the American Academy for the Advancement of Science, and the Association of State and Territorial Air Pollution Control Officials. As the titles indicate, these papers include critical evaluations of current research and technology in the pollution control field that are especially relevant to the Department of Energy's nuclear disposal requirements.

Responses to the Executive Core Qualifications required for all members of the Senior Executive Service. As reflected on the enclosed Federal resume, my three most recent positions have involved increased complexity, supervisory responsibility, and budget authority, even though all have been graded at the GM-15 level. I am scheduled to complete the course of study at the Federal Executive Institute in May, which would provide additional demonstration of my SES capabilities prior to the anticipated starting date of this position.

(continues)

(continued)

Detailed statements addressing both the mandatory and optional qualifications announced in the advertisement. In all cases, my extensive experience is especially suited to the engineering and physical science technical requirements identified as vital to this position.

I have requested that Mr. Robert Quinones, who served as my supervisor in my immediate previous position, complete the required supervisory appraisal. He will forward the form under separate cover. As indicated on this Federal resume, I have not informed my current supervisor of my employment search, and I request that she should not be contacted until an offer is made.

A completed SF-181, Racial and National Origin Identification, as requested.

A copy of my DD-214, confirming three years of active duty in the United States Army and qualifying me for a five-point veterans' preference.

Thank you for your consideration. I will call your office in two weeks to confirm receipt of this material and to ascertain your procedures for evaluating applications and filling this position.

Sincerely,

Joseph T. Johnson

International Affairs Officer, GS-11

CHAGRI SADAT-FERRELL, Ph.D.
5610 Wisconsin Ave. #1501 • Chevy Chase, MD 20815
(301) 718-8333 • cs_ferrell@msn.com

July 10, xxxx

U.S. Department of Labor
200 Constitution Ave., NW
Washington, DC 20210
ATTN: Terri Copeland

Dear Ms. Copeland:

This letter transmits my application for the position **International Relations Officer, Announcement Number ILAB-03-046.** I believe my education and experience provide an excellent understanding and background for the position.

My academic training is extensive. I have just graduated in spring xxxx at the top of my class with a Ph.D. in International Affairs from the School of Foreign Service at the American University. This rigorous program prepared me well to work with individuals and organizations around the world. Prior to that, I completed an M.A. in International Affairs *Summa Cum Laude* from the Elliot School of International Affairs at the George Washington University. My bachelor's degree, *Magna Cum Laude,* is in English. I am an accomplished writer and public speaker in English as well as in other languages. My public school education was first-rate; I graduated with honors from an internationally renowned school in Geneva, Switzerland.

I speak, write, and read five languages fluently: English, French, Spanish, Farsi, and Arabic. I am an excellent translator and have substantive experience utilizing these languages to build and cement strong international client relationships. Throughout my graduate training, I was employed summers in international organizations, where I had the opportunity to work with clients with diverse social and cultural orientations. I have traveled the world, and have either resided in or visited Europe, the United States, Canada, the Middle East, South America, and Central America.

I find working in an international arena to be extremely stimulating. I have great sensitivity to and knowledge of international cultures, including customs, languages, foods, religions, and way of life. I derive great pleasure from communicating with individuals from different nations and cultures in their native languages. I am quick to establish rapport and trust. I am diplomatic and learn about people very quickly.

I wish very much to apply my training, experience, and skills to new challenges. Thank you for your consideration for this position. I look forward to hearing from you soon.

Sincerely,

CHAGRI SADAT-FERRELL

Technical Support Specialist—Customer Support, GS-2210-7/12

Robert L. Walker
8916 Datapoint
St. Paul, MN 78229
(651) 777-7777
robert_walker111@yahoo.com

June 14, xxxx

USDA, Marketing and Regulatory Programs (MRP)
Human Resources-Staffing
100 N. 6th Street, Suite 510C
Minneapolis, MN 55403-1588
Attn: Lisa Heath

Dear Ms. Heath:

Please find enclosed my resume for the position of **Information Technology Specialist-Customer Support, GS-2210-07/12, Announcement: 2462-2003-0017.**

My relevant qualifications include the following:
- I am an analytical, bilingual, creative, results-oriented professional with extensive desktop, hardware, and application support experience. Experiences include systems maintenance, management, and customer-oriented support; excellent communication skills with both technical and end-user communities; and extensive PC component installation, configuration, and troubleshooting skills.
- I have had the opportunity to work on a number of computer-related projects. I have been a part of several successful projects ranging from USAA to the University Health Systems, and most recently Brooks Army Medical Center. I have had excellent exposure to a variety of operating systems, hardware, and network connections.
- While working as a contracted computer consultant, I have been fortunate to have excellent exposure to a variety of operating systems, software, and hardware while perfecting the highest level of customer support.

I would be an asset to your organization because:
- I have attained a high level of knowledge and expertise while working on past projects with cross-cultural teams and customers.
- I have six years of past work-related experience, providing level I and II support in a large-organization enterprise environment.

Thank you for your time and consideration. I look forward to your response.

Sincerely,
Robert L. Walker

Legal Assistant (OA), GS-986-5

Debra Jasper
3256 Roxborough Ave.
Philadelphia, PA 33762
(727) 572-9054
(727) 560-6204
debrajasper696@hotmail.com

September 16, xxxx

U.S. Attorney's Office
615 Chestnut Street, Suite 1250
Philadelphia, PA 19106
Attn: Chris Atkinson, Human Resources Specialist

Dear M. Atkinson:

Please find enclosed my resume for the position of **Legal Assistant (OA), GS-986-5, Announcement Number 03-EDPA-06.**

My relevant qualifications include the following:

- Currently enrolled at St. Petersburg College in the Legal Assistant program studying Legal Research, Lexis/Nexus, Editing, and Document Management. I will graduate from this two-year program in May.

- Computer skills include: Microsoft Office 2000; MS Windows NT, 2000, and Me; MS Outlook; system back-ups and file-management practices.

- Typing skills of 12,000 ksph in Ten Key Data Entry; keyboard speed of 35 wpm and 9,500 ksph in Alphanumeric Data Entry.

I would be an asset to your organization because:

- I am a quick learner and eager to learn more about the law, especially in a government agency. I would like new opportunities to use my current knowledge and expand my knowledge of the law.

- I am available to meet with you to discuss your objectives and my background. You can contact me at either telephone number above.

Thank you for your time and consideration. I look forward to your response.

Sincerely,

Debra Jasper

Enclosures

Program Officer/Knowledge Exchange, GS-343-11/12

Akin A. Okun
30 E. Elm St., #3H
Linden, NJ 07036
(908) 486-7574
(973) 275-2976
akinaokun@hotmail.com

9/4/xx

U.S. Office of Personnel Management
ATTN: Vacancy Identification Number DD169306
DENVER SERVICE CENTER
P.O. BOX 25167
DENVER, CO 80225

Dear Human Resources Specialist:

Please find enclosed my resume for the position of **Program Analyst, GS-0343-11 /12, Announcement Number DD169306.**

My relevant qualifications include:

Grants and Budget Experience: Disseminating information on funding opportunities to Seton Hall University faculty members who wish to carry out research during their sabbatical leaves or simply to obtain research fellowships to further their professional careers.

Research and Project Experience: Administrative and research skills that increased my ability to work well in groups and solve complex problems, and improved my confidence in dealing with the public.

My educational background in International Affairs has provided knowledge and information on international programs, support, and financial lending plans.

I have a strong passion for and belief in the mission of the United States Agency for International Development for providing assistance to disadvantaged members of developing countries.

Thank you for your time and consideration. I look forward to your response.

Sincerely,

Akin A. Okun

Materials Handler, WG 6907-5/5

John T. Van Hassent
29784 Vincent Circle ▪ Mechanicsville, MD 20659
(301) 884-2612 ▪ (703) 883-6616
jtvanhassent@hotmail.com

9/3/xx

Ms. Maria Canales
VA Medical Center
2002 Holcombe Blvd.
Mechanicsburg, MD 77030

Dear Ms. Canales:

Please find enclosed my resume for the position of **Materials Handler, WG-6907-05/05, Announcement Number TA 35-03.**

For the past three years, I have worked as the Warehouse Manager, Work Control Manager, and most recently the Construction Field Superintendent for Johnson Controls, Inc., at the McLean, Virginia, site for the Mitre Corp.

For the previous two years, I was the Material Coordinator for Johnson Controls at the Naval Security Station in Washington, D.C.

Prior to that for approximately seven years, I was a buyer/warehouse lead at the Naval Air Station, Patuxent River, Maryland, and also for Johnson Controls.

I would be an asset to your organization because:

- I have a demonstrated leadership ability. I am self/task motivated. I believe in looking into what needs to be done and getting it accomplished.
- I am very familiar with database operations. I have used Access as well as Deltek and Maximo. I have used Microsoft Office and am familiar with creating reports from databases and spreadsheets.
- I come from a blue-collar background and can relate well to all levels of company staff. As I previously stated, I am task oriented and not afraid to "roll up my sleeves."
- I am a team player and believe in "cross-training." I am willing to "pitch in" wherever help is needed.

Thank you for your time and consideration. I look forward to your response.

Sincerely,

John T. Van Hassent

Enclosures

Claims Assistant, GS-0998-05/05

Jennifer Shimek

1826 First St. N.W. ◊ Rochester, MN 55901

(507) 529-5354 ◊ (507) 255-1799 ◊ shimek.jennifer@mayo.edu

08-23-xx

Department of Veterans Affairs
Delegated Examining Unit
P. O. Box 24269
Attn: Angela Verdick
Richmond, VA 23224-0269

Dear Ms. Verdick:

Please find enclosed my letter of interest for the position of **Claims Assistant, GS-0998-05/05, Announcement Number VAR-BA-3-1814.**

My relevant qualifications include:

Extensive experience setting up files for a number of different nurse managers and modeling them to match the personal preference of the requester. File subject matter varies from highly confidential medical information to clerical.

I am responsible for recording and maintaining the confidential data for the Patient Receiving Unit. The information that I enter is then prepared for statistical reports at the end of the year. This responsibility has minimal supervision.

I receive direction from many different people and areas, including nurse managers, nurse manager secretaries, administration, and research secretaries.

I am an effective team member assisting six different nurse managers daily. This is the key to coordinating patient and staff projects efficiently.

I would be an asset to your organization because:

The experience I have from my current position is excellent for the Claims Assistant position. I am a very outgoing person and have a strong desire to learn more and achieve new challenges and skills.

I work harmoniously and professionally with many people on a daily basis.

Thank you for your time and consideration. I look forward to your response.

Sincerely,

Jennifer Shimek

Summary

Your cover letter is optional, but as you can see from the samples, it is a great "cover" to your application. The important points you have to sell, present, and explain can be written in a few short paragraphs. If you have the time to write the cover letter, it could impress the selecting official or hiring panel.

Part 4

Resumes and Guidance for Specific Federal Careers

CHAPTER 16

Applying for the Senior Executive Service

In an effort to develop a corps of executive managers with the talent, foresight, and flexibility required to lead a soon-to-be-reformed Federal service through a new era, Congress, through enactment of the 1978 Civil Service Reform Act, created the Senior Executive Service (SES). Congress envisioned the SES as a cadre of exceptional leaders recruited from the top levels of government and private industry, who would move among agencies and share their broad backgrounds and experience to create new efficiencies and innovations government-wide.

Managerial experience gained solely in the Federal government would no longer be the most important criterion for gaining a senior position in an agency, nor would the "best qualified" new leader necessarily be the career civil servant who spent his entire career in one agency. The reality, however, is that the majority of SES positions continue to be filled by career civil servants. Nonetheless, it is remarkable that unlike virtually all other governments around the world, high-level professional positions within the United States government still remain open to those who have gained their experience outside the Federal civil service.

A Profile of the SES

The SES has changed in many ways during the past 20-plus years, but it is still the leadership cadre of the Federal service. Of the 6,600 members of the SES, 92 percent are career civil servants. The remainder are noncareer appointments (usually political) or appointments for a limited term. Almost half of SES positions are based in the Washington, D.C., metropolitan area. The composition of the SES reflects various Federal agencies' functional requirements. Forty-two percent are in administrative or management fields. Another 13 percent provide legal services. Engineering, science/math, and other fields each account for 12 to 14 percent. Twenty-five percent of the SES are women, and nearly 14 percent are minorities.

The first word of "Senior Executive Service" is appropriate: It *is* a senior service, with 30 percent of its membership eligible for retirement between now and 2005. Retirement remains the primary method of attrition in the SES.

Ten years ago, the National Performance Review formally recommended that the SES develop a "corporate perspective" that supports government-wide cultural change. This recommendation might have been a veiled acknowledgment that Congress's vision of the SES as a mobile corps of flexible executives had yet to be implemented in practice. Several years later, the Office of Personnel Management revised the Executive Core Qualifications (known as ECQs, listed later in this chapter), which are the five main rating factors used to evaluate an SES candidate's "corporate perspective." The OPM currently has no plans to modify these ECQs, which is a reflection of the OPM's commitment to guide the SES toward the model originally envisioned by Congress.

The Changing Competition for SES Positions

Competition for SES positions will become more intense in the next 10 years. It is not unusual for HR professionals to report receiving 55 to 60 applications for each SES announcement. Not only are numerous baby boomers seeking the promotions that will cap careers that began in the late 1960s, but agencies reduced the number of SES positions during the mid-to-late 1990s as a result of the National Partnership for Reinventing Government—the successor to the National Performance Review.

Most SES reductions were achieved by cuts in the Department of Defense (closures of major installations resulted in many workforce cuts) or by eliminating positions that were on the books but had not been filled. In other instances, agencies eliminated one position only to create another—redesigning jobs to align with "reinvention" initiatives. Such restructuring, however, tended to be at the margins of the SES. Most executive positions lead core agency programs that would require statutory changes to modify or eliminate. In an era of divided government, such changes are difficult to effect.

Who Should Apply?

In most cases, new SES members rise through career-development ladders within single agencies or departments. They might serve within different agency components during their careers, but the Federal service generally still adheres to the principle of advancement within a profession. A new SES manager in the

Environmental Protection Agency's water program, for example, is more likely to come from within that program than from any other program in the EPA. Although most agencies have SES attorneys, an immigration law attorney is unlikely to transfer into an SES position in the antitrust division at the Department of Justice. Demonstrating relevant skills is the surest route to entering the SES, and that is usually done most credibly at the agency where the position will be filled.

There is no substitute for substantial experience. Entrants who rise through career ranks to the SES frequently have 15, 20, or even 30 years of experience, most of which was gained within their own agencies. They typically have at least a college education, and frequently possess graduate degrees and other forms of professional development training. Many will be identified and nurtured—or mentored—through their agency's SES candidate-development programs or through other well-recognized channels, such as the Federal Executive Institute and the Women's Executive Leadership Program. Their experiences will include broadening through a number of detail assignments at other agencies. Nearly all successful SES applicants will have a succession of outstanding performance evaluations and demonstrate a record of developing other people to ensure that their organizations continue to work well in their successors' hands. In addition to this sustained superior performance, it usually helps to have pulled one or two major projects out of the fire under emergency or adverse circumstances.

An important dimension of an SES application, as with most Federal positions, responds to the question, "What have you done lately?" Federal personnel officers and selecting officials are looking for progressively responsible performance at or near the level for which one is applying. Typically, the SES applicant will be able to describe five to seven years of experience at the GS- or GM-15 level.

Successful SES applicants must demonstrate an ability to think at least two bureaucratic levels above the advertised position. An SES appointment usually requires the approval of an agency head, so a Senior Executive applicant must be able to speak that executive's language.

An SES opening in any agency signals some organizational change—maybe an experienced executive is retiring or agency leaders are creating a new position to address a perceived problem. Knowing the agency and its needs is critically important. You can strengthen your SES application if you know what the agency leadership believes its problems to be and can demonstrate that you have the experience to tackle those issues. You need not be an insider to gain familiarity with an agency's mission and requirements; however, you bear the burden of demonstrating that the experience and knowledge you gained elsewhere provide enough background for you to perform effectively.

Finally, senior executives at or above the SES job level being filled usually rate SES applicants. You will be a stronger candidate if these executives already know you and are familiar with your significant accomplishments, and if you effectively represent these accomplishments in your ECQ statements.

If the preceding description fits you, consider applying for the SES. Vacancies for SES positions are listed on the www.USAJOBS.opm.gov Web site. The vacancy list is updated regularly. Many individual agencies also advertise SES positions on their Web sites.

If you are already a member of the SES, an SES reinstatement eligible, or an OPM-Certified Candidate Development Program graduate and are looking for new job challenges, visit the OPM's Senior Opportunity and Resume Systems Web site (SOARS). This site is an online exchange between government agencies seeking to recruit candidates for SES jobs, and SES members who are interested in new opportuni-

ties. Agencies can post their SES vacancy notices on the site and read SES candidates' resumes. SES candidates can post their resumes and view other agencies' vacancy notices. This system offers SES candidates and recruiting agencies an additional opportunity to review their options outside the formal recruiting and staffing process.

Requirements for Successful Applicants: Remember the Basics

As you begin to develop your SES package, keep in mind that, regardless of the Federal agency to which you apply, staffing an executive position is much more complex than staffing other types of Federal jobs. Because of the high visibility and broad impact to the agency, nearly all SES selections require agency-level approval. Before you can even hope to get an interview, your application must survive the initial and secondary screening phases it will pass through in the agency's HR office. One seasoned HR professional who has staffed many SES jobs and has reviewed hundreds of applications offers the following advice to those applying from both within and outside the government.

Read and Follow the Instructions

Follow the application instructions. As obvious as this might seem, an appalling number of applicants are eliminated at the initial screening phase because they simply fail to submit the required documents.

"We received 55 applications for our agency's SES General Counsel position last year," our HR professional reports. "Of those 55, over half were eliminated because they did not submit proof that they were licensed to practice before a state bar—even though the announcement stated clearly that applicants who did not submit such documentation would receive no further consideration."

If you're an attorney applicant with many years of service, you might think such a requirement is unnecessary, or perhaps even nitpicky: After all, you've worked as a civil-service attorney for 30 years. Surely the personnel office "knows" you're licensed to practice before a state bar. Or, at worst, if they don't have record of this, surely the personnel office will call you or your agency's personnel office and ask for it. Remember this: Forty to sixty candidates are applying for only one job. It is an enormous task for the HR specialist to review these applications and whittle them down to a manageable number of candidates for senior managers to interview. If you fail to include the information required in the vacancy notice, it is an easy way for them to disqualify you from further consideration. Don't let this be you. Follow the application instructions to the letter.

Make the Length "Just Right"

Think Goldilocks. Or maybe Procrustes (the mythological host who adjusted his guests to the size of the bed). Make sure the length and substance of each document in the package is neither too long nor too short. "Internal applicants tend to submit way too much information," our HR advisor says. "They've been with the government a long time and think they have to include everything they've done since they were a GS-5." On the contrary, statements should describe experience that is directly relevant and closely focused to the job requirements. "On the other hand," our advisor continues, "external candidates tend to submit only one-page resumes, often with no cover letter, and seem to feel we are lucky to get even that."

The SES selection process, a very daunting one even for internal candidates who are familiar with lengthy staffing procedures, is often incomprehensible to external candidates. "The government loses a lot of good talent because of the process," our advisor notes. "They simply get frustrated and go away. OPM is working on streamlining the process, so we hope it will get better." In the meantime, external candidates must take the time to describe their experience in-depth and explain how it relates to the vacant position. Otherwise, HR professionals simply will not have enough information to determine that an external candidate is highly qualified for the job.

Balance the Strengths and Weaknesses of Your Background

Both internal and external candidates need to balance the inherent strengths and weaknesses of coming from either a Federal or private-sector background. To be effective as a senior leader, SES positions require a mix of both worlds: Candidates must know the internal workings of government systems—how the bureaucracy works—but they also must have the ability to bring new ideas and approaches to the agency.

What Does the SES Announcement Require?

The normal SES package contains a cover letter (see chapter 15), a strong Federal resume (study parts 1 and 2), special statements addressing as many as three sets of technical and managerial factors listed in the vacancy notice, and most importantly, statements showing that the candidate possesses the five Executive Core Qualifications (ECQs) established by the OPM—the managerial skills that are the prerequisites for entry into the SES. Unless the resume and the statements demonstrate that you possess the Executive Core Qualifications, even exceptional technical qualifications will not be enough to develop a successful SES application.

The five Executive Core Qualifications (ECQs) are as follows:

★ Leading Change

★ Leading People

★ Results Driven

★ Business Acumen

★ Building Coalitions/Communication

In addition to the five ECQs, each agency can define both mandatory and desirable technical qualifications for any SES position advertised. These qualifications vary according to the position. For example, an applicant for Assistant Administrator of the Federal Aviation Administration for airway facilities must be able to demonstrate professional knowledge of the design and engineering of radio navigational systems. Firsthand flying experience using this system might strengthen those qualifications, but that would be a desirable, rather than a mandatory, technical requirement.

Nearly one-third of SES applications are rejected for not describing the advertised qualifications for the position. Of the remaining two-thirds, the quality of the ECQ statements determines who will be grouped among the "well qualified," and ultimately, who will gain interviews for the position. It is not unusual for agencies to report a final list of only 3 to 12 "well qualified" candidates from a pool of 60 applicants. With competition this intense, your core qualifications statements must stand above the crowd.

Are All ECQs Created Equal?

A frequently asked question we receive from SES candidates is "Are some ECQs more important than others?" In a recent government-wide survey, the OPM asked career senior executives how the ECQs ranked in order of importance to their current Federal jobs. The majority responded as follows:

1. Leading People
2. Building Coalitions/Communication
3. Results Driven
4. Leading Change
5. Technical Competence
6. Business Acumen

These results confirm that communications and "people skills" continue to be the most important characteristics required of senior leaders in the Federal service. The survey went on to conclude that Business Acumen was also emerging as a more desirable characteristic of future government leaders.

The core qualifications demand more than managerial experience. A candidate must demonstrate keen business acumen, the ability to foresee and overcome challenges to successfully lead change, and the ability to gain others' support and cooperation to reach results. It is not enough to discuss the duties of positions you have held or to make conclusory statements that you have managed large staffs or held jobs that gave you these abilities. You must provide concrete examples of the problems you faced, how you solved them, and how your effort improved the organization. As one personnel officer responsible for SES positions commented, "I want to know not merely what the applicant claims to have done; I need to know when and where it was done to make the case credible." In short, to be a successful SES applicant, you must master the art of writing powerful ECQs. Let's get started!

Writing Executive Core Qualifications

Writing Executive Core Qualification statements is like writing KSAs for other types of Federal jobs. Unlike the KSA statements, however, the ECQs are exactly the same government-wide. Consequently, the statements will be applicable to virtually any SES position for which you apply. Although writing and polishing the statements require significant time and effort, your initial investment will pay off, particularly if you apply for more than one vacancy.

Writing ECQs is no different from any other writing challenge: Well-written material that keeps the reader's interest gets more attention than sleeper prose. Still, the challenge of consolidating 20 years of accomplishments into five pages is significant—especially if you have had too many successes to fit in the allotted space.

Basic Principles

Here are some basic principles that will help you write successful ECQ statements:

1. **The basics of effective writing still apply.** Use the active voice. Your responses must convey what you did and what difference it made. Avoid passive constructions and bureaucratic phrasing: Say "I decided and directed" instead of "I was given responsibility for."

2. **Demonstrate the application of your knowledge.** Whereas KSAs require you to state what you know (knowledge) and what you have done or can do (skills and abilities), Executive Core Qualifications require you to demonstrate effective *application* of what you know. Effective statements require more than an explanation of your personal growth. In each ECQ, describe the effects you and your work have had on other people, other organizations, and agency policies. If you have held a job that required interagency coordination, bring it to the evaluators' attention.

3. **Demonstrate executive performance.** This is not the place to write about how you gained your skills. Many of the KSA statements written for lower-level positions are effective because they show "progressive responsibility"—that is, they describe how increasingly complex work assignments prepared them for the next job up the ladder. The SES needs people who can demonstrate through what they have already done that they are in a position to take charge *now*. Well-qualified applicants must be able to describe how they used or obtained available resources to bring about significant changes or accomplishments while heading agency programs. In addition, OPM suggests explaining how recent education or training enhanced your skills in particular factors. If you mention education or training courses, detail work assignments, or other skills-enhancement efforts, make the link specific and stress the recentness of the information or experience gained.

4. **What have you done for me lately?** The SES needs people who are ready to lead in today's environment. Use recent examples as much as possible. Examples within the past three years are fine, but if you have to go back more than five years, the achievement must be spectacular. If an applicant's responses to Executive Core Qualifications dwell on accomplishments at the GM-13 level, the description will be less favorably received than comparable accomplishments at the GM-15 level.

Helpful Hints for Developing ECQs

Executive Core Qualifications are most effective if they are consistent continuations of the resume and any other documents in the application package. They should summarize—concisely—a record that demonstrates that you are ready for SES responsibilities. Effective statements of the Executive Core Qualifications combine breadth of accomplishments, a record of supervising other people in the successful completion of substantial tasks, and a record of applying current skills and training to challenging circumstances.

In describing your achievements, try to give different examples for each of the ECQs. A candidate with a true likelihood of success will have numerous achievements in each category. As you sift through your experience, you must ask yourself, "Will this example will be a better illustration of Leading People, Results Driven, or Building Coalitions/Communications?" Review the core qualifications as a group, sort through your resume and supporting notes, and make the hard choices about where your achievements best fit into the factors.

Remember that most SES applications are reviewed by agency Executive Resources Boards, whose members are familiar with your accomplishments and the conditions facing the agency at the time. Your responses need to remind people of these achievements in a credible, consistent way.

---

5. **Be concise.** The OPM seeks one to one-and-a-half pages for each qualifications statement. You are writing executive summaries, not autobiographies. If you need more than one page, make certain that every word is important to convey your full leadership abilities. As much as possible, avoid repetition and use different achievements for each of the ECQ statements.

6. **Be specific.** Use precise numbers to describe budget, personnel, dates (time frame), and other factors. Avoid the "various," "numerous," and "several" quantifiers that make people guess about how much. You need to show that you are familiar

with the results and how they were achieved so that your reader can understand the environment you were working in and the significance of the accomplishment.

7. **Keep the scanner in mind.** Some automated resume scanners are programmed to read nouns that identify key skills. If you believe that an SES package might have to pass through a scanner, use more nouns and skill categories than you might otherwise include. See chapter 12 for details on writing a scannable resume.

Here's an example of a nonscannable Profile statement from a Federal resume:

PROFILE:

Senior program manager with 20-year background creating and managing innovative, cost-effective large-scale and long-term programs. Extensive governmental reengineering and streamlining experience. Strong strategic sense with the ability to balance short-term priorities against long-term organizational mission and goals. Excellent communication, leadership, and negotiation skills. National network of professional contacts in and out of government.

Here's a scannable Profile statement with emphasis on the nouns and key skills the scanner would search for in a senior government executive:

PROFILE:

Senior Program Manager. Reengineer. Innovator. Strategist. Communicator, Negotiator, Connected. Mission Planner. Leader. Cost Analyst. Budget Manager. Sets goals, priorities. Organizational representative with government and industry.

Use the OPM's Recommended Format

The OPM recommends that SES applicants use a structured format to address each Executive Core Qualification factor. Using this format helps candidates focus the relevancy and impact of their own experiences on the five ECQs all agencies expect their senior leaders to bring to the table. The format is known by the acronym *CCAR*, which stands for

- ★ Challenge
- ★ Context
- ★ Actions
- ★ Result

Let's analyze the components of this format to learn the best way to write your ECQs.

Challenge

What was the specific problem you faced that needed to be resolved?

- ★ The problem should have existed at a large organizational level, with agency-wide, government-wide, or national effects.
- ★ Resolution of the problem should have required more than one individual's actions. Leadership means, at minimum, that you have the ability to get other people to follow when you set direction.

Context

Define the other factors or limitations (people, institutions, procedures) that made the challenge of executive caliber.

- ★ The problem should require redefinition of goals, changes in conditions, or the need to persuade other people/organizations to comply with your changed direction.
- ★ Be specific about factors that made the challenge substantial: resources, people, laws, regulations, deadlines, and complexity.

Actions

What did you do that made a difference?

- ★ Express your achievement in a team environment, but focus on your leadership role with the team.

Result

What difference did it make?

- ★ Performance and accountability are the key factors. Your participation must be seen as the critical factor in realizing some goal or action that someone else wanted and/or needed done.

As we take an in-depth look at the five ECQs, keep the CCAR format in mind. The format will prompt you to write about specific results instead of citing general information about job responsibilities.

The Anatomy of an ECQ

Now that you're familiar with the fundamentals of writing the ECQs, let's take an in-depth look at the five ECQs and the specific types of information you should include in the statements.

ECQ 1: Leading Change

> The ability to develop and implement an organizational vision that integrates key national and program goals, priorities, values, and other factors. Inherent to it is the ability to balance change and continuity—to continually strive to improve customer service and program performance within the basic government framework; to create a work environment that encourages creative thinking; and to maintain focus, intensity, and persistence, even under adversity.

Your *Leading Change* statement needs to articulate an understanding of the mission and vision of the organization that you have led. Think up the organizational ladder. Describe your achievements in terms of how the head of the agency would have seen the challenge and why it should have been considered important.

If you have participated in a major transformation of an organization—for example, taking a nuclear weapons program from a production focus to an environmental clean-up mission—this is the time to highlight your account of how you achieved the change.

Emphasize the continuity factor here. It is important to realize that sometimes missions change even when authorizing laws and regulations stay the same. Convey the scope of the challenge and describe your role in transforming the organization.

Sub-factors of the *Leading Change* ECQ are the following:

★ **Continual Learning:** Have you acquired recent education, training, or interagency assignments that have helped you lead change? How did you apply that newly acquired knowledge?

★ **Creativity/Innovation:** Have you implemented a new way to solve an old problem?

★ **External Awareness:** What is or was happening outside your agency that affected your programs, or how did your agency's programs affect others, and what did you do to improve the situation?

★ **Flexibility:** Did you identify and work different options to reach a desired result? Was it possible to use one authority versus another to get around a longstanding problem?

★ **Resilience:** Did you overcome obstacle after obstacle to change an agency policy, program, or operating procedure?

★ **Service Motivation:** Did you identify a problem and take responsibility for doing whatever needed to be done to solve it?

★ **Strategic Thinking:** Did you develop and execute a long-range plan to improve the agency?

★ **Vision:** Did you predict a cause-and-effect situation and then act to take advantage of changing circumstances? Or, did you propose and then implement a change?

The questions attached to each of these sub-factors are not the only way to address the ECQs; they are just examples to get you thinking about how you can describe what you've done to lead a substantive change in your agency.

ECQ 2: Leading People

The ability to design and implement strategies that maximize employee potential and foster high ethical standards in meeting the organization's vision, mission, and goals.

Leading people includes supervisory responsibilities—but you should express these in terms of coaching, mentoring, and motivating for success. Stress good communication skills, the ability to convey instructions, the ability to delegate responsibilities, and your success in planning for the professional career development of your subordinates.

Working across organizations is vital. Your ability to reach out, gain the support of other organizations, integrate the working of other managers, and represent your organization is critical. Your description of this ECQ should signal the reader to expect a strong statement about coalition building in the fifth ECQ factor.

Workforce diversity is part of the *Leading People* factor. Government requires an ability to work with all races, creeds, sexes, colors, religions, and nationalities. This factor should affirm a solid commitment to the professional development of women and minorities, describe affirmative employment achievements, and discuss overcoming challenges in this arena. Recruiting and retaining highly qualified people is one dimension of the presentation. Demonstrating your ability to train other team members who are highly regarded in the organization is also a big help.

Diversity also should highlight the need to integrate a complex range of professional skills. Scientific, human resources, legal, public affairs, and other talents need to be melded to achieve complex missions. If you are a mathematician, how did you get your public affairs office to understand the importance of what you accomplished? If your skill is legal, how did you develop a mastery of the technology that your agency uses?

Sub-factors of the *Leading People* ECQ are the following:

★ **Conflict Management:** Have you effectively resolved conflicts between working groups, either within or outside your organization? What happened to cause the conflict, and how did you resolve it?

★ **Leveraging Diversity:** Have you used the diverse makeup of your staff to understand the perspective and needs of both your incumbent work force and the customer base the agency is designed to serve?

★ **Integrity/Honesty:** Have you and your organization's dealings with others resulted in high credibility for the agency's programs?

★ **Team Building:** Have you been able to foster trust and support among staff members to achieve a better program?

ECQ 3: Results Driven

Stresses accountability and continuous improvement. It includes the ability to make timely and effective decisions and produce results through strategic planning and implementation and evaluation of programs and policies.

This factor relies on presenting strong numerical achievements. When possible, cite before-and-after data. In defining challenges, use performance indicators that were considered unsatisfactory (that is, things you had to change). When describing results, compare the differences and describe the resources that you brought to bear to make a difference.

You don't need to base changes solely on program results; they also can be brought about in terms of context. If your actions built alliances, strengthened relationships, or overcame resistance, that too is a result.

Mention successes during organizational changes—for example, sustaining productivity despite reduced resources. Mention policies and procedures you developed to incorporate new assignments while sustaining the organization's current productivity.

Describe methods you developed to define nonessential factors and reduce or eliminate bureaucracy while sustaining results. For example, if OSHA currently measures an agency's performance by how well it complies with rules, and you are successful in changing that approach to now measuring agencies in terms of reductions in accident rates or reductions in time lost due to illness and injury, you should highlight this change in focus here.

What changes or processes did you institute—for example, monitoring mechanisms—to identify future opportunities for improvement and to provide incentives to sustain improved performance? What measures did you take to correct performance problems that preceded your leadership?

Sub-factors of the *Results Driven* ECQ are the following:

★ **Accountability:** What did you do to ensure that performance or outcomes could be measured or quantified? What happened?

★ **Customer Service:** How did you improve it?

★ **Decisiveness:** Were you forced to make a difficult decision? How did you decide which option was best? What happened as a result of taking that approach versus another?

★ **Entrepreneurship:** How have you shown your ability to make smart business decisions?

★ **Problem Solving:** What was the problem and how did you resolve it? If various solutions were possible, don't forget to discuss why you used the approach you selected and why the outcome using this particular approach was superior.

★ **Technical Credibility:** Why did this particular result work better than other alternatives? Did the solution help give customers confidence in your program or agency?

ECQ 4: Business Acumen

Involves the ability to acquire and administer human, financial, material, and information resources in a manner that instills public trust and accomplishes the organization's mission, and to use new technology to enhance decision-making.

Highlight budget data, numbers of people, size of the constituency served, and methods of reducing costs/increasing efficiency here. You should also discuss your familiarity with procedures for establishing and justifying budgets, securing resources, and managing finances.

Demonstrate the effective use of information technology for your activities. The critical factors here are not the abilities to use word processors and spreadsheets, but to define System Development Life Cycle strategies and other factors associated with the acquisition and management of technology resources. The Executive Review Board must be able to see that you know how to apply information technology to the design and management of the organization that you will supervise.

If you have corrected major administrative weaknesses—financial management and accounting procedures, security deficiencies, or potential vulnerabilities of organizations—this is the place to discuss those achievements.

Sub-factors of the *Business Acumen* ECQ are the following:

★ **Financial Management:** Have you managed large program budgets to reach agency goals?

★ **Human Resources:** Have you reorganized or restructured your human resources to better the organization and the services it provides to customers?

★ **Technology Management:** How have you applied information technology to the design and management of your organization?

ECQ 5: Building Coalitions/Communication

> The ability to explain, advocate, and express facts and ideas in a convincing manner, and negotiate with individuals and groups internally and externally. It also involves the ability to develop an expansive professional network with other organizations and to identify the internal and external politics that impact the work of the organization.

Just as the *Leading People* factor addresses your ability to communicate down the organizational chart, this one emphasizes your ability to reach out to other organizations. This factor should highlight your ability to work with nongovernmental organizations, the media, professional associations, and at least other substantial organizations within your agency.

Written and oral communications are both required here. The question should not focus on your ability to write, but on your ability to set direction for others who will draft the correspondence, memoranda, speeches, and other material.

Working on interagency committees and coordinating multi-agency policy development and reporting groups are examples of achievements that you should describe in this factor. Effecting change might require bringing other agencies' perspectives back to your organization and winning support for something that serves the public interest, even if it generates resistance within the agency.

This factor asks you to convey that you are in charge of an organization and that you can convince others that your agency's positions on critical issues are well based. If you have testified before Congress or other legislatures, have spoken to state and local governments, or have represented the U.S. on international working groups, these are the experiences to include here. Again, the focus needs to be on the results that were realized from your efforts.

Sub-factors for the *Building Coalitions/ Communication* ECQ are the following:

★ **Influencing/negotiating:** How were you able to bring together two or more factions to reach a mutually acceptable resolution to a problem?

★ **Interpersonal skills:** How has your ability to relate to diverse groups with diverse needs impacted the organization?

★ **Oral communications:** Have you delivered presentations to high-level audiences both within and outside the organization?

★ **Partnering:** Have you been able to establish solid working relationships with groups that might have been at odds with your organization or agency?

★ **Political savvy:** Were you able to broker a desired outcome or make your organization look good in the face of a potentially nasty outcome?

★ **Written communications:** How have you effectively managed your organization's official communications?

Sample ECQ Statements

The following pages contain samples of core qualifications statements developed for various jobs. Some are actual statements taken verbatim from SES applicants. Others are composites of various statements. Study these samples to get an idea of how to compose your ECQs.

Two Examples in the CCAR Format

You will notice in the first two examples that the statements are broken out into the CCAR format. The later examples, however, drop the specific "challenge-context-actions-result" labels. They flow as one narrative describing the challenge the candidate faced within a limiting context and the action(s) the candidate took to reach the desired results.

As you are first learning to write the ECQ statements, it might help you to organize and label the information under each of these specific CCAR headings. After you work and re-work the material into polished narratives, however, the format will come to mind automatically and you will no longer need the CCAR "training wheels." The final product should resemble the last two examples at the end of this chapter.

ECQ 1: Leading Change
or
ECQ 3: Results Driven

This is an example of an accomplishment that could be categorized under either the *Leading Change* or the *Results Driven* ECQ. Which category do you think it fits best? The answer might depend on the resume, the technical qualifications statements, or other types of accomplishments the candidate plans to use in the application package. The answer might also depend on the problems or perceived problems the senior leaders in this specific agency will expect the selectee to address: Does this program already operate behind the power curve and need leadership to bring it up to speed, or have agency plans been in place for several years and now agency leaders need to see results? This is where knowing the agency and its needs is critical.

[BRIEF INTRO]: I led major organizational changes to improve the agency's performance in meeting its EEO and Civil Rights goals.

[CONTEXT]: As Branch Chief for Equal Opportunity and Civil Rights, National Institutes of Health,

[CHALLENGE]: I discovered that the agency needed to establish the parameters for, design, and implement a comprehensive study of the agency-wide affirmative-action program.

[RESULT]: Within six months, I was able to develop a multiyear employment plan for the central (headquarters) EEO Office.

[Action 1]: I directed a staff of six specialists to elicit and analyze information from 22 component organizations that comprised the National Institutes of Health. The information was consolidated into a comprehensive document, which outlined a long-range plan for increasing minority representation by 10% within a five-year period. I presented this plan to key agency officials, who approved the plan and submitted it without changes to the Public Health Service for implementation.

[ACTION 2]: In carrying out this project, I established strong and compatible working relationships with agency managers and staff in the 22 components (Personnel, EEO, and Executive Officers in each component). *(Provide specific examples of what you did to establish these relationships.)*

[ACTION 3]: I also led a similar effort for the preeminent Biomedical Research Institution, garnering the respect of key management officials in the agency, the Public Health Service, and the Department of Health and Human Services.

[RESULT]: As a result, the agency established a series of employment objectives for a five-year period between xxxx and xxxx. During the first two years of the plan, employment of women and minorities rose 6% agency-wide.

[RESULT]: As senior agency leadership continued to emphasize the importance of affirmative action and hold the 22 components accountable through interim assessments and annual evaluations, the NIH was lauded by the OPM for its successes and has since served as a model for the rest of the department.

[RECOGNITION]: As a result of my efforts, I received the Public Health Service's EEO Special Achievement Award.

ECQ 2: Leading People

This candidate used specific percentages to support her results statements. Anytime you can quantify the outcome of your efforts, it will strengthen your credibility with the reader and make you stand out over other applicants who claim their actions resulted in non-specific "overall improvements."

[INTRO]: Throughout my career, I have recognized the value of motivating and rewarding employees. For the past 15 years, I have developed performance plans, training plans, professional development plans, and counseling; taken disciplinary actions; worked with unions; and hired and promoted employees.

[CONTEXT]: As the Director of the Office of Affirmative Action and Human Resources Special Programs, Library of Congress, my initial assignment was to

[CHALLENGE]: completely restructure and refocus the entire organization. I was advised that the organization was not productive, lacked skills, and had low morale.

[ACTION]: I developed a plan to identify the organization's resources and needs, analyze the work flow, increase productivity, improve service, enhance communication, and improve morale. My challenge was to get the staff to buy into the study and contribute to its development.

I worked hard to get the staff involved. Using positive feedback and active listening techniques, I was able to establish good rapport with all staff members and get them to buy into the process fully. Together we identified specific staff responsibilities. I worked with staff to increase their understanding of the tangible benefits of an organizational assessment. For example, I was able to persuade each staff member that assessing individual and overall program responsibilities and resources would provide critical information for future budget requests.

[RESULTS]: I was able to complete the study and achieve major organizational changes within three months. The major changes were I (1) established an automated work-flow analysis and tracking system to manage, measure, and monitor responses to requests; (2) strengthened internal communications by establishing regular staff meetings; (3) strengthened external communications by providing monthly briefings on programs and activities to clients and agency leadership; (4) developed an interactive, dynamic Web site to further communicate goals and

(continues)

(continued)

advertise accomplishments; (5) promoted team-building activities to strengthen group cohesiveness and maximize organizational resources; (6) trained staff in their new responsibilities and arranged for cross-training to enhance flexibility and mobility; and (7) established production standards and submitted staffing proposals to supplement existing resources.

[RESULTS]: Over a two-year period, and based on documented surveys and feedback I received, I measured a 65% improvement in service to clients. My staff exceeded the established production standards by 25% in all critical functional areas. As a result, morale went up, customer service improved, and I was able to regain our organization's credibility with our agency's senior managers.

The Author's Own Leading Change ECQ

Coming from private industry and wondering how to compete with Federal applicants on the ECQs? Here's an example of the "Leading Change" ECQ from my own experience. Can you see the CCAR format in this writeup?

Leading Change

My track record as a leader of change and an innovator is characterized by one success story after another. I have a reputation as an entrepreneur who thinks "outside the box." Consequently, my thought process as I approach a problem is guided by creativity and strategic vision. During my three decades as a successful change agent, I have eagerly accepted challenges—often working with large Federal organizations that required substantial change in their human resources processes. In this regard, I am one of the few private innovators who can truthfully boast that I have brought about change in the Federal personnel system *from the outside!*

As a small-business owner specializing in Federal careers with an emphasis on writing and word processing the long, verbose, cumbersome, and unflattering SF-171s, I was prepared to take on the challenge of making the Federal application process better. Consequently, when the door opened to significant change in the mid-1990s, I was thrilled with the news and was anxious to see what the new resume would look like. To place my challenge into its proper context, what opened the door to change was when, in 1995, Vice President Gore and his reinvention of government organization, National Performance Review (NPR), enacted an important piece of Federal personnel legislation. One of the by-products of this legislation was that resumes would be accepted in government, and the badly outdated Standard Form 171 (SF-171) would be eliminated. In light of this critical legislative step forward, I took the following actions:

- I spoke with personnel expert Betty Waters at the United States Department of Agriculture (USDA), who was on the panel that determined that resumes would be accepted. She told me that the panel had authorized the development of a small brochure with printed guidelines for the new resume, the Optional Form 510, or OF-510. Although this brochure would affect almost 2 million Federal employees and their careers, it would NOT contain a sample format for the new resume.

- I met with Dick Whitford, Director of Employment Information Services at the Office of Personnel Management (OPM), to discuss the format of the new "Federal resume." He had no specific ideas as to how the resume should be formatted and presented. I then waited for the OPM to create a style guide, or manual, for employees to follow. Nothing was forthcoming.

- As an expert in the "old style" Federal application process (i.e., SF-171s), I decided to take matters into my own hands and design a "user-friendly" model of the Federal resume that would meet the required OF-510 guidelines referred to above. I wasted no time in setting up interviews with Federal human resources experts concerning their preferences for the new Federal resume. I compared the SF-171 and the instructions in the Optional Form 612 (OF-612) with the conventions of a standard private-sector resume and designed the new resume for the Federal government. This new Federal resume would be different from the private-industry resume in that it would be longer, include more details, and have a consistent, conservative chronological format. This consistent style would please Federal human resources professionals, who were accustomed to systematic forms that contained a great deal of "regulatory compliance" information.

- After I developed the first Federal resume format, I proceeded to write a book to support my theories about the new Federal resume, along with its features and benefits. The book included 10 hard-copy samples as well as a cutting-edge PC disk, with Word samples/templates. I mortgaged my house for $50,000 to finance publication of the first 5,000 copies of my 250-page book in July 1995. The copies sold in two years (despite severe Federal cutbacks and two separate government furloughs during the same time period). I subsequently negotiated a publishing agreement with JIST Publishing of Indianapolis, a successful career book publisher. The book, entitled *Federal Resume Guidebook,* is now utilized in human resources offices, libraries, and career centers throughout the U.S. to help job seekers apply for Federal jobs. JIST will publish the third edition in 2003.

As a direct result of my initiative, I brought about a major change in a critical Federal process that Federal insiders were essentially unable to achieve. Specifically, the large and cumbersome Federal human resources bureaucracy saw the need for major change in hiring practices when the Clinton/Gore administration announced the National Performance Review. But, despite their awareness of the need for rapid systemic change, they were unable to act quickly from "within" the system. In contrast, my entrepreneurship and desire to help Federal employees write their first Federal resumes enabled me to move out and develop the process that is used across the Federal government today. I am now recognized as the pioneer designer of the Federal resume throughout government, including the Office of Personnel Management, Federal human resources offices, career centers, and training offices. I am introduced in a variety of forums as the "Federal resume guru," and am regularly hired as a "sole-source trainer" in more than 100 government agencies. Since 1995, I have written six books on the subject and have been published or quoted in more than 150 national newspapers, Web sites, and columns. I am interviewed on radio stations more than 200 times per year and travel extensively in the U.S. and Europe, conducting training on the subject of Federal resume writing. Finally, I am now a keynote speaker for Federal training; professional associations on careers, resume writing, and training; and human resources recruitment conventions.

Thousands of Federal employees and first-time applicants have now gained the confidence as well as the tools to write consistent Federal-style resumes to apply for jobs as a result of my books, training, and media presence. In recognition of the outstanding results of my innovative approach, countless Federal human resources experts now see me as an unofficial government spokesperson for recruitment and Federal jobs. My ability to communicate on the subject of Federal hiring procedures, and my ability to sell audiences on the need for excellent employees and high morale in government, is both unique and understandable to the average person who wants to serve his/her country through Federal employment. I am an advocate on behalf of working for the Federal government and continue to support recruitment while advocating for the applicant, making the hiring process easier through a streamlined, systematic, and flattering resume format and career-motivation printed materials.

Finally, in recognition of the long-term and significant impact of my writings on the Federal hiring process, Mr. Paul Light, Vice President and Director of Government Studies, The Brookings Institution, recently wrote the following about my latest publication, *Ten Steps to a Federal Job:*

"Despite all the efforts to the contrary, finding a Federal job is still a tough climb. *Ten Steps to a Federal Job* is the best guide you can find for the challenge."

Two Sample ECQ Statements from the Federal Sector

The following sample write-ups, taken from a Wildlife Biologist and a Financial Analyst, show how candidates with very different technical backgrounds approached the ECQ process.

Example 1: Wildlife Biologist

This Wildlife Biologist was applying for a job with the Environmental Protection Agency.

In addition to the five ECQs, this sample includes a sixth "additional qualification" factor that was required by the vacancy notice. Note that the candidate includes the definition of each ECQ before addressing it. Although there is nothing technically wrong with doing this, it takes up valuable space you might need to elaborate on your own experiences. You must stay within the page limit specified in the vacancy announcement.

Margaret T. Wingsong, SSN: 000-00-0000

ENVIRONMENTAL PROTECTION AGENCY, Washington, DC

DEPUTY ASSOCIATE ADMINISTRATOR, ES-0340-01/04

Announcement No: EPA-03-SES-OA-6299

Candidate: Margaret T. Wingsong, SSN: 000-00-0000

    1.   **Leading Change**

Through active involvement in the operations of the Forest Service in the field and through major reform programs coordinated by the Washington office, I have consistently demonstrated the strategic vision necessary to assess the strengths and weaknesses of an organization and then to develop a course of effective change that improves substantial vulnerabilities affecting both the agency and the public it serves.

Context and Challenge: While serving in the Arapaho-Roosevelt National Forest (ARNF), I conducted risk analyses of fire-prevention efforts and identified key system vulnerabilities in two areas. First, we had not dedicated sufficient resources to the treatment of sections of the forest that had especially high risk of fires. Second, even though the National Forests surrounded significant urban developments, the Forest Service bore disproportionate risks associated with fire prevention and excessive costs of fighting the fires that did occur.

Actions: To improve our fire-prevention efforts, I began more systematic identification of the fuels inventories and established land-management programs—including measures to improve treatments at a landscape scale—that would reduce risks in areas that the Forest Service controlled directly. I then initiated discussions with the Colorado State Forest Service; local government agencies; affected timber industry organizations; and conservation, wildlife, hunting, and other organizations to identify fire-management priorities and to refine previous strategies for preventing and managing forest fires that might endanger the urban-forest interface. I involved wide participation in the revision of the Forest Land Management Plan and the associated Environmental Impact Statement, enabling the ARNF to adopt a state-of-the-art document that has since become a model replicated by other forests.

RESULTS: Our new plan reduces risks to firefighters and to the public, improves the allocation of cost sharing in fighting fires, and strengthens the community's sense of "ownership" of both the forest and its responsibilities for effective treatment and firefighting procedures. This service earned a Forest Service award for Exemplary Team Leadership that led to the Forest Plan Revision.

Context: In addition to this initiative, I also demonstrated effective leadership in the adoption of the new Financial Foundation Information System (FFIS) at the national level. **Challenge**: During three detail assignments to the national office during 1999, I led task groups contributing to the development of the Primary Purpose policy within FFIS, which will standardize major portions of the agency's financial-management practices. Using expertise that I had developed implementing the Unified Budget system at the local level, I developed and delivered presentations to Washington-level Staff Directors, budget and accounting managers, and regional budget officers. **RESULTS**: These briefings—of the Primary Purpose Task Group (May xxxx) and the Multi-Funding and Program Management Task Group (June xxxx)—earned me stature as the agency's leading expert on Primary Purpose. In addition to earning two certificates of merit, I was selected to lead the national training video supporting implementation of the Primary Purpose component of the FFIS implementation. This new financial system strengthens our use of technology, linking policy priorities and our financial-management capabilities, and thoroughly demonstrates my ability to link national programs with the people and equipment necessary for effective implementation. *I believe that the leadership I have provided in organizing local, state, and national fire-prevention programs and coordinating the development of national modifications of financial information systems reflects my ability to lead change as a Deputy Associate Administrator.*

Margaret T. Wingsong, SSN: 000-00-0000

2. Leading People

I learned innovative team-development techniques in a Total Quality Management environment and lead by example, teaching courses to the staff to develop, refine, and implement this approach to management together. I employ open, candid approaches when dealing with employees and the public. **For example**, I played an active role in the Civil Rights Action Group (CRAG) as the Idaho Panhandle National Forest (IPNF) leadership team representative and as Bridger-Teton NF, Jackson District representative. As District Ranger, I supported my District CRAG representative to join, participate, and use our facilities for the *North Idaho Task Force on Human Relations* to work with the community. This also **improved the Forest Service's employee and family networks for recruiting and retaining minorities in the Coeur d'Alene area.**

I contribute to a Federal workforce that reflects the nation's diversity while sustaining the commitment to merit in our civil-service system. I am a member of the Creek Tribe, Muskogee Nation of Oklahoma, and work effectively with the Native American communities who live in and near national forests. I successfully cooperated with non–Forest Service families to house minority students in communities where they were working on the district during FYXX (four students) and FYXX (five students) field seasons. **The student program is a central element of our efforts to improve diversity within the Forest Service.**

My supervisory experience includes a variety of forests, and I have effectively blended the temporary, seasonal, contract, and full-time employees who are important to Forest Service operations.

Challenge and Actions: As District Ranger and Ecosystem Group Leader from xxxx to the present, I have maintained the temporary workforce to include 20 to 25% minorities, an additional 25% women, and 5% disabled. My supervisory responsibilities have included managing a workforce as large as 55 full-time employees and 75 seasonal staff. **RESULTS**: The professional development that I provide to all components of the workforce has assisted several employees to convert into the permanent workforce and enabled other employees to develop effective skills for use in other employment. I have mentored three employees to District Ranger positions in other regions and three others onto Forest Level staff. I have hired eight coop-education employees over the last eight years, including seven females and two minorities (one female/minority). I have ensured diversity in each work group and promoted effective upward-mobility programs for numerous employees, including women, minorities, and persons with disabilities.

I work effectively in partnership with the National Federation of Federal Employees (NFFE) in developing responsive approaches to our operations. **Context and Challenge**: During xxxx and xxxx, the IPNF initiated downsizing and consolidation of districts, and I led my district through a 35% reduction in personnel. **Actions**: I learned the value of keeping employees informed, and learned and used a variety of tools to communicate and involve the employees. District-wide meetings, NFFE meetings and negotiations, one-to-one discussions, and inter-district meetings with both rangers/staff and functional teams provided myself and others on the District/Forest with several options to reduce employees and meet logistical needs. **RESULTS**: We used a variety of reduction processes, including buyouts, merit promotions, directed reassignments, and the Employee Placement System. **The key was early and constant communication with all employees and NFFE while providing support processes that eased transition to other careers. This ability to work with diverse staff through difficult conditions while sustaining vital public performance reflects my ability to lead people by motivating them toward continuous individual improvements that serve the organization well while enlarging personal opportunities.**

2

(continues)

(continued)

Margaret T. Wingsong, SSN: 000-00-0000

3. Results Driven

Large national forests invariably require a balance of a multitude of economic, recreational, resource-management, environmental, and community interests. During the past 10 years, in several different forests, I have organized and relied heavily on teams representing the full range of interests served by these forests in accomplishing a variety of objectives.

Context and challenge: I have managed large forests where communities depended upon substantial timber production to sustain the local economy. In these circumstances, development and implementation of an effective sales strategy requires personal commitment by key staff and myself working closely with other agencies and the public, and using a wide variety of both routine and innovative procedures to achieve understanding, compromise, and satisfaction and to avert costly and acrimonious appeals and litigation.

Actions: During fiscal years xxxx–xxxx, the Fernan District team produced 21 major Decision Notices, including two Environmental Impact Statements (EIS), and analyzed approximately 150,000 acres that provided a potential 125 MMBF of timber. **RESULTS**: From those plans, the Forest Service realized sales of more than 100 MMBF. One of the EISs required during this period covered a roadless area with extensive habitat for wildlife and fish resources. During these years, the Forest Service achieved a harvest of 160 MMBF, carefully planned to include long-term ecological goals. Revenue from these harvests financed numerous miles of road closures, and 5,000–10,000 acres of wildlife improvement and security. *By the end of my tour as District Ranger, I had also instituted watershed rehabilitation projects valued at $500,000 to $1 million per year*. These performance levels were uncommon even in the early '90s, and ranked Fernan District among the top 10 districts in the nation in accomplishments in timber sales and watershed rehabilitation. This performance met or exceeded all Idaho Forest Practices Act regulations, as well as Forest Plan Standards and Guidelines.

In addition to harvest and sales performance measures, I work with community organizations to develop and implement sustainable activities within forests' capabilities. Some of this success results from my ability to recognize opportunities based on my extensive and varied background. **Challenge**: For example, a community of Laotian immigrants living near one forest wanted beargrass—which we considered a weed—to use in weaving. **Actions and RESULTS**: Using experience gained elsewhere, my negotiations led to a resolution that enabled the Laotians to **successfully** begin harvesting the beargrass for weaving and significantly enhanced revenues returned to the forest, more than any other miscellaneous-products program in the region.

Frequently, vegetation management on lands adjacent to urban areas requires complex assessments of the scenic values associated with vistas; and we coordinate strategies with community interests in these areas. **Context and Challenge**: While on the Fernan Ranger District, I developed an outstanding vegetative management plan for a hillside that was visible from nearby population centers. We went the extra mile to ensure full community participation in all stages of the planning. Our outreach enabled full understanding of the purpose of the chosen management strategies. **RESULTS**: We achieved the project's full range of goals, and the public was pleased its vistas were not damaged. I received the *Forest Supervisor's Award for Excellence in Implementing New Perspectives* for this project. These interactions with the interested communities provide the sustained feedback necessary to measure the success of performance and to anticipate community concerns when we initiate new projects.

These community-centered approaches to forest management reflect well my commitment to developing and using both performance measures and feedback mechanisms essential to attain effective results in Federal programs.

3

Margaret T. Wingsong, SSN: 000-00-0000

4. Business Acumen

Throughout my Federal career I have practiced sound management practices in the development and stewardship of the human, financial, natural, and technological resources that I have administered.

Context and Challenge: As an official who has led the Ecosystem Group, I have recruited and developed a highly effective workforce through systematic training of employees under my supervision. **Actions**: In addition to developing highly effective teams, employees whom I have supervised are recruited actively and sought by other Forest Service managers for the breadth of their skills. **RESULTS**: In addition to serving as career mentor to several professionals who have advanced to supervisory ranks, I work effectively in partnership with all employees through their designated representatives in the National Federation of Federal Employees.

In managing forests, I work closely with community organizations to establish objectives for sustainable, comprehensive management of forest resources. My leadership has been demonstrated through innovative methods of incorporating performance measures to monitor wildlife, rehabilitation, scenic vistas, and other community concerns. In addition to innovative, community-based performance goals for operations, I have a solid business sense in managing fiscal resources.

Context and Challenge: I have developed and justified budget-execution plans of as much as $4.2 million per year. **Actions**: My financial-management abilities are reflected through my ability to manage forests to make effective use of appropriated funds while generating a diverse stream of revenues to support a comprehensive plan for managing each forest consistent with sustainable management principles. I am widely recognized as the regional expert on the unified budget system and have delivered nearly 20 training presentations on the unified budget in other district offices. My knowledge of the unified budget and skill in presentations provided a strong foundation for the Washington Office to recruit me for participation on the national team developing the Financial Foundation Information System (FFIS). **RESULTS**: This system is essential to integrate our operations with government-wide accounting and cash-management requirements overseen by the General Accounting Office, and is essential to full implementation of the Chief Financial Officers Act. I chaired three of the Task Groups participating in FFIS development and played a leading role in the videotape, distributed nationally, to explain a key component of the system, Primary Purpose policy.

In addition to this financial expertise, my participation in developing FFIS reflects my ability to develop information technologies to improve management wherever I serve. **For example**, I regularly use the Incident Command System to maintain records of our annual objectives and monitor performance in dealing with the full range of programs administered in each forest. **RESULTS**: Through intensive team focus on **improving the financial health of systems** within our responsibilities, we substantially improved financial reporting in a two-month period and have sustained that improvement as we move toward becoming a financial-management model.

This combination of effective human resource management, leadership in matters of financial management, and successful use of information technology to support operations demonstrates the business acumen essential to a Forest Supervisor.

4

(continues)

(continued)

Margaret T. Wingsong, SSN: 000-00-0000

5. Building Coalitions/Communication

I am an active participant in the communities surrounding the forests where I work, and am adept at reaching out to the full range of business, civic, recreational, conservation-environmental, and other groups and agencies with interests in Forest Service programs and policies. I have formed effective partnerships at a long succession of National Forests, adjusting local priorities to address community concerns within the umbrella of national laws and policies.

Example: Specifically, I convened a "sounding board" that met 14 times during a two-year period to secure approval of an Environmental Impact Statement authorizing roadless entry to the Idaho Panhandle National Forest. (This occurred in the early '90s before "collaboration" was being used in the Forest Service.) These formal meetings were supplemented by numerous informal consultations to secure agreement among all interested groups.

RESULTS: In addition to effective partnerships with community organizations, I have **forged strong alliances with related Federal agencies such as the National Park Service, the Fish and Wildlife Service, and the Bureau of Land Management**. I have also worked effectively with several state departments of fish and game (especially in California, Wyoming, Idaho, and Colorado) on coordination of improvement projects for wildlife and fish; review and modification of timber, range, and recreation projects; cooperative wildlife monitoring; animal transplants; analysis of game, non-game, threatened, and endangered species; and law enforcement.

RESULTS: These agencies contributed to significant projects, including a multi-year elk transplant from Redwood National Park (CA), a major wildfire control and prescribed burning program adjacent to Grand Teton National Park (WY), and many other wilderness, recreation, and law-enforcement programs. In Idaho, I worked effectively with the Bonneville Power Authority—a Department of Energy agency—to improve power line rights-of-way maintenance, enhance road usage, and coordinate burning strategies to manage fire conditions.

I have also worked effectively with the **Environmental Protection Agency, Idaho's Department of Environmental Quality, and its Departments of Land and Water Resources, as well as natural resource and environmental agencies in California and Colorado**. These partnerships have enhanced specific programs and contributed to the agency's ability to deliver desired public services while providing **effective mixed-use management of valuable natural resources**. In coordinating these relationships, I have enhanced my understanding of relationships between state and Federal responsibilities in these areas, mastered complex details of states' laws as well as the national laws that I administer, and consistently demonstrated an ability to bring people together in pursuit of common objectives.

PUBLIC SPEAKING: I speak before numerous organizations each year to ensure that the communities understand national policies, and I have been recruited to serve on national committees developing key financial-management systems for these operations. In the course of developing these systems, I have conducted briefings for senior Washington officials and presented the training for the Financial Foundations Information System on a nationally distributed videotape.

My abilities to build coalitions, develop cooperative approaches to community concerns, and represent the agency effectively before the public are among the high points of my professional qualifications. *This broad balance of experiences reflects an ability to move into a new community, recognize both strong relationships and opportunities for improvement, and build consensus where it is essential to accomplishment. These traits reflect well my ability to serve as a Deputy Associate Administrator.*

5

Margaret T. Wingsong, SSN: 000-00-0000

6. Natural Resource Management

My professional career includes experience managing a wide range of forests, fields, streams, plants, wildlife, and other dimensions of natural environments. Through more than 20 years of experience after earning my bachelor's degree in wildlife management, I successfully operated a variety of forest, rangeland, and wildlife-management programs in California, Wyoming, Idaho, and Colorado. I have worked closely with community and industry organizations to achieve substantial timber harvests while completing the reforestation, preservation, and restoration of watersheds and their associated wildlife and fisheries habitats. **Other programs I have successfully led are District Lands and District Business Management functions, Forest Air Quality, Recreation/Wilderness, and Heritage functions.**

Context and Actions: I have established leadership throughout the Forest Service in my aggressive, analytical approach to the prevention of forest fires and restoring the landscape within natural fire regimes. I have conducted intensive risk analysis of forests, most recently Arapaho-Roosevelt National Forest (ARNF), and sparked substantial increases in the acreage receiving preventive treatment each year. Where the ARNF had treated 700 to 1,000 acres annually before my arrival, through intensive efforts within the Forest Plan revision and through on-the-ground workforce efforts we are now treating over 5,000 acres and are on target to treat over 7,000 acres per year, a five- to ten-fold increase. **Challenge**: This approach builds on my success resolving a treatment backlog at the Fernan District of the Idaho Panhandle National Forest (IPNF). Here my District was treating less than 500 acres per year and adding to a 10,000-acre backlog each year due to indecision and inaction. **RESULTS**: As District Ranger, I shifted workload to ensure treatment of a minimum of 700 to 1,000 acres annually, steadily reducing the backlog. Both situations included innovative approaches to landscape management to reduce risks, especially at the forest's urban interface. In addition to treatment, I have worked with local communities to provide better evaluation of the risks associated with fires—developing inclusive formulas that ensure full consideration of resource values—and to institute more equitable cost sharing for fire prevention and firefighting efforts.

My experience includes over eight years as field biologist responsible for wildlife, range, noxious weeds, botany, and fisheries, with two different agencies, at four stations and covering a wide range of habitats and animals. These included high-elevation forests, desert grasslands, and temperate rain forests. I have also coordinated responses to numerous sensitive, threatened, and endangered plants, animals and fish, including spotted owls, goshawks, endangered non-game warm-water fish, anadromous steelhead trout, and salmon. This breadth of experience provides a strong basis for understanding effective ecological principles and provides a strong record of success.

My successes in these areas build upon effective community relations. **RESULTS**: When restoring an elk herd to the Klamath National Forest, I involved local tribes in identifying suitable locations for placing the herd, in the building of prerelease holding and capture pens, and in long-term monitoring. I have worked closely with other Federal, state, and local agencies; tribal organizations; environmental organizations; and organizations of hunters and fishers who gain substantial recreational benefit from the wildlife inhabiting the national forests. *This strong range of experiences and ability to apply contemporary management tools to monitoring and enhancing these national resources fully demonstrates my ability to address the full range of natural resource needs in the context of major national policies.*

6

Example 2: Financial and Cost Analyst

This candidate, a Financial and Cost Analyst applying for an SES position with his own agency, does a good job of addressing the five ECQs. The candidate could have strengthened the statements by using more "plain language" and writing in the active voice. Specific numbers, rather than general statements such as "I hired several" or "my system optimized investments," also would have helped the reader grasp measurable results.

Department of Homeland Security, Transportation Security Administration

DIRECTOR OF BUDGET AND PERFORMANCE, SW-0501-00/00

Announcement No: TSA-TSES-05

Candidate: NATHAN LEVINE, SSN 000-00-0000

EXECUTIVE CORE QUALIFICATIONS

1. Leading Change

My 18-year career in the Department of Defense reflects sustained professional growth integrating key risk-analysis factors in the development and deployment of a multitude of advanced aerospace weapons systems. Refinement of cost estimation requires a progressively more precise understanding of proposed weapons systems in the national security strategy, as reflected in emergent technologies and policies. Thorough assessment of the life-cycle risk factors associated with any long-term plan requires accurate understanding of national missions in the context of a global environment that experienced substantial changes during the period. **I believe that my sophisticated understanding of the relationship of risk assessment to strategic thinking enhances my ability to lead change in the future Federal workforce.**

Challenge: Industries supporting government programs were intensely suspicious at the government implementation of the Cost/Schedule Control Systems Criteria (C/SCSC) during the 1980s. While leading more than 50 C/SCSC validation reviews, I noted that the review criteria allowed for only "satisfactory," "marginal," and "unsatisfactory" ratings. The score sheet, in effect, provided neither incentives nor opportunities to recognize excellence.

Result: Accordingly, I used my responsibilities as a C/SCSC Review Director working for Air Force Systems Command to gain support for adding "good," "very good," and "excellent" to the ratings. More than fostering competition for higher ratings, the additional factors encouraged the government to be more forthcoming about evaluation criteria and strengthened the exchange of information between the agency and its contractors, which fostered an atmosphere of continuous improvement.

Today, the government and defense industry have developed from criteria controlled and maintained only by government to standards established and maintained by industry. My early work promoted an environment where the common management goals of Earned Value Management (EVM) are achieved to the benefit of both government and industry. **I continue to apply this mutually beneficial approach in advancing integration of the cost estimating and earned-value communities by including insight from cost-risk identification and reporting in earned-value management implementation.**

Context and Challenge: In the early 1990s, as a Space and Missile Systems Center (SMC) Cost Branch Chief, I recognized that our cost estimates did not adequately account for risks.

Actions: In xxxx, under an agreement between local program managers and contractors, I arbitrated disagreements related to a congressionally driven study into infrared satellite systems.

NATHAN LEVINE, SSN 000-00-0000, TSA-TSES-05

The Air Force planned to acquire two separate infrared satellite systems that appeared duplicative, so a committee proposed consolidation of the two systems. Working with an Aerospace Corp. cost engineer, we developed the cost-risk positions of each satellite system but produced estimates that were considered too high. This experience confirmed the need for a better system of "risk-to-cost impact" translation. With my experience in prioritization systems, I developed a proposal to hire a cost-support contractor to help develop an approach, using such a prioritization system that would reduce the ambiguity in cost-risk impacts. I secured local funding to develop a mechanism to credibly translate risk into cost impact, called the Cost-Risk Identification and Management System (CRIMS).

Results: This $60,000 investment in refined methodology strengthened the analysis supporting a multibillion-dollar contract for engineering manufacturing development. This methodology continues to support development of the Evolved Expendable Launch Vehicle and the Space-Based Infrared Satellite Systems as they meet the funding challenges posed by the technical risks today. *My role in the development and promotion of this risk-assessment methodology thoroughly demonstrates my ability to lead change*.

2. Leading People

For the past 15 years, I have orchestrated ad hoc teams with members from geographically dispersed DoD-wide locations, led teams organizing nationally attended conferences, directly supervised employees, and spearheaded the cultural transformation for Air Force implementation of acquisition reforms.

Context: As Chief of the Air Force Cost Center's Information Systems Branch, I promoted effective research to improve performance of the Air Force's cost mission. I chaired the DoD Cost Research Working Group—composed of senior Air Force, Army, Navy, and OSD representatives—and directed intensive efforts to identify research redundancies between services. **Challenge**: This evaluation and prioritization used a team approach to ensure that the research was balanced between the services and OSD. I managed the execution of the Air Force's research plan, which involved creating new, automated tools for software cost estimation, economic analysis, and basic interactive cost analysis training. I convinced my staff of the importance of our mission and their contribution's importance to its success.

RESULTS: We produced tools in xxxx that are effective today. I made sure my management was aware of the great work done by the people in my branch, and secured a promotion to GS-13 for one of my civilian employees and promotion to Major for an Air Force officer. I recommended and received maximum bonuses for the deserving civilians. Their professionalism and dedication has continued to enhance their careers.

Context and Challenge: As the Communication Satellite Cost Branch Chief for the Space and Missile Systems Center Cost Division in xxxx, I had the opportunity to build up the branch to a staff of 12 civilian and military personnel. **Actions**: I supervised professional civilian employees from GS-7 through GS-13, and military employees up to the rank of Major. During the interviews I conducted, several minority candidates stood out, and I hired them consistently through merit-system procedures. I ensured appropriate training and on-the-job experiences vital to enhance their opportunities. I have consistently maintained open communications with all

2

(continues)

(continued)

NATHAN LEVINE, SSN 000-00-0000, TSA-TSES-05

members of my staff and have worked in partnership with employee union representatives. I have initiated conversations, provided information about organizational developments, and anticipated potential concerns to provide a sound foundation for cooperative action in support of the Air Force's mission. **RESULTS**: They have all been promoted since then, some two whole grade levels.

3. Results Driven

Context: As an Analyst for Cost Programs at the Pentagon in xxxx, I coordinated development of a more equitable means of distributing budget cuts during the FYxx–xx POM Space and C3I Resource Allocation Team disconnect exercise. **Challenge**: The panels had previously spread reductions across all programs. This technique produced inequitable cuts from most programs. **Actions**: To assist the panel chairman, I devised a system that optimized investments in cost-research projects by adapting a system I developed for the AF Cost Center that optimized the cuts proportionally across the panel's programs. **RESULTS**: The technique proved very successful and minimized the impacts of the cuts in the Air Force's FY xx–xx research program.

Challenge and Context: When downsizing hit the SMC cost division in xxxx, the Acquisition Management Directorate led implementation of acquisition reform. They recruited me from SMC/FMC for my strengths in CAIV, cost-risk systems analysis, entrepreneurship, and innovation leadership. Space budgets had been cut and SMC had to reduce its System Program Office (SPO) without jeopardizing the workload. As we implemented acquisition reform, we reinvented systems and procedures to acquire space systems more affordably, with substantial reliance on risk management to enhance our cost assessments.

Actions: First, I structured the technical framework to identify best processes and to convince the SMC workforce to utilize the tools. I adapted cost-risk analysis to the life-cycle cost-estimating process, earned value management, cost as an independent variable (CAIV), and the reduction of total ownership cost. I leveraged my position at the RFP Support Office to build awareness of the affordability tools available during development of RFPs. I convinced the leadership of both the EELV and SBIRS High programs to utilize this tool set. I trained the staff of their Aerospace Corp. engineers in the use of the tools, convincing them of the importance of applying these tools for acquiring the most affordable systems during source selection.

RESULTS: The Cost-Risk Identification and Management System (CRIMS) that I have developed and refined provides the framework for risk estimation as a project is being developed, risk management during implementation, and post-facto risk assessment to strengthen accountability and build data for better risk assessment in future programs. *This comprehensive approach to risk management and cost analysis provides an accurate reflection of my drive to achieve continuous improvement in agency programs.*

3

NATHAN LEVINE, SSN 000-00-0000, TSA-TSES-05

4. Business Acumen

Context and Challenge: As Chief of the Air Force Cost Center's Information Systems Branch, I realized that a tool was needed that would enable the Center Commander to optimize the available budget. **Actions**: Based on a concept for such a tool using new commercial prioritization and optimization software, I hired a decision-support software firm to assist development and produced a tool the Center Commander used to prioritize research and data-collection projects. Knowing the skepticism associated with computer-generated solutions, I chose tools that were sufficiently sensitive to provide flexibility in exploring options and likely consequences.

RESULTS: This approach defused initial objections to using a computer and ultimately facilitated consensus. The commander was very satisfied with the results, confident that he optimized the use of his scarce financial resources, and we institutionalized the process for subsequent years.

Context and Challenge: In xxxx, the National Polar Orbiting Environmental Satellite System (NPOESS) program manager requested my help in evaluating the technical cost-risk impacts for this ambitious new weather-satellite system. The task was a Joint Program Office (AF, NASA, and NOAA) with two program offices: one in Los Angeles, CA, and the other in Silver Spring, MD. I needed to get the consensus of both groups of sensor engineers. Initially, the West Coast engineers' results were disputed by the East Coast, who had not participated in the West Coast cost-risk evaluation.

Actions: To break the deadlock, I utilized a software program and telephonic connection that allowed me to facilitate the risk evaluation from a computer network in Los Angeles, with a simultaneous broadcast of the computer program images to the Silver Spring, MD, office.

RESULTS: This approach proved enormously successful, with both groups of engineers reaching a consensus that there was much more risk in developing the sensors than was initially believed. The program acquisition strategy was reconsidered after the risk evaluation, resulting in multiple sensor-development study contracts prior to advancing into Engineering Manufacture and Design. This use of an available, advanced information management system assisted the program in avoiding a premature EMD start, strengthening program performance and reducing long-term risks that could have proven wasteful.

4

(continues)

(continued)

NATHAN LEVINE, SSN 000-00-0000, TSA-TSES-05

5. Building Coalitions/Communication

Context and Challenge: As the president of the Southern California chapter of the Society of Cost Estimating and Analysis (SCEA) in xxxx, I was asked by the Missile Center's advanced planning organization to sponsor a Cost as an Independent Variable (CAIV) workshop.

Actions: I had been very active, personally, in presenting "Cost" seminars on at the xxxx–xxxx Acquisition Reform Weeks at SMC, and knew of the interest of the defense community in understanding CAIV and the government's plan for implementation. We anticipated attendance of 20 people from the local government and defense industry. We convinced expert speakers with experience in this policy from Air Force HQ to speak and recruited comparable people from industry. We also recruited industry personnel who were implementing this cost process to share their experiences. **RESULTS**: We held the workshop in March xxxx and over 110 people attended. We had attracted representatives from the defense industry and government from all over the country. The workshop was so informative that there was immediate consensus to hold another workshop within six months.

Context and Challenge: In October xxxx I presided over the second "Cost" workshop. I persuaded the Society Board that the focus of the second workshop should be the development of a *Government/Industry CAIV Guide*. Between the first workshop and this one, Air Force HQ had selected Space and Missile Systems Center (SMC) as the focal point for reinventing the CAIV process within the Air Force. **Actions**: I was also asked to be a part of that team. One of the outputs required of the Reinvention Team was a product, and I convinced the lead to utilize the second SCEA CAIV Workshop Guide as the Reinvention Team's product. He agreed.

We recruited the OSD Cost as an Independent Variable lead official as our keynote speaker, as well as other service subject-matter expert directors and the Air Force's leader. This time the workshop attracted over 140 attendees. We produced the outline for the Guide, and as tenets for Cost as an Independent Variable were taking shape, the Reduction of Total Ownership Costs (RTOC) office requested our assistance in shaping their Guide. The Cost as an Independent Variable Reinvention Team leader and I realized that there was enough similarity between CAIV tenets and RTOC processes that I recommended merging the two concepts. We discussed this with the team lead and formed an operating coalition between the two teams built on government and industry communication that I sponsored using the Society of Cost Estimating and Analysis organization.

RESULTS: The consolidated *RTOC/CAIV Guide* can be accessed today from the RTOC office Web site. My leadership in this area earned me positions on the Cost-Estimating Reinvention team, the Earned Value Management team, and the Cost as an Independent Variable integrating group for the Air Force. I retain an active interest in these issues as I expand my skills in budget areas. **This experience fully demonstrates my ability to build coalitions within the Department of Defense and with its contractors to enhance the effectiveness of government operations.**

5

A Sample Executive Federal Resume

See the appendix for more Executive Federal resumes.

Harvey Allen
221 S. 9th Street
Oklahoma City, OK 73159
H_allen@aol.com

Day: (505) 555-7525   Cell Phone: (505) 333-4701

SSN: 000-00-0000
Citizenship: United States
Federal Status: FAA Career
Highest Grade Held: FM-905-15
Veterans' Status: U.S. Navy Veteran

OBJECTIVE   Chief Counsel, Senior Executive Level (SES); Department of Energy,
                  Albuquerque, NM, Announcement Number: AL-SES-01-02

PROFILE: Senior Attorney and legal expert with mastery of complex federal acquisition as well as budgetary, business and political aspects of Federal Aviation Administration Aeronautical center management. Exceptional strategic vision and leadership skills, with systematic approach to organizing information and prioritizing work schedules. Well-established ability to evaluate standard legal practices and corresponding results. Extensive record of writing for large audiences, and familiarity with managing controversial situations. Adjunct professor with teaching experience at three separate universities in Aviation Law, Space Law and MBA programs. Currently completing Ed.D. degree studies, pending dissertation. Naval Reserve Captain (0–6) with experience in senior Staff Judge Advocate positions between Oct. 1993 and Sept. 1999.

PROFESSIONAL EXPERIENCE

Senior Attorney for Acquisition   Sept. 1992–Present
Department of Transportation, FAA   40–50 hrs/week
Aeronautical Center Counsel (AMC-7)   Grade Level: FM-905-15
Oklahoma City, OK 73125
Supervisor: Joe Randell, Phone: (505) 653-3296 (Supervisor May Be Contacted)

As Senior Attorney for Acquisition, carry out daily responsibility for national, international, agency-wide and local contract litigation and mediation efforts on behalf of the Federal Aviation Administration. Analyze requests for legal opinions and associated financing documents relative to issuing advisory opinions regarding registration of aircraft at the U.S. Aircraft Registry. Serve as a team member, tasked to draft the Federal Aviation Administration's Acquisition Management System. Served on several challenge boards for that effort.

Accomplishments:
• Proactively identified and proposed several cost recovery centers for the Office of the Chief Counsel in response to the Administrator's cost recovery policy.

(continues)

(continued)

- Assisted the Equal Employment Opportunity Commission's initiation of its current mediation process by providing initial training for third-party neutrals.

- Sponsored training associated with Early Neutral Evaluation in the U.S. District Court for the Western District of Oklahoma.

- Prosecuted enforcement cases on behalf of the Federal Aviation Administration and defended the Agency in Equal Employment Opportunity Commission cases and Environmental Law cases.

Government Contracting/Litigation Attorney   July 1991–Sept. 1992
Department of Transportation, U.S. Coast Guard   40+ hrs/week
2100 Second St., SW   Grade Level: GM-905-14
Washington, DC 20593-0001
Supervisor: RADM Paul Evers, Telephone number unknown

Developed goals and objectives to resolve challenges related to legal, budgetary, ethics and business problems and other corporate issues affecting U.S. Coast Guard acquisition efforts. Coordinated goals and objectives for management, and resolution of complex legal challenges, as well as business anomalies in the aftermath of the Exxon Valdez oil spill in Prince William Sound, AK. Was tasked to lead the U.S. Coast Guard's acquisition planning efforts to install a Global Positioning System on the ground, and in airborne platforms, to enhance shipping safety. Coordinated U.S. Coast Guard work with the Department of Justice for Coast Guard and contractor claim resolution through negotiations and litigation, while performing risk analysis in conjunction with associated budget austerity. Served as Trial Attorney for matters related to Acquisitions and Contracts.

Accomplishments:
- Managed, negotiated and eventually litigated highly complex automated data processing (ADPE)—Federal Information Processing Systems (FIPS) post award bid protests before the General Services Board of Contract Appeals, and the U.S. General Accounting Office.

- Managed and litigated Government contract appeal cases before the Department of Transportation's Board of Contract Appeals, the U.S. Claims Court, Court of Appeals for the Federal Circuit and other Federal courts of appropriate jurisdiction. Researched and prepared legal opinions for the Director of Contracting and the Chief Financial Officer.

- Teamed with the Director of Contracting and Chief Financial Officer to investigate and eventually remove a contracting officer's representative at a U.S. Coast Guard site in Louisiana.

- Managed and litigated Freedom of Information Act (FOIA) request appeals and related claims.

Attorney
Franklin, Stringer and Webster, P.C.
101 N. Broadway, Suite 800
Oklahoma City, OK 73102
Supervisor: Parry Hage, (505) 373-1536

Jan. 1989–July 1991
40+ hrs/week
Salary: $75,000/yr

Served as Chairperson, American Bar Association, Government Contract Section, for the States of Oklahoma and Texas. Conceptualized and co-sponsored training related to acquisition, Small and Economically Disadvantaged Business and Section "8-A" Contractors. Developed and taught a course related to Small and Economically Disadvantaged Business and *Crossen v. City of Richmond* for a broad range of participants, including national and international contractors, business leaders, legal counsel, and national acquisition experts from the academic community. Instructed and taught for Federal Publications (now known as West Publications), the National Contract Management Association and Associated General Contractors—teaching and training participants in the basic elements of federal acquisition, advanced federal acquisition, bid-protests, disputes, cost accounting and procurement integrity. Coordinated the development and implementation of the firm's government acquisition Vision and Mission Statement for the business section of the firm.

Accomplishments:
- Successfully resolved the firm's client workload in acquisition claims and contract disputes before the General Services Board of Contract Disputes, the Armed Services Board of Contract Appeals, the Postal Service Board of Contract Appeals, the Government Printing Office Board of Contract Appeals, and the Housing and Urban Development Board of Contract Appeals. Also resolved the firm's workload in acquisition claims and contract disputes before the U.S. Federal District Courts, the U.S. Court of Federal Claims and the U.S. Court of Appeals for the Federal Circuit.

- Negotiated, mediated and litigated acquisition matters involving International Business claims; "85-804" claims; disbarments; and pre/post award bid protests at the U.S. General Accounting Office, the General Services Board of Contract Appeals and the U.S. Federal District Courts.

- Authored numerous professional articles, including those listed under WRITINGS/PUBLICATIONS below.

(continues)

(continued)

Government Contracting/Business Law and Litigation Dec. 1981–Dec. 1988
A. L. Murray, P.C. 40+ hrs/week
8890 South Eastern Ave. Salary: $125,000/yr
Oklahoma City, OK 73160
Supervisor: Frank Jones, (505) 654-5655

Engaged as legal practitioner in Oklahoma City metropolitan area. Conducted all aspects of legal practice, including marketing, client intake, case development, litigation, billing and collection of accounts. Focused on representation of clients whose businesses included government contracting, oil, gas, real estate, business and securities, engineering and entertainment challenges. Served as active member of the American Bar Association, Government Contracts—Bid Protest Committee and authored articles for the Association's Government Contract Law Review.

Accomplishments:
- Managed office operations for a 3-attorney practice.

- Mediated and litigated government contracting cases before the Boards of Contract.

- Appeals, including complex fiscal law and automated data processing cases before the General Services Board of Contract Appeals and in U.S. District Courts.

- Litigated bid protests at the U.S. General Accounting Office and the General Services Board of Contract Appeals.

- Government Contracts Instructor for West Publications (formerly Federal Publications, Inc.).

EDUCATION

- Oklahoma State University, Ed.D. Degree, 2002 (Degree pending dissertation)
- Southern Nazarene University, M.S. Degree, 1995
- University of Tulsa, J.D. Degree, 1977
- Illinois State University, B.S. Degree, 1973
- Ottawa Township High School, Ottawa, IL, Diploma, June 1966

UNIVERSITY TEACHING EXPERIENCE

Adjunct Professor   Jan. 2001–Present
Southeastern Oklahoma State University
Durant, OK
Supervisor: Don Lemming, (683) 549-4563

Instruct undergraduate and graduate students in aviation management curriculum.
Also teach Business Law and Aviation Legal Problems.

Adjunct Professor   Mar. 1998–Present
Oklahoma State University, Graduate College of Education   12 hrs/week
Stillwater, OK 74078-0050
Supervisor: Dr. Norman Stanley, (505) 644-9989

Instruct undergraduate and graduate students in aviation and space law and
management, including Leadership, Management, Acquisition and Contracting,
Support of National Air Space Systems, Analysis of Air Traffic, Aircraft Certification,
Airman Certification, Medical Certification, Flight Standards, Aviation Systems
Standards, Security, FAA National and International policies, U.S. Business and
Government Interaction and Team Building with International Entities,
Governments and Businesses. Have developed/taught curricula involving Building
Consensus and Cooperation between the FAA and the U.S. Congress, as well as
between the FAA and International Aviation governing bodies. Also taught the
Development of Leadership skills and habits in the worldwide Aviation Community,
as well as Analyzing U.S. and International Security Measures.

Adjunct Professor   Oct. 1996–Present
Southern Nazarene University, Graduate School of Management   6 hrs/week
Bethany, OK 73008
Supervisor: Dr. Stanley Smith, (505) 695-6645

Instruct graduate students in the Master of Business Administration and Masters in
Management, including the following academic areas: Business Leadership—
Cultural Difference; Influence Building Across Organizational Lines; Teaming in the
International Community; Dealing and Negotiating with High-Level Government
Officials; Dealing, Negotiating and Teaming with High-Level Industry Officials;
Market Analysis of the International Community; Promoting Acceptance of U.S.
Standards of Safety and Quality Production in the International Market.

WRITINGS/PUBLICATIONS

- Author: "The Government Contractor Defense in Tort Liability, a Continuing
  Genesis," American Bar Association Public Contract Law Journal, Vol. 19, No. 1,
  1990.

(continues)

(continued)

- Author: "The Government Contractor Defense in Tort Liability, a Continuing Genesis," Federal Publications, Inc. (West Publications), Vol. 26-B, December 1990.

- More than 70 published and reported trial and appellate cases, including topics of Government Contract Law, Fiscal Law, Aviation Law, Military Law and Criminal Law.

- Selected to write Federal Aviation Administration's Acquisition Management System replacing the Federal Acquisition Regulations for Federal Aviation Administration contracting personnel.

ACADEMIC HONORS

- Kappa Delta Pi Honor Society in Education, Oklahoma State University

- Delta Mu Delta Honor Society in Business Administration, Southern Nazarene University

- Phi Alpha Delta Legal Fraternity, University of Tulsa, College of Law

- Phi Eta Sigma Honor Society, Illinois State University

- Robert G. Bone Scholar, Illinois State University

- President's Honor Roll, Illinois State University

OTHER HONORS

- Recipient of Special Achievement Award from Federal Aviation Administration, Aeronautical Center Director for successful completion of protracted information resource management litigation in support of the Center's Information Resource Management Division.

- Recipient of Special Achievement Award from the Director, Federal Aviation Administration, Aviation System Standards for conceptualization and implementation of results-oriented agreements and other transaction training, and computerized data bank for cross-organizational use and transaction tracking.

- Recipient of the Rear Admiral Hugh H. Howell, Jr., Award for Outstanding Meritorious Service as Commanding Officer, Naval Reserve Legal Service Office, Great Lakes, IL 113.

- Recipient of the Senior Judge Advocate Commendation for service as National Director of the Naval Reserve Voluntary Training Units comprised of more than 30

Naval Reserve Units worldwide and for design and implementation of Judge Advocate General's Corps computerized performance-based tracking system.

- Recipient of the Senior Judge Advocate Commendation for service as Commanding Officer, Naval Reserve Legal Service Office, Great Lakes, Illinois 113.

- Recipient of the Senior Judge Advocate Commendation for service as Executive Officer, Navy–Marine Corps Appellate Review Activity 110 and 111.

CIVIC ACTIVITIES

- President of the Federal Bar Association, Oklahoma City Chapter. Former President-Elect, Vice-President of Membership, Vice-President of Programs and Secretary.

- National Director of World of Wrestling. Public address announcer for the University of Oklahoma wrestling program and numerous other events, including the Lone Star Duals—Dallas, Texas; Cliff Keen Kickoff Classic—Tulsa, Oklahoma; Grand Gator Grapple—Shreveport, Louisiana; Tulsa Nationals—Tulsa, Oklahoma; Cliff Keen Reno World Championships—Reno, Nevada; Amateur Athletic Union's Folkstyle International Championship; the Big XII Wrestling Tournament; and various Olympic qualifying tournaments.

- Adjunct professor, Oklahoma State University, Aviation and Space Education—Aviation Law, Legal and Ethical Problems in Aviation and Business Law.

- Adjunct professor, Southern Nazarene University, Graduate School of Management—International Business and Legal Environment of Management.

- Adjunct professor, the University of Oklahoma, Military Science Department—Uniform Code of Military Justice.

- Founder of the Kimberly Kay Clark Award, awarded in memory of Kimberly Kay Clark, who was killed in the April 19, 1995, bombing of the Alfred P. Murrah Federal Building, Oklahoma City, Oklahoma.

MILITARY SERVICE

Captain, United States Naval Reserve, Judge Advocate General's Corps. Director of VTU Law comprised of 31 Navy Judge Advocate Units and more than 300 officers (1997–1998). Commanding Officer of Navy Legal Service, Great Lakes (1995–1997) and Executive Officer of Navy–Marine Corps Appellate Review (1993–1995).

Summary

As you develop your specific application package for each SES job, review and study this chapter on writing the ECQs. Developing these statements is a challenging process, but it is supported by a formula that you can learn. Because mastering the ECQ statements is critical to qualifying for an SES job and being selected for an interview, the time you spend learning how to structure your statements is an investment that has the potential to pay huge dividends.

CHAPTER 17

Federal Job Survival: CareerProofing™

By Michael Dobson and Debbie Singer Dobson

Is your 401(k) or your Federal retirement account your biggest financial asset? Is it your house? How about your IRA or your stock portfolio? For most people, it's none of the above. The biggest financial asset you have is your career. It's easy to see why if you run the numbers. A GS-12/1 with 30 years until retirement is looking at over $3.5 million in total salary—not counting the cash value of benefits (or, for that matter, promotions)!

If you received that kind of money in any other area of your life (or even felt you had a good chance of getting that kind of money), you'd certainly think about how you could maximize your opportunities, protect the assets, and make them grow. Yet only a small percentage of professionals truly regard their careers as a multimillion-dollar asset and behave accordingly. You'll find the ones that do clustered disproportionately at the upper end of most organizations, and that's no coincidence.

The CareerProofing System

CareerProofing is wealth management for your most important financial asset. From securing your fundamentals to increasing the return on your investment, you should look at fitting a range of strategies and tactics into your professional life. In the same way that it's a bad idea to start your retirement planning for the first time when you're 62, it's an equally bad idea to wait until the downsizing, reorganization, commercial activities study, or buyout announcement is made to check to see that your Federal resume is up-to-date.

Level One: Protect Your Assets

Like any good financial-management strategy, the first level of CareerProofing is to safeguard and protect the asset itself. What do you need to do to improve your job security, your promotability, your ability to change jobs or agencies, the quality of your references, the scope and level of your assignments and special projects, and the range of your personal network?

Level Two: Add Value to Where You Work

In the same way that the ultimate value of a share of stock is related to the value of the company itself, your value—and therefore your career security—is related to the contribution you make. The second level of CareerProofing is to find out how you can add the most value to your organization, your agency, your program, and your office. Are your performance goals in alignment with the mission of your organization? Do you understand the goals and objectives of those in your management chain, and are you seen as contributing to the achievement of their goals and objectives? Ultimately, real job security and real advancement are given to those who are seen as contributing to larger value. This level also involves understanding office politics, organizational dynamics, and the people strategy that is part of every successful career path.

In the case of commercial activities studies in many government agencies, the better you know your value to your organization; the organization's programs, policies, and procedures; and your performance goals, the more competitive you will be against the private-sector bidders.

Level Three: Improve the Value of the Assets

Building further on this idea, the third level of the CareerProofing system is to improve the value of the asset, both inherently and in terms of contribution. You increase the potential value of a career through developmental activities. These include obtaining training, learning and practicing new skills, seeking out developmental job assignments that fit you to take on new responsibilities, and working on areas that might be weak or troublesome for you. In addition to increasing the innate asset value, you want to look for ways to put the new value to work for the organization and for the mission, vision, and values of those in your chain.

Level Four: Make Job Hunting and Upward Mobility a Regular Practice

Of course, upward mobility generally requires job hunting; thus, seeking out new positions and new challenges forms the fourth level of CareerProofing. The critical difference between normal job hunting and a CareerProofing approach is that it's much better to seek out new opportunities when you don't desperately need a new job. Unfortunately, at the times you most need an opportunity, they are most scarce. Instead, develop options when you don't need them. That way, you can pursue only those opportunities that form a clear step upward.

By the way, it's important to remember that although for many people job changing is part of career development, there are others who find that the same job or the same program can provide a career's worth of satisfaction. If that describes you, your concern in job hunting is not so much to seek out a better position, but rather to learn how to protect yourself in the event that your job, your program, or your office becomes part of commercial activity studies, or suffers a cut or reorganization that could leave you hanging when you have only two to five years before collecting your Federal retirement.

Level Five: Get Involved in Your Profession

Parallel with job hunting is a fifth level of the CareerProofing system, which is industry or professional involvement. Besides your job, your program, or your agency, you are often part of a field. Professionals in that field often have organizations, conferences, networks, and other structures that can help you achieve multiple goals in your career. In addition to the obvious opportunities for job hunting that these organizations provide, they also provide educational and training opportunities, the stimulation of like-minded professionals with similar enthusiasms and passions, a wider perspective on the work going on in your field, a source of new ideas and directions to bring back to the office, and much more. Contributing to the development of your field or profession is a success strategy that can be powerful in the same way as contributing to the value of your organization or program.

A Closer Look

Let's take a closer look at CareerProofing and learn how to do it. Like most ideas worth acting upon, there is a minimum level of time and effort you need to spend on a regular basis in order to reap the benefits that await you.

We started by comparing your career to financial assets such as a 401(k) or a stock portfolio. Financial assets can be acquired, conserved, invested, grown, and used. All these things have analogues from a CareerProofing perspective. Our first and most serious recommendation to you is to make CareerProofing a weekly requirement in your life, as important as exercise, investment, or other long-term ways you build your future.

Of course, if you're like many busy two-career professional families today, the idea of adding an extra obligation to an over-stressed, over-committed life sounds a little ludicrous, no matter how well-intentioned or well-argued it might be. We don't want to add a burden to an over-burdened life, and fortunately, it doesn't have to take a lot of extra effort. In fact, some valuable CareerProofing activities are things you likely do anyway for other reasons. By looking at these things in a slightly different light, you can get extra value out of the same work, which is a more realistic goal for a lot of us.

One important idea in making life-change investments is that relatively small amounts of time add up dramatically, the same way that small amounts of money invested regularly and earning compound interest turn into surprisingly large amounts of money over time.

For example, investing one hour a day in an activity might be challenging but probably not impossible. It also doesn't seem like it would make that big a difference. Over the span of a single year, however, an hour a day (we'll add in weekends on the assumption that this is something to benefit you at home as well as at the office) adds up to 365 hours. That's the equivalent to 45 eight-hour days with five hours left over! That's over two months of five-day-a-week office time, which is a tremendous resource. Imagine what you could get done if someone would leave you alone for two months at the office! Of course, that's unlikely to happen, and interrupted time isn't quite as efficient as uninterrupted time. Still, small amounts of time do add up to significant blocks if you stay at it.

A fundamental rule for building a financial nest egg is "Pay yourself first." In other words, take out of your paycheck the money you plan to invest *before* you pay your bills, rather than pay your bills and then invest what's left over. The reason, of course, is that you're going to have too much week left over at the end of your check. Set a regular weekly goal of completing CareerProofing activities. To increase your likelihood of success, make appointments with yourself in your calendar. Keep a log of what you've accomplished and review it from time to time. Although the first few entries in the savings account of a new investor often don't look inspiring, as the numbers mount up, so does the incentive to keep with the program.

Because CareerProofing activities can also be normal work activities, list these normal activities as well. Take credit for them on the CareerProofing side of the ledger. You deserve it, and it also helps build good habits.

Protect Your Assets

As we discussed, the first part of a CareerProofing strategy is improving your job security where you are. The more secure you are, the more valued you are, the more productive you are, and the more attractive you'll be to other prospective employers. Nothing can replace having strong fundamentals, yet some people neglect this central concept in their career-management strategies.[1]

[1]*For amplification and additional suggestions, see Dobson, Michael, and Deborah Singer,* Managing UP: 59 Ways to Build a Career-Advancing Relationship with Your Boss, *New York: AMACOM, 1999.*

Do Good Work

"Do good work" sounds far too obvious to repeat; however, the concept of "good" can be slippery in certain situations. A mismatch between your idea of "good" and your boss's idea of "good" can lead to disaster in short order.

Consider the following:

★ **Performance objectives.** Do you have negotiated performance objectives for the current rating period? Are some of them in the form of special projects or objectives? Often, such projects become "OBE," or "Overtaken by Events," swept away in the flood of daily crises. Unfortunately, at rating time, these can come back to haunt you. When the situation and your objectives must change, sit down with your boss and get your objectives formally changed.

★ **Quality and priority areas.** Are you delivering in all the critical quality areas in your job description? Many professionals deliver outstanding results in several areas but fall short in others, perhaps because they consider them secondary or unimportant. Does your boss view priorities in the same light you do?

★ **Key relationships.** How are your relationships with the people with whom you have to work? In measuring perceived quality, customers report that the quality of service and attitude is often at least equal in importance to the quality of the product or technical performance. A person who is outstanding on the latter but not

satisfactory on the former might be shocked at how low his or her job performance is rated by peers or superiors. Do a brief review of how you are getting along with different parts of the organization, with special attention to the power brokers. Determine where you might need to mend fences; then get to work.

★ **Position description issues.** What does your job description actually say, and how does it relate to the position as it is actually performed? If there are major discrepancies (which is not unusual), is it appropriate to propose a rewrite?

By the time performance appraisal season rolls around, it's often too late to do anything constructive. At best, you'll be repairing damage. First, have your boss describe behaviorally what exceeding expectations and goals looks like. Try to get regular, ongoing feedback and show that you are the kind of professional who welcomes it and profits from it.

Your success in an organization depends on many factors, but the hard-to-quantify concept of "organizational fit," which is largely subjective, plays a huge role in decisions about promotions, retention, layoffs, and dismissal. Although that role might sometimes be offstage, it nevertheless has significant impact on your career prospects and job security.

It's vital to remember that you are seldom the sole arbiter of what "good work" means in your office. Your boss, your boss's superiors and peers, your own peers, subordinates, colleagues in other departments, customers, and stakeholders outside the organization might all get a vote.

Be a Team Player

It's perfectly legitimate and appropriate to seek career rewards. Organizations offer incentives, raises, and promotions as ways to motivate certain types of performance. At the same time, we become suspicious and resentful of people whom we perceive are gaming the system to maximize their rewards at the expense of other people.

The most successful go after the legitimate rewards, but at the same time remember that they are team players and take care of the needs, goals, and aspirations of others as well. In most cases, there is little conflict between behaving decently and supportively toward your colleagues and pursuing your own ambitions. In the cases where conflict exists, sometimes being too career-focused will come back to haunt you when people who feel injured by your activities have a later opportunity to do likewise. The more decent approach is often the smarter and more practical one as well.

Regardless of your career ambitions, you have responsibilities toward your current job and your current colleagues. Take care of those responsibilities in an ethical, positive, open, and honest manner. Actively look for concrete ways to help your colleagues advance and develop. Not only does that count toward doing today's job well, you can also mark it down as a CareerProofing activity!

Add Value to Where You Work

When the organization knows the unambiguous value you provide, your security is at its highest. Only if the entire program is in jeopardy is your personal career on the line. In addition, people who add value are on the top of the list of those considered for promotion, for two important reasons. The first is, of course, the value itself. The second is a bit more subtle: A person who adds real value is also a person who understands what the real mission of the organization or program is all about. Notice in this case "real" means "in accordance with the beliefs of those in charge," which might not always be the same ideas you hold.

Understand and Manage Priorities

It's normal—but not always wise—to consider the assignments that you have been given to be your #1 priority. In reality, sometimes assignments of relatively minor importance are shifted from a superior's desk to yours not because they have priority, but precisely because they do not. Dropping everything to take care of those assignments does not necessarily add value; sometimes it shows that you don't have the requisite understanding of the big picture. When you're given assignments from your boss's desk, ask where the assignment ranks in priority with your other regular work and objectives.

Know When "Good Enough" Really Is

A vital—and often overlooked—principle in organizational effectiveness is the concept of "good enough." You'll often hear the concept dismissed as associated with poor performance, but that's sloppy thinking. All the projects in our organization take place within an environment known as the Triple Constraints, the intersection of *time* (how long have we got), *resources* (how much can we spend, including both dollars and resources, such as person-hours), and *performance* (what the output must achieve).[2]

[2]*For a thorough discussion of this vital concept in the worlds of both single and multiple project management, see Dobson, Michael,* Practical Project Management: The Secrets of Managing Any Project On Time and On Budget, *Mission, Kansas: SkillPath Publications, 1996; and Dobson, Michael S.,* The Juggler's Guide to Managing Multiple Projects, *Newtown Square, Pennsylvania: Project Management Institute, 1999.*

In a complex world, normally one leg of the Triple Constraints takes precedence. Let's say you're writing a report. If the purpose of the report is to provide the Assistant Secretary with backup on his or her Congressional testimony on Tuesday, then *time* is likely the driver. Missing the hearing is not an option. Therefore, you will do some combination of spending additional resources/person-hours, or limiting the scope covered in the report. Depending on the type of hearing, either strategy might have its place.

If there are only two qualified people available to write a certain report, then it will either take longer to write the report, or the scope or depth of the report will have to be limited. *Resources* in this case are the driver. If the accuracy in the financial data must be in the range of ±1%, there is a measured *performance* driver, and it will either take more time or more resources to achieve it, and so on.

If you can identify what part of "good" is mandatory and what part is flexible, your ability to achieve balance within the bigger picture is dramatically improved.

Objective Versus Subjective Quality

The picture is made more complex by office politics. All professionals quickly learn that a CareerProofing strategy must take office politics into account. One key predictor of how unpleasant or dangerous the office politics tend to be in a given organization is how objective or subjective is the definition of quality performance. When it's unambiguous and relatively nonnegotiable who is performing and who isn't, some of the nastier varieties of office politics tend to remain in abeyance. If, on the other hand, quality is largely a subjective characteristic, or is substantially determined by political affiliation or perspective, infighting tends to take on a more negative cast.[3] In such an environment, making sure that you're seen as a performer in all quality measurements that are objective is one critical element in demonstrating that you add value.

[3]*For more on office politics and the unofficial organization, see Dobson, Michael, and Deborah Singer,* Enlightened Office Politics: Understanding, Coping with, and Winning the Game—Without Losing Your Soul, *New York: AMACOM, 2001.*

In such an environment, negotiate performance expectations and goals clearly and up front. Unclear and indefinite goals and projects are likely to be interpreted through a filter of subjectivity. In such an environment, you're more likely to lose than to win.

Be Principled, Even When Others Are Not

Although some principles are a function of one's political beliefs or positions on one or more of the issues of the day, other principles, such as honesty and fair dealing, are relatively independent of party lines. Principles are not, as some suppose, synonymous with weakness. They are a source of long-term strength. Someone who does not keep his or her word might achieve occasional short-term tactical advantage, but someone known to be reliable and consistently honest has credibility in difficult situations. Such a reputation takes time to build and is a long-term strategic asset.

Be realistic about other people. It is perfectly principled to keep your word but withhold trust from someone who has demonstrated unreliability. Give people the benefit of the initial doubt, even though some will let you down. As your reputation grows, people who might not always be honest with others might find your trust an asset worth preserving. Look around the organization. You'll often find a few people who tend to be treated better than average. What is it that they do that is different?

Putting It All Together

The concept of CareerProofing exists to remind you that there's more to career management than job hunting, and more to doing a job well than getting today's work assignments off your desk. Professionals are normally entrusted with the care of organizational assets and important Federal missions. We are responsible for ensuring that they are used properly, not wasted, and not prematurely worn out and thrown away.

We, too, are organizational assets, and we must be used properly, not wasted, and not prematurely worn out and thrown away. Ideally, our bosses and our managers consider this one of their obligations, but it is not solely their obligation; it is first and foremost our own. We are expected as professionals to take the primary responsibility for self-management, if for no other reason than we are the people in the best position to know our true situation.

We deserve and have a right to professional self-development, growth, and advancement in line with our potential and our desires, but we are also the primary force that must act to achieve what we deserve. Our career goals are not incompatible with doing our jobs, and many work activities support both at the same time.

That's why you should think in terms of CareerProofing rather than in terms of career management or job hunting. Your career is certainly about the money you make, the promotions and respect you earn, and the recognition you receive. It is also about the work you do, the benefit you provide others, and the value that you leave behind. As professionals, we do not have to choose between these goals; we integrate them. In the process, we achieve greater security, greater growth, greater satisfaction, and greater results.

CHAPTER 18

Federal Jobs in Science, Medicine, and Health Policy: Converting a Curriculum Vitae into a Federal Resume

By David Raikow, Ph.D.

Scientists and graduate students are very familiar with the Curriculum Vitae (CV), which differs substantially from business resumes and Federal resumes. Whereas a business resume is usually limited to two pages and is highly focused or tailored to a job ad, the CV has no length limit and is meant to catalog the sum total of your experience. You can add a description of yourself in the form of a tag line or brief profile statement to a business resume; however, that type of information is usually included in the cover letter when you're using a CV to apply for scientific jobs outside of government. Business resumes are meant to be quickly scanned, whereas CVs are meant to be studied. Both the format and actual information presented in a business resume vary widely. CVs in general have standard sections; additionally, discipline-specific CVs have their own standard sections. Federal resumes fall between these two extremes.

As a scientist or graduate student, you should already have a CV. Indeed, it's a good idea to update your CV every time you do something new such as publish, get a grant, or present a paper at a meeting. Some things never leave your CV (such as your publications); however, you might decide that other things are too old or are no longer relevant to include on your CV as you advance professionally (such as the committees you served on as a graduate student). Even then, it's a good idea to save those deleted items in a separate file because you never know when you'll need to remind yourself of what you actually did in the past (such as now, as you write a Federal resume!). Building a CV is a continual process and should be taken seriously; that's why spending a few minutes to update it whenever necessary is important.

The good news is that it's easy to convert a CV into a Federal resume. CVs have standard sections, including contact information and affiliation, education, professional experience, publications, and so on. Some of these sections can go by different names. Whether you use a section labeled Professional Activities or Academic Service; Teaching Experience or Courses Taught; or Grants, Grants and Funding, Selected Grants, or Competitive Grants is not important here. You might even have sections that are not discussed here or sections that are particular to your field of study. Just match the sections discussed here with your own and follow the examples for sections with similar kinds of information in lieu of an exact match.

The following table is a quick comparison between what sections a typical CV contains and what a Federal resume contains.

Curriculum Vitae	Federal Resume
No length limit	Maximum of 5 pages
Contact information and affiliation	✓ + additional information
No	Objective
Research interests	Profile statement
Education	✓ + high school
Honors	✓
Grants	✓ (or incorporated into project descriptions)
Employment	✓ (combined with job or project descriptions)
Research experience	Project experience descriptions
Teaching experience	No, incorporated into skills
Professional activities/ academic service	No, incorporated into skills
Extension and outreach/ community service	No, incorporated into skills
Current/professional memberships	✓
Contributed papers/presentations at meetings	✓
Collaborators	No, incorporated into project descriptions
Students advised	No, incorporated into skills if relevant
References	No, usually asked for separately
Book reviews/other publications	✓ (or incorporated in skills)
Scientific publications	✓
No	Skill lists by class

Section-by-Section Conversion Instructions

The following sections step you through converting each section of your CV to a Federal resume.

Contact Information and Affiliation

Use your name, affiliation, and contact information as you would on a CV, but add your citizenship, Social Security number, Veterans' Preference, and Federal civilian status (they're required).

Objective

State the position for which you are applying, including title and job application reference number, just below your contact information.

Profile Statement

Include a Profile statement just below your objective. State what kind of scientist you are; in other words, your field of expertise and the kind of experience you have. (See chapter 10, "The Magic of Page 1.") Also state how many years of hands-on experience you have, if it is more than four years.

Education

List your degrees, majors, and school name as you would on a CV, but add the school addresses. Also list your high school (it's required).

Honors

List your fellowships, awards, and honors as you would on a CV.

Grants

These can be listed as you would on a CV if you want to highlight them. Otherwise, you can incorporate grants into the project descriptions (see "Research Experience/Project Descriptions" later in this chapter) if you don't have many or are a graduate student.

Employment

List your positions but add descriptions of your duties. This is where you'll need to add keywords or phrases from the job announcement. You shouldn't need to embellish here; after all, you should be applying for jobs for which you have relevant experience. You will, however, need to phrase your descriptions so that the human resources personnel who are grading your application can see that you are indeed qualified. (See chapter 8 for more on writing work experience descriptions.)

If you're a graduate student or a recent graduate, delete the Employment section and highlight your experience under the Project Descriptions section.

Research Experience/Project Descriptions

It can be useful to organize your scientific or technical experience in terms of the major projects you have undertaken. Many scientists do this in their CVs early in their careers. In Federal resumes, project experience descriptions can substitute for a series of specific jobs or job titles that you don't have. The concept is the same as describing previous jobs. You need to name the project, state where you conducted it, state when you conducted it, state the number of hours a week you spent on it, and describe what you did. (See chapter 8, "Writing Your Work Experience.") You might also have other relevant experience, such as a college internship, which could have its own separate section and short description.

Teaching Experience

Unless the job is a teaching position or contains a major teaching component, you can incorporate teaching experience into your skill lists (see "Skill Lists by Class" later in this chapter).

Professional Activities or Service

Do not include a Professional Activities section on your Federal resume. Activities such as organizing workshops or giving guest lectures can be incorporated into your skill lists. If the advertised position is administrative, you can include a specific Administrative Skill List (see "Skill Lists by Class" later in this chapter).

Extension and Outreach

Do not include an Extension and Outreach or Community Service section. You can include these activities within your skill lists.

Current Memberships in Societies or Professional Organizations

List your memberships as you would on a CV.

Presentations Given at Meetings or Conferences

Some people list all of their presentations by title on the CV. I don't recommend this because it takes up a lot of space, especially if you have given many presentations. Instead, list the name of the society or meeting followed by the years in which you have given presentations for it.

Collaborators

Do not list your collaborators in a separate section. Instead, name collaborators if relevant within job or project descriptions.

Students Advised or Mentored

Do not list your students in a separate section. You can summarize your mentoring activities within a skill list.

References

Some people include a list of references in their CVs. Employers usually ask for lists of references separate from the resume. This is the case for government positions. Consequently, do not include a list of references in your Federal resume.

Book Reviews, Non-Scientific, or Non-Peer-Reviewed Publications

You might want to list such publications on your Federal resume as you would on your CV. Use your field's standard notational format. If you are running out of space, summarize this type of writing within skill lists, unless the job description specifically calls for this kind of experience.

Scientific or Peer-Reviewed Publications

List your peer-reviewed publications as you would on a CV. Include papers in review.

Skill Lists by Class

As a scientist, you have amassed many skills. Chances are, though, you've never had to actually think about it and list them all. Listing your skills can take some time, but it is extremely important in the Federal resume. These skill lists can be presented in the Federal resume as either individual top-level sections or subsections within a section labeled "Skills."

I recommend grouping your skills into classes that are relevant to your field of study and the job announcement. For example, you might have laboratory skills, field-data-collection skills, and computer skills. You might want to group specific types of computer skills together. It's up to you. The different skill sets you organize give you a chance to creatively customize your Federal resume to yourself and the job announcement.

To figure out exactly what skills you have, I recommend walking through the steps of the various projects that you have done and cataloging the skills necessary to do each step. For example, an ecologist might have studied the ecosystem of a stream. In order to do this, she took water samples, measured temperature and other parameters, collected organisms, and brought them back to the lab for analysis. Later she compiled her data and analyzed it. What specific skills were necessary to do all this? She had to collect water samples without contaminating them. She had to run specific chemical tests in the lab. She had to know how to collect specific organisms, handle them, identify them, and preserve them. She had to manage her data in spreadsheets or databases and then analyze them statistically. The skill set derived from this project and listed on the Federal resume will be specific and lengthy; and perhaps will contain discipline-specific terminology (more on jargon in the next section). Be careful not to lump different skills under general titles. For example, "microscopy" is too vague. Instead, do you know how to prepare samples for microscopy, operate specific types of microscopes, identify microscopic organisms or tissues, or all of these things?

You should also include a section or sections that describe your communication skills and experience. In this section, include your writing skills (grants, reports, protocols, papers, and so on); oral presentation skills (workshops, presentations at national meetings or conferences, guest lectures, and so on); teaching (unless it's in a separate section); and interactions with the public, the media, and students.

Other Hints for Crafting Your Federal Resume

There are a few other considerations to keep in mind as you convert your CV into a Federal resume. These include tailoring the writing to your audience and how to compensate for a lack of formal experience outside of college.

Balancing Jargon and Clarity

Scientists are used to speaking in their own technical language. The problem is that the people who evaluate applications are not scientists. Indeed, your application will be evaluated by human resources personnel who will not have

technical training in your discipline. If the HR personnel cannot understand the language you use, you might not be rated as highly as you could be. So, make it easy for them to understand your qualifications. At the same time, it is probably impossible to adequately describe your experience without some degree of technical specificity. Also, once you get past the first cut, your Federal resume will be evaluated by someone with scientific or technical training. Additionally, resumes might be scanned for technical keywords. Thus, it is important to balance technical language or jargon with clarity for non-scientists.

You can achieve balance between jargon and clarity in several ways:

★ First, scan the job announcement for keywords and phrases, and use them to describe your experience. Again, you don't need to embellish if you are applying for a job for which you have relevant experience and which is at the appropriate GS-level. You're simply choosing to phrase your experience so that the HR personnel can recognize it.

★ Second, simplify the titles of projects if they are very technical. If you are using project descriptions, title the projects descriptively, but more simply than publication titles. For example, a project entitled "Cellular mechanisms of protein transport" is better than "Binding homologue identification using affinity purification in lymphocytes." You can then get a bit more detailed and technical in the description as well as in your KSAs.

★ Third, if the job announcement calls for knowledge of something specific, such as statistics, do not simply list the statistical tests with which you have experience. Instead, say "Statistical analysis" in a skill list and then briefly list the tests you have performed, grouped and identified by type.

Graduate Students and Recent Grads Versus Established Scientists

Graduate students or recent graduates face some issues that established scientists do not. Foremost is the fact that you have spent all your time in graduate school and not in different jobs with separate titles. To deal with this, list your experience as specific projects you've undertaken. If you don't have many grants, delete the Grants section and incorporate the grants you have into project descriptions. Another issue is how to quantify your hands-on experience. The human resources personnel who will evaluate your application have strict guidelines concerning the calculation of time spent on the job. If you've just graduated, how do you quantify your experience in terms of hours spent per week? The solution is to count the semesters that you have been earning graduate-level credits for research and total them into years. You can count this as full-time work experience (40 hours per week) and your statements are supported by your transcripts.

All Federal resumes should include narrative descriptions of past jobs or projects. But as scientists advance and gain experience, their skill sets increase, and established scientists might find that listing all their skills is redundant with detailed job or project descriptions. Because you should avoid redundancy in your Federal resume, I recommend that you reach a balance between skill lists and narrative descriptions. Scientists early in their careers should certainly have narrative descriptions, but they should stress skill lists. As you advance, the number and size of narrative descriptions should increase while skill lists become smaller and more general. Senior scientists should have a minimum of skill lists, if any. In addition, the Major Accomplishments section is best used by more senior-level scientists. If you include a Major Accomplishments section early in your career, it might backfire by implying that, for example, all you've done is get your degree.

Before-and-After Sample CV and Federal Resume

Here is a real example of a CV and its Federal resume counterpart.

Curriculum Vitae

1234 Bryant St.   **DAVID F. RAIKOW**   123-456-7890
Pittsburgh, PA 15213   draikow@kbs.msu.edu

Profile and Research Interests

A broadly trained community and ecosystem ecologist with experience in streams, lakes, and wetlands; knowledge of ecological principles underlying physical, chemical, and biological components and processes of ecosystems including nutrient cycling, food webs, and assemblage structure; practice with ecosystem disturbance including biological invasion; training in teaching and course development at the college level; research interests in landscape-level ecosystem connectivity including terrestrial-aquatic linkage, using food web structure as an organizing principle, continuing the development of stable isotope ecology, and the ecology of environmental problems such as habitat fragmentation and biological invasion.

Education

Ph.D. 2002   Zoology and Ecology, Evolutionary Biology and Behavior (dual degree), Michigan State University, Department of Zoology and W. K. Kellogg Biological Station. Advisor: Stephen K. Hamilton. Dissertation: "How the feeding ecology of native and exotic mussels affects freshwater ecosystems."

M.S. 1996   Biological Sciences, Ecology and Evolution Program, University of Pittsburgh, Department of Biological Sciences. Advisor: William Coffman. Thesis: "Macroinvertebrate diversity and substrate heterogeneity in Linesville Creek."

B.S. 1993   Biological Sciences, University of Pittsburgh.

B.A. 1993   History and Philosophy of Science, University of Pittsburgh.

Honors and Fellowships

Certification in Teaching College Science and Mathematics Teaching Fellowship   2001

Research Training Group (RTG) Fellowship, W. K. Kellogg Biological Station   1997–1999

Graduation Cum Laude, University of Pittsburgh   1993

Departmental Honors, Biological Sciences, University of Pittsburgh   1993

Departmental Honors, History and Philosophy of Science, University of Pittsburgh   1993

David F. Raikow   2

Research Publications In Preparation / In Review

Raikow, D. F., A. E. Wilson, O. Sarnelle, and S. K. Hamilton, In Prep, Exotic zebra mussels promote dominance of the noxious cyanobacterium *Microcystis aeruginosa* in low-nutrient lakes. To be submitted to **Limnology and Oceanography.**

Raikow, D. F. In Revision. Food web interactions between native larval fish and exotic zebra mussels. Submitted to **Canadian Journal of Fisheries and Aquatic Sciences.**

Research Publications In Press / Published

Hamilton, S. K., J. L. Tank, D. F. Raikow, E. Siler, N. Dorn, and N. Leonard. In Press. The importance of aquatic production to stream food webs: Modeling the results of a nitrogen isotope addition experiment. **Journal of the North American Benthological Society.**

Raikow, D. F., and S. K. Hamilton. 2001. Bivalve diets in a Midwestern U.S. stream: A stable isotope enrichment study. **Limnology and Oceanography** 46: 514–522.

Hamilton, S. K., J. L. Tank, D. F. Raikow, W. M. Wollheim, B. J. Peterson, and J. R. Webster. 2001. Nitrogen uptake and transformation in a Midwestern U.S. stream: A stable isotope enrichment study. **Biogeochemistry** 54: 297–340.

Raikow, D. F., S. A. Grubbs, and K. W. Cummins. 1995. Debris dam dynamics and coarse particulate organic matter retention in an Appalachian mountain stream. **Journal of the North American Benthological Society** 14: 535–546.

Searcy, W. A., S. Coffman, and D. F. Raikow. 1994. Habituation, recovery, and the similarity of song types within repertories in red-winged blackbirds (*Agelaius phoeniceus*) (Aves, Emberizidae). **Ethology** 98: 38–49.

Book Reviews

Stevens, M. H. H., D. F. Raikow, M. R. Servedio, R. J. Collins, T. L. Schumann, A. N. Tipper, and W. P. Carson. 1996. Hutchinson's Chariot: A Review of Species Diversity in Space and Time, by M. L. Rosenzweig. **Plant Science Bulletin.**

External Grants

$21,650   "Can zebra mussels suppress bluegill and promote the toxic   1999
             algae Microcystis?" Kalamazoo Community Foundation.

$600   "Migration patterns of adult insects emerging from streams: 1997
             a 15N tracer study," Sigma Xi Grants-in-aid-of-research.

(continues)

(continued)

David F. Raikow　　　　　　　　　　　　　　　　　　　　　　　　　　　　　3

Internal Grants

Numerous	Department of Zoology	1996–2002
Numerous	Research Training Program (RTG)	1996–2002
Numerous	Ecology, Evolutionary Biology and Behavior Program (EEBB)	1996–2002
$350	Lauff Research Award, Kellogg Biological Station	1997
$900	McKinley Research Fund, University of Pittsburgh	1995
$1,000	Howard Hughes Medical Institute, University of Pittsburgh	1993

Teaching Experience

Certification: Teaching College Science and Mathematics Program, Michigan State University. Attended 10 teaching workshops, completed a class on teaching techniques, and conducted a mentored teaching project: "Improving links between the elements of a field ecology course."	2002
Guest lectures: "The Ecology of Biological Invasions," for the graduate course Community and Ecosystem Ecology, Michigan State University.	1999–2002
Genetics: Recitation instructor. Led discussions, answered student questions, wrote and evaluated quizzes, graded tests.	2002
Introductory Biology Lab: Michigan State University and University of Pittsburgh. Ran labs, created tests, evaluated student presentations.	1994–1997
Ecology Lab: Michigan State University and University of Pittsburgh. Ran campus-based labs and assisted in field-based courses.	1995, 2001
Ecology: Assisted lecture classes at Michigan State University and University of Pittsburgh field stations. Wrote and evaluated tests.	1995, 2001
Ecology of Fishes: Assisted University of Pittsburgh field course.	1996

David F. Raikow   4

Professional Service

Manuscript review: *Limnology and Oceanography, Journal of the North American Benthological Society, Marine Biology, Hydrobiologia.*	Current
Student representative to faculty, Kellogg Biological Station.	2000–2002
Invited seminar: "The Lotic Intersite Nitrogen Experiment," Ecology and Evolution Program, Dept. of Biological Sciences, University of Pittsburgh.	2001
Workshop organization: "Stable isotopes in aquatic food web research: pitfalls and potentials," Long Term Ecological Research All Scientist Meeting.	2000
Design and administration of websites: Pymatuning Laboratory of Ecology; Lotic Intersite Nitrogen Experiment, others.	1995–2003
Planning and hosting of meeting: First Biennial Western Pennsylvania Symposium of Ecologists, Evolutionary Biologists, and Systematists, Powdermill Nature Reserve, Carnegie Museum of Natural History.	1995

Collaborations

Kenneth W. Cummins, William A. Searcy, Stephen K. Hamilton, Orlando Sarnelle, Scott A. Grubbs, Alan E. Wilson.

Contributed Papers

Ecological Society of America	2002, 2000, 1997
North American Benthological Society	2001, 2000, 1999, 1997, 1993
Long Term Ecological Research (LTER) All Scientist Meeting	2000
Freshwater Mollusk Conservation Society Symposium	1999

Memberships

American Society of Limnology and Oceanography	joined in 2000
Ecological Society of America	joined in 1997
North American Benthological Society	joined in 1993
Society for Ecological Restoration	joined in 1993

(continues)

(continued)

David F. Raikow   5

Community Service

Founder, www.creationism.com, a website dedicated to rational thought   2003
and debunking creationism.

Interviews with local newspapers, radio, and television.   1999–2002

Science fair judging, Zoology & Grand Awards   2001
- Science & Engineering Fair of Metropolitan Detroit.   2000
- International Science and Engineering Fair.

Invited lectures, "Zebra mussels and other local exotics"
- Three Rivers Rotary Club.   2001
- The Seedlings Garden Club.   2000

Mentored local 7th grade student with school project: "Will turtles eat   1998
zebra mussels?"

Volunteer Emergency Medical Technician, medical supply officer,   1989–1993
secretary, Foxwall Emergency Medical Service, Fox Chapel, PA.

Employment

Current   The Resume Place, Inc.
Writer. Write federal resumes, Knowledge, Skills, and Abilities statements, and Senior Executive Service Executive Core Qualifications for clients; write columns for company website; contributing author to *Federal Resume Guidebook*; currently writing a book on how to write CVs and co-authoring another book on career document preparation.

1996–2002   Michigan State University (Ph.D. program).
Grant recipient (2 semesters) Kalamazoo Community Foundation; *Fellow*, Research Training Group (2.5 years); *Research Assistant* in my advisor's biogeochemistry lab and as a technician for zebra mussel experiments (4 semesters); and *Teaching Assistant* (4 semesters).

1994–1996   University of Pittsburgh (M.S. program).
Teaching Assistant.

1991   Center for Hazardous Materials Research.
Intern, Government Programs Division. Evaluated reports for the EPA Pollution Prevention By and For Small Business Program. Co-authored fact sheets. Trained on environmental and hazardous materials regulations, agencies, and information sources.

Federal Resume

DR. DAVID F. RAIKOW
1234 Bryant St., Pittsburgh, PA 15213
Phone: 123-456-7890, Fax: 123-456-7890, Email: draikow@kbs.msu.edu

SSN: 123-45-6789
Citizenship: The United States of America

Veterans' Preference: N/A
Federal Civilian Status: N/A

OBJECTIVE

Ecologist, GS-0408-11, Environmental Protection Agency,
Announcement # SAMPLE 01-23

PROFILE

A broadly trained community and ecosystem ecologist with 7 years of hands-on graduate-level experience in streams, lakes, and wetlands; knowledge of ecological principles underlying physical, chemical, and biological components and processes of ecosystems, including nutrient cycling, food webs, spatial ecosystem connectivity, and community structure; education in environmental stressors including habitat fragmentation, eutrophication, biological invasion, and responses such as ecological restoration; and experience independently designing and coordinating scientific studies, ecological field sampling, experimental design, protocol development, data exploration and statistical analysis, and publication and presentation of results to scientific and general audiences.

EDUCATION

- Ph.D. 2002 Ecology, Evolutionary Biology, & Behavior, and Zoology (dual degree), Michigan State University, East Lansing, MI 48824.
- M.S. 1996 Biological Sciences, University of Pittsburgh, Pittsburgh, PA 15260.
- B.S. 1993 Biological Sciences, University of Pittsburgh, Pittsburgh, PA 15260.
- B.A. 1993 History & Philosophy of Science, University of Pittsburgh, Pittsburgh, PA 15260.
- Diploma 1988 Peabody High School, Centers for Advanced Study, Pittsburgh, PA 15206.

HONORS

- Fellowship, Certification in Teaching College Science and Mathematics   2001
- Fellowship, Research Training Group (RTG), Kellogg Biological Station   1997–1999
- Graduation Cum Laude, University of Pittsburgh   1993
- Departmental Honors, Biological Sciences, University of Pittsburgh   1993
- Departmental Honors, History & Philosophy of Science, Univ. of Pittsburgh   1993

(continues)

(continued)

SCIENTIFIC EXPERIENCE

THE ZEBRA MUSSEL INVASION OF INLAND LAKES

Michigan State University, Kellogg Biological Station, Hickory Corners, MI 49060; August 1997 to August 2002, 50 hrs/week, Ph.D. dissertation. Designed, executed, analyzed, documented, presented, and submitted for publication several ecological studies of how the biological invasion of zebra mussels (*Dreissena*) perturbs inland lake ecosystems. Supervised assistants in the field. Collected, preserved, identified, and enumerated phytoplankton and zooplankton. Collected water samples and analyzed nutrient levels and related water quality parameters. Designed, constructed, and ran a field mesocosm experiment using larval fish collected directly from nests. Identified zebra mussels as cause of impairment of larval fish growth rates through food web interactions. Identified zebra mussels as cause of perturbation to phytoplankton community structure and shift to dominance of the toxic cyanobacteria *Microcystis aeruginosa*. Secured over $21,000 in grant funding from the Kalamazoo Community Foundation. Worked with a local research team and collaborated with the Great Lakes Environmental Research Lab (NOAA). Major Advisor (Supervisor): Dr. Stephen K. Hamilton, whom you may contact at 123-456-7890.

THE LOTIC INTERSITE NITROGEN EXPERIMENT

Michigan State University, Kellogg Biological Station, Hickory Corners, MI 49060; June 1998 to June 2000, variable hours overlapping with project above. Designed, executed, analyzed, documented, presented, and published an ecological study of stream freshwater unionid mussels and helped analyze and publish ecological studies of biogeochemical cycling and food webs. Collected macroinvertebrates in streams of Arizona, Tennessee, and Michigan. Collected periphyton, phytoplankton, organic matter, sediment, and water samples. Designed, constructed, and ran an in-situ field experiment. Identified cause of perturbation to the mussel population as increased terrestrial predation facilitated by lowered water levels during drought conditions. Documented biological invasion of Asiatic clams (*Corbicula*). Worked with the local sampling team and the national synthesis team.

MACROINVERTEBRATES AND SUBSTRATE DIVERSITY

University of Pittsburgh, Pittsburgh, PA 15260; August 1994 to August 1996, 50 hrs/week, M.S. thesis. Designed, executed, analyzed, documented, and presented an ecological study of how stream macroinvertebrate assemblages respond to substrate composition. Collected macroinvertebrates using a box sampler of my own design and construction. Supervised assistants in the field.

WOODY DEBRIS AND ORGANIC MATTER IN STREAMS

University of Pittsburgh, Pittsburgh, PA 15260; January 1993 to May 1994, 10 hrs/week, Undergraduate thesis. Designed, executed, analyzed, documented, presented, and published an ecological study of organic matter retention, geomorphology, and woody debris. Conducted field experiments.

David F. Raikow
SSN: 123-45-6789

page 4
Announcement: Sample 01-23

Writing:
- Writing of grants, scientific publications, progress reports, budgets, protocols.
- Contributing author to *Federal Resume Guidebook,* 3rd Ed.
- Freelance writing, federal resume and curriculum vitae consultation.
- Reviewing of manuscripts for *Limnology and Oceanography, Journal of the North American Benthological Society, Marine Biology,* and *Hydrobiologia.*

Public Speaking:
- Organizing and running of a workshop at national scientific ecology conference.
- Organizing and hosting regional meetings with several hundred attendees.
- Certification in Teaching College Science and Mathematics.
- Assisting or teaching of numerous classes including Genetics, Ecology, Ecology Lab, Biology Lab, and Ecology of Fishes.
- Numerous informal presentations to scientific peers.
- Lecturing to scientists at an invited seminar at the University of Pittsburgh.
- Lecturing to students on the ecology of biological invasions in a class.
- Public seminars at local community groups (e.g. The Rotary Club).
- Lecturing to Congressional delegates on environmental issues at site review.
- Interaction with local media (e.g. newspapers, TV, radio).

ENVIRONMENTAL CONSULTING EXPERIENCE

Intern, Government Programs Division
Center for Hazardous Materials Research, Pittsburgh, PA

Summer 1991
$1000/ mo.

Evaluated EPA Pollution Prevention By and For Small Business Program reports. Co-authored fact sheets (e.g. Leaking Underground Gasoline Storage Tanks, Spill Notification Reference, Clean Air Act Amendments). Trained on environmental & hazardous materials regulations (e.g. RCRA, CERCLA, SARA, TSCA, FIFRA, CAAA), agencies (e.g. PADER, EPA, OSHA), and information sources (e.g. CFR, BNA Environment Reporter, Inside EPA, Federal Register). Certified in Hazardous Waste Operations and Emergency Response (29 CFR 1910).

MEMBERSHIPS

- American Society of Limnology and Oceanography — joined in 2000
- Ecological Society of America — joined in 1997
- North American Benthological Society — joined in 1993
- Society for Ecological Restoration — joined in 1993

PRESENTATIONS AT SCIENTIFIC MEETINGS

- Ecological Society of America — 2002, 2000, 1997
- North American Benthological Society — 2001, 2000, 1999, 1997, 1993
- LTER All Scientist Meeting — 2000
- Freshwater Mollusk Conservation Society Symposium — 1999

(continues)

(continued)

SKILLS

Field:
- Experimental and field survey design.
- Sampling of lakes, streams, and wetlands for limnological water quality.
- Collection of benthic macroinvertebrates, freshwater mussels, zooplankton, periphyton, phytoplankton, and fish (by seining, electroshocking, and direct harvest of larvae).
- Sampling of suspended sediment, sediment coring, use of sediment traps.
- Measurement of physical ecosystem parameters using probes (e.g. YSI multisensor, Hydrolab, flow meter, quantum meter, pH meter, Hobos, etc.).
- In-situ tracer additions (e.g. ^{15}N).
- Construction of mesocosms, field experiments, and sampling equipment.
- Use of the Global Positioning System (GPS).
- Surveying of elevation and mapping.
- Operation of boats (e.g. canoes, johnboats, pontoon boats).

Laboratory:
- Filtration and preparation of water samples for chemical analyses.
- Preparation of chemical reagents.
- Nutrient/chemical analyses (e.g. Chlorophyll-a, Dissolved Organic Carbon, Ammonium, Phosphate, etc.).
- Operation of HPLC, GC, IC, Spectrophotometer, Mass Spectrometer, etc.
- Stable isotope analyses.
- Preparation of samples for microscopy.
- Operation of compound, dissecting, and inverted microscopes.
- Identification of macroinvertebrates, zooplankton, and phytoplankton.

Computer:
- Windows and Macintosh operating systems.
- Word processing (e.g. MS Word, Adobe Acrobat).
- Presentation & poster creation (e.g. MS PowerPoint).
- Data management (e.g. MS Excel, Access).
- Model creation (e.g. Stella).
- Image manipulation (e.g. Adobe Photoshop).
- Graphics creation (e.g. Adobe Illustrator, Appleworks).
- Website creation and administration (e.g. Macromedia Dreamweaver).

Statistics:
- Statistics programs including SAS, SPSS, Systat, and Statview.
- Basic statistical analysis (e.g. ANOVA, ANCOVA, Repeated measures ANOVA, Regression).
- Multivariate statistical analysis (e.g. Correspondence Analysis, Principal Components Analysis, Multi-Dimensional Scaling, Linear Discriminant Analysis).
- Geostatistical analysis (e.g. Spatial autocorrelation).

PUBLICATIONS

• **Raikow**, D. F., A. E. Wilson, O. Sarnelle, and S. K. Hamilton. In Preparation. Exotic zebra mussels promote dominance of the noxious cyanobacterium *Microcystis aeruginosa* in low-nutrient lakes. To be submitted to *Limnology and Oceanography*.

• **Raikow**, D. F. In Revision. Food web interactions between native larval fish and exotic zebra mussels. Submitted to *Canadian Journal of Fisheries and Aquatic Sciences.*

• Hamilton, S. K., J. L. Tank, D. F. **Raikow**, E. Siler, N. Dorn, and N. Leonard. In Press. Using stable isotope tracer additions to study food webs: A model to interpret results from a woodland stream. *Journal of the North American Benthological Society.*

• **Raikow**, D. F., and S. K. Hamilton. 2001. Bivalve diets in a Midwestern U.S. stream: A stable isotope enrichment study. *Limnology and Oceanography* 46: 514–522.

• Hamilton, S. K., J. L. Tank, D. F. **Raikow**, W. M. Wollheim, B. J. Peterson, and J. R. Webster. 2001. Nitrogen uptake and transformation in a Midwestern U.S. stream: A stable isotope enrichment study. *Biogeochemistry* 54: 297–340.

• **Raikow**, D. F., S. A. Grubbs, and K. W. Cummins. 1995. Debris dam dynamics and coarse particulate organic matter retention in an Appalachian mountain stream. *Journal of the North American Benthological Society* 14: 535–546.

• Searcy W. A., S. Coffman, and D. F. **Raikow**. 1994. Habituation, recovery, and the similarity of song types within repertories in red-winged blackbirds (Agelaius phoeniceus) (Aves, Emberizidae). *Ethology* 98: 38–49.

VOLUNTEER COMMUNITY SERVICE

• *Science Fair Judge*   2000–2001
   Judged high school science projects at regional and international science fairs as Zoology and Grand Awards Judge.

• *Mentor to local 7th grader with science project*   1998
   Helped student design, build, execute, and analyze a science project involving whether turtles will eat zebra mussels.

• *Emergency Medical Technician, Foxwall Emergency Medical Service*   1989–1992
   Manned base; responded to emergency dispatches; drove ambulances; assessed, treated, and transported patients from the scene to hospitals; purchased ambulance supplies; served as Medical Supply Officer, Secretary, and Crew Representative to Board of Directors.

CHAPTER 19

Writing a Federal IT Resume

By Evelin Letarte

The IT field has gone through many changes over the past few years, and the market for IT workers has varied as well. The perception of job and earnings potential has soured, and IT workers are faced with fewer jobs and greater job insecurity. The one exception is in the Federal government, which is hiring IT workers at a greater rate than in earlier years. The good news is that the market for Federal IT workers has remained solid. A recent quick search on USAJOBS revealed 118 active jobs in the GS-2210 series. The many positions available are in a range of grade levels. Wages and benefits are competitive. In addition, the new Department of Homeland Security will require a massive IT infrastructure. For workers seeking a new or better position in the Federal government, this is good news.

Job seekers will find that the Federal government has also recently made updates to its job classification system. In May 2001, the Federal government renumbered the group and series to more accurately reflect the modern IT market and the skills needed to competently perform those jobs. The old series, including GS-0334—Computer Specialist and GS-0391—Telecommunications, were folded into the new GS-2210—Information Technology Management Series. Job titles have also been updated and job descriptions have been clarified and updated to make it easier for the job seeker.

The GS-2200—Information Technology Group includes only two series: GS-2210—Information Technology Management Series and GS-2299—Information Technology Student Trainee Series. But the real bulk of the series is GS-2210 because the GS-2299—Information Technology Student Trainee is described and classified under the General Student Trainee Series, GS-0099.

According to the Office of Personnel Management, the GS-2210—Information Technology Management Series covers two grade-interval administrative positions that manage, supervise, lead, administer, develop, deliver, and support information technology (IT) systems and services. This series covers only those positions for which the paramount requirement is knowledge of IT principles, concepts, and methods; for example, data storage, software applications, and networking.

Information technology refers to systems and services used in the automated acquisition, storage, manipulation, management, movement, control, display, switching, interchange, transmission, assurance, or reception of information. Information technology equipment includes computers, network components, peripheral equipment, software, firmware, services, and related resources.

The GS-2210 series includes, but is not limited to, the following[1]:

★ **Security:** Work that involves ensuring the confidentiality, integrity, and availability of systems, networks, and data through the planning, analysis, development, implementation, maintenance, and enhancement of information systems security programs, policies, procedures, and tools.

★ **Systems Analysis:** Work that involves applying analytical processes to the planning, design, and implementation of new and improved information systems to meet the business requirements of customer organizations.

★ **Applications Software:** Work that involves the design, documentation, development, modification, testing, installation, implementation, and support of new or existing applications software.

★ **Operating Systems:** Work that involves the planning, installation, configuration, testing, implementation, and management of the systems environment in support of the organization's IT architecture and business needs.

★ **Network Services:** Work that involves the planning, analysis, design, development, testing, quality assurance, configuration, installation, implementation, integration, maintenance, and/or management of networked systems used for the transmission of information in voice, data, and/or video formats.

★ **Data Management:** Work that involves the planning, development, implementation, and administration of systems for the acquisition, storage, and retrieval of data.

★ **Internet:** Work that involves the technical planning, design, development, testing, implementation, and management of Internet, intranet, and extranet activities, including systems/applications development and technical management of Web sites. This specialty includes only positions that require the application of technical knowledge of Internet systems, services, and technologies.

★ **Systems Administration:** Work that involves planning and coordinating the installation, testing, operation, troubleshooting, and maintenance of hardware and software systems.

★ **Customer Support:** Work that involves the planning and delivery of customer support services, including installation, configuration, troubleshooting, customer assistance, and/or training, in response to customer requirements.

[1]Handbook of Occupational Groups and Families GS-2200 Definitions, *August 2001, Office of Personnel Management.*

You can find comprehensive descriptions of the skills needed for IT jobs at each GS level in the GS-2200 series at www.opm.gov/fedclass/html/gsseries.asp#2200. The information contained in this document can be extremely useful when you're writing your resume and evaluating your skills and abilities.

There is a wide range of positions to be filled. With a focused, thoughtful resume, a candidate has a good opportunity to acquire one of those jobs.

IT Resume Writing Challenges

Writing a resume for the IT field can be especially demanding because of the range of skills you need to market. Resumes in the IT field have a unique challenge: Not only must you present yourself as technically proficient, you also need to illustrate your nontechnical aptitude as well. In addition to knowing what nontechnical skills are important for the jobs you are applying for, you also need to thoroughly explore and realistically evaluate your skills in areas such as management, customer service, and teamwork. Combining technical and people skills on your resume is challenging; however, if you do it right, you and your job search will benefit greatly.

To help integrate your technical and nontechnical skills into your resume, ask yourself the questions that we expand upon in the following sections.

Is Your Resume Too Technical?

Many IT job seekers focus exclusively on their technical skills, using too much unnecessary technical jargon that might be meaningless to the average reader, including numbers, acronyms, and shorthand instead of complete sentences.

It is essential to use keywords and IT-specific language appropriately, but it is equally important to make your resume accessible to everybody. It is important to remember that the person who initially reads your resume might not be as technically proficient as you are. You can enhance the readability of your resume if you consciously write for a more general audience. This doesn't mean that you should cut out your technical information; you need to include that information. But it is important to make sure that your overall resume is reader-friendly.

Having your spouse or a friend who is not in your field read your resume can help ensure that you have eliminated technical jargon and slang that is exclusive to your field.

Are You Emphasizing Teamwork Enough?

Teamwork has become an important keyword for today's job seeker. Hiring managers want employees who can work collaboratively with current personnel with little or no guidance. Technical skills can be learned, shared, or

researched with relatively little effort; however, successful integration into a team is more difficult and critical, especially in the IT field. For example, essentially all large software and programming projects are developed collaboratively. Without effective cooperation, such projects could not be completed.

Articulating teamwork and effective collaboration skills on a resume can be difficult. A good place to start is to brainstorm about the important characteristics of teamwork, such as flexibility, reliability, dedication, enthusiasm, commitment to the team and project, leadership, the ability to listen, the ability to accept criticism, tact, honesty, frankness, and so on. When you've done that, you can determine what aspects of teamwork are most important in the position you are seeking. Then you can concentrate on communicating the important qualities that you want to emphasize in your resume.

For example, if the new position will require you to write part of a large computer program, you might want to focus on your ability to listen to others, your ability to accept constructive criticism, and your commitment to the team and project. School projects, previous programming experience, or collaborative writing projects are good examples of when you might previously have used and demonstrated these skills. An individual working as a team member to provide help-desk support would emphasize her flexibility and reliability, as well as her previous experiences providing customer service in a team environment, even if the experiences were not in the IT field.

Have You Included Your "People Skills?"

More and more frequently, employers are looking for individuals in the IT field who have people skills. Almost everyone has encountered a manager or supervisor who is an expert in his or her field but who lacks managerial and leadership skills. Companies have taken note of the problems this practice creates and are hiring individuals with people skills in addition to technical skills.

A hiring manager usually has criteria other than technical proficiency. The first and most important thing to do is to identify what skills they are looking for and which you should emphasize on your resume. For example, you would want to emphasize your managerial and leadership skills if you were looking to move into a leadership position in the IT field. If you want a position in policy and planning, you might want to emphasize your communications and research skills. Each position is different and requires a unique skill set.

By researching the job description, you will get a clear picture of what skills are needed; then you can focus on addressing those needs. In your resume and KSAs, you should identify and write about the experiences you have had that demonstrate how you possess the required skills. By effectively communicating that you are more than just a compilation of technical skills, you will be more likely than another candidate to get an interview.

Have You Given Specific Examples?

Specific examples in a resume help paint a picture of your experiences so that the reader has a clear idea of what you have done and have accomplished. It is much easier for the reader to understand what you have achieved if you can provide examples, both in your resume and in your KSAs. It is tempting to just list the skills you have (for example, Java, C++, C, UNIX, HTML); however, a simple list cannot adequately illustrate what you can do with those skills. You need to give specific examples of how you use your skills.

For example, instead of writing "Skilled at performing team management," which is a very

passive way of saying you managed a team, you could write "Manage a team of seven programmers to write, create, and revise Java programs supporting the entire State Department" or "Manage, supervise, and provide feedback to team of seven programmers providing programming support to the State Department." Depending on what you want to emphasize, there are multiple ways of writing about any skill you might have.

It is important to remember that the clearer the picture you paint, the better the reader can realize what you do and how you can meet the organization's needs.

Have You Clearly Defined Your Accomplishments?

No matter how much you do and how vivid a picture you paint of your work, it is most important to be specific about the outcomes of your work. Your day-to-day duties can help clarify what you do and the skills you have, but it is your accomplishments that will sell you.

It is very powerful to give results rather than just actions. This might include monetary values (for example, "Designed and wrote new program that saved the company $200,000 a year in postal fees"), time ("Initiated new team-based procedures that lowered the response time from an average of 48 hours to an average of 8 hours"), satisfaction rates ("Implemented new tracking system resulting in a 15% rise in satisfaction based on customer surveys"), and so forth.

A simple way to determine the outcome of a task is to ask yourself "So what?" after reading each sentence of your resume. For everything you do, there is a result, although it might not always be spectacular. In fact, sometimes your work might seem routine and boring. If so, start to look outside the boundaries of your job. If by keeping the network up and running you ensure that 300 people have uninterrupted access to essential data and can keep working, you should point it out. Ask yourself, without you or your position, what would happen? What would *not* happen?

Did You Proofread Your Resume and KSAs?

The ability to express yourself in writing is essential to all jobs. When writing a resume, your English teacher was right: Spelling counts, as do grammatical errors, typos, and other mistakes. Your experience will not speak for itself if the reader is distracted by poor writing skills or a sloppy resume. Don't rely on the spell and grammar checkers on your word processor alone; only a human can pick up certain spelling and grammar mistakes.

Quick List of Final Steps to a Great IT Resume

With many Federal IT positions being offered in the coming years, your resume should stand out so that you will be interviewed. Follow these final tips to create the best possible package of your qualifications:

1. Research the two to three top skills you need to succeed at a specific position, both technical and nontechnical, by reviewing the job description carefully and by using the information provided by the Federal government. Use these general skills in your Summary of Qualifications or Profile.

2. Identify strong examples from your experiences to demonstrate that you have particular skills and use those examples in your resume and KSAs.

3. Quantify your accomplishments. This is the best way to convince an employer that you are qualified for a job and should be interviewed.

4. Review your resume with a very critical eye. Ask yourself the following questions:

    a. Is my resume attractive, easy to read, and concise?

    b. Is my resume free of technical jargon?

    c. Did I include my education, certificates, and training information?

    d. Does my resume list accomplishments, not just job duties?

    e. Have I written about my people skills in addition to my technical skills?

    f. Have I shown that I am the best-qualified candidate for the job?

5. Finally, review your resume to make sure that it reflects who you want to become, not who you were in the past.

The most important thing to remember is that your Federal resume is your tool to market yourself and your skills. By taking the time to be sure it adequately and accurately represents you and the skills you possess, you can raise your chances of securing the Federal position that you deserve.

Federal IT Resume Examples

Patricia Davis is changing her career. She was a science teacher for nine years until she decided to go back to school to complete her M.S. degree in Computer Information Systems. She is focusing her resume on education and training on page one, with a complete list of her teaching positions as well, to demonstrate communications, planning, and teaching skills.

Patricia Davis

3695 Water Point Drive • Kissimmee, Florida 34741 • (407) 555-1212 • patriciadavis@hotmail.com

Personal Statistics:

Citizenship: United States of America
Social Security number: 000-00-0000
Veterans' and military status: n/a

Objective:

Position title & Series/Grade: Computer Specialist – Networking, GS-2210-09
Announcement number: STS-9338-B

Professional Summary:

Certified Network Professional: Certified MCSE and CCNA technician. Skilled with researching and analyzing problems and recommending effective solutions. Demonstrated experience in Microsoft Windows 2000, Microsoft NT, Microsoft Back Office, SQL Server 7, and UNIX environments.

Technically Proficient: Qualified professional finalizing master's degree in Computer Resource and Information Technology Management. Skilled in analyzing and resolving hardware and software problems. Trained to test new releases of applications software prior to distribution and provide installation and operations assistance.

Excellent Communications Skills: Professional with over 15 years experience teaching and training individuals of diverse backgrounds about technical and scientific principles. Exceptionally skilled at communicating with non-technical personnel to facilitate the appropriate use and operation of computer components and employment of network capacities. Exceptionally adept at analyzing policies and operating procedures and recommending standards and solutions to management.

Experienced Leader and Manager: Lead teams of educators and technical professionals to carry out team projects. Provide technical leadership as Team Sales Representative. Provide guidance to help team take advantage of technical tools. Excellent project management skills, including development and production of master's thesis with Systems Development Life Cycle, and Microsoft Project software.

(continues)

(continued)

Education:

Master of Arts in Computer Resource and Information Technology Management **2002**
Webster University, Orlando, Florida GPA: 3.57

Associate of Science in Computer Network Administration **2001**
Keiser College, Melbourne, Florida GPA: 4.00

Bachelor of Science in Education **1981**
Southwest Texas State University, San Marcos, Texas

Certifications:

MCSE 2000 (Microsoft Certified Systems Engineer), CCNA (Cisco Certified Network Associate)

- Adept at planning, implementing, maintaining, and supporting information systems in a wide range of computing environments with Microsoft NT, Microsoft Windows 2000, Microsoft Back Office, SQL Server 7, and UNIX.
- Analyzed alternative networking service infrastructure designs to supported system requirements.
- Scored 847 / 900 points on Microsoft Infrastructure Design Exam 70-219.
- Skilled at identification of components, media, and protocols of a LAN to configure static and dynamic routing tables for network traffic.
- Experienced planner of directory services structure and the implementation and analysis of system performance in a Windows NT environment.
- Accomplished at identification of components, implementation, configuration and troubleshooting of TCP/IP protocol, domain name system, and Windows Internet Name Services environment.

Related Coursework:

Integrated Studies in Computer Resources & Information Management; Information Systems Applications; Developing and Managing Human Resources; Project Management of Information Systems; Computer Security; Systems Analysis, Design and Implementation; Database Management; Internet Management Applications; Organizational Behavior and Leadership; Computer Resources & Information Management; Networking & Telecommunications Management

- Planned, designed, and published Web site, http://www.seashellnames.com, using Microsoft Publisher.
- Researched administrative workflow infrastructure in Information Systems, and how it compares with Business Process Reengineering and Enterprise Resource Planning.
- Planned, built, and implemented dropout-prevention Web site using Microsoft FrontPage as part of a team.

2

Professional Experience:

Office Manager   1/2002–12/2002
Unity Christ Church
771 Holden Avenue
Orlando, Florida 32811   Salary: n/a
Supervisor: Tona Craviato, (407) 478-5896   Hours per week: 28

- Organized office; answered phones, e-mail, and written correspondence on daily basis.

Team Sales Representative   2/2001–12/2002
Media Outsource Services
4071 L.B. McLeod Road
Orlando, Florida 32811   Salary: $10/hour
Supervisor: Chris Roe, (407) 554-1256   Hours per week: 30

- Consistently met and exceeded organizational sales goals.
- Used Linux operating system and UNIX commands to track customer demographic information and sales.

Science Teacher   10/1999–1/2000
Vero Beach High School
1707 16th Street,
Vero Beach, Florida 32960   Salary: $29,000/year
Supervisor: Mrs. Moran, Vice Principal, (561) 559-3689   Hours per week: 40

- Produced and implemented cooperative lesson plans and student assessments taking state learning regulations into account.
- Increased Spanish-speaking students' reading comprehension by at least one grade level with a combination of ESOL lessons and one-on-one tutoring.

Substitute Teacher   8/1998–9/1999
Cypress Fairbanks School District
10300 Jones Road
Houston, Texas 77065   Salary: $10/hour
Supervisor: Mrs. Hastings, (281) 669-4000   Hours per week: 30

- Independently implemented absentee teacher's lesson plans and maintained uninterrupted learning in the classroom.
- Provided quality instruction to classes of 25 to 35 children in all subjects and grade levels.

3

(continues)

(continued)

Science Teacher   4/1996–7/1998
Bahrain Bayan School
P. O. Box 32411
Isa Town, Bahrain   Salary: $33,000/year
Supervisor: Mr. Troyist, 01 (968) 666844   Hours per week: 40

- Improved workflow efficiency by automating the process of documenting student performance using the school's electronic grading application.
- Prepared and implemented cooperative lesson plans and student assessments for a student body where 70% of the students scored above average on standardized exams.

Science Teacher, Head of Science Department   8/1991–4/1996
Anglo American School of Sofia, U.S. Embassy
1 Suborna, 1000 Sofia
Bulgaria   Salary: $30,000/year
Supervisor: Mr. Price, (359) (2) 668425   Hours per week: 40

- Produced and implemented lesson plans and student assessments conforming to school regulations where 65% of the students achieved above-average performance on standardized tests.
- Managed $3,000 annual budget, prepared departmental inventory, and acquired resources.
- Presented monthly reviews and reports to over 45 teachers and administrators.
- Advised elementary school teachers curriculum committee and worked with teachers to implement curriculum for third and fourth graders.

Additional Professional Activities:

- Designed and presented Microsoft PowerPoint presentations to audiences of 10 to 20 students and professors.
- Planned and designed Web site for Master of Arts thesis project: http://www.seashellnames.com.
- Student council member at Keiser College. Organized fund-raising activities with up to 600 participants in attendance, generating over $7,500 for local charities.

Professional Memberships:

- ABWA, American Business Women's Association
- ASIST, American Society of Information Science and Technology

4

Bill Cavdek was laid off because of the bad economy in Silicon Valley, California. He is seeking an IT position in government where he can use his INFOSEC experience, certifications, and skills.

BILL CAVDEK

2206 Inverness Ct., Oxnard, CA 93030 • Home: 805.485.7575 • bill.cavdek@aol.com

Social Security number: xxx-xx-xxxx • US Citizen • Federal Civilian Status/Veterans' preference: n/a

OBJECTIVE: Information Technology Specialist (Security) GS-2210-14/15
Announcement Number: ARN 090-A
Agency: Department of Justice

SUMMARY OF QUALIFICATIONS:

Certified Information Systems Security Professional (CISSP)
Cisco Certified Network Associate (CCNA)

- **Experienced Systems and Network Administrator.** Eight and nine years experience, respectively, performing Windows NT and UNIX systems and network administration. Extensive experience administering NT 4.0/3.51, WIN 98, WIN 95, WFW, WIN 3.1, and DOS. Substantial expertise supporting Silicon Graphics IRIX, including operating system upgrades and security patch installations. Actively learning Sun Solaris 8, Linux (Mandrake 8.1), WIN XP, and WIN 2K on home network, including researching and implementing recommended security practices and evaluating newly released security applications.
- **Skilled Leader and Manager.** Unsurpassed creativity, resourcefulness, and leadership in three high-tech startup companies. Excellent communications skills, including proficiency preparing written reports and spreadsheets, and superior ability to communicate with individuals at all levels of technical expertise. Adept at promoting teamwork among employees. Outstanding rapport with subordinates and all levels of management. Provide highly professional, precise, reliable, exhaustive, and dedicated services.
- **Professional with Cutting-Edge Skills.** Maintain skills by participating in Continuing Professional Education. Active member of Computer Security Institute and Information Systems Security Association. Subscribe to various Information Security (INFOSEC) advisory groups. Monitor federal government security web sites for latest advisories and new developments. Attend pertinent security conferences to stay abreast of the rapid evolution of INFOSEC.

PROFESSIONAL HISTORY:

Senior Information Systems Engineer   12/00–3/01
Parthus Technologies, Inc., 2033 Gateway Place, Suite 150, San Jose, CA 95110
Supervisor: Patrick O'Connor   Telephone: 408-514-2929
Salary: $92,500 per year   Hours: 40+ per week
- Assessed computer, network, and physical security vulnerabilities, and reported findings to senior management with recommended corrective action.
- Collaborated on security issues with systems and network administrators at Ireland headquarters.

(continues)

(continued)

- Supported and managed Virtual Private Network (VPN) accessibility to company intranet for traveling sales force and telecommuters.
- Configured and managed user access, passwords, permissions, and restrictions on Sun Solaris and Windows NT local (LAN) and wide area network (WAN).
- Configured tape autoloaders, verified backed-up data integrity, and initiated offsite data storage and tape-rotation service with special vendor.

Network & Security Administrator *(at now-defunct Internet startup)*   4/00–12/00
ePlanning, Inc., 550 N. Winchester Boulevard, San Jose, CA 95128
Supervisor: David Bakhtnia   Telephone: 650-224-7297 (cell)
Salary: $70,000 per year   Hours: 40+ per week

- Installed and configured Cisco 3640 router, including configuration and deployment of standard and extended Access Control Lists to protect LAN from hacking.
- Configured packet filters for Netopia Synchronous Digital Subscriber Line (SDSL) router to restrict external access into network, and installed router as T1 line outage backup.
- Researched, installed, configured, and assessed evaluation copies of WebTrends Security Analyzer, Sniffer Pro LAN, VisualRoute Traceroute Utility, HP TopTools, and SolarWinds Network Management Tools for overall applicability and security utility.
- Installed, configured, and maintained secure heterogeneous network, involving direct, hands-on work with servers, hubs, routers, switches, and all communications resources.

NT Network Systems Administrator *(at now-defunct Internet startup)*   11/99–3/00
PointConnect, Inc., 340 Pine Street, San Francisco, CA 94104
Supervisor: Paul Linares   Telephone: unknown
Salary: $70,000 per year   Hours: 40+ per week

- Installed and configured Watchguard Firebox II firewall to create Demilitarized Zone (DMZ) for company web server and to restrict and log external access, and attempted access, into company LAN.
- Configured VPN using Point-to-Point Tunneling Protocol (PPTP), lmhosts files, and PC Anywhere to provide secure transmissions for traveling employees and local employee telecommuting.
- Reconfigured existing NT Workstation LAN with NT Server to create NT domain for robust, centralized security features.
- Transitioned company LAN from one Internet Service Provider (ISP) to another for increased reliability and performance, requiring all-new Class C network and reassignment of Internet Protocol (IP) addresses on all network nodes.

NT/UNIX Network Systems Administrator   7/93–11/99
Cyber F/X, Inc., 615 Ruberta Avenue, Glendale, CA 91201
Supervisor: Dick Cavdek   Telephone: 818-246-2911
Salary: $56,000 per year   Hours: 40+ per week

- Created, cultivated, and managed Information Technology Dept. for start-up company, including researching, selecting, purchasing, installing, configuring, maintaining, troubleshooting, repairing, and upgrading all hardware and software.
- Wrote security policy governing access rights to computers and network; configured and managed security levels, passwords, and restrictions.
- Configured Network Address Translation on Covad SDSL router to protect LAN.
- Installed Anti-Virus Protection, automated routine nightly scanning, proactively monitored virus bulletins and alerts, and regularly downloaded and installed latest virus signatures.
- Sourced, installed, and configured Redundant Array of Independent Disks (RAID) Level 5 server for failover protection and to facilitate LAN backups.
- Utilized various third-party tools for checking, optimizing, monitoring, securing, and troubleshooting Windows NT.

Senior Material Planner   3/87–7/93
Continental Airlines, Inc., 7300 World Way West, Los Angeles, CA 90045
Supervisor: Ed Leigh (retired)   Telephone: 213-646-7405
Salary: $36,000 per year   Hours: 40+ per week

- Conceived, created, and maintained electronic spreadsheet for mathematical analysis of detail parts requirements for high-profile, cost-saving, provisioning project to move overhaul of aircraft components in-house.

EDUCATION:

B.S. Aeronautical Operations, San Jose State University, School of Engineering 1976
Information Technology Certificates, University of California, Santa Cruz (UCSC)
    Network Engineering Certificate (6 courses)   7/01
    Internet Security Certificate (5 courses)   6/01
    Network Management and Administration Certificate (7 courses) 5/01

Additional Security Training
    Intrusion Detection, Attacks, and Countermeasures—CSI / NSA 2-day seminar 3/02
    Advanced UNIX Utilities and Shell Programming—UCSC—28 hours 5/01
    UNIX Security for System Administrators—UCSC—21 hours 3/01
    Solaris 8 System Administration I—Sun Microsystems 5-day class 2/01

PROFESSIONAL CERTIFICATIONS and AFFILIATIONS:

CISSP—Certified Information Systems Security Professional—cert. no. 26095
CCNA—Cisco Certified Network Associate—cert. no. CSCO10337410
Member—Computer Security Institute (CSI)—I.D. 748803
Member—Information Systems Security Association (ISSA)—I.D. 17520

Susan Clowney is seeking an IT Specialist position where she can utilize her network management, security, systems analysis, and customer service experience. Her diverse and creative IT systems setup experience with Internet firms could be useful with changing government organizations and new information technology systems.

Susan Clowney
800 North Way • Hyattstown, Maryland 20871
Home: (301) 414-5546 • Work: (301) 298-3271 • sclowney@aol.com

Personal information:
Social Security number: 000-00-0000
Military & federal service: n/a
Citizenship: United States of America

Objective: **Information Technology Specialist—Help Desk Support, WA-TB-2-008**

Summary of Qualifications:

Network Professional: Install, maintain and troubleshoot desktop and mini computers, personal computers, computer peripherals and Local Area Network (LAN) and Wide Area Network (WAN) devices. Install/upgrade application programs.
Communication Skills: Support users in the effective use of PC application software and operating systems. Resolve user problems on Hewlett-Packard and IBM personal computer clones running Windows 95/98, Windows 2000, Windows Millennium and Windows NT. Provide first- and second-level technical support to internal customers in computer use, and hardware and software problems.

Work Experience:

Systems Engineer   June 2000 to March 2003
Collaborative Services Group, Vertis, Inc.
250 West Pratt Street, Baltimore, Maryland 21201   30+ hours per week
Supervisor: Mary LeFrank, Phone: (800) 755-3569   Salary: $32,000/year

- Managed, maintained and troubleshot systems for corporate office and 32 remote locations with a six-member system engineers team.
- Monitored remote backup, restoration system, security concerns, day-to-day upkeep of system and special projects.
- Administered advanced Windows NT & 2000 system.
- Optimized servers' performance through upgrade software and hardware.
- Set up and configured NAS devices for corporate and remote sites.
- Monitored and troubleshot the Kronos time and attendance system.
- Responded to first- and second-level trouble tickets from Helpdesk.
- Redesigned, with senior engineers, the Citrix infrastructure to stabilize enhanced usage for 250 remote users.
- Integrated application in a diverse Citrix Metaframe environment including ADP, PeopleSoft, Kronos, Lotus Notes and Microsoft Office.
- Developed an active directory design and rollout plan with senior engineer.
- Diagramed corporate data center servers and networking equipments with Visio 2000.

LAN Administrator   March 1997 to August 1999
IT Group, Digicomlab, Inc.
2000 Rockville Pike, Rockville, Maryland 20850   40+ hours/week
Supervisor: Steven Lucas, Phone: (301) 212-4345   Salary: $35,000

- Built, administered and troubleshot Intel-based Microsoft NT 4.0 and Sun Solaris Servers with a three-person team.
- Created and purged users and group accounts on NT and Solaris servers.
- Planned, designed, implemented and documented new systems and servers in an organized and efficient manner.
- Installed, integrated and supported an Internet-based company including Web, exchange and RAS servers, and standard Windows NT services in LAN environment.
- Configured and supported servers and desktops for mission-critical sectors.
- Set up, configured and maintained DNS, DHCP and WIN Servers.

Education:
University of Maryland, College Park, December 2001
Bachelor of Science in Information Systems Management, GPA: 3.38

Professional Certifications:

Microsoft Certified Systems Engineer (MCSE)	CompTIA A+
Microsoft Certified Systems Engineer	Mar 14, 2000
Microsoft Certified Professional + Internet	Mar 14, 2000
Microsoft Certified Professional	Nov 23, 1999

Training:

Advanced Database Using Oracle, 12/01	Communication Network Mngmnt., 12/00
WAN Mngmnt. Using Cisco Router, 5/01	LAN Management Using NT, 12/00
Survey of Telecommunication, 5/01	LAN Management Using UNIX, 12/00
C Programming, 12/00	Database Program Development, 8/00
Structure System Analysis/Design, 12/00	Software/Hardware Concepts, 5/00

Implementing and Supporting Microsoft Internet Information Server 4.0	Mar 14, 2000
Internetworking with Microsoft TCP/IP on Microsoft Windows NT 4.0	Jan 20, 2000
Networking Essentials	Jan 12, 2000
Implementing and Supporting NT Server 4.0 in the Enterprise	Dec 21, 1999
Implementing and Supporting NT Server 4.0	Dec 07, 1999
Implementing and Supporting NT 4.0 Workstation	Nov 23, 1999

Computer Skills:
Hardware: Compaq, HP, IBM, Dell and Sun servers; 3Com Switch, Cisco Router, various desktop and laptop personal computers, multimedia products, modems, DAT and DLT tape drives, polycom video and autoloaders.
Software: DOS, Windows NT, Windows 95/98, Windows Millennium, Windows 2000, Linux, Solaris, Exchange, DNS, DHCP, WINS, Microsoft Office Package, Lotus Notes, Sendmail, Apache, ArcServeIT, Legato Networker, Compaq Insight Management, Visio, Internet and TCP/IP.

2

Summary

Your resume is an opportunity to show off your skills, both technical and nontechnical. While writing your resume, reflect upon the skills for which employers are looking. Working in the IT industry demands that you stay abreast of current technology and future trends, and outdated education and skills do not impress employers.

It is your responsibility to get the training you need to stay current. Seek out and create opportunities to get involved with new technology, to take on new assignments, to get technical training, to begin a degree program, or to take on management responsibilities. Change is the only constant in the IT field; stay ahead of the curve by transforming yourself to meet the evolving demands of the IT field.

CHAPTER 20

Wage-Grade Resumes: Staying Employed, Getting Promoted, or Going to General Schedule (GS) Jobs

When writing "keyword and skill" electronic resumes, job seekers are concerned that they will not be able to write a career-change resume. Because the electronic resume system is read by a computer initially, rather than a human resources professional, the words in the resume must be clear. There will be little chance to influence a reader with an entire package presentation.

Can a Supervisory Submarine Hatch Mechanic get unstuck from his current series? The answer is *yes*. In this chapter, you'll find out how. The example of the Hatch Mechanic's ability to select skills, nouns, and verbs that are transferable from the specialized field of submarine hatch work to general maintenance, supervision, and team leadership in a production shop environment is interesting and can help you learn how to target new jobs with selected relevant skills.

Case Study: Ship Fitters at Pearl Harbor

Ten ship fitters attended one of my Resumix resume-writing workshops at Pearl Harbor Naval Base. They were positive they were stuck for the rest of their careers as hatch mechanics. And they were determined not to use "flamboyant language" that was meaningless in their resumes to change jobs. But could it even be done?

Jeff is the Pearl Harbor Naval Shipyard's expert on submarine hatches. He has had 16 years of repairing, installing, troubleshooting, upgrading, scheduling, training, quality assurance, purchasing parts, and endless communication to schedule the on-board ship repairs. But he wants to do something new now. He really wants to move out of the specific submarine-hatch area. How can he refocus his skills away from the submarine-hatch world and into a different mechanical world where he can use his transferable skills? What job would that be? And what are his transferable skills? He would consider an inspector or quality-assurance job, or a production controller job in a Navy shipyard. He has many transferable skills in addition to the specialized ones in the area of submarine hatches.

But the second challenge is the Resumix system. How can Jeff "fool" the Resumix system into thinking he can do something besides work on sub hatches? Does he have to fool the system? Will the human resources recruiters and managers find him if he tries to present himself as someone other than a submarine-hatch mechanic? He doesn't want to be lost forever in the database. Can he come up with a good set of skills that will be truthful for his new career-change objectives?

Together in the workshop we analyzed the transferable skills that a supervisory hatch mechanic uses every day to see whether the skills would fit in another career—without being flamboyant or untruthful. Then we made a list of keywords and skills.

I asked the 10 ship fitters "What percentage of time do you spend fixing stuff versus talking to people?" They said 70 percent talking and 30 percent fixing. "Wow," I said, "70 percent?" (This demonstrates extensive use of **communications skills.**)

Then I had to know more. "Who are you talking to?" I asked. One said "It takes about two hours to do a 30-minute job because I have to talk to the ship captain, engine mechanics, and plant operators to schedule the on-site repair with security, parts, and other trade cooperation." (This demonstrates **customer service, liaison, scheduling, coordination,** and **planning skills.**)

"All right," I said, "this is communications skills, teamwork, interpersonal skills, customer service, job planning, and scheduling. These are some of the keywords you can add to your resumes. And they are all transferable skills that you could use in any mechanic or mechanic supervisor position."

We were getting somewhere. So we kept making this list. Here's what we created. These keywords and skills should be integrated into a career-change Resumix resume, along with some of the technical descriptions.

Teamwork–Team Leader (40%)

★ Leadership
★ Project coordination and planning
★ Planning and scheduling
★ Contractor liaison and oversight
★ Training

Customer Service (30%)

★ Problem-solving, negotiating solutions
★ Systems and problem analysis; devising solutions

Quality Control (30%)

★ Quality assurance
★ Research (parts, warranties, new equipment)
★ Purchasing/ordering
★ Inventory and equipment control
★ Security systems implementation

After you have your list of keywords, you should create an outline with three to five major work areas. Then describe your duties in each area. This is the best way to create a great skills list that will be transferable to your next field. You can also add percentages to each of your major skill areas so that the human resources staff can see how you spend your time at work.

The submarine-hatch mechanic now feels like it is possible for him get away from being the "hatchman." As long as he analyzes the duties of his target position and adds those skills to the list, he should qualify for a new position.

Note: In today's facilities services operations departments, many employees are competing to keep their jobs and offices. If you believe that your organization will become privatized, you should begin to write your resume and plan for your next career now. Research the jobs that are not being privatized and target these positions so that your job will be safer.

Strategies for Writing a Winning Wage-Grade Resume to Compete to Keep Your Job

With the advent of computer technology and the reduction of personnel office staff, applying for Federal jobs as a first-time applicant or for promotion/career change for current Federal employees has changed drastically over the past five years. Application forms that ask specific questions and are completed with pen and ink are practically obsolete. The Federal sector now utilizes software called Resumix, USAJOBS, and other online applications. What each has in common is the requirement for the individual to be proactive in seeking employment or in managing his or her career by submitting an online resume.

The software applications make qualification determinations. If the applicant does not use the correct language on the resume, he or she might miss the opportunity for employment or promotion. Federal Wage System (FWS) employees are sometimes at a disadvantage in using these systems because they often do not have access to computer terminals at work and do not have the time to do research to properly prepare a resume.

Also, many tradesmen/women are not writers. They work with their hands, building, fixing, and maintaining things. They are not writers, editors, or job analysts. So, online resumes, transference of skills, and job analysis of new positions are difficult, to say the least. But it is a *must* for anyone who wants to survive in government after privatization activities or to be promoted.

It is vitally important that the resumes of current Federal employees in the FWS classification, seeking promotion or a change in career field, reflect the correct language tailored to the applicable software. Another stumbling block is that "one size does not fit all." Your resume must be targeted toward the position for which you are applying; therefore, you might need to rewrite it depending on the type of position that is vacant.

Journeyman wage-grade employees, due to their extensive shop-floor experience, are often sought as prime candidates for some GS positions, such as Equipment Specialists and Production Controllers. However, they must stress in their resumes the correct knowledge, skills, and abilities they possess if they are to be considered for these career changes. FWS employees are an extremely valuable asset. They often have the capabilities to progress into production-chief positions and high-grade general-schedule positions; but in today's environment, that might be more difficult if the employee doesn't take a proactive approach.

The Most Desired Jobs for Former WG, WS, WL, WD, and WN Employees

In many cases, foremen, work leaders and planners, and estimators are usually WS, WL, WD, or WN grades, which are blue-collar positions. Some activities have converted these schedules to GS grades. Here are some GS jobs that blue-collar workers can move into most effectively by transferring their existing skills:

★ Administrative Clerk

★ Data-entry positions

★ Production Controller

★ Material Specialist

★ Buyer

★ Planner/Estimator

★ Work Leader/Supervisor

★ Quality Assurance Specialist

★ Surveillance Specialist

★ Occupational Safety and Health

If WG workers go into GS jobs, they can expect to be in an office environment, even if they are in the shop, because they will be sitting at a desk working on a computer. That means for a WG to be successful as a GS, he or she will need some sort of computer and keyboarding skills.

Researching Your Transferable Skills and Keywords

Look for position descriptions, vacancy announcements, and the skills they list. A great source for position descriptions or a classification standard is the army's Civilian Personnel Online site at www.cpol.army.mil. Follow the Tools link and then the FASCLASS link.

Another excellent source is the Classification Standards from the Office of Personnel Management at www.opm.gov.

As examples, we'll make a list of keywords and skills from the Position Description and Classification Standards for the following three occupational series and incorporate them into the sample Resumix resumes later in this chapter:

★ Heavy Mobile Equipment Mechanic

★ Power Support Equipment Mechanic

★ Air Conditioning Equipment Mechanic

After you create your list of skills, make sure that the statements and skills are true. For example, there is a statement in the introduction for Heavy Mobile Equipment Mechanic that might or might not be true of an employee's job: "…and assisted heavy mobile equipment mechanics in the complete overhaul and repair of major systems, such as engines, transmissions, drive lines, and hydraulic utility systems." If you did not assist mechanics, or if there are some systems listed that you did not work on, you should delete these. Also, do you assure proper "calibration"? We included this word in the keyword list, but it does not appear anywhere in the materials. Is another word more accurate?

Here is a list of keywords from three WG-10 announcements that we will try to integrate into the resume:

Pre-shop analysis

Major systems and components

Disassembly

Diagnoses malfunctions

Places in operable condition for preinspection

Utilizes gauges and instruments

Performs rebuild, repair, assembly, adjustment, troubleshooting, applicable functional test of major mechanical systems and components for…

Defective units

Repairs/replaces

Assembles

Performs limited functional test

Hand tools

Measuring instruments

Micrometers

Dial indicators

Torque wrenches

Blueprints/schematics

Technical publication

CMWR

Checkout

Adjustment

Tune-up

Examines vehicles; starts, performs operations checks

Detects malfunctions

Here's a list of keywords and skills from the KSAs in the announcements:

Mechanical makeup operating and working relationship of heavy mobile vehicles

Troubleshooting

Analysis

Vehicle systems

Assemblies

Parts

Diesel

Gasoline

Transmissions

Hydraulic systems

Technical manuals

Diagrams

Schematics

DMWRs

Work orders

Micrometers

Dial indicators

Dial bore gauges

Ignition timers

Fuel pump testers

Here are the keywords from a second announcement that are different from what we've already listed:

[Listing of types of heavy equipment]

Traces and locates defects, causes of mechanical problems

Determines type and extent of repairs

Selects repair specs and procedures

Routine welding

Transitioning from a WG Career to a GS Career

What does it take to change career paths from a WG career to a GS career? It might take going backward in grade so that you can begin a new career track. It might take some education and specialized training (read the announcements and occupational series to find out what is required). It will take specialized experience in your selected area. You must make a concerted effort to develop the skills and gain the experience needed while you're in your current job. Ask for and take on additional projects in order to gain specialized skills.

You might have to perform two jobs while you are transitioning from one career to another—the one you are paid for and special projects in your new career area. Analyze skills, training opportunities, and project opportunities; network with people who are in the new area; and build your resume to support the job change.

Checklist for Writing a Wage-Grade Resume

The following checklist was created by Mark Reichenbacher, who specializes in writing WG civilian resumes for the Resumix system. He is highly analytical in developing keyword lists and skills from classification standards and announcements. He selects the keywords that will best fill the "skills bucket" for the target grade and announcement. He then carefully crafts a three-to-five-page resume with good descriptions of job functions, specifics of jobs, accomplishments, awards, and recognitions.

You can use this checklist to write a wage-grade resume for a lateral position, as well as one geared toward a promotion. The analysis and keywords can also be developed so that you can target a GS position. The GS positions require less "hands-on" technical skills and more planning, estimating, project-coordination, communications, and problem-solving skills. Write your resume to include the skills that will be required in your *future* position.

1. Assess Your Skills and Research Relevant Positions That Fit These Skills

A WG employee (or any other employee) should make an assessment of his or her skills and then look for relevant positions that fit those skills. You can make a list of your skills based on your position description and the services you provide to your customers.

2. Review Your Work Experience for Relevance

Look at each position in your work experience. Are they relevant to the target positions? Should they be combined? Should the resume be arranged in reverse-chronological order for the most relevant presentation of the jobs? Should any positions be left out? How many jobs have you had over the last 20 years?

3. Analyze Your Work Experience for Jobs, Grades, and Special Assignments

Target the resume to qualify for two grade levels if that is appropriate. You can capture extra job skills in "special assignment" sections that can help you qualify for a higher grade level. Add hours per week to the special assignments.

4. Analyze Work Experience for Numbers

How many employees, square feet, numbers of items, numbers of helicopters, numbers of job tickets, dollars, budgets, percentages, money saved, hours billed? These numbers help describe the work in context and are also important in describing accomplishments and special projects in specific terms.

5. Write Accomplishments and Special Assignments

Write about specific projects that resulted in performance awards or customer-service letters. Have you improved the efficiency of your shop operations? Write about new projects and complex situations. Did you work on special projects? Were you a member of a team to redesign a work process? Were you involved with new construction, capital improvements, or tenant build-outs? If so, describe them in the corresponding work experience block, using the CCAR formula, which is explained in chapter 14, "Boosting Your Employment Chances with Great KSAs."

6. List Education

Add your college course hours and list your college or professional training programs in the education section. You might have to consider returning to college in order to change careers. If you have a college degree, even if it is an associate's degree from a community college, you will have a big advantage over other WG employees with no college degrees.

7. Include Job-Related Training

Computer and keyboard training will be helpful in any desk or trades job. You might need to give a quote, pull up an order, create a receipt or bill of sale, or research a manual for repair. New training can help you change occupational series.

8. List Certifications

Under the Certifications heading, list training courses that resulted in professional licenses or certifications, and include the month and year when the certification was achieved. List first those that are current and essential to your current work.

9. Cite Awards

When listing awards, list them by importance. Check to see whether the order of "importance" is accurate. For instance, it's difficult to tell how an "Official Commendation" is regarded in terms of importance unless you state the reason for receiving the commendation. Also, a Letter of Appreciation is received for a reason. If you have room in the Awards section, write a sentence about why you received the award.

10. Remove Redundancies in Work Descriptions, Awards, and Training Courses

Because the Army resume format is only three pages, you will have to be concise and to-the-point when writing your duties, skills, and accomplishments. Maximize your three pages by avoiding redundant information.

11. Include Other Experience and Summary of Important Experience

In a Summary statement, you can summarize your experience, knowledge, skills, and abilities (one for each sentence). This is a good place to pick up anything that might not be covered elsewhere. Also, you can include the strongest statements from your appraisal. Put them in some logical sequence. You can add volunteer, nonprofit, association, and community activities in this section.

12. Core Competencies

Don't forget any core competencies that can be added to this section; for example, flexibility, resourcefulness, proficiency in oral and written communications, or being a valuable team member. Refer to chapter 5 to determine your competencies that would be impressive to the selecting official.

13. Talk to Your Human Resources Office

Ask about other occupational series that will be available (not privatized) for people with skills that match your experience. Ask about positions that can lead to a promotion.

14. Get Help from Professionals

If writing is not one of your best skills, get professional help with writing, editing, and determining your skills and accomplishments. Your resume is your future and career. It's worth your time and investment.

Sample Resumix Resume for a Wage-Grade Transition

This Electrician, WG-10, is seeking a new position in Planning, Inspection, and Supervision where he can utilize his technical skills as well as his teamwork, planning, inspection, and supervisory experience.

Edward C. Alvarez   SSN: 000-00-0000
3000 Lancaster Boulevard
California City, CA 93505

Home Phone: 760 333-3333
Work Phone: 661 333-3333
Mobile Phone: 661 333-3333

E-mail address: edward.alvarez@usa.net

WORK EXPERIENCE:

08-2000 to Present; 40 hours per week; ELECTRICIAN; WG-2805-10; $20.95 per hour; 95th Air Base Wing, 95th Civil Engineer Group, 795th Civil Engineer Squadron, Edwards Air Force Base, CA 93524-6745; Mr. Robert Blackwood, 661 277-4411; may contact supervisor.

JOURNEYMAN LEVEL ELECTRICIAN: One of seven electricians performing for all non-contracted electrical work at Edwards AFB. TRAIN AND DEVELOP new electricians.

PROJECT LEADER: Plan and coordinate work needed with customer or building manager. Discuss needs, provide feedback, give project status updates, and determine materials to be ordered. Plan schedule with customer, other trades, and team members.

FACILITIES SERVICED: Exchange services, commissary, base headquarters offices, security forces, child development center, officers' housing, lodging facility, temporary lodging facility, morale, welfare and recreation facilities, base communications (electrical), and Federal Aviation Administration. Restricted and security areas.

INSTALLATION AND TESTING: Install, service, modify, repair, test, and troubleshoot new and existing electrical systems, circuits, devices, control circuitry, and conduits "thru 4." Work on systems and associated equipment 600 volts or less; explosion-proof systems; industrial lighting; battery chargers; water, sewage, and fuel pumps; and commercial and domestic appliances.

ELECTRICAL REPAIR: Calculate voltage, amperage, watts, resistance, and other units of measurement in the electrical field using mathematical formulas. Utilize wiring diagrams, schematics, manufacturer instruction leaflets, and blueprints for the troubleshooting and installation of single and three-phase electrical motors, controls circuits, and other associated equipment that is vital to prevent work stoppage of other agencies. Set up and operate a variety of portable test equipment: network tester, amptector tester, power supply, precision instrument, shop standard and multiamp tester such as SR-51, SR-76, SR-78, TV-2, frequency generator phase shifter, phase angle, and K-Dar tester.

INTERPRET AND APPLY THE FOLLOWING GUIDELINES: National Electric Code, Air Force Standards and Procedures, Occupational Safety and Health Regulations. Possess working knowledge of various fittings, types and sizes of wire, and types of conduits associated with electrical work. Skill and ability to use and select proper trade tools such as crimpers, soldering irons, wrenches, socket sets, benders, wire pullers, various pliers, screwdrivers, multimeters, meggers, and other tools in conjunction with Personal Protective Equipment.

SPECIAL PROJECTS: OUTDOOR SWIMMING POOL—Ran new incoming feed from a disconnect on a utility pole to the swimming pool main breaker, due to the loss of one leg on the existing feed. Ordered materials, contacted appropriate agencies for digging permits, completed all phases of project from start to finish. COURTHOUSE—Surveyed, procured, and installed new outlets and materials for new audiovisual equipment for the courthouse.

01-2000 to 07-2000; 40 hours per week; RELAY TECHNICIAN; $9.60 per hour. Guam Power Authority, P.O. Box 2977, Hagatna, GU 96932; Mr. Leon Hanna, 671 666-6666.

Performed preventive maintenance and troubleshooting; installed, tested, repaired, overhauled, and calibrated mechanical, electrical, electronic, or pneumatic instruments, electronic components, automated equipment, test equipment, and control devices associated with power generation, distribution, and power system protection, such as indicating and recording meters, voltage, current, frequency, differential and impedance relays, current, and voltage transformers. Accomplished set up, operation, testing, repairing, and calibration using a variety of test equipment, power supplies, precision instruments, and industry standards under simulated or actual operating conditions, while understanding the operating characteristics, electrical operation relationships, sequence, and impact of malfunction on related components. Documented test reports and interpreted results of the work on the basis of trade knowledge and experience. Applied visual-motor skills to make precise adjustments required by complex instruments and devices due to equipment deterioration or malfunction throughout the interrelated units or the requirement to obtain exact output.

Applied knowledge of "Theory and Standards of Electrical Principles" and electrical equations or formulas that are associated with the protective relay field. Applied specifications that included wiring diagrams, schematics, blueprints, and manufacturer instruction leaflets for the installation or troubleshooting of new and existing electrical systems, controls circuits, battery chargers, pneumatic and hydraulic operating mechanisms, power system protection networks, zone relays, circuit breakers, and generator control systems.

10-1994 to 01-2000; 40 hours per week; INSTRUMENT MECHANIC; WG-3359-11; last promoted 11-1998. U.S. Navy, Public Works Center, Utilities Department, PSC 455, Box 195, FPO, AP 96540-2937; Ms. Marie Turner, 671 333-3333.

Same as Relay Technician, described above. Performed testing, troubleshooting, calibration, and preventive maintenance on pneumatic devices, air compressors, pressure switches, 600-volt circuit breakers, single and three-phase pump motors, Sluice Gate Controls, various types of gauges, and water purification monitoring equipment and controls. Researched, identified, and procured materials with the Government I.M.P.A.C. credit card.

Special Assignment: Assigned on loan for two years to the Guam Power Authority. Tested analog and digital instrument meters and protective relays. Performed troubleshooting on circuit breakers and transformers while on stand-by and reported findings to the power system dispatcher.

11-1991 to 10-1994; 40 hours per week; INSTRUMENT MECHANIC APPRENTICE; WT-3359-11; U.S. Navy, Public Works Center, Utilities Department, PSC 455, Box 195, FPO, AP 96540-2937; Mr. Rudy Smith, 671 333-3333; may contact supervisor.

(continues)

(continued)

Received training through the U.S. Navy Apprenticeship program in the protective relay field as an Instrument Mechanic. During that time I passed courses that were required by the apprenticeship program. Courses included "Theories and Standards of Electrical Principles," Trade Theory classes, On-the-Job Training (3 years), Technical Math I and II, Physics I and II, and Technical Drawing I and II.

EDUCATION:
George Washington Sr. High School, Los Angeles, CA. High School Diploma, 1988.

U.S. Navy Apprenticeship Program, Naval Station, GU 96540-2937. Department of the Navy Certificate of Apprenticeship, 1994. Department of Labor Certificate of Completion of Apprenticeship, 1994. 520 Quarter Hours. GPA: 3.0 out of 4.0.

Guam Community College, Mangilao, GU 96926. 25 Semester Hours. GPA: 3.0 out of 4.0.

PROFESSIONAL TRAINING:
Fall Protection Course, 8 hrs, 1999. Confined Spaces Course, 8 hrs, 1999. Sexual Harassment Awareness, 3 hrs, 1995. Instrument Mechanic Apprentice, On-the-Job Training, 3 yrs, 1994. Instrument Mechanic Apprentice, Trade Theory Courses, 3 yrs, 1994. Instrumentation and Control Training, 40 hrs, 1993. Reading Schematics and Symbols, 40 hrs, 1993. Fundamental Pole Climbing, 40 hrs, 1993.

PROFESSIONAL LICENSES AND CERTIFICATES:
The United States Department of Labor Certificate of Completion of Apprenticeship—Instrument Mechanic, Guam USA, 1994. Department of the Navy Certificate of Apprenticeship—Instrument Mechanic, Guam USA, 1994.

PERFORMANCE RATINGS, AWARDS, HONORS, AND RECOGNITIONS:
Performance Rating of Superior, 12-2000. Special Act or Service Award, 1999. Special Act or Service Award, 1998.

U.S. MILITARY SERVICE INFORMATION:
10-1988 to 08-1990; U.S. Army; Honorable Discharge.

OTHER INFORMATION:

Profile: Journeyman-level electrician. Quick learner, dependable, responsible, and independent in carrying out assignments. Supervisory Appraisal indicates: "Mr. Alvarez is an excellent electrician. He has a vast knowledge of the electrical field. His troubleshooting of electrical systems has aided the section tremendously. He adapts well to mission-required changes and has had no lost time while performing those changes. He maintains all required vehicle operation items."

Project Leader: Train and develop new electricians. Provide customer service as point of contact for work needed.

Summary

Resume writing is challenging for trades professionals. They are highly skilled in a variety of hands-on tasks, but writing, marketing, editing, and salesmanship are usually not part of their daily activities. But without a good resume, promotions might not occur, jobs might disappear, and job offers might not happen. It's worth the time and effort to create lists of skills, accomplishments, training, and customer comments when a promotion or job change is near.

CHAPTER 21

Resumes for Business Contracts and Purchasing

By Michael Ottensmeyer

In this chapter, we look at Federal business specialists in the contracting series. In private industry, these business specialists are called account executives, purchasing agents and directors, contract managers and negotiators, account managers, and other business-related titles.

The contracting series, GS-1102, is part of the Business and Industry Group (GS-1100) in government for a very good reason. The "group" includes all positions in government where the primary duties include advising on, administering, supervising, or performing work that requires knowledge of business and trade practices, products, or industrial production methods and processes. The business group involves a great deal of investigative work as well as detailed studies, collection, analysis, and dissemination of information. This group also includes the establishment and maintenance of contacts with industry and commerce. Finally, it includes advisory services, examination and appraisal of merchandise or property, and administration of regulatory provisions and controls. For all of these reasons, the Federal government needs experienced people with solid business and industry backgrounds to handle the job responsibilities of business- and industry-related jobs.

Understanding business and industrial concepts and frames of reference has been important to the United States Government since World War II, when the military came to rely heavily on industry to deliver the goods during wartime, as well as subsequent peacetime and then throughout the "Cold War" period from about 1948 until 1989 when the Berlin Wall fell. People who work in Federal contracting (or "Acquisition," as it is likely to be called now) must have a solid grasp of the ways of the business world outside government because they interface on a daily basis with large and small businesses. For instance, contracting and purchasing agents in government are the linchpins between their agencies and industries that supply goods and services to keep them running. Contracting professionals work with internal customers to learn about the requirements; then they work with external vendors/suppliers to buy what is needed. Communication is a big part of the job of the Federal contracting specialist, because both parties (inside experts and outside companies) need to know what goods and services must be delivered at the right time (and for the right price) to meet the Federal agency's mission. In short, the contract specialist/purchasing agent in the Federal government must be a business-savvy negotiator who has the ability to communicate in business terms that are understood by both parties to major government contracts.

The "Government to Business" Imperative

The newest imperative in Federal contracting is shifting work functions from government to business. President Bush announced in November 2002 that up to 850,000 additional Federal jobs would be contracted out. This bombshell announcement means that the already changing field of government contracting has changed even more dramatically. Now, contract specialists in government must know how to buy entire government functions from the outside to take over huge chunks of what the government agencies used to do in-house! For example, outside corporations are now contracted to provide millions upon millions of dollars worth of military base maintenance functions (repairing roads and buildings, replacing electrical wiring, doing plumbing, and so on) that used to be performed by military members or full-time permanent Department of Defense career civilian employees.

As thousands upon thousands of former Federal jobs have been contracted out to private industry across all government agencies, Federal contracting professionals have learned to approach their jobs not only from the perspective of "how to buy goods and services," but also from the perspective of purchasing entire functions to increase their agency's work efficiency. In the past, an agency would look to purchase materials only to perform internal ("organic") agency functions. Today's Federal agency looks for alternative methods of getting the bulk of the work done as well. Agencies are ever vigilant for the potential to "contract out" their work to get it done better, faster, and more efficiently than before. This is so important that Federal executives at the highest agency levels are now evaluated in their yearly performance reviews based on their openness to contracting out inefficient functions to the private sector.

As a direct consequence of the new Federal imperative to achieve real-world business results, and the continual improvement of processes for getting the work of Federal agencies accomplished, contract specialists have been forced to go back to school and learn more about the technical aspects of business itself. Some agencies, such as the Department of Defense, have demanded that contract specialists have a college degree that includes no less than 24 semester (or equivalent) hours of business coursework.

When internal promotion candidates apply for advancement to higher levels of pay and responsibility, their resumes and KSA statements have become far more detailed and sophisticated. Candidates must be able to demonstrate their business savvy in writing! Outside job candidates for positions as Contract Specialists (GS-1102 series), Purchasing Agents (GS-1105 series), and Contracting Support employees (GS-1106 series) must show that they are true business professionals who work with and manage contracts. They need to clearly demonstrate a keen insight into the essential elements of government contract management, as grounded in essential business concepts.

Skills for Contracting Experts

What skill sets do contracting experts in Federal agencies need to demonstrate? The following sections list these skills by candidate type.

Federal Employees Seeking Positions in the Contracting Series

You need to know the technical skills of contracting, as well as the transferable business management and communications skills required to negotiate and monitor large-scale service and product provision contracts. It will help if you can show that you have done investigative work as well as detailed studies, collection, analysis, and dissemination of information in your present job or in recent jobs. You also need to demonstrate that you have studied business at the associate or bachelor's degree level. Include this information in your resume and in KSA statements.

Federal Contract Specialists Seeking Advancement or New Positions in the Same Field

An important first step is to carefully examine exactly what you do in your job every day! This sounds a bit obvious, but you'd be surprised how many contract specialists in government are so busy performing the work of their positions every day that they don't think about highlighting their acquired business skills in their promotion and advancement applications/resumes. Because most Federal agencies now use some form of "self-nomination" for promotion actions, contract specialists are well advised to stop and think occasionally about what skills they can bring to the table when it comes to applying for promotion. You will be amazed to learn that it's really a lot! You are a key person when it comes to providing essential services to the American public and the internal customers you serve each day. Write your resume and KSAs with the dual focus of managing contracts and making sure that the high-quality services you bring to your agency have a positive effect on bottom-line business outcome.

Military Members with Contracting Experience Considering Federal Jobs in Contracting

Good news! If you are about to exit the military service and have professional contracting experience, you might qualify for the GS-1102 series in the Federal government based on your experience and expertise gained in the military, even if you have not completed a college degree and even if you do not have 24 semester hours in business. This is a relatively new waiver procedure based on the fact that Federal agencies are hurting for qualified professionals with experience. (See the first sample resume at the end of this chapter.)

Private-Industry Professionals Considering Federal Jobs in Contracting

It helps to understand exactly how contract specialists do their work, and to understand that, even though the title of the job is "Contract Specialist," the position involves more than contracting. In private industry, this work involves the same skills needed by business managers, operations managers, financial managers, senior accounts managers, program managers, or professional staff persons in a contracting department. If you have this kind of experience, there is a good chance that the Federal government can use your skills now more than ever!

You need to write a great resume that highlights your business experience and makes you stand out as someone the Federal agency of your choice wants to hire to negotiate contracts with private firms. You can do it, and you can compete successfully for these excellent career opportunities in government! (See the second sample resume at the end of this chapter.)

The OPM's Classification Standards

To write an outstanding Federal resume, it helps to study the official classification standards for the occupation itself. The official Office of Personnel Management (OPM) Occupational Standards, although not new, are written broadly enough to cover the work that is done today. Here is an abstract from the online version of the GS-1102 series classification standard, as published by the OPM, describing the typical duties of the 1102 series:

"The procurement process begins with the determination of requirements needed to accomplish the agency mission. The program office is responsible for the initial determination that the requirements can or cannot be fulfilled from within the Government, such as from existing stock or in-house capability, for preparing preliminary specifications or work statements, for recommending delivery requirements, and for assuring the availability of funds. The document transmitting this data to the contracting office is a procurement request. The contracting office provides assistance in developing acceptable specifications, work statements, and evaluation criteria; determines the method of procurement and contractual arrangement appropriate to the particular requirements; and conducts the contracting process.

"The contracting office first screens the procurement request to assure its completeness for contracting purposes, then develops an overall plan designed to obtain the requirements in the most economical, timely, effective, and efficient manner.

"The plan embraces the entire procurement process from the inception of a program to completion of the contract. It may be simple or complex, depending on the circumstances of the particular requirement. It includes such fundamental considerations as funding, contracting method, contract type, source competence, number of sources, source selection, delivery, Government-furnished property, possible follow-on requirements, and contract administration. It should include the means to measure accomplishments, evaluate risks, and consider contingencies as a program progresses. It should also include market research and analysis and other considerations as necessary to achieve the program objective."

New Competencies Needed for Contract Specialists in Government

Two of the most important competencies for government contract specialists are computer literacy and the ability to work independently.

★ **Computer literacy:** As in any other career field in government or the private sector, contract specialists today need computer literacy. This is the biggest new requirement, in addition to what I have addressed earlier in this chapter. Computer literacy is necessary because contracts in the Federal government today are accomplished on computers. Each system for contracting is different. Some agencies use more complex computerized contract-writing software than others; however, the bottom line is that contract specialists are "administratively independent" in the 21st century and do not have contract clerks to type up lengthy contracts for them, as in the old days.

★ **Ability to work independently:** Along with the new administrative independence comes more professional independence, as well as heavier workloads with fewer people in the typical contracting office. Today's specialists need to be true self-starters who are willing to learn the process extremely well and take a contracting requirement from start to finish pretty much on their own. Contract specialists who expect to take their time and learn while others carefully supervise their work are not going to be happy in government today. There is simply no need for professionals who cannot take the ball and run with it!

Other important competencies and skills include the following:

★ **Quality assurance:** Continual review of the Statement of Work against the services being provided. (This is not done by contract specialists. It's done by QA specialists, GS-1150 series, who interface with contract folks.)

★ **Problem-solving and follow-up:** Answering questions concerning performance, expectations, timing, and cooperation with government employees. (This is not new; it has been done all along.)

★ **Customer service:** Continual communication with project managers and contract officer technical representatives (the government employees who work "hands-on" with the contractor). (This is not new; it has been done all along.)

★ **Teamwork:** Working in combination with project managers, employees, and supervisors. (This is not new; it has been done all along.)

★ **Creativity:** As daily problems occur, contract specialists resolve them with contractors and other government employees to keep projects going for the good of the project and the government's investment. (This is not new, it has been done all along.)

Examples of the Types of Contracts Negotiated and Managed

Once again quoting from the online version of the GS-1102 series standards, contracting work in the Federal government includes the following specialty areas:

- **Supplies:** Commodities range from commercial off-the-shelf products, components, or spare parts, to unique items requiring fabrication to specification.

- **Services:** Services include professional or nonprofessional, such as research for a specified level of effort, field engineering work requiring specialized equipment, the delivery of a series of lectures, or provision of janitorial services to perform specific tasks in specific locations. When contracting for services, competition may be based on both price and technical considerations.

- **Construction:** This includes construction of public buildings and repair or alteration of building structures, hospitals, prisons, mints, dams, bridges, power plants, irrigation systems, highways, roads, trails, and other real property. Construction contracts have a variety of special requirements which must be followed.

- **Automatic Data Processing Equipment and Telecommunications:** ADPE acquisition with supporting software, maintenance, and services is governed by a separate statute and special regulations. Telecommunications consist of local and intercity telephone services, radio service, audio and visual service, and equipment associated with these services. In ADPE and telecommunications contracting, competition is based on both price and technical considerations.

- **Research and Development:** Research and development contractors are selected primarily for technical considerations, although a thorough evaluation and comparison of all relevant business, price, and technical factors are required for meaningful source selection. Technical evaluations are directed both to the proposal itself and to the contractor's capabilities in relation to it.

- **Major Systems:** Major systems are the combination of elements, such as hardware, automatic data-processing equipment, software, or construction that will function together to produce the capabilities required to fulfill a mission need. Major systems acquisition programs are directed at and critical to fulfilling an agency mission; entail the allocation of relatively large resources; and warrant special management attention. No two are identical and involve such differences as time, cost, technology, management, and contracting approach. Major systems are designated as such by the agency head according to a variety of criteria established by the Office of Management and Budget and by the individual agency. Examples of large procurements, some of which are designated as major systems and are subject to major systems acquisitions policies and procedures, are Federal office buildings; hospitals; prisons; power-generating plants; dams; energy demonstration programs; transportation systems; ship, aircraft, or missile systems; space systems; and ADP systems designated as major systems.

Examples of Good Contracting Resumes

The following are two examples of contracting resumes. The first is for a military person who wants to transition to a job as a civilian contract specialist. The second is for a person in the private sector who wants to become a Federal contract specialist.

Military to Civilian Contract Specialist

CHARLES CHAMBERS
PSC 5 Box 55555
APO, AE 09050
e-mail: chambers@hotmail.com

Home Phone: 011-49-69-6999-3333	Home Fax: 01149-69-6909-5555

Social Security Number:	000-00-0000
Country of Citizenship:	U.S.
Veterans' Preference:	5-Point Veteran
Highest Federal Civilian Grade:	N/A
Clearance:	Top Secret

PROFILE:

Dynamic, energetic, results-oriented professional with outstanding independent experience in Air Force Acquisition. **Warranted Contracting Officer** with an excellent grasp of Federal Acquisition Regulations (FAR), as well as proven track record in negotiating and administering complex contracts. Persuasive communicator, team builder, problem solver, and motivator. Comfortable working in both large and small organizations. Outstanding management, networking, presentation, and follow-up skills. Always accessible to provide excellent customer support in line with mission goals. Excellent troubleshooter and self-starter. Flexible, loyal team player with strong work ethic who embraces new challenges.

OBJECTIVE:

Contract Specialist, GS-1102-12, Shaw Air Force Base, Announcement Number AF-25-45-2003

PROFESSIONAL EXPERIENCE:

Deputy, Operational Contracting Chief	August 2001 to Present
469th Air Base Group / LGC	40+ hrs per week
Rhein Main Air Base, Germany	USAF; Tech Sgt.
Supervisor: Tom Jones, GS-13; 01149-69995-8888 (may be contacted)	

Provide oversight of operational contracting flight construction, services, and supply acquisition on ad-hoc basis. Independently perform the full range of duties as warranted U.S. Air Force Contracting Officer. Work side-by-side with other professional Contract Specialists, both military and civilian, preparing solicitations and awarding large-dollar services and construction contracts. Analyze contemplated awards to ensure price, quality, and delivery factors are in the best interest of the government. Prepare bid abstracts and review bids for responsiveness and compliance with purchase description, as well as specifications, performance requirements, and terms/conditions. Conduct contract negotiations. Independently prepare contract modifications as needed. Monitor contract progress and advise contractors on all compliance matters. Prepare and conduct pre-construction briefings. Provide contracting support and training for non-appropriated fund instrumentalities and customers. Personally coordinate the government-wide purchase card program, continually providing training and monitoring nearly 100 agency credit card holders in services and supply acquisition.

Major Accomplishments:

- In spite of the disruptive effects and challenges presented by the events of 9/11, executed $2.7 million in error-free end-of-fiscal-year commitments.

- Skillfully managed all assignments while acting as Operational Contracting Chief with oversight of $750,000 of procurement actions. Made sure all procurement actions were appropriately distributed and purchased, and commodities and services were delivered on time.

- Diligently reviewed, obtained revisions, and negotiated 5 Military Housing, Quality of Life Improvement Projects in less than 45 days! Ensured 100% acquisition, and no loss of Fiscal Year (FY) funding.

- Negotiated a major base gymnasium renovation project, bringing cost down to $327,000 from an original estimate of $495,000. Saved nearly $170,000 in the fiscal year.

- Oversaw the growth of the government-wide purchase card program at the Rhein Main Air Base from yearly expenditures of $1.1 million in 1999 to nearly $2.5 million by 2002, while significantly reducing agency workload and paperwork.

Services and Construction Buyer   August 1998 to August 2001
469th Air Base Group / LGC   40+ hrs per week
Rhein Main Air Base, Germany   USAF; Staff Sgt.
Supervisor: Tom Jones, GS-13; 01149-69995-8888

Performed the full range of duties of a warranted U.S. Air Force Contracting Officer. Prepared solicitations and awarded large-dollar services and construction contracts. Analyzed contemplated awards to ensure price, quality, and delivery factors were in the best interest of the government. Prepared bid abstracts and reviewed bids for responsiveness and compliance with purchase description, as well as with specifications, performance requirements, and terms/conditions. Conducted contract negotiations. Independently prepared contract modifications as needed. Monitored contract progress and advised contractors on all matters concerning contract compliance. Prepared and conducted pre-performance

(continues)

(continued)

briefings. Provided contracting support and training for customers. Personally coordinated the government-wide purchase card program, continually providing training and monitoring nearly 100 agency credit card holders in services and supply acquisition. Performed duties as required for the smooth operation of Standard Procurement System (SPS), including training of others.

Major Accomplishments:

- Provided outstanding support to the Rhein Main Air Base (469th ABG) by awarding over 65 contracts and 350 line items totaling more than $1,200,000.

- Effectively managed the highly visible government purchase card program, consisting of 93 cardholders, 30 separate approving officials, and purchases of over $925,000. Accurately tracked all monthly reconciliation, resulting in no delinquent payments to vendors.

- Independently devised new liquidated damage rates to be applied to construction contracts, allowing for fair payment deduction, and ensured government protection in the event of delinquent performance on the part of contractors.

Contract Administrator/Management Analyst November 1995 to August 1998
3rd Contracting Squadron   40+ hrs per week
Elmendorf AFB, AK   USAF; Staff Sgt.
Supervisor: Roy Smith, GS-12; (345) 627-5555

Over a two-and-a-half-year period, held a variety of challenging assignments in contract administration, negotiation, and information systems administration. For instance, between November 1995 and November 1996, administered and enforced all formal construction contracts written by the base Operational Contracting Office. Then, between November 1996 and November 1997, took responsibility for solicitation, development, and awarding of construction projects. Finally, between November 1997 and August 1998, served as systems administrator for the Base Contracting Automated System (BCAS). In the latter assignment, coordinated, supervised, and obtained funding for agency computer system infrastructure shortfalls and required upgrades. Streamlined the agency local area network (LAN), improving access by interagency, agency, and prospective customers. Developed agency Web site, which provided quick Internet access to a full range of information on contracting actions.

Major Accomplishments:

- Negotiated a major contract modification when asbestos was located at Galena Air Station, AK, precluding costly delays that would have exceeded $1,000 per day in field overhead charges due to remote location.
- Negotiated $2,000,000 renovation of historical facilities.
- Negotiated $800,000 renovation of Seward, AK, Armed Forces Recreation Center.
- Saved over $400,000 in overall project costs during negotiations.
- Procured and administered eight separate projects totaling in excess of $13 million.

EDUCATION:

- Community College of the Air Force
  Projected: October 2003, Associate of Arts Degree in Contracts Management

- Chauncy High School, Cleveland, OH, Diploma, May 1982

LICENSES/CERTIFICATIONS:

Warranted Contracting Officer, July 2000

PROFESSIONAL TRAINING:

- Acquisition Professional Development Program Level II, August 2001
- Construction Contracting Course, May 2001
- Contracting Craftsman Course, April 2000
- Government Contract Law Course, January 2000
- Quantitative Techniques for Contract and Price Analysis Course, June 1999
- Acquisition Professional Development Program Level I, September 1997
- Contract Pricing Course and Principles of Contract Pricing Course, May 1997
- Operational Level Contract Pricing Course, February 1997
- Base Level Contracting Fundamentals Course, March 1997
- Apprentice Contracting Specialist Course, May 1996

COMPUTER SKILLS:

Extensive knowledge of Microsoft Office (Word, Excel, Access, PowerPoint, and Outlook) and most Microsoft Windows and DOS software.

Private Sector to Federal Contract Specialist

GEORGE A. DAIMLAR
7555 Effington Circle
Alexandria, VA 22315
Day: (246) 555-4794 * Evening: (703) 555-1011 * E-mail: daimler@aol.com

Citizenship: U.S.A.
Federal Status: N/A
SSN: 000-00-0000

Veterans' Status: 5 points
Military Status: U.S.A.F., 1987–1991

OBJECTIVE

Contract Specialist, NH-1102-12/13, United States Air Force, District of Washington, Bolling AFB. **Announcement No: DD-2-0131.**

SUMMARY OF QUALIFICATIONS

Contract Attorney with 15+ years of progressive, professional experience in private industry, government, and the U.S. Military. Outstanding record of performance in contract administration and procurements, including four years of experience as Judge Advocate General for the U.S. Air Force, Strategic Air Command (SAC). Currently administering over $1 million in contracts for five U.S. military installations. Juris Doctorate and Master of Law degrees. Licensed to practice law in four states and the District of Columbia.

Key competencies include:

- Expert knowledge of federal contracting laws, regulations, policies, and procedures, including Government Procurement Procedures and Federal Acquisition Regulations (FARs).

- Demonstrated ability to manage and administer all facets of the contract process from pre-award to post-award, including proposals, price/cost analyses, expenditure evaluations, and determining reasonable cost. Experienced in all contracting/procurement methods and types.

- Successful track record as an advisor and legal counsel to government agencies, military organizations, and administrative boards.

- Direct and decisive. Skilled in all aspects of contract negotiations.

- Strong oral and written communications skills. Excellent organizational, analytical, and research capabilities. PC proficient.

PROFESSIONAL EXPERIENCE

Subcontract Administrator   July 2002 to Present
Brown & Root Services, a division of Halliburton Company   40–60 hours/week
6452 Landsdowne Centre, Alexandria, VA 22315   Current Salary: $60,000
Supervisor: Greg Jones (703) 555-7552; may be contacted.

Recruited to Brown & Root, a federal government contractor, to manage and administer all facets of the competitive contract process for the Military District of Washington (MDW) Job Order Contracts (JOC). Provide leadership and expertise for contract administration and procurements for five U.S. military installations. Manage over 30 multi-year contracts in excess of $1 million. Negotiate, draft, and administer contracts for diversified goods and services, repairs, construction projects, contractor services, and professional services, including architectural, engineering, and consulting. Key responsibilities include:

- Contract Administration: Manage and administer all contractual actions from pre-award to post-award, including initial planning, contract awards, and administration. Initiate, create, manage, negotiate, and manage Master Agreements with subcontractors. Prepare bid proposal packages. Initiate formal change orders, contract amendments, invoicing, and certified payrolls.
- Market Research: Analyze and research market conditions, contractors, and services to monitor changing costs and to obtain best prices for goods and services.
- Cost Price Analysis: Format and abstract bids. Draft bid tabulations to determine best-qualified bidder. Review proposals against previous history, actual and estimated expenditures, and established rates. Determine price reasonableness or negotiation position. Calculate pricing using the *R.S. Means Facilities Construction Cost Data Book.*
- Negotiations: Negotiate best value. Conduct post-proposal and pre-evaluation meetings. Initiate requests for purchases/invitations to bid. Over 85% of bids are competitive; the remaining 15% are divided between fixed bids and sole-source selection.
- Quality Control: Monitor QC performance to ensure timely closeout of delivery orders and contracts. Coordinate project specifications and requirements with the QC and Delivery Order Managers. Draft Statements of Work (SOW) and Price Breakdown Sheets.
- Post Award: Execute post-award actions, including cost reimbursement and incentive arrangements. Provide business advice and contract guidance. Review and analyze settlement proposals and recommend allowable costs. Lead post-award conferences.
- Procurement Administration: Build and maintain a procurement system to support the real-time financial needs of the project. Analyze all procurement requests to determine requirements, contracting methods, and types.

(continues)

(continued)

Key Accomplishments:
- Minimize contract response time through efficient subcontract management and fast-track selection.
- Initiate agreements with subcontractors to respond within two hours to minimize response time for corrective actions.
- Establish and administer internal Quality Control and Improvement programs.
- Mentor and consistently utilize successful local area subcontractors. Improved work performance, ensuring quality consistency by using pre-qualified, proven performers.
- Gained a thorough knowledge of Indefinite Determination/Indefinite Quantity (IDIQ), FARs, Competition in Contracting Act (CICA), Buy American Act, Balance of Payments Program, the Contract Work Hours and Safety Standards Act, and the Davis-Bacon Act.

Contract Attorney	September 2000 to July 2002
LawCorps	50–70 hours/week
1819 L. Street, NW, Washington, DC 20036	Starting Salary: $45,000
Supervisor: Lee Fox, (202) 555-5996; may be contacted.	Ending Salary: $70,000

Researched, analyzed, and evaluated legislation related to antitrust, acquisitions, and mergers. Prepared written and documentary responses to regulatory review of large-scale corporate transactions. Oversaw document production for government and regulatory investigations and civil discovery. Researched complex legal and factual issues. Reviewed contracts and trade-secret, non-disclosure, licensing, and patent agreements for legal sufficiency.

Key Accomplishments:
- Chosen as project leader for complex acquisition case. Supervised 25+ attorneys.
- Selected for Privilege Review Team for FTC/DOJ antitrust and mergers/acquisitions.
- Based on successful track record for document review and preparation, selected as member of Quality Control review team.
- Consistently rated as "excellent" on performance evaluations.

Assistant Attorney General	September 1993 to May 1999
New Hampshire Office of Attorney General	50–60 hours/week
Consumer Protection & Antitrust/ Transportation &	
Construction Bureaus	Starting Salary: $43,000
33 Capitol Street, Concord, NH, 03301	Ending Salary: $58,000
Supervisor: Charles Plowman, (603) 555-3658; may be contacted.	

Attorney for seven licensing and disciplinary agencies. Conducted legal research for cases involving consumer protection, antitrust, and construction. Presented before trial and appellate courts, and administrative tribunals with quasi-judicial powers. Handled a broad range of legal and managerial assignments. Supervised 44+ administrative and support employees.

- Worked with Department of Transportation engineers and contractors to delineate scope of work. Reviewed construction, dredging, and demolition contracts. Helped ensure that pre-bid documents met specifications. Monitored post-award conferences and drafted contract amendments.
- Official representative for the licensing state agencies at hearings. Expert for administrative subpoenas, specialized expert testimony, quality of care, professional competence, and other legal issues.
- Conducted training classes for volunteers and interns. Researched, developed, and presented cases involving professional misconduct or malfeasance.
- Drafted position papers, policy statements, and memoranda relating to current and pending legislation, decisions, and orders of government agencies.

Key Accomplishments:

- Streamlined the investigatory and hearing phases of disciplinary hearings.
- Devised a reusable package of step-by-step processes in the administrative resolution of disciplinary actions, ensuring uniform and consistent procedures.
- Successfully handled a caseload (45) for seven licensing and disciplinary agencies while increasing the turnaround time efficiency.
- Established the use of legal interns, volunteers, and non-legal professionals for review of cases involving specialized issues, thereby reducing cost.
- Successfully argued three novel issues before the N.H. Supreme Court.
- Appointed to the Lawline Honor Roll for providing free legal services to New Hampshire citizens.

Judge Advocate General (JAG)	October 1987 to January 1991
U.S. Air Force, Office of Judge Advocate General	60 hours/week
Pease AFB, Newington, NH 03801	Ending Salary: $42,000
Supervisor: Lt. Frank Skinner; DSN: 555-3552; may be contacted.	

High-profile, high-visibility law position supporting top-level command personnel regarding base policies and command objectives, including personnel, regulatory issues, Uniform Code of Military Justice, civil law, procurement, and acquisition contracts. Government counsel, defense counsel, and investigator for general courts-martial and administrative disciplinary hearings.

- Managed a legal assistance program serving a community of 15,000 military and dependent personnel. Litigated cases before trial and appellate courts and administrative tribunals. Supervised staff of seven.
- Reviewed procurements, contracts, and acquisitions for the SAC. Provided general technical and administrative direction of Staff Judge Advocate for protests and problems for contracts awarded or administered within the Pease complex. Managed an average of 10 contracts up to $1 million. Interpreted FARs.
- Provided legal guidance for acquisitions and procurements, including business strategy, acquisition policy, source solicitation, contract formation, negotiation (in

(continues)

(continued)

accordance with TINA), preparation and interpretation of contractual documents, modifications and changes, and contract change notices.

- Reviewed contracts and purchase requests for legal sufficiency. Advised the base contracting office as to status of pending bid protests.
- Provided legal counsel for personnel and disciplinary matters and inquiries relevant to the Freedom of Information and Privacy Acts.
- Performed legal research in the areas of military and veterans' law, civil rights, employment discrimination, domestic law, torts, criminal law, and contracts.

Key Accomplishments:

- Gained an extensive knowledge of the Contract Disputes Act (CDA), Armed Services Procurement Act (ASPA), Federal Property and Administrative Services Act (FPASA), and Competition in Contracting Act (CICA).
- Received commendation for uncovering contractor fraud. Evaluation stated: "Provided outstanding services as base legal advisor on contracting matters; cited by HQ AF/JA for efforts enabling the government to assert counterclaims of fraud without a final determination by the contracting officer."
- Initiated a program to reduce time spent reviewing legal sufficiency in the pre-award by improving coordination through the Base Contracting Office. Streamlined a checklist for acquisitions and procurement's review for legal sufficiency.
- Promoted to Area Defense Counsel, serving five bases.
- As a result of demonstrated knowledge and ability, was selected as Chief Legal Advisor and Consultant within the Office of the Judge Advocate General of complex and unusual matters.
- Prevailed in an Unfair Labor Practice case involving a recalcitrant employee and an Armed Services Board of Contract Appeals case involving fraudulent claims submitted by the contractors.
- Developed necessary management controls that ensured quality performance in office operations and improved legal services.

EDUCATION

Master of Law, 2000
Major: Law
Semester Credit Hours Earned: 84
University of Dayton School of Law
Dayton, OH 45419

Bachelor of Arts, 1982
Major: Political Science &
International Relations
Semester Credit Hours Earned: 128
Boston University
Boston, MA 02215

Juris Doctorate, 1985
Major: Intellectual Property
Semester Credit Hours Earned: 30
Franklin Pierce Law Center
Concord, NH 03301

Springfield North High School, 1978
Springfield, OH 45504

PROFESSIONAL LICENSES & CERTIFICATES

Licensed to practice in:
The State and Federal Courts of Ohio, 11-85, and New Hampshire, 04-94
The State Courts of Massachusetts, 02-94, and Colorado, 05-01
The District of Columbia, 05-02

MILITARY SERVICE

U.S. Air Force, 10/87 to 1/91, Honorable Discharge
Highest Military Grade Held: Captain

AWARDS & HONORS

Military Honors & Awards:
Air Force Commendation Medal, 1992
Air Force Achievement Medal, 1988
Top Gun Award for litigation and advocacy skills, 1988

Professional Honors & Awards:
Lawline Honor Roll, 1996 (donating time and legal services to the needy and indigent).
Speaker, Continuing Legal Education presentation in 1994.
Selected by the New Hampshire Bar Association to teach courses in Continuing Legal Education (CLE) in the areas of Administrative Law and Procedures.
Appointed Legal Customer Service Representative for LEXIS/NEXIS, Mead Data Central, 1985 to 1986.
Certificate of Appreciation, University of New Hampshire for Presentation on Trial Advocacy and Constitutional Rights.

TRAINING

- Federal Forfeiture of Assets, 3 hours, 1999
- Criminal Law and Procedure, 12 hours, 1998
- How to Draft, Negotiate and Enforce T-M, Copyright and Software, 1999
- Licensing Agreements, 6.25 hours, 1999
- Sexual Harassment in the Workplace, 2 hours, 1996; 12 hours, 1998
- Ethics for Government Lawyers, 2 hours, 1995
- Appellate Advocacy CLE, 3.5 hours, 1995
- Practical Skills for Windows, 5 hours, 1995
- MS Word I, 14 hours, 1994
- Administrative Law, 6 classroom hours, 1994
- Ethics CLE, 3.5 hours, 1994
- Practical Skills for Lawyers, 6 hours, 1995

Summary

A final thought on Federal contracting resumes: As you develop your business-focused resume, keep in mind that the Federal government really needs your *business-based* perspective as agencies move into the future. Don't be afraid to stress your *corporate* knowledge and your unique understanding and insight into working with both vendors and suppliers. Emphasize your knowledge of acquisition, and use the description of your current job to show how you can lead others in achieving cost-effective results for the public sector.

CHAPTER 22

Resumes for Administrative Assistant and Secretarial Series Jobs

By Carla Waskiewicz, CPRW

Employment opportunities for administrative, secretarial, and clerical professionals are abundant in the Federal government. Why? Because these important support positions are essential to the operations of virtually every government agency. A recent search of the USAJOBS Web site for Clerical positions (0303) generated nearly 200 openings in various grade levels. A search for Management Assistant generated an additional 20 job openings.

A resume for clerical and administrative positions should focus on your abilities to carry out the duties and responsibilities detailed in the position description. However, because many other applicants might share similar skills and qualifications, your resume should highlight the unique benefits you will bring to the position and emphasize your accomplishments. This chapter contains four case studies that offer excellent examples of how you, too, can make your clerical/administrative resume a real standout!

CASE 1: State to Federal Career Change

Mary Stone, an Inspection Aide for the State of Connecticut, was seeking a Federal position as a Secretary, GS-06 grade level, in the U.S. Attorney's office, Department of Justice. Although she had selected several potential administrative positions for which to apply, this position moved to the top of her priority list because of her extensive law-related clerical experience.

To match her resume to the position and use the right keywords, I analyzed the duties and qualifications requirements in the posting and organized them into focusing sections to be incorporated as part of her Summary of Qualifications. I used this "profile statement" to showcase her core competencies and qualifications at the start of the resume to better catch the Federal hiring manager's eye. With hundreds of applications, hiring managers must quickly scan the first page of a resume to look for the most qualified candidates. I like to compare the Qualifications Summary to a billboard on the highway. You have less than 15 seconds to capture that hiring manager's attention. Why not make his or her job easier and improve your chances during the initial screening? Add impact to your resume by summarizing your best skills and qualifications right at the start! This summary also gives you the opportunity to develop a precise and targeted response to the "duties" section of the announcement.

Here's an excerpt from Mary's "before" resume. As you can see, her resume includes basic duties, responsibilities, and compliance information, such as salaries and starting dates, but does not effectively highlight her qualifications or accomplishments.

MARY A. STONE
P.O. Box 269008
West Hartford, Connecticut 06127
(860) 570-8522
e-mail: mstone@aol.com

PROFESSIONAL EXPERIENCE

STATE OF CONNECTICUT

Inspection Aide—Consumer Trades Division   (04/94–Present)
165 Capital Avenue, Room 110/Trades Division   40 hrs/week
Hartford, CT 06106   Starting Salary: $28,200
Supervisor: Linda Brown (860) 712-6123   Current Salary: $29,200
You may contact present employer.

Serve as the first point of contact for consumer inquiries and complaints involving work performed in the State of Connecticut by trades professionals. This includes, but is not limited to, carpenters, plumbers, electricians, painters and other home improvement workers, as well as ordinary everyday complaints.

Intake initial information and verify its accuracy with the complainant. Handle complaints by phone, by mail or from walk-in citizens. Evaluate the seriousness of the complaint. Make a preliminary decision as to whether or not to investigate further. Forward complaints for further investigation and/or mediation. Perform all data entry so that information is entered correctly onto computer database. Handle case files. Follow up through resolution of case. Assist in onsite inspections of home improvement work. Perform Notary Public duties as required.

Court Monitor—Connecticut Superior Court   (01/00–04/01)
20 Franklin Square   40 hrs/week
New Britain, CT 06051   Starting Hourly: $14.25
Supervisor: Mimi Palmer (860) 515-5343   Final Hourly: $14.25
You may contact this employer.

Recorded both Criminal and Civil Proceedings through the use of stenography machine and audio recording equipment. Utilized CD-ROM technology. Prepared certified transcripts of trials, appeals, hearings and motions. Prepared billing and tax statements. Performed general administrative and clerical duties. Set up equipment. Maintained records. Provided auxiliary and administrative support to attorneys and court personnel.

Due to performance and to fulfill the needs of the Court, asked to perform independent contractual work for (described in detail later in resume). Operated this position as an adjunct to the Court Monitor Recording position (while working full 40 hours/week in Court Monitor Recording position).

The "After" resume presents her key skills and abilities and the top duties requirements at a glance in bold type for greater emphasis. Her work experience follows in reverse-chronological order. The new resume format and design, with a prominent qualifications summary, make her a standout candidate for the secretarial position.

MARY A. STONE
P.O. Box 269008
West Hartford, CT 06127
Home: (860) 570-8522 • Work: (860) 715-6887
E-mail: Mstone@aol.com

Social Security No.: xxx-xx-xxxx	Citizenship: United States of America
Veterans' Preference: 10 points	Federal Status: N/A

OBJECTIVE

Secretary, Office Assistant, Justice Department, United States Attorney's Office, New York City, NY; Announcement #02-SDNY-19D, GS-0318-06.

SUMMARY OF QUALIFICATIONS

Experienced Office Administrator with 11+ years of diverse experience in government and private industry. Outstanding organizational and office administration skills, including financial management, personnel management, database expertise, and technical support capabilities. Excellent oral and written communications skills. Skilled in all aspects of office operations. Able to establish priorities and implement decisions to achieve both immediate and long-term goals.

- **Administrative Expertise:** Maintain administrative office flow. Track and maintain files; manage correspondence and information; maintain inventory. Procure office equipment and supplies.
- **Secretarial Skills:** Keyboard 69 words per minute with an error rate of 3. Experience with stenography, audio recording devices, and duplicating and facsimile machines.
- **Computer and Database Skills:** Create, establish, and maintain databases in support of operations using a LAN and desktop computers. Proficient in Word, PowerPoint, and Excel.
- **Finance and Accounting:** Experience with budget, payroll, and accounting.
- **Specialized Training:** AA degree, Liberal Arts; Certificate of Secretarial Science; Certificate of Court Reporting; Notary Public.

PROFESSIONAL EXPERIENCE

INSPECTION AIDE   April 1994 to Present
State of Connecticut, Consumer Trades Division   40 hours per week
165 Capital Avenue, Room 110, Hartford, CT 06106   Current Salary: $29,200/year
Supervisor: Linda Brown, (860) 712-6123. May be contacted. Starting Salary: $28,200/year

Provide administrative, technical, and customer service support for all consumer inquiries and complaints for work performed by trades professionals in the State of Connecticut. First contact for all customer complaints. Coordinate all administrative functions and manage customer service complaint process to ensure smooth and efficient operation and problem resolution.

- Receive telephone calls and walk-in visitors, record intake information, and verify accuracy of information with complainants.
- Review all complaints to determine level of action. Respond to inquiries and recommend further investigation and/or refer complaints to managers for further investigation or mediation.
- Prepare and maintain all data entries and ensure accuracy of entries to computer database.

CASE 2: Transitioning from Private Industry to Government

Barbara Taylor was working as a Business Process Analyst for a Federal contractor that provides administrative support services for special events, meetings, and conferences. She was seeking to transition to a Federal position as a Management Assistant with the Department of Housing and Urban Development. Here is a summary of the target skills from the description of duties for the announcement:

> Coordinates administrative matters.
>
> Works with senior staff to consolidate administrative reports.
>
> Initiates necessary correspondence.
>
> Develops methods of operation or improvements in administrative practices and work routines.
>
> Performs research and gathers background data for use by senior staff.
>
> Researches and assembles materials for meetings, conferences, and presentations...

There were also four KSAs required for the application, including knowledge of office procedures and filing systems; knowledge of quantitative methods and research methodologies; knowledge of computer software sufficient to create tables and graphs; and skill in oral and written communication to effectively communicate with managers, employees, and the public.

Take a look at Barbara's "Before" resume. You can see that it begins with her education and then includes short summaries of her qualifications and previous positions. The summary for her current position as Business Process Analyst is brief and does not effectively showcase her many qualifications.

Barbara Taylor
2000 Quarters Apt. E
Quantico, VA 22134
703-699-8888

EDUCATION:

Park University, B.S. degree candidate (Management)
Dale Carnegie Training (12-week course)
Situational Leadership Training (2-day course)
Merchandise Assistant Training Program (6-week course, JCPenney)
U.S. Navy Administrative Data School, Meridian, MS
Event Management Training (1-week course)
Calvert County Community College, LaPlata, MD (1994–1995); Completed Computer Courses

---

EXPERIENCE SUMMARY:

18 years of professional experience.

- Experience with various computer software systems including MS Office 2000 (Word, Excel, Access, PowerPoint), MS Project, Lotus Notes, WordPerfect, Quicken, Harvard Graphics, MS Publisher, FoxPro, R-Base, dBASE, Flowcharting 3, TSO/ORACLE, Group Systems, Scheduling System, Internet, and e-mail.

- Developed and maintained company employee database in Access to track employee reviews, goals, and personal information.

- Several years of experience managing events from concept to completion.

- **Business Process Analyst,** 2002–Present:

   Provide required resources and expertise to support the planning and execution of events; conduct AGC events and presentations and provide facilitation and process support in diverse areas to ensure smooth and successful execution. Determine the purpose and requirements of the customer including, but not limited to, identification of the participants and any unique support required, and appropriate technology systems. Prepare an activity security plan and prepare a plan outlining the resources and staffing required to meet customers' requirements/objectives.

Now, take a look at her new resume. Here are some of the improvements we made to make her qualifications really stand out.

Because Barbara had more than 18 years of valuable administrative experience, her new resume needed to focus on her core qualifications and career accomplishments. Her education was still important, but it needed to go at the end of the resume instead of at the beginning.

To better market Barbara's qualifications, we started her resume with a comprehensive Professional Profile section, a summary statement that encapsulated all of her best administrative management skills. Then, under a Core Qualifications subheading within this profile, we organized her skills and abilities in separate categories. These categories were highlighted in bold, italic type to add impact.

Next, within those categories, we incorporated keywords from the duties description in the job posting, as well as some of the knowledge and abilities from the KSAs, such as Communications Skills. This great focusing section now makes it easy for the selecting official to see at a glance just how qualified Barbara is for this job.

Finally, one of the most important additions to her resume was a list of accomplishments for each position she held. Showcasing accomplishments is the most effective way to set yourself apart from the competition and show a potential employer what you have achieved on the job. Just think about it; if you were a hiring supervisor with dozens of resumes to read, which candidate would you select for an interview: the candidate who simply lists what they do each day on the job, or the one who clearly shows quantifiable accomplishments or project successes? A resume is a marketing document. Marketing yourself as the best candidate will increase your chances of landing an interview *and* a new job!

BARBARA N. TAYLOR

2000 Quarters, Apt. E
Quantico, VA 22134

Day: (202) 781-1000   E-mail: Btaylor@yahoo.com   Evening: (703) 699-8888

Social Security No.: XXX-XX-XXXX   Citizenship: U.S.A.
Federal Status: N/A   Veterans' Preference: N/A

OBJECTIVE

Position: Management Assistant. **Grade:** GS-0344-07. **Announcement No:** 00-DEU-03-0002

PROFESSIONAL PROFILE

Organized, articulate Administrative Professional with 18+ years of progressively responsible experience in the strategic areas of administrative operations, information management, and events/meeting planning. Excellent organizational, research, and communications capabilities. Demonstrated ability to prioritize tasks, meet time-sensitive deadlines, and work independently to achieve goals.

CORE QUALIFICATIONS

- *Administrative Expertise:* Comprehensive executive-level administrative and technical expertise. Skilled in developing, implementing, and managing office procedures and systems, with extensive experience providing informational, logistical, and technical support for meetings, conferences, and special events.

- *Computer Skills:* Broad-based computer software knowledge and database management expertise. Proficient in MS Word, Excel, PowerPoint, Access, Outlook, Publisher; GoldMine; and Graphic User Interface (GUI) systems. Extensive expertise creating tables, graphs, charts, spreadsheets, reports, specialized correspondence, and multimedia presentations. Valued for ability to organize computer data files to improve productivity and manage information.

- *Research & Analysis:* Adept at researching, analyzing, extracting, and archiving data for development reports and subject-matter files.

- *Communications Skills:* Polished oral and written communications skills. Well-developed interpersonal skills. At ease interfacing with top executives, government leaders, clients, customers, and vendors.

EDUCATION AND TRAINING:

Park University, B.S. degree candidate (Management), Quantico, VA 22134
Dale Carnegie Training (12-week course), June 2002
Situational Leadership Training (2-day course), March 2002
Merchandise Assistant Training Program (6-week course, JCPenney), May 2001
Event Management Training (1-week course), August 1999
U.S. Navy Administrative Data School, Meridian, MS, March 1995
Calvert County Community College, LaPlata, MD, 56 credit hours, 1994–1995

PROFESSIONAL EXPERIENCE

BUSINESS PROCESS ANALYST
COMPUTER SCIENCE CORPORATION (CSC.COM)
1201 M Street, Washington, DC 20376
Supervisor: Erin Gantt, (202) 675-4993, may be contacted.
(A federal contractor providing conference/special events services)

May 2002 to Present
40 hours per week
Current Salary: $47,000

Act as Administrative Assistant and Events Representative. Provide comprehensive administrative, clerical, and technical support for the Admiral Gooding Center, Command Events Planning Branch of the Naval Sea Systems Command (NAVSEA). Manage and coordinate administrative functions to ensure the smooth and efficient operation of conference facilities and services. Report to the Director of Events Planning.

- Organize and coordinate logistics and provide administrative and technical support for special events, meetings, conferences, and seminars at the Center. Maximize use of software applications to create project correspondence, support materials, and record program documentation.
- As Events Assistant, serve as key client interface and on-site technical representative from pre-event planning to post-event follow-up. Use state-of-the-art computer technology (GUI) to hyperlink client information to PowerPoint and other software to create multimedia presentations. Play integral role in planning meetings. Key contact for high-ranking military personnel.
- Assist with basic accounting/finance functions. Track bank card transactions and purchase orders. Review financial reports to ensure accuracy.
- Answer and screen telephone calls, greet and register incoming visitors, and disseminate information to customers, the public, and staff. Conduct facility tours.
- Administer workflow, and establish and maintain subject-matter files. Provide secretarial/clerical support. Track and document project status using spreadsheet applications.

Key Accomplishments:

- Improved data collection, documentation, and access, and reduced errors by consolidating six spreadsheets into one. Also created pivot tables to extract requested data more efficiently.
- Utilized Word and Excel to create and implement a more efficient system for tracking and documenting conference/meeting project status and follow-up.
- Assisted with financial report review and uncovered a $30,000 calculation error. Revised and improved the report implementing Excel software.
- Consistently exceed performance standards. Valued by management and staff for increasing internal efficiencies and cutting administrative costs by creating new ways to automate office procedures and duties.

CASE 3: Moving Up from One Federal Job to Another

Experienced administrative professional Carol Deeter had worked for the U.S. Department of Agriculture for more than 10 years. Prior to working in the Federal government, she had also worked for more than 20 years in private industry. Her goal was to move from a Grade 7 position to a Grade 8. When applying for previous grade changes, Carol had always submitted her government form SF-171. OPM officially eliminated this form in 1995, but many Federal employees are still using it. A paper resume is a much more effective way to present a candidate's job history and skills. To apply for the new grade level, Carol wanted to convert her lengthy SF-171 to a Federal resume to better showcase her experience and qualifications.

Carol's new Federal resume starts with a comprehensive Skills Summary. As detailed in the previous examples, this section incorporates many of the duties from the job posting she selected, such as market research, database analysis, and statistical analysis. Also included are important administrative/office-management skills that she will bring to the job, such as "Valued by senior executives for ability to manage offices, improve systems, meet deadlines, and develop and implement new administrative procedures."

Within the Skills Summary, we also high-lighted her important "soft skills," such as "self-motivated," and her desire to expand her computer software knowledge. This helps to demonstrate that she is an experienced and competent administrative professional, and that she also has drive and initiative. She not only gets things done, but she makes things better. She achieves results and is always willing to take on new responsibilities. Those are just some of the qualities that make her stand out!

Finally, in the summary of her present job, we featured her responsibilities using a subhead format. Instead of providing a long list of job duties, this approach helps to better organize her responsibilities and makes the resume easier to read. Her accomplishments are clearly highlighted in a separate section. With the new resume format, it is easy to pinpoint her most significant accomplishments and skills.

CAROL F. DEETER

3535 Signal Road
Alexandria, Virginia 22304
Home: (703) 755-6555 • Work: (202) 699-1111
E-mail: carol.deeter@wdc.usda.gov

Social Security No.: xxx-xx-xxxx
Citizenship: United States of America
Veterans' Status: None
Federal Status: Secretary, GS-318-6

Objective:

Secretary, GS-0318-08, U.S. Department of Agriculture, Farm Service Agency, Washington, DC, Announcement #F2-FSA-042.

Skills Summary:

Secretary, Administrative Specialist, and Office Manager with more than 30 years of Federal and private industry experience. Excellent oral and written communication skills, demonstrated interpersonal skills, and proven organizational and administrative expertise. Skilled in market research, statistical analysis, and database management. Valued by senior executives for ability to manage office, improve systems, meet deadlines, and develop and implement new administrative procedures. An integral staff professional, skilled in assisting with program functions, training personnel, and supporting and communicating with program director. Coordinate work load and projects, ensuring compliance and quality control. Effectively serve staff needs for information, scheduling, and administrative support.

- **Finance/accounting support expertise.** Formulate, justify, and execute budgets. Proven experience preparing budget reports, cash-flow analysis, accounts payable and receivable, and payroll.

- **Maintain smooth flow of paperwork.** Research, analyze, process, and track files, documentation, correspondence, and information. Maintain inventory. Procure office equipment and supplies.

- **Self-motivated.** Able to establish priorities and implement decisions to achieve both immediate and long-term goals.

- **Eager learner.** Wish to increase knowledge base, particularly in the areas of computer software applications.

- **Database expertise.** Create, establish, and maintain databases in support of operations. Implement filing systems to improve internal operations.

(continues)

(continued)

Carol F. Deeter, XXX-XX-XXXX

Employment History:

SECRETARY (GS-0318-7/10)   December 1997 to Present
U.S. Department of Agriculture   40 hours per week
Farm Service Agency, Outreach Programs Staff
1451 Rockville Pike, WOCII, Room 2009, Rockville, Maryland 20850
Supervisor: Cindy Harn, Director; yes, please contact at (202) 722-2222
Ending Salary: $38,954 per year; Starting Salary: $28,000 per year

Provide broad-based administrative support to the Supervisor and multi-cultural support staff. Primary responsibility includes coordinating administrative functions to ensure the smooth and efficient operation of the office and its programs. Provide the Women's Outreach Coordinator with essential information and resources to promote the staff's outreach efforts to women's farm organizations.

Responsibilities:
- **Coordinate internal and external office communications and documentation:** Review and analyze incoming mail and distribute mail to director and staff. Evaluate all correspondence to ensure conformance to administrative and security requirements. Review and type all correspondence, reports, publications, and other materials from rough draft to final form, ensuring accuracy, proper formatting, spelling and grammar. Maintain and update files supporting State Quarterly Reports and programs.

- **Supervise support staff:** Control and expedite work assignments to staff members. Prepare, maintain, and transmit time and attendance reports. Train and supervise summer intern staff.

- **Create and manage schedules and workflow:** Maintain supervisor's calendar and use own initiative to prioritize and schedule appointments.

- **Manage multiple administrative requirements:** Receive visitors, screen and field incoming telephone calls, and direct inquiries to proper departments. Monitor and maintain office supply and operating forms inventories. Administer travel arrangements for all staff members, including travel orders and airline, hotel, and car rental reservations.

- **Support meetings and presentations:** Arrange and coordinate monthly meetings with National Outreach Council Members, including setup and participation in the monthly teleconference with State Executive Directors (SEDs) and Outreach Coordinators. Assist in preparation of outreach training documents.

    Accomplishments:
    ➤ Volunteered to serve as interim Women's Outreach Coordinator when position was vacant. Independently researched women's farm organizations nationwide and prepared statistics that helped establish a women's program file. When new coordinator joined staff, provided orientation and resources, and developed information in support of the staff's outreach efforts.
    ➤ Assisted in the preparation of SED's Outreach Training documents in Atlanta, St. Paul, and Washington, D.C.
    ➤ Created database of state directors and contact information for office distribution.

CASE 4: Transitioning from Nonprofit to a Federal Job (Electronic Resume)

In this example, Tammy Dean, an Administrative Assistant with a Baltimore nonprofit organization, was seeking an entry-level position as a Records Management Assistant (0303) with the National Security Agency. The duties and responsibilities of her current job, as well as experience gained through a previous position, were a perfect match for the Federal job she was seeking. To apply for the position, she needed an electronic Federal resume (or Resumix) that could be cut and pasted into the agency's online resume builder.

To build her resume "skills summary," we incorporated keywords from the announcement's Duties summary into her resume as the headings for short blocks of copy describing her knowledge, skills, and job experience. They included Database Management, Communications, and Travel and Schedule Management. We incorporated additional target skills into the blocks of copy describing her job history, such as "Worked independently to accomplish administrative

tasks," and "Answered, screened, and routed as many as 100 daily telephone calls." Note that in this sentence she quantified how many calls she answered each day. Quantifying your skills helps to more clearly demonstrate what you do best, in measurable terms.

As with paper Federal resumes, electronic resumes should always include accomplishments. In Tammy's resume, the accomplishment from her current job clearly demonstrates her "records management capabilities." This will help to set her apart from other candidates who do not include accomplishments in their resumes.

In many resume builders, it is not possible to start a resume with a profile statement. So, rather than exclude this information, take advantage of the general heading in the builder called Other Information to provide that great summary profile. You will notice that Tammy's summary includes key computer and office equipment proficiencies, as well as important soft skills, such as energetic, flexible, and detail-oriented. This profile statement incorporates additional keywords from the job posting and ensures that all of her best skills are featured in the resume.

@@@@@@@@@@@@@@@

TAMMY DEAN
SSN: XXX-XX-XXXX

1500 East Biltmore Street
Baltimore, MD 21233
Home Phone: 410-567-0219
Work Phone: 410-799-4900
E-mail: Tdean@aol.com

Country of Citizenship: United States of America
Highest Grade: N/A

VACANCY INFORMATION

Vacancy I.D. No.: PH147170
Job Title: Records Management Assistant, GS-0303
Grade(s) Applying for: GS-04, GS-05

EXPERIENCE

October 2001 to present; 40 hours per week; ADMINISTRATIVE ASSISTANT, $14,586 per
year, Empower Baltimore Management Corporation, EBMC, 3 South Frederick Street, Suite
800, Baltimore, MD 21202; Supervisor: Tisha Edwards, Chief Operating Officer, (410) 783-
4400; may contact.

Executive Administrator for the Chief Operating Officer. Provided comprehensive, direct
executive-level administrative support to the COO. Coordinated administrative functions to
ensure smooth and efficient operation of the office and its programs. Worked independently to
accomplish administrative tasks. Organized, collected, analyzed, and distributed information
related to EBMC programs and projects.

DATABASE MANAGEMENT: Utilize office automation, database management, word
processing, and financial software programs. Establish and maintain electronic and paper files.
Enter and retrieve data files. Use manual and automated filing systems to establish and
maintain administrative files.

COMMUNICATIONS: Create and distribute correspondence and reports using office automation
tools. Perform various clerical duties. Answer recurring questions and resolve administrative
and clerical problems. Provide backup front-desk support on multi-line telephone system.
Receive and refer visitors. Greet customers. Answer, screen, and route as many as 100 daily
telephone calls. Disseminate customer information. Distribute mail and messages.

TRAVEL AND SCHEDULE MANAGEMENT: Manage executive schedules and appointment
calendars. Schedule reservations and travel arrangements.

ACCOMPLISHMENT: Instrumental in the creation and organization of the first EBMC Policy
Database, a historical database created in Access summarizing six years of funding history,
board actions, and policy changes. Created the database and researched, analyzed,

categorized, summarized, and consolidated hundreds of pages of written source documents to create automated records and summary data for use as a historical reference.

December 1999 to September 2001; 40 hours per week; STIPENDS CLERK, $14,586 per year, Empower Baltimore Management Corporation, EBMC, 3 South Frederick Street, Suite 800, Baltimore, MD 21202; Supervisor: Steve Davis, CFO, 410-783-4400; may contact. (Intern, 12/1999 to 5/2000)

ADMINISTRATIVE SUPPORT: Provided administrative-level accounting support to the Chief Financial Officer. Monitored and maintained daily documentation and computation of contractor and trainee information, stipends, vouchers, invoices, and payments. Ensured timely processing. Reviewed documents for completeness and accuracy of information. Reviewed payment checks and support documents for errors or omissions. Began as intern in December 1999 and began working full time in June 2000.

Prepared data entry using MIP accounting software. Converted paper documentation to electronic formats. Verified contractor and trainee eligibility. Documented and ensured accuracy of computer entries. Ensured the effective and efficient maintenance of stipend administrative records for contractors and trainees.

Received, analyzed, verified, and validated expenditure and stipend submissions. Provided information support and assured timely processing of stipends for the accounting department. Maintained detailed records.

June 1999 to August 1999; 40 hours per week; ACCOUNTING ASSISTANT, Klacik & Associates, 829 E. Baltimore Street, Suite 101, Baltimore, MD 21202; Supervisor: Jeffrey Klacik, 410-528-1100; may contact.

Provided information and data support for internal audits. Provided administrative and secretarial support, including typing, filing, faxing, photocopying, mail distribution, appointment scheduling, and telephone support.

EDUCATION

Strayer University, 9409 Philadelphia Road, Baltimore, MD 21237
Pursuing B.S. in Business Administration; Completed 72 Credit Hours
Courses completed to date:
PowerPoint, Principles of Marketing I, Business Ethics, Introduction to Sociology, Principles of Management, International Business Environment, Principles of Organization Behavior, History and Methods of Science, Introduction to Networking, Introduction to College Math I, Introduction to Business, Accounting I, Communications I, Fundamentals of Math, Introduction to Computer Information Systems, Access

Merganthaler Vocational Technical High School, Baltimore, MD.
Concentration: Business Administration. High School Diploma, 6/2000.

(continues)

(continued)

OTHER INFORMATION

COMPUTER PROFICIENCIES: Proficient in MS Office 97 and 2000 (Word, Excel, Access, PowerPoint), WordPerfect, and MIP non-profit accounting software. Strong database management skills. Create, copy, edit, store, print, and standardize documents using templates, form letters, and mailing lists. Prepare spreadsheets, databases, and word-processing documents.

PERSONAL STRENGTHS: Competent, professional, proficient, attentive to detail. Team player with proven oral and written communications skills, interpersonal skills, and multiple task coordination and management capabilities. Energetic, flexible, and detail-oriented with a proven ability to handle multiple tasks efficiently and professionally.

ORGANIZATIONAL SKILLS: Expertise scheduling executive-level meetings and appointments, and maintaining and establishing a complex filing system.

ADMINISTRATIVE EXPERTISE: Progressively responsible administrative expertise. Experience preparing documents, memos, reports, and other documentation. Excellent typing skills: Typing speed, 50 WPM.

OFFICE EQUIPMENT: Broad knowledge of all types of office equipment, including personal computers, scanners, facsimile machines, and photocopying machines.

With a few adjustments to this electronic resume, this candidate will be ready to apply for other administrative positions, as well.

Summary: Six Key Ways to Improve Your Administrative Resume

Now that we've given you some examples of how other candidates improved their Federal administrative resumes, here are the most important points to remember:

1. Analyze the posting for keywords and make a list. Many administrative positions share similar descriptions. Be sure to include those keywords in your new resume.

2. Make a list of qualifications unique to you. Think about what sets you apart and include that information in your resume.

3. Create a strong Profile statement.

4. Make sure your critical skills are on page 1 of your resume.

5. Try to list at least one accomplishment in each position.

6. Be sure to include information on your resume in the following areas:
   * Professional Memberships
   * Licenses, Certificates, and Military Service
   * Education and Training
   * Computer Expertise
   * Language Proficiencies
   * International Travel
   * Special Skills
   * Volunteer/Community Service

CHAPTER 23

Applying for Program/Management Analyst Positions

By Jacqueline Allen

A few of the questions most frequently asked about positions as Program/Management Analysts by those seeking a job in the Federal government include the following:

- ★ What exactly is this position?
- ★ What are the job requirements?
- ★ Is it important work?

To the untrained eye, this position description might appear vague and perhaps be viewed as a "catch-all" job title for employees whose job requirements are not clear. However, nothing could be further from the truth. In fact, Program/Management Analysts play an instrumental role in the process of passing and implementing laws. The work these specialists perform is critical in the decision-making procedure for obtaining funding and for establishing and evaluating programs that Federal agencies implement and administer.

According to Ligaya J. Fernandez, Senior Research Analyst for the Office of Policy and Evaluation at the U.S. Merit Systems Protection Board,

The Program/Management Analyst positions are very important in government...yes, these positions are critical in government. The government does not provide products to the public. The government provides services. These services are based on programs that government policymakers have determined the American public needs and wants, and so they pass laws to make sure that these services are provided to the people. Once the laws are passed, the executive branch of government implements them. Program/Management Analysts are involved in the process of passing and implementing the laws...they actually do the analytical work required, from which important decisions are made.

Decisions are based on information. Information (or data) has to be gathered, organized, and analyzed. And Program/Management Analysts do the gathering, the organizing, and the analyzing of information so that decisions can be made. Many are involved in program funding; and so many program analyst jobs require an understanding of financial management.

*Once a law is passed and implemented, the government also needs to know if the program is working the way Congress said it should work. They need to know if the program is cost-effective or if improvements are needed. Answers to these and other questions are very important to the policymakers. And the people who are assigned the task of answering questions like these are the **Program/Management Analysts**. They gather essential information, organize and study it, analyze it, and then make recommendations to government officials by way of formal reports.*

The requirements for, and responsibilities of, a Program/Management Analyst differ from job to job depending on grade, organization, location, etc. Reading the vacancy announcement very carefully is key to understanding what the job is all about. Some will require specialized subject-matter knowledge; but generally, they don't. What is required is knowledge and skill that would enable them to perform analytical and evaluative work regarding the agency's operation or management of its programs.

The basic qualification needed for these types of jobs is the knowledge of the theories, function, and processes of management so that

analysts can identify problems and recommend solutions. (And so, there really is no specific education required for these jobs, although coursework that includes math, statistics, economics, accounting, and finance is very helpful.) These types of jobs also require knowledge of the different analytical tools and evaluative techniques needed to analyze qualitative and quantitative data.

In sum...I would say the importance of this series is this: Important government program decisions are made based on what Program/Management Analysts recommend, so candidates for these jobs better be good!

Now *that* is an important position!

What Is a Program/Management Analyst?

We have heard from a government expert about how important the Program/Management Analyst is in terms of keeping the "wheels of government" rolling and on track. So now let's examine the actual basic position description for this critical government employee.

 Note: Please be mindful of the fact that every agency advertising a job typically details additional explicit requirements in the individual vacancy announcement. Carefully read the announcement to identify agency requirements before applying for a specific job.

The following is taken from the OPM's USAJOBS Web site (www.usajobs.opm.gov). To learn more about the information available there, click on the Explore Career Interests section. Then from the list on the Web page to which you are led, scroll down to the title for Management and Program Analysis (Series No.

0343) positions and click on it. You will be directed to a Web page that highlights the requirements for Entry, Intermediate, and Full Performance levels for this job category. Click on the level that best suits your qualifications to read about the specific requirements for positions as a Program/Management Analyst:

Management and Program Analysis Series include positions which primarily serve as analysts and advisors to management on the evaluation of the effectiveness of government programs and operations or the productivity and efficiency of the management of Federal agencies or both. Positions in this series require knowledge of: the substantive nature of agency programs and activities; agency missions, policies, and objectives; management principles and processes; and the analytical and evaluative methods and techniques for assessing program development or execution and improving organizational effectiveness and efficiency. Some positions also require an understanding of basic budgetary and financial management principles and techniques as they relate to long-range planning of programs and objectives. The work requires skill in: application of fact finding and investigative techniques; oral and written communications; and development of presentations and reports.

Translated into nonprofessionals' terms, some of the key qualities needed to be a successful Program/Management Analyst are the following:

★ The ability to identify the things that are not working right in an organization and the knowledge of how to create a way to make things better.

★ The ability to see the need for some procedure or process that does not currently exist, which would make for a more efficient operation.

★ The ability to conceptualize a plan to make an organization's mission a reality by attaining specified goals, which in the case of the Federal government means developing new services or modifying existing ones.

Now, how many times have you or someone you work with ever said, "You know, if only the boss would try 'this' or 'that,' this place would run so much better! If I were in charge, I would do 'this' or 'that' to make things more efficient… more effective…and everyone working here would be a lot happier!" To a certain extent, this is the kind of person it takes to be an effective Program/Management Analyst. It requires having a somewhat "critical" eye. An effective Program/Management Analyst is able to see the big picture and yet narrow his or her focus to examine the "devil in the details" to see how things can work better or how services can be improved. The best Program/Management

Analysts might actually be considered "value-added employees."

Furthermore, a good Program/Management Analyst also needs to be able to work well with all kinds of people and with all levels of staff. Routinely, the work of the Program/Management Analyst involves the potential for change. Change is not always welcome or well received by everyone affected by it, even if it is for the better. So the Program/Management Analyst must be able to build confidence and trust, to persuade, and to effectively obtain required information without ruffling too many feathers in an organization.

Above all, an effective Program/Management Analyst must be able to communicate well both verbally and in writing. He/she needs to be able to develop plans and studies that are clear and that make sense to those who are involved in them. The Program/Management Analyst also needs to exhibit effective communication skills so that any evaluations of existing programs, proposals for new programs, or recommendations for procedural modifications can be presented well and can be understood and approved.

Job Requirements for a Program/Management Analyst

There are a number of critical and specific qualifications candidates need to be competitive. Following is a list of the competencies required for a Full Performance level (GS-12 and above)

Program/Management Analyst. This information was taken directly from the USAJOBS (Office of Personnel Management) Web site's Explore Career Interests section, which details the requirements for positions as a Program/Management Analyst. (To obtain information on the entry and intermediate levels for this series, go to http://career.usajobs.opm.gov/explor/occprof.asp?jobno=0343&level=F).

Competencies Required for a Program/Management Analyst

★ **Integrity/Honesty:** Contributes to maintaining the integrity of the organization; displays high standards of ethical conduct and understands the impact of violating these standards on an organization, self, and others; is trustworthy.

★ **Reading:** Understands and interprets written material, including technical material, rules, regulations, instructions, reports, charts, graphs, or tables; applies what is learned from written material to specific situations.

★ **Writing:** Recognizes or uses correct English grammar, punctuation, and spelling; communicates information in a succinct and organized manner; produces written information, which may include technical material, that is appropriate for the intended audience.

★ **Self-Management:** Sets well-defined and realistic personal goals; displays a high level of initiative, effort, and commitment towards completing assignments in a timely manner; works with minimal supervision; is motivated to achieve; demonstrates responsible behavior.

★ **Interpersonal Skills:** Shows understanding, courtesy, tact, empathy, and concern; develops and maintains relationships; may deal with people who are difficult, hostile, or distressed; relates well to people from varied backgrounds and situations; is sensitive to individual differences.

★ **Attention to Detail:** Is thorough when performing work and conscientious about attending to detail.

★ **Oral Communication:** Expresses information to individuals or groups effectively, taking into account the audience and nature of the information; makes clear and convincing oral presentations; listens to others, attends to nonverbal cues, and responds appropriately.

★ **Problem Solving:** Identifies problems; determines accuracy and relevance of information; uses sound judgment to generate and evaluate alternatives, and to make recommendations.

★ **Reasoning:** Identifies rules, principles, or relationships that explain facts, data, or other information; analyzes information and makes correct inferences or draws accurate conclusions.

★ **Teamwork:** Encourages and facilitates cooperation, pride, trust, and group identity; fosters commitment and team spirit; works with others to achieve goals.

★ **Planning and Evaluating:** Organizes work, sets priorities, and determines resource requirements; determines short- or long-term goals and strategies to achieve them; coordinates with other organizations or parts of the organization; monitors progress and evaluates outcomes.

★ **Decision Making:** Makes sound, well-informed, and objective decisions; perceives the impact and implications of decisions; commits to action, even in uncertain situations, to accomplish organizational goals; causes change.

★ **Flexibility:** Is open to change and new information; adapts behavior or work methods in response to new information, changing conditions, or unexpected obstacles; effectively deals with ambiguity.

★ **Information Management:** Identifies a need for and knows where or how to gather information; organizes and maintains information or information-management systems.

★ **Customer Service:** Works with customers to assess needs, provide assistance, resolve problems, and satisfy expectations; knows products and services; is committed to providing quality products and services.

★ **Self-Esteem:** Believes in own self-worth; maintains a positive view of self and displays a professional image.

★ **Technology Application:** Uses machines, tools, or equipment effectively; uses computers and computer applications to analyze and communicate information in the appropriate format.

★ **Creative Thinking:** Uses imagination to develop new insights into situations and applies innovative solutions to problems; designs new methods where established methods and procedures are inapplicable or are unavailable.

★ **Stress Tolerance:** Deals calmly and effectively with high-stress situations (for example, tight deadlines, hostile individuals, emergency situations, or dangerous situations).

★ **Memory:** Recalls information that has been presented previously.

★ **Learning:** Uses efficient learning techniques to acquire and apply new knowledge and skills; uses training, feedback, or other opportunities for self-learning and development.

★ **Arithmetic:** Performs computations such as addition, subtraction, multiplication, and division correctly using whole numbers, fractions, decimals, and percentages.

The general duties and responsibilities for a Program/Management Analyst are additionally described on the USAJOBS Web site in the Explore Career Interests section. The routine tasks for this position are defined as explained in the following section.

Routine Tasks for a Program/Management Analyst

Following is a list of basic daily work activities for this position:

★ Contacts others orally to obtain information.

★ Serves as a primary point of contact for a specific subject area.

★ Uses computer systems or applications to access, create, edit, print, send, retrieve, or manipulate data, files, or other information.

★ Reads and understands nontechnical materials (for example, letters, memoranda, electronic mail, and simple instructions).

★ Collaborates with others or works on teams to accomplish work-related activities.

★ Discusses results, problems, plans, suggestions, terms, or conditions with others.

★ Notifies individuals or offices orally of decisions, problems, or further actions needed.

★ Operates standard office equipment other than computers (for example, telephone, typewriter, fax, photocopier, and calculator).

★ Analyzes or interprets data or other information.

★ Collects, compiles, and organizes information.

★ Informs supervisor or other official of issues or problems.

★ Enters data or other information into computer.

★ Contacts others in writing to obtain information.

★ Promotes or develops and maintains good working relationships with key individuals or groups.

★ Initiates and maintains contacts with individuals outside the organization.

★ Uses addition, subtraction, division, or multiplication.

★ Composes simple correspondence or other written work (for example, memoranda, or form letters).

★ Notifies individuals or offices in writing of decisions, problems, or further actions needed.

★ Uses fractions, decimals, percentages, or averages.

★ Explains or justifies decisions, conclusions, findings, or recommendations.

★ Provides or disseminates information orally (for example, responds to inquiries concerning claims status or provides job information).

★ Reads charts, graphs, diagrams, or tables.

★ Receives office telephone calls or visitors.

★ Monitors, maintains, or updates data, records, or other information.

★ Reviews reports, documents, records, data, or other materials to verify completeness, correctness, consistency, compliance, or authenticity.

★ Questions, interviews, or confers with others to obtain or verify information.

★ Explains nontechnical information orally.

★ Processes or analyzes data using computer systems or applications.

★ Provides technical advice in subject matter area to others.

★ Searches for and extracts information from files, documents, reports, publications, recordings, or other materials.

★ Motivates others (for example, subordinates, patients, clients, or team members).

★ Monitors programs, projects, operations, or activities.

★ Makes improvements, solves problems, or takes corrective action when problems arise.

★ Manages, leads, or administers programs, projects, operations, or activities.

★ Reads and understands technical or other complex materials required for the job.

★ Records information.

Gearing Your Resume Toward a Program/Management Analyst Job

If you want to break into the Federal job market and feel you have all the right qualifications, including the required competencies, but your current professional history does not contain one job description that is titled Program/ Management Analyst, do not be discouraged. There are a number of positions in the private sector that the Office of Personnel Management recognizes as the equivalent of a Federal Program/Management Analyst position.

How Does Your Private-Sector Job Compare?

The OPM Web site has a great cross-reference called Public/Private Sector Crosswalk for comparing Federal and private-sector job descriptions. (Go to http:// career.usajobs.opm.gov/explor/cross1.asp for more information on this subject.) The following is a direct quote from the Public/Private Sector Crosswalk section:

...Crosswalk is based on a comparison of public and private sector job titles conducted by the Department of Labor, Bureau of Labor Statistics. A crosswalk was performed between the Dictionary of Occupational Titles (DOT) and titles used for Occupational Employment Statistics (OES) 1994. The Federal Job Classification was crosswalked to the OES. The bridge between the DOT and The Federal Job Classification is the OES; therefore, some of the occupations that you see may seem inappropriate for your position. The OES is a much broader classification system than The Federal Classification System. It has very broad categories which cover several jobs.

The following are the private-sector occupations that match the public-sector Program/Management Analyst job:

★ Analyst, Food and Beverage

★ Clerical-Methods Analyst

★ Director, Records Management

★ Forms Analyst

★ Freight-Traffic Consultant

★ Library Consultant

★ Management Analyst

★ Manager, Forms Analysis

★ Manager, Records Analysis

★ Manager, Reports Analysis

★ Preventive Maintenance Coordinator

★ Records-Management Analyst

★ Reports Analyst

Obviously, a number of private-sector jobs have performance skills and qualifications that easily convert to Federal requirements for a Program/Management Analyst. So just compare your background and job titles to the Public Sector Job Classification reference and determine whether you do have the required qualifications. If you determine that you do have the qualifications, move forward and apply for a Program/Management Analyst position in a Federal agency with an advertised job vacancy. Read the vacancy announcement carefully and identify agency-specific requirements. If you are qualified, be sure to incorporate the vocabulary of the announcement into your resume and KSA (Knowledge, Skills, and Abilities) narrative.

Are the Qualifications for All Program/Management Analyst Positions the Same?

As stated previously, individual agencies generally have specific requirements when they advertise a job vacancy. Everything that has been discussed in terms of qualifications for Federal Program/Management Analysts up to this point has been *general* requirements. If a candidate has the basic qualifications, that is good; but to be really competitive and to be able to make the "first cut" in the selective process, a candidate must also possess the job-specific qualifications as defined in individual vacancy announcements. The following relevant portions of some vacancy announcements for Program/Management Analysts demonstrate how requirements can vary from agency to agency.

Vacancy Announcement Example 1: Architect of the Capitol

Position: MANAGEMENT AND PROGRAM ANALYST

GS-0343-12/13

DUTIES: Assists the senior analyst in the development of an Agency-level Strategic Plan. Participates in defining the Strategic Planning process and long-term goals that serve as the starting point and unifying framework for AOC's various business units and jurisdictional planning. Assists Agency Strategy Teams in the development of annual performance goals and ensures linkage of long-term strategic goals with day-to-day activities of managers and staff. Participates in the development of an effective proactive strategic planning system—consisting of a strategic plan and performance plan—for agency program activities to enable the agency to develop long-term strategies. Utilizes engineering analysis techniques to measure the overall effectiveness of the organization's business performance. Provides guidance to Strategy Team Champions and Jurisdictional Head on development of input to the annual performance plan, setting forth the performance indicators established in the agency performance plan, along with the actual program performance achieved compared with the performance goals expressed in the plan for that fiscal year. Predicts and evaluates agency business systems to determine the impact of long-term strategies against resources, employees, materials, and equipment. Develops, analyzes, evaluates, and advises on improvements to the effectiveness of work methods and procedures, organizations, staff utilization, distribution of work assignments, delegations of authority, management controls, information systems, and similar functions of management. Analyzes individual programs, functions, and business processes to determine whether the management systems in current use efficiently accomplish objectives sought and whether they provided controls necessary for sound management. Analyzes and prepares program status reports for review at all levels. Establishes baseline measurements for strategic goals and objectives.

SPECIALIZED EXPERIENCE is defined as experience which has equipped the applicant with the particular knowledge, skills, and abilities to perform successfully the duties of the position, and that is typically in or related to the position to be filled. To be creditable, specialized experience must have been equivalent to at least the next lower grade level in the normal line of progression for the occupation.

INSTRUCTIONS FOR THE SUPPLEMENTAL STATEMENT (Optional):

Listed below are some of the knowledge, skills, abilities, and other characteristics (KSAOs) necessary for successful job performance. Your application should provide sufficient information describing your work experience, training, education, and knowledge that demonstrates your ability to successfully perform the duties of the position. As such, you do not have to write a supplemental statement addressing the KSAOs.

1. Comprehensive knowledge of strategic planning and performance measurement in order to enable the AOC to achieve program goals, to set program goals, to measure program performance against those goals, and to report publicly on their progress; to improve program effectiveness and public accountability by promoting a new focus on results, service quality, and customer satisfaction; and to help managers improve service delivery by requiring that they plan for meeting program objectives and by providing them with information about program results and service quality.

2. Expert knowledge of the latest innovative analytical techniques, with emphasis upon planning systems, design, analysis, and improvement, of integrated systems such as financial, management information, procurement, and facility management systems.

3. Knowledge of facilities planning, acquisition, and management process to help prepare long-range (five-year) and short-range planning guidance in accordance with broad agency program policies and objectives.

4. Skill developing agency performance metrics for key mission and business functions and provides guidance for subordinate activities. Knowledge and skill in adapting mathematical and analytical techniques and evaluation criteria to the measurement and improvement of business operations and associated processes.

5. Ability to communicate effectively, both orally and in writing. Ability to express Strategic Planning goals and objectives in quantifiable and measurable form through the development of graphs and charts.

Vacancy Announcement Example 2: Department of Transportation, Federal Aviation Administration

Position: MANAGEMENT AND PROGRAM ANALYST

FG-0343-13/14

Duties:

The incumbent is responsible for performing special studies pertaining to the implementation, conduct, revision, or modification of the airport planning program and for investigations and evaluations directed toward the development and improvement of a national system of airports. Formulates, defines, and develops the scope of studies; evaluates the validity of program assumptions and the sufficiency of available data; correlates conclusions concerning benefits, alternative choices, and resource availability. Formulates and coordinates Government Performance Results Act (GPRA) compliance, strategic planning, and work plan management. Prepares studies to support strategic planning and work plan management. Prepares studies to establish, support, or defend the agency position on legislative initiatives, official inquiries, audits, and similar inquires. Through administrative review or on-site visits, monitors the preparation and production of the National Plan of Integrated Airport Systems, develops and disseminates instructions to regional and district offices for collection and submission of data, and evaluates data received from these offices. Participates in the development of standards for airport system planning, intermodal transportation interfaces, airport capacity analysis, evaluation of regional effectiveness, and related activities. Represents the organization on panels, committees, meetings, and symposia.

Evaluation criteria:

Eligible candidates may be ranked based on the knowledge, skills, abilities, and other characteristics (KSAOs) described below.

RATING AND RANKING FACTORS:

1. Skill in communicating and disseminating information through written reports, memos, procedures, etc., as well as through presentations and briefings.

2. Ability to review and analyze complex and novel situations, collect and analyze data, develop insights, and formulate recommendations.

3. Knowledge of the roles of Federal, state, and local government and private industry in planning, developing, and maintaining the airport system.

4. Skill in developing and/or providing guidance on performance measurements and work plans.

5. Ability to serve as a member of a small group and to participate in a wide range of activities.

We cannot overemphasize the importance of carefully reading the vacancy announcement. Doing so is critical to a candidate's successful application for a Federal position. As the previous examples demonstrate, although a position title might be the same, the individual agency's description of required qualifications can sometimes be subtly different—but more often will be clearly diverse—than another agency's ad for the same type of job opening. So when preparing a resume for a Program/Management Analyst position, it is most important to reflect the individual agency's requirements in the vocabulary you use to describe experience and qualifications.

Sample Resume for a Program/Management Analyst

The following is an example of an effective resume for a Program/Management Analyst position.

Resume for Vacancy Announcement # 000000000

Sallie Mae Federal

1098 N. 30th St.
Arlington, VA 22203

Business: (202) 123-3456
Residence: (703) 987-6543
E-mail: salliem@house.com

Social Security No.: 000-00-0000
Citizenship: U.S.A.

Federal Civilian Status: GS-0301-13
Veterans' Preference: N/A

QUALIFICATIONS & SKILLS SUMMARY

Offers more than 15 years of successful experience as a manager responsible for analyzing programs from many aspects, including operational and financial perspectives. Extensive expertise conducting studies to evaluate policies, procedures, and existing programs to identify issues of concern and operating inefficiencies. Demonstrated competence in developing strategies and designing plans to resolve conflicts and to implement new and/or more effective programs. Adept at recognizing sensitive issues and skillfully employing proven and innovative techniques to address them. Established reputation for conducting effective briefings, imparting critical information, and providing reliable and substantiated advice and guidance on specific subject matter. Proven ability to effectively write analytical reports, performance standards, policies, and procedures.

PROFESSIONAL HISTORY

Chief, Compliance Branch   **August 1998 to Present**
Federal Election Commission (FEC)
999 E Street, N.W.
Washington, DC
Salary: $65,095 per year
Hours Worked: 40/week
Supervisor: Sam Goodfind, (202) 321-7654

Analyze and develop procedures for new Administrative Fines Program as well as manage and direct staff of six analysts and two administrative assistants responsible for implementation of program and review of all compliance matters referred by the Reports Analysis Division (RAD). Program authorizes FEC to impose civil money penalties on political committees that fail to file, or fail to timely file, campaign finance reports. Duties include:

- Evaluating effectiveness and efficiency of existing programs and processes of Compliance Branch, including the Non-Filer program, Debt Settlement review process, and review of referrals to the Office of General Counsel and Audit Division.

(continues)

(continued)

- Representing RAD before the commission in its deliberation of all compliance matters initiated by division's analysts.
- Conducting briefings for commissioners in Executive Session (closed) and open meetings and responding to commissioner inquiries concerning division procedures and policies.
- Recruiting, interviewing, and hiring new employees.
- Creating and assessing effectiveness of training programs.
- Developing performance standards and evaluating employees' work.
- Recommending cash awards, step increases, and promotions.
- Addressing sensitive issues related to performance warning notices, suspensions, and removals.

Accomplishments:

Processed over 300 cases and collected in excess of $130,000 in civil money penalties in first six months of the program's operation.

Increased production levels and developed highly motivated staff as result of cross training of staff, reassigning tasks and duties (on a rotating basis, where possible), and rewriting procedures to omit unnecessary steps and duplication of effort.

Chief, Unauthorized Branch   **October 1985 to August 1998**
Federal Election Commission
999 E Street, N.W.
Washington, DC 20463
Salary: $58,904
Hours Worked: 40/week
Supervisor: Bill Corleone, (202) 727-8989

Supervised 15 analysts responsible for reviewing and analyzing campaign finance reports filed by political committees for compliance with Federal Election Campaign Act (FECA) and Code of Federal Regulations (CFR). Duties included:

- Conducting studies to examine effectiveness of branch policies and procedures.
- Providing advice and guidance on required revisions to increase quality and consistency of reports review process.
- Developing performance standards and evaluating employees' work.
- Creating methods and standards for evaluating and assessing staff workload and performance.
- Reviewing, analyzing, and approving all compliance matters prepared by staff analysts.
- Conducting briefings for commission.

- Responding to inquiries from commissioners regarding branch procedures and practices and providing guidance for developing and designing plans to make changes or create new policies and procedures.
- Recruiting and hiring new analysts.
- Developing training programs and analyzing effectiveness.
- Recommending cash awards, step increases, and promotions.
- Addressing sensitive issues related to performance warning notices, suspensions, and removals.

Accomplishments:

Developed and presented highly effective training seminars on various campaign finance subjects at regional conferences sponsored by FEC.

Developed new procedures and policies resulting in 45% increase in staff productivity and 80% increase in staff morale.

Senior Reports Analyst   **September 1983 to October 1985**
Reports Analyst   **July 1978 to September 1983**
Federal Election Commission
999 E Street, N.W.
Washington, DC 20463
Salary: $54,780
Hours Worked: 40/week
Supervisor: Manual B. Tipton (no phone number available at this time)

Analyzed campaign finance reports of political party and political action committees for compliance with FECA and CFR. Duties included:

- Providing guidance and training to committees regarding interpretation and application of the FECA and CFR.
- Identifying issues related to violations (e.g., prohibited contributions, omitted information, and discrepant activity) and writing letters recommending appropriate corrective actions to political committees to address concerns of FECA and CFR.
- Developing and producing written referrals to Office of General Counsel and Audit Division Committees demonstrating substantial non-compliance with FECA and CFR.

Accomplishments:

Resolved 93% of non-compliance issues.

(continues)

(continued)

EDUCATION / RELEVANT TRAINING

– Management Analysis: An Overview, 2002
USDA Graduate School, Washington, DC

– Principles of Criminal Investigation, 1993
Towson State University, Towson, MD

– Bachelor of Arts, Political Science, May 1978—3.5 cumulative GPA
Georgetown University, Washington, DC

– Phi Beta Kappa graduate, June 1974
Red Hills High School, Lansing, MI

AWARDS

Performance Awards (Cash Awards) received each year from 1986 through 2000.

References provided upon request.

Summary: Final Advice for the Program/Management Analyst

Use concrete examples of the kind of work experience or formal training you have had to illustrate that you do have the required capabilities. And above all, tailor your resume to respond to the exact requirements described in the vacancy announcement for the job you are pursuing. If you do this, you will be on a level playing field with the competition and your chances of making it through the "first cut" are excellent.

CHAPTER 24

Human Resources Management: An Occupation in Transition

By Laveta Casdorph

Perhaps no other career field within the Federal government has been called upon to redefine and reinvent itself this past decade as extensively as the Human Resources Management (HRM) career field. Formerly known as and titled the "Personnel Management" occupation, the OPM published new classification standards in 2000, renaming the GS-200 job family to reflect the occupational title commonly used in the private sector. The changed job title is only one indication of the major restructuring the career field has undergone.

The HRM work situation—and thus the role of the HR specialist—changed significantly during the 1990s in both the public and private sectors. The shifting national economy and major downsizing affected all administrative functions; however, the OPM reports that the HR career field suffered a 20-percent cut, which is disproportionately higher than overall reductions government-wide. As HR staffs shrank and many experienced specialists retired or separated from Federal service, HR offices reorganized and many positions were restructured from specialists to generalists. By 1998, 60 percent of HR jobs were generalist positions.

In 1999, Congress voted to cut 272,000 Federal jobs, offering $25,000 buyouts to employees who agreed to retire or resign. Unfortunately, many of the buyouts were indiscriminate and ill-considered. Representative Steny Hoyer, D-Maryland, admitted, "Frankly, folks…we took a number. We did not make an analogy between the programs that we wanted accomplished and the level of personnel that would be required to accomplish those objectives." Naturally, the best employees left government service, and today many agencies don't have people with the skills needed to do the work.

The impact of these dynamics on the HR career field, as well as the technological changes in office automation, is largely responsible for the broader knowledge, skills, and abilities now required of HR practitioners. Management's needs have changed. The role of the HR professional as a technical authority and the gatekeeper of rules and regulations is no longer viable. Today, managers need the HR professional to understand their agency's mission and their organization's business requirements in order to advise them of available options and the regulatory flexibilities they have for meeting those requirements. The HR professional must understand the line manager's world and the realities that impact that world, such as the role finance plays in staffing, performance management, training, awards, and other agency operations. Far beyond traditional management advisory services, the HR professional in today's environment must be able to offer managers more thoughtful, cross-functional solutions, and recommend ways to respond to changing priorities and the ambiguities created by government policies that are still shifting.

As the career field continues to evolve, the challenge for the HR professional will be to understand and better-define how to consult with managers and employees—the clients and customers—to carve out a valued consulting role in what is now a moving target for everyone. To successfully play this role, HR professionals must develop new and effective behavioral competencies and be able to portray these competencies when responding to KSAs and updating their resumes.

Addressing the New HR Competencies

Before we discuss how to develop and portray the HR competencies described in the OPM's new classification standard, you need to be aware that some agencies define the term *competencies* differently than the OPM does. As you work through your resume and write KSA statements in response to job announcements, be sure that you understand how the agency is using that term.

The OPM uses the term *competencies* as a broad umbrella that includes the concepts of both KSAs and work behaviors. In other words, the OPM defines a competency as something you know, something you know how to do, or something you have gained experience doing. Such knowledge and abilities can be measured somewhat objectively by customer feedback, in performance evaluations, or through some other measurement device that captures the quantity and quality of your work. Without getting into

the controversial topic of whether performance evaluations are objective or subjective measurements of work behaviors, be aware that job announcements that ask you to describe your *competencies* in terms of the stated job requirements are asking you to write KSAs based on your work experience. Other agencies use the term *competencies* to mean something quite different than KSAs or work behaviors. For these agencies, a "competency" can be a personal characteristic, a level of response to a set of circumstances, or the way in which someone approaches a problem-solving exercise. One senior HR Manager in the Department of Energy explained it this way: "If I were to hit on any competency that a good HR specialist must have these days, it would be dealing with ambiguity —my staff continues to look for ways to make things 'black and white' in a very gray world!"

We all have different responses—behavior competencies—when working in situations where there is a high degree of ambiguity: Do you function happily and effectively in an environment where few guidelines exist, or are you more comfortable with structure and direction? How would you go about setting up a staffing and recruitment program in an agency that is not subject to Title V statutes and regulations? Your response to this situation is an example of your *competency* in dealing with ambiguity. How flexible are you? Do you look for all possible ways to solve a problem, or do you interpret rules and regulations very narrowly, thus limiting the number of solutions you present to your clients? There are no right or wrong answers to these questions. Everyone is different, and everyone behaves differently in these circumstances. Although it is difficult, if not impossible, to measure behaviors objectively when defining competencies in this way, be aware that interviewers or job raters who ask you to describe or give examples of your responses in certain situations are using the term *competencies* to mean your defined behaviors within a given context.

Most agencies define *competencies* as the OPM does, to mean KSAs and related work behaviors, such as the ability to work on a team. The point is, be sure you know how the agency to which you are applying is using the term.

Developing New HR Competencies on Shifting Sands

There is no doubt that skills shortages in the Federal service will continue in the next decade. Therefore, superior HR practices will be the key to attraction, retention, and successful mission accomplishment for many Federal agencies. The new OPM classification standard contemplates the HR professional operating in a government-wide context of decentralized personnel policies and delegations of authority, in which agency managers collaborate with HR to justify expenditures, help them design economic staffing and pay practices, and advise them on employee development and work technologies. The OPM envisions that over time, the HR professional will be called upon to become an overall resource advisor and to show managers how to hire the right people, train them, retain them, and help them develop an overall "performance culture" that enables the agency to achieve its mission. In other words, HR systems, policies, and products will be valued more for their contribution to the organization's mission and performance culture and less for the policies and regulations as ends in themselves.

For many agencies, this vision might not become the reality for many years in the future; and for some agencies, it might never be. Although some agencies indeed have decentralized their personnel policies and operations and established more generalist positions as a result of government downsizing, others, such as the Department of Defense, have taken the opposite

approach and have centralized many functions such as staffing, classification, pay, and benefits, leaving few HR specialists remaining in the field to provide advisory services to managers. Both types of changes reportedly have caused lengthy delays in delivering basic HR services. Former specialists sometimes struggle with the shift in mentality and the learning curve required to change from a specialist role to a generalist role; and specialists now operating at large, under-staffed, centralized HR centers often report management work-request backlogs of 90 days or more. Both situations will make it more difficult for HR professionals to operate as consultants or strategists. One line manager, listening to an HR executive trying to advise him on manpower issues, said, "How about getting my open positions filled before giving me advice on strategic staffing issues?"

Regardless what state of transition your agency is in, the HR occupation will continue to evolve. How do you, as the HR professional, plan to find the right work situation to develop the required competencies—both KSAs and defined behaviors—to play your emerging role as a consultant and advisor? How will you portray these new skills in your KSA statements?

Take Stock of Changes You Have Experienced Already

First, take stock of changes you have probably already experienced in the job you have now. Think about how you can work these new developments into your KSAs. Have you been to any HR training programs or workshops within the past two years? You have probably noticed an important shift in the focus of the training. Many HR specialists report that staffing workshops, for example, are not based as much on enhancing technical and functional expertise anymore. Instead, workshops now focus more on strategic planning and how to enhance management consulting skills.

Cross-Training Is a Good Thing

See cross-training as a good thing. The more skills and abilities you develop, the more marketable you become. This is true not only from a technical standpoint, but from a behavioral one as well. It is often easier to move up by first moving over—meaning, the broader your background and the more adaptable you are to change, the easier it will be to stand out from the crowd during the selection process.

Commit to Change

With the HR career field shifting as it is, it will be very important that you commit to challenging yourself in terms of personal change. You cannot afford to wait for the agency to send you to training to develop these new skills.

Have you applied to gain your certification from the private-sector Society for Human Resource Management (SHRM)? This organization has online workshops and great information that Federal HR professionals can apply to their own jobs. For example, private-sector HR professionals often wish they had the processes and procedures found in the Federal government; however, Federal HR managers covet the flexibilities of the private sector. Both sides can learn from each other, and the SHRM organization is a good place to start. In addition, SHRM certification is highly valued, and knowledge of private-sector HR practices is becoming a more-and-more important credential in both the public- and private-sector HR career fields.

 Note: As a Federal HR professional, are you aware that the new Department of Homeland Security will generate controversial issues around—and could change—some longstanding HR policies and rules affecting veterans' preference? Such a change could have a big impact on the OPM's traditional watchdog role of ensuring agencies do not try to get around veterans' preference under delegated examining authorities. The current administration has also gone on record that its goal is to see about half of government jobs channeled through the A-76 process—a push that could result in closing the gap between public- and private-sector HR rules and practices.

Have you taken on any self-assessment exercises, such as the Myers-Briggs test, or the Colby Index, to understand how you react to or manage ambiguity and change? Are you alarmed at "breaking rules" you perceive to be black and white? Are you able to find ways to redefine problems and use other available authorities—such as awards and recognition rules—to accomplish something you couldn't do under staffing rules? These are the types of competencies the OPM envisions that the HR professional will be required to develop in the future. You might be surprised to discover that you already have desirable behavioral competencies that you can highlight in your KSAs.

The HR Paradigm Shift

Third, building your credentials as a new HR professional requires making what is commonly referred to as a "paradigm shift." In the not-so-distant past, many HR professionals had self-defined, cut-and-dried roles and goals, defining themselves as the gatekeepers of the rules and regulations, the managers as clients, and employees as the enemy. The HR professional's role was to give advice to the manager about what to do, much as an attorney or doctor tells his clients what to do. The employee was not the client, but merely a "customer" coming to the personnel office to apply for a job, get information about pay or benefits, or to complain about his supervisor. There was no need to develop an ongoing relationship with the employee because the important long-term relationship was the one with the manager.

In today's environment of reduced staffing levels, the HR professional is still required to deliver traditional HR services, plus learn the new management consulting and strategic planning roles. To have time to do both, HR staffs must increase efficiency, streamline operations, link performance to organizational objectives, and establish sound relationships with clients and customers. But most of all, HR managers and professionals must redefine the word *strategic*.

HR offices must get rid of what's unnecessary. Not all programs and practices add value to the organization's objectives. By focusing on those that do, HR professionals free up time to provide more management consulting and strategic planning services.

Reevaluate Automated Processes

Automated processes and services should also be reevaluated. When HR technologies became widely available several years ago, many agencies automated as much information and as many processes as possible. The assumption was that the faster HR services were automated, the more efficient the organization would become. Unfortunately, some agencies have discovered that implementing technology without a clear objective in mind has increased, rather than decreased, operating costs and has not helped managers or employees get better HR service. The OPM's new HR classification standards now include a parenthetical title for Information Technology (IT), underscoring the importance of determining which functions are best automated and will help the agency achieve its mission.

Before labeling managers as the HR "client" and employees as the HR "customer," agency HR offices should implement an overall IT strategy

that takes into account what each of these groups wants and needs from the HR function. For example, employees often communicate with the HR professional just to find out the status of a recruitment action or to ask questions about how to apply for a job.

The key to building credibility with these customers, while freeing up time to perform consulting work, is to use technology to design and implement an overall communications strategy. Employees want to know how things work and what is going on with a personnel action. If they don't know, they will fill in the blanks and assume bad things are happening or that the HR staff has ulterior motives for not telling them what they want to know. How difficult would it be to post the status of job-fill actions on the agency's Web site? Is the action at the rating and ranking step or at the interview step? The manager who is trying to fill the vacancy could also visit this Web site to learn this information. Has a selection been made? Who was the selectee? One senior HR manager who recently implemented this system reported a substantial reduction in the number of telephone calls to her staff. "The more information you push out to employees, the less calls, and more time we have to devote to management consulting," she said. More HR offices should take the hint. A recent survey conducted by the OPM revealed that only 10 Federal agencies sent letters to job candidates announcing who was selected for vacant jobs.

Strategy Versus Implementation

These are the new strategic planning and management consulting roles contemplated by the OPM's new HR classification standards. But HR professionals need to be realistic and face the fact that not every HR manager, professional, associate, and assistant can be focused solely on strategy. The core HR services and processes must still be delivered, yet everyone still wants to be seen as a "strategist."

The solution to this problem is to broaden the definition of "strategic" to include both the formulation *and* the execution of a strategy to accomplish organizational goals. The HR organization must clearly define roles and expectations for people in its HR positions. The percentage of time any given staff member spends formulating strategy versus executing it should be calculated, and it should be clear that meeting operational objectives is a top priority.

At the same time, it is important that HR professionals in all positions understand how their work affects the bottom line. Employees must know that their individual contributions have a measurable effect on the agency's ability to meet its business goals, and how their work fits into the achievement of those goals.

The foregoing discussion highlights the main points the OPM makes in its new classification standards about the changing HR career field. It would be well worth your time to read the new standards, along with the OPM's explanatory comments, to gain a thorough understanding of the HR career field's new occupational demands. The standards are written in the Factor Evaluation System format (FES), which describes and distinguishes the different KSAs required at different job levels in factors such as

★ Knowledge Required by the Position

★ Guidelines

★ Complexity

★ Scope and Effect

★ Personal Contacts/Purpose of Contacts

By reading these factor-level descriptions, you will be able to identify the critical KSA statements you will need to include with your application package for vacant HR jobs. Log on to www.opm.gov to locate these standards. As a bonus, the OPM has incorporated links into the online standards. These links provide specific examples of the knowledge, skills, and abilities

required of each of the HR specialties, giving you even more detailed guidance about the KSAs.

In the next section, let's take a closer look at the standards to see how you can use them to best design your new KSAs.

Two Contexts, Three Roles, and Ten Specialties: Using the HR Classification Standards to Focus Your KSAs

As you study the HR classification standards, you must understand the three most important factors that affect how to best focus your KSA statements. Before you sit down to prepare your application package, ask yourself these three questions:

1. What is the job context, or work situation? Will I be functioning as a "generalist," or as a "specialist?"

2. Of the three possible HR roles identified in the OPM's new standards, how many does the job require and what knowledge, work behaviors, and personal competencies are required to carry out these roles?

3. If the job carries a specialty designation, what KSAs do I currently have that are related to the job's functional requirements?

After you answer these questions, you can turn to the factor levels in the classification standard that will help you most in structuring your KSAs. For example, the factor-level description of *Knowledge Required by the Position* will help you describe the information you must know and understand to do your work, such as the procedures, rules, and policies you use and apply daily. Are these procedures, rules, and policies "like" or "different than" those called for in the vacant job? How can you describe your knowledge in a way that is more "like" the knowledge called for in the job announcement?

The *Guidelines* factor will help you describe how extensive or scarce the guidance is that applies to your work, which affects how much interpretation and judgment is required to do your work. Does the job announcement describe a work situation that requires a lot of judgment and discretion? The standards will tell you that you need to develop your KSAs in a way that illustrates your resourcefulness in adapting available guidelines to your work.

The *Complexity* factor will help you explain the variety and intricacy of processes or methods you use to do your work, and how difficult it is. Is your work more of a technical or an advisory nature? Can you describe different situations or problems that you had to resolve that involved conflicting or incomplete information? The factor-level descriptions will give you plenty of examples of the types of information you can use to write your KSAs.

What effect does your work have on others? Does your work affect only the internal processes of your own office, or does it determine the "bottom line" in some other organization? The *Scope and Effect* factor states that how your work products and services impact those both within and outside your organization is an indicator of how broad or narrow your work assignment really is. Do your recommendations influence the decisions of others? This is one way to address an "advisory services" KSA.

Finally, the *Personal Contacts/Purpose of Contacts* factor is a good source of information on how to portray your communications skills, describe the setting in which the communications take place, and highlight special communications skills such as the ability to negotiate or mediate.

These examples show you how the OPM's FES classification standards can help you write KSAs. Although this technique works for almost any job series, there is a special reason that HR applicants should work with these standards when applying for HR vacancies. The OPM's standards for the HR occupation use the "job family" approach to classifying jobs. This means that the standards centralize and describe—in one place—the core skills required of *all* HR specialties. Instead of reissuing the HR standards in separate specialist or assistant series, the OPM canceled over 10 individual job series and replaced them with two basic standards covering HR specialist work (the two-grade interval positions) and HR support work (one-grade interval, or "assistant" positions). The jobs are all given the same basic title (for example, Human Resources Specialist, Human Resources Assistant). If the duties are limited to one specific type of HR work, a parenthetical title is added to denote the specialty.

This job-family approach, along with the FES format, offers the HR job applicant a tremendous advantage in structuring KSA statements: The knowledge, skills, and abilities required of *all* HR jobs are consolidated and described in general terms that are common to all specialties. This means that if you are applying for a job in a different specialty, or want to broaden your experience by doing generalist work, it will be easier for you to show how your KSAs are related to similar work within the same job family. The factor-level descriptions can also provide a framework for preparing examples of your work and may prompt you to recall accomplishments that illustrate the required KSAs.

Answering Question 1: Identifying the HR Work Context

The OPM recognizes 10 different specialties and two work contexts within the HR occupation. As we've seen, these two factors are interrelated. The overall work context (in other words, the HR office's staffing level and whether the operation is centralized or decentralized) usually has a big impact on whether a job is structured as a *generalist* position or as a *specialist* position.

Generalist jobs are more often found in smaller, decentralized offices or at a headquarters level. These jobs require the applicant to work in and apply the KSAs of two or more HR functions. For example, a generalist job might require the incumbent to deliver services in the Recruitment and Placement, Classification, and Employee Relations functions. These multispecialty jobs usually are titled and advertised as Human Resources Specialists without a parenthetical title. If you see a generalist job title advertised, you will need to read the announcement carefully to discover the work context and see which HR specialty skills the employer is seeking. The FES factors that might help you write KSAs addressing the overall context you will be working in are Knowledge Required by the Position and Scope and Effect.

Within the generalist work context, you will also need to discover how the agency's HR guidance is structured. For instance, some agencies have very few regulations and impose no policy restrictions beyond what laws and government-wide regulations require. This leaves the HR generalist in a very key role, with frequent opportunities to interpret guidance, collaborate with managers, and advise on and design creative solutions to operational problems. In other agencies, such as the Department of Defense, HR guidance is highly regulated and agency-wide policies are frequently updated, publicized, and controlled. Generalists in these agencies, although having multifunctional knowledge to draw on to help managers solve problems, are limited to making recommendations that fall within the bounds of published policies. The factor-level descriptions that will help you address this aspect of the generalist context are Guidelines and Personal Contacts/Purpose of Contacts.

The second work context is that of the more narrowly focused HR specialist. These jobs are usually found in HR offices that are large enough to support a number of specialists who each work exclusively within an HR function. A specialist job requires the incumbent to service clients in only one or two of 10 possible

functional areas. These jobs are titled Human Resources Specialist followed by a parenthetical title denoting the specialty, such as Human Resources Specialist (Classification) or Human Resources Specialist (Classification/Recruitment and Placement). If you see a specialist job advertised, it will be easy to go to the OPM Web site, find the HR classification standards, and go to the appropriate link for illustrations of the knowledge, skills, and abilities required of positions at the advertised grade level. The factors that will help you the most in structuring KSAs for a specialist job are Knowledge Required by the Position, Guidelines, Complexity, Scope and Effect, and Personal Contacts/Purpose of Contacts.

Answering Question 2: What Roles Are Required?

The HR job standards and the OPM's explanatory materials discuss three roles demanded of the HR professional in today's world. They are the following:

★ **Technical expert,** delivering the core HR products and services to the agency.

★ **Management advisor,** providing consulting and strategic planning services to help managers decide how to best use HR processes to achieve the agency's overall objectives.

★ **Services to applicants and employees,** focusing work effort more on communications to customers rather than "gatekeeping" functions.

The OPM states that these three functions constitute the "emerging roles" of the HR career field. In its "Appendix H—Historical Record and Explanatory Material," published as a companion to the new HR standards, the OPM candidly admits that most positions surveyed were still working in "traditionally structured roles," and that very few examples of properly classified "new role" positions turned up while they were developing the standards. Nonetheless, such positions do exist, and the OPM expects the trend toward this model to continue.

What should you do if the vacancy notice provides no information about which of the three roles you would be expected to perform? First, refer back to the overall context of the job. A generalist job probably offers more opportunities for you to play an advisory role, if for no other reason than the broader knowledge requirement—the more you know, the more options you can see to offer your clients. The job's grade level is also a clue—the higher the grade, the more likely it is you will be required to provide some type of consulting or planning advice. Is the job located in a centralized HR service center? Your role in this type of work situation may be the much more traditional one of delivering core HR processes and services.

Try to discover as much as you can about the role you will be expected to play before writing your KSAs. If you are lucky enough to spot one of the "new role" positions and have a chance to apply, refer to Factor Level Description 1–8, Knowledge Required By the Position, for examples of the types of experiences that characterize the management consultant/strategic planning roles.

Answering Question 3: How Are My KSAs Like Those in the Job Announcement?

The OPM has arranged the list of the 10 new HR specialties into a hierarchy of subgroups based on the similarities or differences in knowledge and skills demanded of each subgroup. By understanding what caused the OPM to group certain specialties together, you can assess whether your KSAs are more similar or more different than those of the job being advertised, and thus, what experiences you need to stress that will make your KSAs more "like" the ones listed in the job announcements.

Subgroup 1: Information Systems and Military

The first two subgroups are the following:

★ **Information Systems,** denoting work that requires developing, delivering, managing, and maintaining HR information systems when the paramount knowledge required is Human Resources Management rather than information technology.

★ **Military,** denoting work that requires knowledge and administration of military personnel management systems within military agencies or organizations.

These two specialties are listed first in the HR standards because they cut across all functional specialties, thus requiring the broadest HR knowledge. Incumbents who serve in these specialties must have more than a passing familiarity with all the HR functions in order to help managers decide how to best meet their organizational and mission requirements.

If you are applying for jobs in either of these two specialties, whether a "traditional" or "new role" situation, you will need to emphasize your breadth of experience across functional lines and highlight any other work experience that shows your ability to direct or coordinate multifunctional projects. You will need to be able to handle a wide variety of issues simultaneously. Almost certainly you will be using automated databases to evaluate work operations and make recommendations.

Subgroup 2: Traditional HR Services

The next subgroup is the largest and is oriented toward the mainstream, or "core" HR functions such as staffing, classification, and human resource development. The functions are the following:

★ **Classification,** covering work that involves the proper grouping, titling, and pay of individual jobs, and advising on position and organization design.

★ **Compensation,** describing work that involves analyzing laws, regulations, and policies that cover pay and leave administration and advising managers on the use of compensation flexibilities to help recruit, retain, and manage employees.

★ **Recruitment and Placement,** covering work that involves recruiting and placing employees, performing job analysis, workforce planning and analysis, and advising managers on how to attract and retain a high-quality and diverse workforce that can accomplish the agency's mission.

★ **Employee Benefits,** denoting work that requires providing guidance and assistance to employees and their relatives on retirement, insurance, health benefits, and injury compensation.

★ **Human Resource Development,** which requires planning, administering, or evaluating training programs and advising managers on employee development.

★ **Performance Management,** describing work that requires helping supervisors and managers establish and maintain effective programs to monitor, develop, and reward employee performance and provide employee incentives and recognition.

These HR specialties are grouped together because they represent the "traditional" HR services and require specialized knowledge of the concepts, laws, policies, and practices that apply to each of these areas. HR services are traditionally process-driven; however, work at higher grade levels often requires that the HR professional help managers analyze their needs and plan how to use the processes to help managers meet their needs.

If you are applying for a job in one of these "core" specialty functions, you will need to emphasize your specialized technical knowledge and describe the complexity of the work

assignments you have handled. You will also want your KSA statement to explain the purpose of your personal contacts, to illustrate the types of HR roles you have played.

Subgroup 3: Employee Relations and Labor Relations

The final HR subgroup is composed of two specialties that the OPM recognizes as having a "special character" within the HR occupation:

★ **Employee Relations,** denoting work that requires analyzing and interpreting a wide range of HR case law, principles, practices, and regulations in order to advise managers about complex legal issues, solve problems, and serve as experts in appeals processes.

★ **Labor Relations,** involving work to establish and maintain effective relationships with labor organizations, to negotiate and administer labor agreements, and to provide guidance to managers on a variety of labor-relations matters.

The OPM states that these two HR specialties are distinct from the others because they require unique knowledge and skills, and require making legal recommendations. In fact, they are so distinct that the OPM has given them separate factor-level descriptions for Factor 1—Knowledge Required by the Position.

Because of the vast amount of administrative and case law, in addition to the rules and processes of other HR functions that incumbents in these two specialties must know, applicants for these jobs will want to emphasize the complexity of various problems and types of cases they have handled. These specialties inherently require management advisory and strategic planning skills, and often involve mediation and negotiation skills as well. Because these jobs directly impact personnel-management practices in all other agency organizations, applicants should also review the Scope and Effect factor in the HR standards.

Putting It All Together: Writing KSAs in the CCAR Format

To write effective KSAs for the HR Specialist or Assistant job, follow the advice outlined in chapter 14. That chapter outlines the "CCAR" format, a special template the OPM recommends for SES candidates who are writing their KSA statements (known as Executive Core Qualifications). "CCAR" stands for Context (what work environment were you in?), Challenge and Actions (what was the problem you faced and what did you do to resolve it?), and Result (how did your actions improve the situation?). The underlying theme of the CCAR format is that specific examples or stories that illustrate problems you've resolved, cases you've handled, actions you've taken, and accomplishments you've achieved will always make you stand out above applicants who merely state that their experience has provided them with the needed KSAs.

As you work with the factor-level descriptions in the HR classification standards, write down the accomplishments that illustrate your knowledge and your ability to perform the tasks the standards call for. What guidelines do you use? If you can't apply them directly, do you interpret them? If you do, how does your interpretation affect the quality of service you deliver? Can you write a paragraph about a work assignment you've had that required you to interpret unclear guidance? With a little practice, you'll soon be giving examples of problems you've solved instead of just telling the job rater, "My job requires me to interpret a variety of guidance that is not always clear."

Eight Emerging KSAs for the HR Career Field

As more and more agencies transition toward the "new role" model of HR management, new KSAs will begin to show up in job vacancy announcements. Although no one can predict

exactly how these KSAs will be worded, the OPM's explanatory material indicates that they will fall within eight broad categories:

★ How HR management and development contributes to the agency's ability to reach its strategic goals and objectives.

★ How HR professionals collaborate with managers to design and implement strategic approaches to overall agency objectives.

★ How HR professionals develop and recommend options best suited to particular missions, labor markets, and work technologies.

★ How HR organizations invent and adapt their processes and programs to the agency's mission.

★ How HR professionals provide advice about the latest practices and developments that might help achieve mission results and maintain a strong performance culture for the workforce.

★ How HR organizations integrate methods and options from different HR functions to streamline operations and make them more relevant to clients and customers.

★ How HR professionals work across multiple functions to tailor solutions to various HR challenges.

★ How HR information systems development is used to affect management's and employees' expectations about timely, quality service; for example, using the Internet to educate the workforce about HR programs and options.

As you develop your KSAs, be aware that in the future many HR candidates will be called on to illustrate how they have played one or more of these roles in their own HR organizations. Look for opportunities within the context of your current job to lead change, and you will automatically become a stronger candidate for the "new role" HR job of the future.

CHAPTER 25

Military to Civilian Resume Conversions

Diane Burns, CCMC, CPRW, is a nationally recognized Military Conversion Authority and author who specializes in coaching military members through their transitions to corporate America. She can be contacted at www.polishedresumes.com or newcareer@polishedresumes.com.

Military members need to prepare Federal resumes to look and speak the same as those of their civilian counterparts. However, after being in the military for many years, they often speak "military," using plenty of military acronyms and jargon that need to be translated to meet corporate or civil-sector requirements.

Translating Your Resume to Civilian Speak

Service members have the added challenge of not only looking for civilian keywords that help their resumes qualify in the Federal system, but they also need to spend extra time learning what their military terms, acronyms, and jargon translate to in the corporate world. Service members should translate military rank, career history, job titles, military occupational specialties and career fields, and training courses; and use their award, training, and performance-rating justifications to glean accomplishments.

The following are a few sample translations for rank, responsibilities, and acronyms. Sometimes service members tell me that they don't know what an acronym means because they never spelled it out. If you don't know what it means, ask someone or look it up. Federal resumes need to have all acronyms spelled out at least once in the first reference. Please note that each branch of service has its own set of acronyms for individual systems. Some acronyms might be the same, but the meaning is very different.

Military Speak	Civilian Speak
Rank	
Senior Officer (Naval Commander, Army or Air Force Major)	Chief Executive, Administrator, Chief of Staff, Senior Executive/Vice President, Chief Administrator, CEO, COO, or CFO
Senior Enlisted (E-7 to E-9) or Junior Officer	Program/Project/Plant Director, Manager, or Coordinator
Enlisted (E-5 to E-6)	Team Leader, Training Manager, or Instructor
Responsibilities	
Commanded	Directed, supervised, or guided
Provisioning Chief	Logistics management
Briefings	Presentations, seminars, or public speaking (communications)
Acronyms and Terms	
Battalion	250 personnel
ANOC	Advanced Noncommissioned Officer Academy (Leadership and Administration Course)
COMSEC	Communications Security
AcofS	Assistant Chief of Staff
OCONUS	Outside continental United States
PCS	Permanent Change of Station (a move or transfer)
PAC	Personnel Actions Center
AORS	Army Reserve Orders Requisition System
ATRRS	Army Training Requirements and Resources System
Pathfinder	Army Intelligence Database System
SGT	Sergeant
CPT	(Captain: very senior officer in the Navy; junior officer in the Army)

Service members are proud of their duties, titles, training, leadership roles, and awards. However, military members need to further translate accomplishments into qualitative and quantitative sentences that are chock-full of keywords. A quality, translated sentence can be very successful in describing years of leadership and management credentials.

Here's a sample translation for operations management (extracted from a resume written by a military member):

> Support the 76th aircraft wing providing services to 12 carrier air wing squadrons and 32 reserve squadrons, supported commands, and a special project unit. Manage inventory and a budget.

To:

> Supervise a staff of 35 shop personnel providing maintenance services to 12 major customers and 32 tenant units encompassing 87 worldwide sites. Orchestrate logistical support and inventory requirements controlling a bench stock of 2,400 items. Execute a $60 million operational budget.

The first sentence includes only three keywords (inventory, budget, and manage), and it is confusing to the reader. A civilian without any knowledge of aircraft wing, reserve squadrons, or supported commands will not fully comprehend the credentials behind the candidate. The sentence will be vague and complicated to a civilian recruiter. With some strong questioning and a thorough review of "what you actually do on the job," you can write a strong qualitative or quantitative sentence that shows the employer what you managed and what value you have to offer his organization.

The second sentence includes at least 11 keywords: supervise, staff, shop, personnel, maintenance, services, customers, logistical, inventory, bench stock, and budget. Moreover, it describes for the reader how vast the needs are to coordinate logistical requirements for the 76th aircraft wing. Additionally, the second sentence captures the reader's attention with specific accomplishments and numbers. This translation is strong and factual.

The second sentence was derived from a line of questioning using the information provided in sentence one:

What is the 76th aircraft wing?

> 12 major customers and 32 smaller customers in 87 sites around the world.

Do you have a team to accomplish this support?

> Yes, I supervise 35 personnel.

Tell me about the inventory you control.

> Well, it is pretty big; I coordinate logistical support for the 87 sites with a bench stock of 2,400 items.

Tell me about your budget. Is it significant?

> Yes, $60 million, which includes pricey aircraft maintenance parts.

This line of questioning helps unfold skills, accomplishments, and credentials that are otherwise lost in military speak.

Also, you need to remember that if you convert your paper copy (formatted resume) to an electronic Resumix version, the Resumix system will not understand the military terms in the first sentence. Furthermore, the second sentence quantifies the military terms and adds keywords that are critical for a candidate seeking employment in logistics or supply discipline management.

Remember, this is only one sentence in a three- to five-page resume. Each sentence needs to carry its weight in order to match the skills required for a specific Federal series. Military members should research private-industry job announcements as well as Federal job announcements to learn how to properly translate military terms.

When a military sentence (full of military acronyms and military terms) is properly converted to a civilian sentence, there is almost no recognition that the applicant is from the military—and private-industry officials will be able to understand and appreciate your qualifications.

Service members who prepare early to exit or retire from military service can learn to write a successful civilian-language, skill-based Federal resume, maneuver the Federal/OPM application process, and land a second career with the Federal government.

Focusing Your Resume

Often, military clients tell me that they can do anything…they are leaders and they have managed personnel, human resources, logistics, computer repairs and LANS, accounting and budgets, supply systems, commissary operations, aircraft maintenance, security requirements, instructors, health care…and the list goes on. Interestingly, they might perform many of these duties under the job title of Ammunition Specialist, Administrative Specialist, or Field Artillery Surveyor. Very often, the work completed on the job and the skills and training acquired are very different from the job title or occupational field.

Unfortunately, the Federal resume system does not favor "jack-of-all-trades" resumes. In order for a candidate to be deemed "best qualified," his or her Federal resume must meet requirements for a position within a Federal series. So, for example, one client told me he was an accountant and was seeking accounting positions based on his work with budgets in the military. However, he began to apply for different positions such as Force Protection Manager and Security Operations Manager. This client was not qualifying for any positions in the security series because his resume was focused toward accounting and auditing. We rewrote his Federal resume to incorporate both accounting and security operations, focusing on his military background and highlighting specific accomplishments in both accounting and security. As a result, he began to qualify for jobs in the security series.

Sample Federal Resume 1: Counterintelligence Specialist Seeking Federal Employment

Most candidates need one resume that targets one to three similar Federal series codes. For example, the following resume highlights an Army Counterintelligence Specialist seeking Federal employment in intelligence operations

(0132) or security management or operations (0080). Her military training and on-the-job experience includes motor-pool manager, instructor, analyst, supply manager with line items, and personnel actions clerk. This candidate also told me that she has a background in retail management and that she could easily see herself as an HR manager.

Realistically, she will qualify and rate the highest in the intelligence and security series with agencies that post for such types of positions. She placed her resume with the CIA, FBI, State Department, Department of Transportation, and others. She submitted both an electronic Resumix for appropriate agencies and a formatted resume for the agencies that do not yet accept the Resumix.

 Note: Each agency has different application and resume requirements; consequently, military candidates need to read the application procedures carefully for each agency to which they want to submit an application.

Introductory Material

Jane's resume begins with a formatted heading and the required Federal elements. Note that she used both her home and work phone numbers to ensure that she can be reached. Because she is leaving the military, her employer knows she is leaving and she does not have to worry about confidentiality.

JANE MYERS

1280 Patriot Lane
Columbia, MD 21451

410.555.1256 (h) / 410.555.4312 (w)
JaneM@hotmail.com

Social Security Number:	xxx-xx-xxxx
U.S. Citizen:	Yes
Veterans' Preference:	5 points; U.S. Army (E-6); Military Service: 05/1998 to Present
Federal Employment Status:	N/A
OBJECTIVE:	Announcement Number: TSA-02-112 Intelligence Operations Specialist, SV-0132-00/00

Jane needs to include her military dates of employment and veterans' preference because some military personnel receive special preference in the hiring process based on service dates, service during wartime, or disabilities.

Professional Profile

Next, Jane's resume includes a profile section that provides an overview of her qualifications in intelligence and security. Note that in the profile section and throughout the resume, Jane spelled out a number of acronyms familiar to counterintelligence. She referred to commanders and generals as high-level delegations or decision makers. She ensured that the resume included reference to the required KSAs on the application (in other words, analysis and presentation skills, coordinating activities with other law enforcement agencies, analyzing and evaluating intelligence programs, policies, and knowledge of software applications). We included a final profile bullet about her interpersonal skills with descriptors.

PROFESSIONAL PROFILE

- Five years' direct experience as a Counterintelligence (CI) Special Agent for the Department of the Army, conducting critical counterintelligence, counterterrorism (CT), counterespionage (CE), and security investigations and operations to protect national security. Engaged in intelligence collection and analysis to develop reports and threat assessments. Initiated and coordinated investigative operations. Conducted interviews and interrogations.

- Specific knowledge of Technical Surveillance Countermeasures, National Security, Foreign CI Investigations & Operations, Human Sources (HUMINT) Operations, Personnel Security Investigations (PSIs), Communications Security (COMSEC), Computer Espionage & Security, Technology Protection, and Force Protection.

- Member of the worldwide foreign surveillance team conducting sensitive investigations and surveillance operations resulting in arrests of suspected terrorists.

- Skilled computer operator. Maintain databases, prepare PowerPoint presentations, write SOPs for data entry, and train users. Proficient with MS Office (Word, Excel, Access, PowerPoint, Outlook), Exchange 5.5, and Windows 98/ME, 2000, and NT.

- Superior oral and written communications. Compose reports, investigative and operational plans, summaries, updates, incident accounts, memos, and briefings. Deliver briefings before high-level delegations, conduct platform instruction and training sessions, and present security awareness seminars.

- Excellent interpersonal skills. Energetic, easily adaptable to changing conditions, determine new and innovative methods to interact positively in difficult situations, relate well with various people and individuals of diverse backgrounds, and apply direct, action-oriented approaches to solving problems.

Security Clearance

A qualifying factor for this critical position is the ability to obtain and retain a TOP SECRET (TS) security clearance with SCI (Secret Compartmented Information) access, having completed an SSBI (Single Scope Background Investigation). Consequently, we included this very important factor at the beginning of her work experience section. We listed her entire current access because the position is dependent on this access level. We also added her last periodic reinvestigation (PR) date so that Federal employers know that she is very current and will not need another periodic investigation for nearly four more years.

CLEARANCE

TS/SCI/SSBI (current/active) PR updated 05/2002

Professional Experience

In the Professional Experience section, Jane included the Federal requirements for each job in reverse-chronological order. Because she is a service member, we included her rank (E-6) and proper dates (MM/DD/YYYY). We were sure to include, "yes, you may contact my current employer." Because there is no threat of a confidentiality breech, Jane gladly listed her current supervisor's name and phone.

Each description entry is broken down into two parts: scope of operations and accomplishments. The scope of operations helps the reader see the special or collateral duties the military member might perform, as well as offers insight to daily responsibilities. The accomplishments section offers specific accomplishments and highlights special activities or projects.

Once again, acronyms are spelled out, except for well-known acronyms, such as CIA and FBI.

PROFESSIONAL EXPERIENCE

Surveillance Case Officer (E-6)
Foreign Counterintelligence Office
U.S. Army, Detachment 26
Fort Belvoir, VA 22340
Supervisor: Matt Eve; Phone: 410-555-5555
Yes, you may contact my current employer.

02/12/2000 to Present
Hours per week: 50+
Salary: $2,500 per mo.
Supervise: 25

Scope of Operations

Plan and conduct worldwide physical surveillance operations against Foreign Intelligence Services (FIS) in support of national-level Human Intelligence (HUMINT) requirements and counterintelligence (CI) operations and investigations to identify suspects involved in compromising national security.

Review surveillance processes, requirements, and cases. Approve or disapprove surveillance measures.

Employ state-of-the-art surveillance equipment to train subordinates. Led and controlled ground operations for a specific mission and supervised 25 team members.

Conduct regular liaison with representatives from various counterintelligence and law-enforcement agencies, including the FBI, CIA, DOA, and other national agencies.

Compose and review reports and other written documents.

Serve as Communications Security (COMSEC) Custodian.

Plan and lead training scenarios. Advise, evaluate, mentor, and counsel students at a CI training school.

Collateral Assignment, Assistant Supply Manager: Manage and account for $1.4M worth of equipment, purchasing requirements, and logistical support for the surveillance team.

Specific Accomplishments

- Since September 11, the surveillance team has worked overtime on additional counterterrorism operations and investigations. We work closely with local law-enforcement representatives to handle multiple arrests.
- Develop Surveillance Detection Routes (SDR) in support of Offensive CI Operations.
- Conduct debriefings.
- Engaged in a number of surveillance activities: foot, mobile, public transportation, map reading, tradecraft and operation activity recognition, note-taking and report writing, aerial surveillance, night surveillance, stakeouts, and boxing.
- Conduct briefings. Prepare PowerPoint presentations for briefings and class instruction.

(continues)

(continued)

Special Agent/Security Specialist (E-5)   02/12/1998 to 02/12/2000
U.S. Army   Hours per week: 40+
Detachment 7   Salary: $2,500 per mo.
Fort Meade, MD 21067   Supervised: 8
Supervisor: Joe Brown, Phone: 455-555-5555

Operations Officer/Training and Operations (S3)

Scope of Operations

Managed and coordinated all CI taskings from subordinate organizations and input all data into the database to include Polygraphs, Technical Support Countermeasures, Information Warfare Branch, and counterintelligence activities in support of the Department of the Army (DoA) and DoD military units and civilian contractors. Enforced Department of Army Intelligence and Security Command procedures and policies.

Supervised the mission database and daily operations stats and provided operational input/reports to headquarters. Managed the in-house database software.

Managed and controlled physical security of sensitive areas and the proper operation of access devices.

Assisted in the local adjudication and granting of access to sensitive compartmented information and assisted in the processing of periodic reinvestigations for DoA personnel.

Provided security and computer forensics to computer investigations and collection efforts.

Trained personnel in the completion of the Electronic Personnel Security Questionnaire and led security training for over 250 personnel.

Maintained excellent liaison with program managers, operations officers, and other unit representatives regarding issues of multi-disciplined CI technical assets.

Prepared regular weekly and special PowerPoint slides for meetings.

Constructed and wrote a weekly operations report, a monthly unit status report, and a quarterly civilian law-enforcement operations report.

Supervised, mentored, and counseled eight subordinates. Fostered a cohesive working team. Assisted personnel with travel orders and requirements.

Specific Achievements

- Selected to supervise a team (normally assigned to a much more senior agent) to support the Presidential mandated DoD War Crimes Disclosure Act declassification project. The project digitized over one million counterintelligence investigative and operational files and then declassified and released over 15,000 of the files to the National Records Administration. Managed all Quality Control reviews for declassification of the files.
- Developed a Fire and Safety Program and prepared for a Safety/Fire Inspection, passing with success. Conducted security inspections ensuring compliance with DoD and Army security policies, procedures, and regulations.
- Located and removed over 300 corrupted computer files within one week of hire.
- Created a Standard Operating Procedure (SOP) for data entry.
- Devised and implemented a cross-training plan for the section, which ensured assignment completion (devised training for agents in Personnel Security Investigations and Subversion and Espionage Directed Against the Army (SAEDA) briefings.
- Maintained and accounted for $600,000 worth of equipment.

Special Agent (E-4)
U.S. Army
A. Co. 518th MI BN Korea
Supervisor: MAJ Donna Merson

02/12/1997 to 02/12/1998
Hours per week: 40+
Salary: $ 2,300 per mo.
Supervised: 6

Scope of Operations

Provided covering agent support and security assistance to all staff sections and elements within the U.S. Forces Korea headquarters. Supported two exercises. Conducted security briefings and answered questions related to suspicious activity to over 20,000 individuals stationed in Korea.

Assisted with cyber-counterintelligence investigations to detect, prevent, and neutralize threats to national security.

Conducted liaison with Federal, state, and local law-enforcement agencies.

Organized and maintained counterintelligence files and databases.

Debriefed or interviewed witnesses and sources to extract pertinent information concerning investigations. Coordinated, implemented, and maintained debriefing programs with Federal agencies. Debriefed DoA personnel for information of intelligence value.

Wrote investigative plans, reports, summaries, updates, and closure reports. Produced intelligence reports to answer national-level intelligence requirements.

Managed barracks requirements: Created a detail roster, enforced standards, and coordinated building work orders.

(continues)

(continued)

Specific Achievements

- Served as the Investigations Team Leader/Personnel Security Investigations (PSIs) Case Control Manager and directed the investigative actions of six agents, completing over 2,000 leads and closing 486 cases.
- Personally closed 120 PSIs and conducted 300 leads, accounting for 40% of the total PSI production.
- Acted as Lead Investigator on six espionage investigations and supported one other by completing two Intelligence Memorandums for Record (IMR).
- Selected among a pool of 37 peers to participate in two counterintelligence surveillance exercises.
- Selected as Soldier of the Quarter (Battalion level).

Education

Because Jane is fairly young, we included her college achievements.

EDUCATION

Pursuing a Masters in Intelligence, enrolled Fall 2002

Bachelor of Science in Health Administration, University of Maryland, MD, 1996 (GPA: 3.8)

    Dean's List

    Women's Business Honor Society

    Who's Who Among American Colleges and Universities

American Military University, Richmond, VA

Diploma, Canyon Area High School, Columbia, MD, 1992

Professional Development

Jane's military training and professional development is very applicable to the security field positions she is seeking. We listed her training in reverse-chronological order and included course length and graduation dates.

PROFESSIONAL DEVELOPMENT

Basic Noncommissioned Officer Course (BNOC), 8 weeks, 2001 (Distinguished Graduate)

Basic Surveillance Course, Joint Training Academy, 200 hours, 2001

Driver Enhancement Training, Police and Correctional Training Commissions, 1 week, 2000

Basic Tactical Pistol Class, 40 hours, 2000

Counterintelligence Training Center Surveillance Course, 2 weeks, 2000

CI/HUMINT Automated Tool Sets (CHATS), 1 week, 1998

Korea Surveillance Training Course, 2 weeks, 1997

Primary Leadership Development Course, Noncommissioned Officer Academy, 4 weeks, 1997

U.S. Army Counterintelligence School, Counterintelligence Agent, 17 weeks, 1996

Awards

Finally we listed some of Jane's awards. The titles of the awards are not as significant as the accomplishments pulled from the award justifications that are incorporated into the resume text. The awards indicate her drive to excel and attain recognition. She can describe the nature of the awards in an interview.

AWARDS

Received special letters of commendation from senior members of the FBI and national-level intelligence agencies for supporting a successful and highly sensitive operation, 2002

The Army Commendation Medal, 2002

The Army Achievement Medal, 2001, 2000

Certificate of Achievement, 1998 (for skillful investigative techniques)

Sample Federal Resume 2: Human Resources Management Candidate

We describe each section of this sample resume in the following sections.

Introductory Material

Marc's resume begins with the standard required information:

Marc Myers

1278 Brookstone Path
Columbia, MD 21044
410-555-1243 (w)
marcm@aol.com

Social Security Number:	xxx-xx-xxxx
U.S. Citizen:	Yes
Military Service:	U.S. Army, Active Duty, 06/05/1982 to 12/30/2002
Veterans' Preference:	5 point
Highest Federal Employment:	N/A

OBJECTIVE:	Announcement Number:
	Title, Series, Grade:

Professional Profile

Marc's profile section includes a skills grid to highlight pertinent credentials related to HR. Many military people who exit service are trained in some HR functions, including performance evaluations, personnel actions, training, and training program coordination. However, when they tell me that they want a position in HR, I ask them whether they have experience with staffing, contacts with recruiters, knowledge of unions, and skills in benefit packages. Most say no to these questions. Then, unless they are interested in an entry-level HR position, we determine a different focus for the resume.

Marc attained his degree in HR during his time in the military. It took many years, but he accomplished the degree. He also maintained a membership in SHRM (Society for Human Resource Management), which adds to his credentials when he applies for jobs in corporate or Federal America.

Even though Marc is seeking employment in HR Administration, he lists collateral duties in the profile section. These additional skills will enhance his qualifications as a leader and well-rounded administrator.

 Note: HR, EO, and EEO are well-known acronyms in both the military and corporate America, and they are seen as acronyms in the Federal announcements. Also note that previous entries become shorter in description content. The most recent positions carry the greatest weight and indicate the highest responsibility levels.

PROFESSIONAL PROFILE

HR Management & Personnel Administration

High-performance administrator with broad scope of responsibility incorporating 20 years of direct experience in Personnel Administration and HR management. Provide strong and solid leadership serving as a technical authority, subject-matter expert, instructor, and advisor.

Planned, initiated, and conduct training programs for Personnel Administration Specialists, technical staff, and clerical staff. Maintain well-organized filing systems.

Handle employee labor relations and equal-opportunity disputes. Create quality, "customer service first" environments. Act as a liaison.

Skilled communicator: excellent report writer and briefer. Manage administrative requirements, prepare presentations and training outlines, compose correspondence, and write reports. Superior ability to assemble talented teams and delegate assignments.

Actively engaged in office administration. Serve as Printing and Reproduction Manager, Savings Bond Representative, Copier Maintenance Manager, Forms Control and Publications Library Manager, Mail and Messenger Services, and Records Manager. Utilize Microsoft PowerPoint, Excel, Access, and Word.

Employment Experience

In this section, Marc describes the work experience for each job he's held, beginning with the most recent and continuing in reverse-chronological order. First, he lists the duties of the jobs, followed by his special accomplishments. This allows the rater to see not only what his assigned responsibilities were, but also what he accomplished personally while he held the job.

United States Army, TOP SECRET Clearance   *1982 to 2002*
Personnel Actions Center (PAC)
Administrative Manager (E-9)   06/12/1996 to 12/12/2000
HHC 1st BN   Hours per week: 40+
Fort Belvoir, MD 20540   Salary: $45,000 per year
Supervisor: MAJ Varin; Phone: 555-555-2501   Supervised: 15

Promoted through a series of increasingly responsible administrative positions supporting the largest and most widely dispersed security organization in the U.S. Army with over 250 personnel in 32 separate locations globally. Supervised all activities in the Personnel Actions Center. Commended for designing and incorporating streamlined administrative functions and maintaining high work productivity.

Analyzed and determined manpower, staffing, and resources requirements. Managed multiple projects and stressful deadlines. Evaluated processes and solved problems. Tackled tough issues. Integrated the flow of business, set office and administrative priorities, and ensured the timely follow-up and completion of daily workloads.

Provided timely customer service and assisted personnel in resolving personnel actions or pay issues, determining benefits, and mediating EEO problems. Reviewed EEO complaints in the early stages and avoided escalation of complaints to higher levels by applying sensitivity to each case, defusing flared angers, identifying the problem, and resolving issues.

Drafted written materials, including policy, instructions, and correspondence. Conducted studies and prepared analyses. Instructed and trained personnel. Conducted briefings and meetings. Interpreted, formulated, implemented, and enforced management and EEO processes, procedures, laws, and regulations.

Reviewed and monitored that all reports and administrative actions—including awards, evaluations, promotions, personnel actions, finance, leave, and legal actions—were completed in a timely manner and of a high quality. Reviewed and consolidated reports, statistics, and personnel actions submitted to higher headquarters.

Oversight accountability for administrative security, copier maintenance, forms control, printing and reproduction, publications, and records management.

Specific Accomplishments
- Effectively reviewed and revised a critical HR Standard Operating Procedures (SOP) manual utilized by 32 subordinate elements.

(continues)

(continued)

- Supervised, trained, and evaluated a staff of 15. Maintained full accountability for equipment and property valued at over $100,000. Fully accountable for office affairs, messenger services, equipment acquisition and allocation, records management, and constantly reworking the administrative infrastructure.
- Anticipated a 50% loss in Personnel Actions Center (PAC) strength and implemented a cross-training program to ensure continuity. Delegated assignments and fostered a sense of teamwork among subordinates.
- Demonstrated technical competence and computer savvy to single-handedly create a well-needed Unit Manning Report database where none existed previously. The database allowed requisitions for shortages of personnel and accurate tracking of nearly 800 personnel in six geographical areas.
- Directed and guided administrative and personnel requirements for the opening and closing of several offices.
- Quickly reviewed, analyzed, and resolved personnel problems.
- Trained junior personnel specialists. Maintained 100% accountability of 59 new personnel associated with six subordinate offices in one year.
- Effectively executed over 100 separate personnel restructure actions on time during a highly stressful and high-tempo period of organizational restructuring.
- Collateral duty: Reviewed and processed over 130 performance evaluations with a submission rate of 99%.

Personnel Manager (E-8)   06/12/1990 to 06/13/1996
Manager Strength Management Division   Hours per week: 40
Personnel Actions Center   Salary: $38,000 per year
Heidelberg, Germany   Supervised: 10
Supervisor: MSG Daila Laner; Phone: DSN: 555-2668

Supervised a staff of 10 personnel specialists and managers supporting a 270-employee organization in six geographical locations. Served as liaison and point of contact for all personnel matters between the units and the headquarters. Provided personnel guidance to senior management/Chief of Strength Management. Executed a full range of personnel actions. Conducted weekly training. Managed Force Reduction units and units moving from Germany to America.

Specific Accomplishments
- Monitored authorized strength replacement flow for specific elements.
- Supervised the turn-in and subsequent destruction of office files for deactivating units.
- Managed the organization and maintenance of thousands of files and records.
- Interviewed personnel and determined appropriate staffing requirements.

- Processed over 2,000 foreign-service tour extensions and hundreds of other personnel actions monthly, including the assignment of 1,000 personnel to 17 subordinate units and 100 reclassifications.
- Full responsibility for a Promotion List with over 900 names.
- Prepared the monthly unit status personnel readiness brief and prepared analyses for the regional briefings.
- Supervised the database management section. Served as Casualty Assistance Coordinator for the community, served as Retirement Files Manager, and sat on the Promotion Board as a member.

Instructor/Writer (E-5 to 7)　　　　06/12/1986 to 06/12/1990
A Co　　　　　　　　　　　　　　　　　Hours per week: 40
Fort Stewart, GA 45698　　　　　　　　Salary: $30,000 per year
Supervisor: MSG Michael Fraley　　　　Supervised: 6

Instructed students to become Personnel Management Specialists at the Primary Leadership Development Academy. Wrote lesson plans and taught courses; wrote and administered practical exercises and tests. Counseled students.

Developed learning objectives, tests, lesson plans, and practical exercises pertaining to Personnel Management and the Promotion System. Taught, administered practical exercises and performance tests, and evaluated students. Counseled students with personal/academic problems.

Personnel Management Specialist (E-5)　　06/12/1982 to 06/12/1986
Manager Promotions Section　　　　　　　　Hours per week: 40
12th BN, HHC　　　　　　　　　　　　　　Salary: $22,000 per year
Germany　　　　　　　　　　　　　　　　　Supervised: 3

Prepared promotion orders for publication for all personnel in a database. Reviewed accelerated promotions. Maintained a promotion standing list of 900 personnel. Processed hundreds of promotion and personnel transactions. Served as board recorder for the promotion board. Interviewed personnel for board appearance.

Managed administrative office procedures and prepared reports, correspondence, and personnel transactions. Managed database files and personnel transactions for a community of 5,000 personnel.

Education

Marc succinctly states his formal education:

EDUCATION

Master of Human Resources, University of Maryland, March 2001

BA in Business Management, University of Maryland, 1990

Professional Development and Awards

Marc lists most of his applicable training and indicates the course content, when it might not be fully recognized by a civilian employer (for example, NCO equals Management).

PROFESSIONAL DEVELOPMENT

U.S. Army Training:

Data Handler Management, 1999 (1 week)
Unit Deployment Officer Course (Logistics), 1998 (2 weeks)
Advanced Noncommissioned Officers Academy (Senior Mgt. and Administration), 1994 (8 weeks)
Computer Training, 1993 (2 weeks)
Personnel Service Center, Basic Noncommissioned Officers Academy (Management), 1992 (7 weeks)
Staff and Faculty Development Training Course, 1992 (2 weeks)
Noncommissioned Officers Development Course (Leadership), 1988 (2 weeks)
Equal Opportunity Training, 1988 (2 weeks)
Primary Leadership Development Course, 1985 (4 weeks)

AWARDS

Meritorious Service Medal × 3
Army Commendation Medal × 2
Army Achievement Medal × 2
National Defense Service Medal
Southwest Asia Service Medal
Kuwait Liberation Medal

CLEARANCE

Top Secret (U.S. Army)

MEMBERSHIPS

SHRM (Society for Human Resource Management)

Summary

The foregoing examples illustrate some of the ways you can convert military experience to "civilian speak." Remember to frame your experience in everyday terms that are familiar to the civilian rater—the qualifications standards. Follow this simple rule and you will be well on your way to developing a winning resume.

Appendix

Federal Resume Examples

Federal Resumes for Students and Recent Graduates

B.S. in Economics, Applying for Economist, GS-9/11

GARY L. BLANKENBURG
SS# 000-00-0000
U.S. CITIZEN

8 WINDSWEPT LANE
COLUMBIA, MD 21030
email: garylblankenburg@yahoo.com

HOME: (410) 744-4324
WORK: (410) 881-9943

VETERANS' PREFERENCE: 5 POINTS   FEDERAL STATUS: N/A

OBJECTIVE:

> **Labor Economist, GS-0110-11, U.S. Department of Labor, Washington, DC
> Announcement: NCSC/ILAB 95-046**

SUMMARY OF RELEVANT SKILLS:

Economics
- Utilize knowledge of economic relationships to advise senior researchers.
- Apply money, banking, and foreign-exchange principles to current research.

Econometrics
- Prepare economic and governmental forecasts.
- Provide information to support policy decision-making.

Computers
- Proficiency with Mini-tab and SAS statistical software.
- Compile data; analyze statistics.
- Produce spreadsheets and reports.

Written Language
- Construct clear, concise, audience-specific reports.
- Conduct extensive research to support team-oriented work projects.

Public Speaking
- Design and present informative, demonstrative, or persuasive speeches.
- Deliver animated conference-level presentations with visual aids.
- Interview specialized professionals and executives on economic research.

EDUCATION:

> **University of Tennessee,** Knoxville, TN 32408
> **B.Sc., Economics,** 1997
> GPA: Overall: 3.4   Economics: 3.5

ACADEMIC AWARDS AND HONORS:

> **Fulbright Grant** in Stockholm, Sweden, August 1997–May 1998
> Research focused on efforts to improve the labor market in the United States by researching historical and current institutions in Sweden. Interviewed Swedish government officials, academicians, and business executives, who provided volumes of data and anecdotal references. Researched, analyzed, and interpreted economic data.
>
> Utilized specialized methods such as sampling, statistics, and economic forecasting to gather data. Tools of analysis included supply and demand, cost benefit, labor market, ISLM equilibrium, inter-temporal external balance methods, 1st and 2nd order condition optimization, and Lagrangian optimization techniques. Procedures for quantifying and measuring economic

Gary Blankenburg, SS# 000-00-0000, Labor Economist, GS-0110-11, ANNCT NCSC/ILAB 95-046

relationships included game theory, econometric forecasting, regression analysis, OLS methods, etc. Utilized Mini-Tab and SAS statistical programs.

Top Economic Award (Przygoda) at University of Tennessee for Exceptional Standard of Economic Scholarship, May 1997

International Honor Society in Economics: Omicron Delta Epsilon, April 1997

Macro Economics Award for Excellence, University of Tennessee, May 1996

Dean's List for Academic Excellence, University of Tennessee, May 1996

Graduate, Oak Ridge High School, Oak Ridge, TN, May 1986. Member, National Honor Society

PAPERS & PRESENTATIONS:

Federal Tax Receipts Associated with Two U.S. Labor Market Improvements: A Proposal. Summary proposal of Fulbright research conducted in Stockholm, Sweden, May 1998. This work anchors itself in progressive-labor economic concepts, innovative childcare modeling techniques, and specialized policies and programs regarding contemporary women's issues.

Economic Systems Analysis: A Case Study Comparing the Economies of Sweden and the United States. Conference paper presented at The Society for the Advancement of Socio-Economics, New School for Social Research in New York City on March 27, 1997.

Economic Systems Analysis: A Case Study Comparing the Economies of Sweden and the United States. Conference paper presented at The Society for the Advancement of Scandinavian Studies, University of Texas at Austin in Austin, Texas, on April 22, 1997.

Structural and Political Analysis of European Economic and Monetary Union. Research paper. April 1997.

Two Labor Market Ideas to Strengthen the American Family: Lessons from Sweden. Research paper. March 1997.

Economic Systems Analysis: A Case Study Comparing the Economies of Sweden and the United States. Extensive 130-page symmetrical study, which critically examined areas for cross-fertilization of economic and social ideas in Sweden and the United States. Academically supervised semester course, August–December, 1996.

Papers published in *Tennessean* (university newspaper), 1996–1997.

EMPLOYMENT HISTORY:

Baltimore Savings Bank
21 N. Calvert Street, Baltimore, MD 21203
Assistant Branch Manager
Salary: $25,000 annually
Supervisor: Greg Summers, (410) 244-3628

July 1998–Present

40 hours/week plus overtime
Please do not contact

Assist with managing retail bank operations, including supervision of 10 tellers and customer service representatives. Train staff in policies, procedures, bank products, cash management, and customer services. Provide account services, bank product sales, and coordination of loan applications. Introduce consumer and mortgage loan services to customers. Assess customer financial and bank service needs and make appropriate recommendations.

2

(continues)

(continued)

Gary Blankenburg, SS# 000-00-0000, Labor Economist, GS-0110-11, ANNCT NCSC/ILAB 95-046

Fulbright Commission
12-1 855 First Avenue, Stockholm, Sweden   June 1997–June 1998
Researcher
Salary: $1,000 per month grant stipend   40 hours/week
Supervisor: Carol Lundstrom, 011-46-08-107-2789

Learning Resource Center at Loyola Marymount University
55 Surrey Lane, Greeneville, NC 40840   January 1996–May 1997
Senior Writing Tutor
Salary: $400 per month   20 hours/week
Supervisor: Kevin O'Connor, (310) 338-7702
    Provided writing support and course-specific tutoring in economics, history, and English to undergraduates.

United States Marine Corps Intelligence Field   January 1991–January 1996
Cryptologic Spanish Linguist
Salary: $1,500 per month   40 hours/week
Supervisor: Edward A. Hall, (202) 736-3259
Top Secret Clearance. Honorable Discharge, 1996.

MILITARY CLEARANCE AND AWARDS:

United States Marine Corps, 1991–1996.
Cleared for Top Secret information and granted access to Sensitive Compartmented information based on a special background investigation completed on 880802 under CCN #88132-1366.

Awards:
- National Defense Service Medal (Operation Desert Shield/Storm)
- Rifle Expert Award
- Good Conduct Medal
- Overseas Service Ribbon
- Letter of Commendation
- Letters of Appreciation

LEADERSHIP ACTIVITIES:

President of the Economics Society at the University of Tennessee, 1996–1997.
Student Selection Committee, 1997.
    Special appointment by the university Academic Vice President for the selection of the new Dean of Liberal Arts.
Student Advisory Council, 1997.
    Special appointment by the university Dean of Liberal Arts.
Vice President of the Sailing Club at the University of Tennessee, 1991.
Vice President of the Oak Ridge High School Student Body, 1985–1986.

3

*GS, Mechanical Engineering, Seeking Mechanical Engineering, GS-0830-07
(Intern Program Student)*

Scott Hampstead

5555 University Blvd., Hyattsville, MD 20783
(301) 333-3333 • scotth20202@earthlink.net

SSN: 000-00-0000; US Citizen; No prior Federal or Military Experience
OUTSTANDING SCHOLAR; 3.7/4.0 GPA

Objective **ENGINEER, MECHANICAL, GS-0830-07**
Defense Contract Management Agency Keystone Intern Program
Defense Contract Management Agency—West, DCMAW-03-KEY-170718

Skills
As Team Leader for more than 10 significant projects, developed skill in analyzing projects, delegating tasks, and establishing timelines. Also developed the following engineering and project management skills:

- Draft project details.
- Devise and recommend alternative methods of standardized analysis as a basis for solving problems.
- Recommend and devise deviations to details.
- Assist in reviews of engineering changes.
- Review compliance to contract during design, development, and production.
- Evaluate control of baseline products.
- Manage and/or witness tests.
- Evaluate quality assurance activities.
- Conduct cost and schedule analysis and estimations.
- Manage engineering data collection and analysis.

Education
B.S. in Mechanical Engineering Honors Program
University of Maryland, College Park, MD
Expected July 2003   Overall GPA: 3.6/4.0   Engineering GPA: 3.7/4.0

Honors and Activities
National Merit Scholar   Maryland Distinguished Scholar
A.P. scholar with honors   Dean's List (four times)
Maryland club lacrosse (1999–2000)   Maryland intramural soccer (2002)

Related Coursework
Calculus, physics, chemistry, differential equations, statistics, dynamics, thermodynamics, introduction to matlab, fluid mechanics, electronics and instrumentation, engineering materials and manufacturing processes, statistical methods of product development, transfer processes, vibrations controls and optimization, product engineering and manufacturing, automotive design, manufacturing automation, technical writing, human resource management, introduction to transportation in supply-chain management.

(continues)

(continued)

Scott Hampstead, SSN 00-00-0000; Mechanical Engineer, DCMAW-03-KEY-170718

Team Semester Projects

Redesign of the DeWalt tradesman drill using the nine-step product development process. Directed the testing and building of a prototype cordless/corded drill. Compared results to necessary specifications to determine effectiveness of the design. Gave PowerPoint presentations on project results. Utilized analytical tools such as the House of Quality, Weighted Decision Matrix, Morphological Chart, and Functional Decomposition to redesign drill. 2002

Design of Hybrid SUV for Future Truck competition. In charge of testing the performance of the electric motor. Analyzed complex schematics to determine connector specifications and location. Negotiated the donation of connectors for the high-voltage system. Researched torque curves for the stock engine and the replacement engine. 2002–2003

Design of Matlab code to model airborne concentrations of dust in turbulent winds. Modeled winds with force vectors. Displayed results in multiple plots corresponding to different wind conditions. Experimented with different mesh densities to determine the degree of computing power necessary for accurate results. 2001

Other projects have included:
Design of portable water pump
Statistical analysis of campus traffic flow
Evaluation of scale wind tunnel testing of a high-rise building
Analysis of stress, bending, and failure in a lug wrench

High School

Centennial High School, Ellicott City, MD, Class of 1999

Academic Honors:
Honor Roll; Cumulative GPA: 3.6/4.0
National Merit Finalist/Scholar; A.P. Scholar with Honor

Significant Courses:
Gifted and Talented English, Social Studies
Math and Science course work
A.P. Psychology, A.P. Statistics, A.P. English 12, A.P. U.S. History, A.P. Calculus One and Two

Computer Skills

Word, Excel, PowerPoint, Pro-Engineer, Matlab.

Work Experience

Sales Clerk, Village Antiques (18 hours per week)
1000 Old Frederick Road, Oella, MD 90909 (1996–1999)
Supervisor: John Jones (410) 444-4444; salary: $12 per hour
Responsible for customer service, sales, daily operation of store.

2

Career Change Federal Resumes

Correspondence Analyst, GS-0301-08, Seeking Program Assistant, GS-0344-09

DONNA M. STEPHENS
9006 Mill Court
Ft. Washington, MD 20744

Home: (301) 248-8831   stephensdm123@yahoo.com   Work: (703) 695-1647

Social Security No.:   000-00-0000
Citizenship: United States
Federal Status: Correspondence Analyst/Expediter, GS-8
Veterans' Preference: N/A

OBJECTIVE   Management and Program Assistant, GS-344-09/9, EVER-DEU-08-08
Department of the Interior, National Park Service, Everglades National Park, Homestead, FL

SKILLS SUMMARY

Fourteen years of administrative experience with the Department of the Navy, including positions as **Correspondence Analyst Leader, Research Assistant,** and **Personnel Assistant.** Skilled in assisting with program functions; supporting and communicating with senior managers; coordinating work load and projects; and ensuring compliance and quality control. Effective at responsively serving customers and constituents regarding activities and information.

- Research, analyze, and track files, documentation, correspondence, and information.
- Communicate with government managers and staff.
- Maintain awareness of program and management functions in order to act as effective intermediary between managers.
- Coordinate office administrative functions.
- Train and delegate assignments to project staff.
- Troubleshoot PCs: Support user inquiries concerning system and software updates for Windows, communications, and other applications.

EMPLOYMENT HISTORY

DEPARTMENT OF THE NAVY, Washington, DC 20350   9/84 to present
Secretary of the Navy (Administration Office)

    CORRESPONDENCE ANALYST/EXPEDITER (GS-8)   2/96 to present
    Allan Grisolm, Supervisor, (703) 744-4324   40 hours/week
    Supervisor may be contacted   Current salary: $41,090

    Analyze, prioritize, and manage correspondence for all professional staff within the Administrative Office of the Secretary of the Navy, the Department of Defense, and other agencies.

- Track documents and maintain information concerning action items and deadlines.
- Retrieve and update status of documents on computer tracking system.
- Ensure quality control of documents for the Secretary of the Navy's signature.
- Serve as representative to the Information Systems Group, providing information to users concerning system and application updates.

(continues)

(continued)

Donna M. Stephens, SSN 000-00-0000; Management & Prog. Assist., GS-334-09, EVER-DEU-08-08

- Liaise with congressional offices, Department of Navy heads, and others for information concerning correspondence and documents flowing through the Administrative Office.
- Write and edit correspondence, and track and report statistics on documents and correspondence utilizing WordPerfect and Outlook. Skilled with Excel.

Accomplishments:
- Developed and implemented a basic internal hands-on training program for the installation of the electronic document archiving systems. Trained the staff, oversaw the archiving of all previously manually maintained files, and met project deadlines.
- Enhanced job-related skills by cross-training and quality reviews.
- Improved efficiency of document control and processing. Improved daily operations, cutting down on duplication of efforts. Analyzed system and improved efficiency of paper flow within Outgoing Mail, Records, and Reference Branch departments.

COLLATERAL PROJECTS:

Representative and Assistant Secretary
NSSORA Recreation Association (1993 to present)
- Serve as liaison to vendors providing products and services for employees of the Department of the Navy.
- Negotiate prices and coordinate procurement and logistics for clothing and movie and event tickets for employees.

Accomplishments:
- Improved the documentation and archiving of correspondence by creating an abstract incorporating key words, cross-references, and relationships to other correspondence and programs.
- Recognized by superiors for initiative and drive and for efforts to maintain an awareness of events, programs, priorities, and issues.

TEAM LEADER (GS-7)   12/90 to 2/96
Ms. U. Schlegel, Supervisor, (703) 695-1648   40 hours/week

Directed operations in the Outgoing Mail Records and Reference Branch. Supervised student aides and clerical employees.

- Provided input into staff performance reviews and implemented training programs to improve productivity and accountability.
- Implemented new systems to increase efficiency and customer service.
- Reviewed all final documents for procedural and format compliance with DoD guidelines.
- Wrote job descriptions for summer hires manpower. Utilized this staff to handle the backlog workload and administrative processes.

RESEARCH ASSISTANT (GS-6)   1/89 to 12/90
Mike James, Supervisor, (703) 695-1648   40 hours/week

Reviewed and analyzed technical, policy, and organizational material; applied classification number according to Standard Subject Instruction Manual.
- Maintained/integrated permanent correspondence with micrographics equipment.
- Maintained and compiled a dossier for the Secretariat and staff.
- Edited and modified data from automated correspondence control system.

2

Donna M. Stephens, SSN 000-00-0000; Management & Prog. Assist., GS-334-09, EVER-DEU-08-08

Accomplishments:
- Assumed additional job responsibilities during a time of reorganization and severe personnel and equipment shortages. Participated in quality-control projects, provided special service to the executive director, and delegated activities to 10 new employees handling the administrative responsibilities of this office.
- Received a Sustained Superior Performance Award.

ASSISTANT FOR AWARDS AND PERSONNEL ACTIONS (GS-5)   1/88 to 1/89
Ms. B. Shephard, Supervisor, (703) 695-1648   40 hours/week

Coordinated support for personnel actions and awards. Researched personnel actions and maintained files, retrieved data from automated system, answered personnel inquiries, and requested information from individuals and agencies.

EDUCATION

University of Maryland, College Park, MD 21205
Bachelor of Arts Degree, 1996
    Courses included:
    Public Policy and Government Relations (24 credit hours)
    Business Management (27 hours)
    Information Systems Management (12 hours)
    Completed BA degree while working full-time; received Naval Scholarships

Homestead Senior High School, Homestead, FL 21280
Graduated, 1987

AWARDS

Superior Scholastic Achievement Award, 1996
Quality Step Increases / Cash Awards, 1991–1996
Sustained Superior Performance Award, 1991
Naval Developmental Scholarship, 1990

PERSONAL

Seeking a position returning to my family residence where I was raised and educated. Willing to relocate at personal cost in order to be near my family.

Very familiar with Everglades National Park, as well as proven federal administrative experience.

3

Executive Secretary, GS-8, Seeking Administrative Officer, GS-9

Emily Anne Layton

310 Frederick Road
Ft. Worth, TX 87987

Office: 604.333.2245   E-mail: ealayton@audit.navy.mil   Home: 604.988.3333

SSN: 000-00-0000
United States Citizen

Federal Civilian Status: GS-8/10, 4/97
Veterans' Status: SFC, U.S. Army Reserve
Security Clearance: SECRET

Objective   Administrative Officer, GS-0341-09, PO-03-40

Indian Health Service, Department of Health & Human Services, Ft. Worth, TX

Profile

Office manager, executive secretary, and instructor/writer with over 25 years' Federal, National Guard, and Army Reserve experience. Excellent communications, organizational, and administrative skills. Valued by senior executives for ability to independently manage offices, improve systems, meet deadlines, and implement new administrative procedures.

Qualifications Summary

Office Reorganization and Design of Administrative Processes:

- As Executive Secretary, Naval Audit Service HQ (1989 to present), developed and implemented improved office administrative systems to meet decreased staffing and growing audit report production requirements. The new systems improved workflow, file management, and communication methods that met deadlines, maintained quality, and ensured satisfaction by 10 audit managers plus the Director.

- As Administrative Assistant to the Director of the IRS Internal Security Division, wrote new procedures for personnel actions that improved time documentation and reduced errors and processing time. Successfully managed an extensive travel and premium pay budget for investigative staff.

Writing and Editing Experience:

- Edited the Department of Energy's (DoE) *D.O.E. This Month,* a monthly newsletter distributed to all departmental headquarters and field offices. (7 years)

- Edited *Public Information Field Report* (on key programs, events, and issues) for daily distribution to 50 top Headquarters officials and 300 field public information officers department-wide. Increased *Field Report* coverage 30% in one month.

Training:

- Senior instructor/writer for the 2970th U.S. Army Reserve Forces School, Ft. Belvoir, VA. Courses include: Basic Computer Operation and Concepts of the Tactical Area Army Computer System (TAACS), Office Management.

- Taught EEO for the Federal Women's Program.

Computer Expertise:

- Word, PowerPoint, Excel, Outlook; WordPerfect; GENUS; TAACS.

Emily Anne Layton, SSN: 000-00-0000   2

Employment History

Executive Secretary, GS-318-8/10   July 1993–Present
Naval Audit Service HQ, 5677 Compton Blvd., Dallas, TX 78732   40 hours per week
Supervisor: Andy McDowell, 604.681.6092; may be contacted   Starting Salary: $25,910
                                                      Current Salary: $42,199

Principal Executive Assistant to the Director of Audit Operations, and sole administrative/audit assistant to 10 department management auditors and their staffs. (The Director monitors worldwide audit activities within the Department of the Navy.)

- Liaise to Congressional staff, government agencies, Navy components, and the public. Direct office administrative activities including workflow, deadlines, correspondence, records, and appointments.
- Receive audit updates by e-mail and PC disk from audit managers. Utilizing knowledge of DoD procedures, policies, and standard formats, produce detailed and timely audit reports and statements in the correct format.
- Research and respond to audit manager's questions for information, scheduling, and coordination matters. Manage multiple projects while meeting stringent deadlines.

Accomplishments:
- Continually analyze systems to meet changing administrative and reporting demands.
- Designed record-keeping systems, calendar, and schedule of projects for audit staff and myself.
- Consistently meet audit report deadlines (3–5 per month).

Administrative Assistant, GS-318-8   September 1990–July 1993
Internal Security Division, IRS, Dallas, TX 78987   40 hours per week
Supervisor: Dan Moneybags, 604.387.8732   Ending Salary: $25,910
Administrative assistant to the Director of the Internal Security Division, a national office with 110 employees, 3 branches, and 7 regional offices.

- Provided supervision and management for all administrative functions in the office including record keeping, appointments, travel, correspondence, and special projects.
- Monitored travel and premium pay budget to support travel and overtime requirements (15%–25%) of investigative staff and ensured all accounts were current and meticulously maintained. By keeping these accounts current, funding was maintained at levels necessary for investigations to proceed in a timely manner.

Personal Assistant/Secretary, GS-318-6   September 1988–September 1990
Defense Contract Audit Agency, Andersonville, TX
Managed office administration for the Chief, Policy Liaison Division. Supervised staff, prioritized workflow to meet deadlines, reviewed and disseminated correspondence, maintained records, scheduled travel arrangements, prepared vouchers, and coordinated and scheduled appointments.

- Initiated, prepared, developed, and edited documents, reports, analyses, and correspondence from contributing staff elements.

(continues)

(continued)

Emily Anne Layton, SSN: 000-00-0000   3

Secretary/Editor, GS-318-7   September 1980–September 1988
Department of Energy, Wallace, TX
Promoted rapidly during transition of U.S. Energy Research and Development Administration into the Department of Energy. Gained knowledge of energy issues and organizational mission that led to a position in the Office of Public Affairs.

- Supervised and managed all administrative and clerical functions in office including record keeping, appointments, travel, correspondence, and special projects.
- Edited *D.O.E. This Month,* a monthly newsletter distributed to all departmental headquarters and field offices.
- Edited the *Public Information Field Report* (on key programs, events, and issues) for daily distribution to 50 top Headquarters officials and 300 field public information officers.
- *Increased distribution of* Public Information Field Report *by 30% in one month.*

National Guard & Army Reserves Service

Joined the 115th Infantry Unit of the Maryland National Guard in 1979 and was the first woman to serve in the unit. Transferred to the U.S. Army Reserves in 1981. Currently serving as (SFC) Senior Instructor/Writer with the 6th BN 80th Division, Dallas, TX. Current Supervisor: Daniel Jacobson, Unit Telephone: 604.233.8777 (20 hours per week). Current annual salary: $5,000.

Education

48 Hours, Education, University of Texas, Lubbock, TX 98789
Diploma, Danville High School, Danville, TX 98787

Professional Development

Technical, Management, Business Training:
Writing, Office Management, Office Productivity Through Individual Leadership, Quality Improvement, Travel Voucher, Executive Secretarial, Instructor Training

Military Leadership Training:
Instructor Training Course, Ft. Worth, TX, 1994, with honors
Advanced Retention NCO Course, Ft. Worth, TX, 2 weeks, 1993
U.S. Army NCO Academic Graduate, Advanced, 1989
Texas Military Academy, Administrative NCO in Charge of Personnel, Texas National Guard, Danville, TX
Army Personnel Management

Honors & Distinctions

Outstanding Performance Evaluations, 1996–2002
Navy Audit Performance Award, 1995
National Defense Service Medal, 1996
Army Achievement Medal with 4 Oak Leaf Clusters, 1988, 1991, 1993, 1995, 1996
Career Counselor Badge, 1991
Army Commendation Medal, 1987

Resume for Promotion

Information Technology Specialist, GS-7, Seeking Promotion to GS-8 with Noncompetitive Promotion to GS-11

Rachel T. Jones

4000 Eighth Street, SW
Washington, DC 20017

Home: (202) 888-8888
E-mail: Jonesr111@yahoo.com

Work: (202) 666-6666

Social Security No.:	000-00-0000
Citizenship:	United States
Federal Status:	Information Technology Specialist, GS-2210-7, 2001 to present
	Office of the Secretary, U.S. Department of State
Veterans' Preference:	N/A

OBJECTIVE: INFORMATION TECHNOLOGY SPECIALIST, GS-2210-8
ANN. # OH-DEU-03-006, GS 7/11
SUPPORT SERVICE UNIT/IRM
Rural Development State Office, Columbus, OH

PROFILE:

Computer Operator and member of computer support team for conversion of Windows operating system. Expert support services provider for e-mail, computer system, hardware, software, networking management, and upgrading to more than 300 users within the Office of the Secretary, Department of State. Hold **Top Secret Clearance.**

Customer Services—System Solutions, Modifications, and Problem-Solving:
- Resolve critical problems in existing or planned systems/projects.
- Anticipate systems changes and prepare users for changes.
- Make minor modifications to computers, networks, and e-mail systems.
- Provide ADP advice and direction to management and program office officials.
- Use innovative methods and techniques for problem-solving.
- Skilled analyst and troubleshooter.

Member, Project / Support Service Team:
- Carry out project assignments, meet deadlines, and provide quality service to customers.
- Determine sequence of actions necessary to accomplish the assignment.
- Independently perform tasks within team environment.
- Assist in development and maintenance efforts.

COMPUTER SKILLS:

Networks:	Networking with Novell Software, Windows NT
Operating Systems:	Windows NT, Windows 2000
Programs:	Microsoft Word 8.0, WordPerfect, PageMaker

EXPERIENCE:

U.S. Department of State
1993 to present

Information Technology Specialist—Support Services, GS-2210-7
Office of the Secretary, 2201 C Street, NW, Washington, DC 20520
Supervisor: John Smith; (202) 666-6666; may be contacted

February 1997 to present
$26,069/year
40 hours/week

- Provide technical support for critical information systems for the Secretary of State and over 800 users at the Secretariat level. Manage the electronic mail system, imaging, and Local Area Networks (LANs).

(continues)

(continued)

Rachel T. Jones, SSN 000-00-0000, IT Specialist, ANN: OH-DEU-03-006, GS-7

- Provide technical and troubleshooting assistance to hundreds of software application package users throughout the entire Department of State.
- Provide technical support for a vital electronic mail and telegram system: Principal Officer's Electronic Mail System (POEMS) and POEMS Automated Telegram Handler (PATH) in the Department of State.
- Monitor and repair problems, rebuild files, and provide ongoing network maintenance. Manipulate paper charts, imaging services, graphics, and improved scanning software.

Accomplishments:
- Installation of Novell NetWare on LANs throughout the entire department.
- Standard plan for software-required modifications to set up and reinstall additional software.
- Installation of software works—PC hardware.
- Installation of Outlook e-mail systems for new offices.
- Installation of 20 to 30 software works on PC hardware for reorganized department.

Information Assistant, GS-5   May 1993 to February 1997
2201 C Street, N.E., Washington DC 20520 $25,370/year
Supervisor: Ricardo Smith; (202) 647-2977   40 hours/week
- Received and analyzed telegrams and mail in the Office of Information Resources Management Remote Automated and Collating System (REARCS) at the Department of State. Distributed sensitive (limited use, official, confidential, top secret) incoming telegrams to State Department employees throughout the 25 bureaus in the department.
- Developed and implemented a plan for processing telegraphic backlogs.
- Operated the IBM computer system to retrieve information; trained staff on the use of the system, including keyboard, operator console, and hardware configurations.

EDUCATION:

Strayer College, Washington, DC 20006   March 1999 to present
Major: Computer Information Systems Science (CISS)

University of the District of Columbia, Washington, DC 20006   August 1988 to March 1992
Completed 115 of 130 credit hours toward B.S. degree in Computer Information Systems Science (CISS). Major courses of study included data processing; COBOL/JCL; business statistics. Attended college while working full-time.

St. Anthony's High School, Washington, DC 20006, High School Diploma   June 1987

AWARDS:
Received cash awards for outstanding performance in 1997 through 2002.

COMMUNITY SERVICE:
Volunteer financial advisor to youth at my church. Manage a savings fund for teenagers, teaching them how to save and manage money. More than $5,000 under management with 30 student members. Also active in the choir and special events coordination.
Personal interests: 10K runner for more than 5 years; focused on health and fitness; member, women's baseball team for 7 years.

2

Resumix Resumes

Navy AC/Refrigeration Mechanic, WG-10, Seeking HVAC Mechanic, WG-12

WAYNE C. HART, JR.
SSN: 000-00-0000

3719 Three Mile Road
Annapolis, MD 21403
Home Telephone: (410) 268-2315
Work Telephone: (410) 293-3850

E-mail Address: wchart@aol.com

EXPERIENCE

09-1988 to present; 40 hours per week; AIR CONDITIONING / REFRIGERATION
MECHANIC, WG-5306-10; last promoted 08-1989; Public Works Department, U.S. Naval
Academy; Jeffrey Bloom, (410) 293-5750; May contact.

CUSTOMER SERVICES AND PROJECT INSTALLATION. REPAIR AND MAINTAIN
domestic and industrial air-conditioning and refrigeration equipment at Naval Station,
Annapolis. Facilities include main campus, Radio Transmitter Facility, Critical Buildings, 255
Townhouse Residences, Apartment Complexes, Single-Family Residences, Small-Craft Facility,
Computer rooms and offices, Enlisted Dining Hall, Research Laboratory, Ice-Skating Rink, and
Exchange Store.

EXPERT KNOWLEDGE of the principles and theories related to refrigeration cycles;
equipment functions; and testing, repair, and maintenance procedures for a variety of equipment
and systems that achieve regulated climatic conditions, including compressors, motors,
condensing units, electric controls, heat pumps, cooling towers and refrigeration liquid
(glycol/water; contractor, relays), and wall converters.

OVER 20 YEARS OF EXPERIENCE DIAGNOSING AND TROUBLESHOOTING equipment
malfunctions and planning and supervising the installation, repair, and maintenance of HVAC
equipment such as chillers; large A/C package units; rooftop commercial A/C units; rooftop split
systems; heat pumps; central air-conditioning systems; window A/C units; air-dryer systems;
computer room A/C systems; dehumidifiers; ice machines; electronic air cleaners; refrigeration
and freezer systems; commercial walk-in boxes; drinking-water fountains; medical centrifugals;
and electrical, pneumatic, and pressure controls. Replace compressors, coils, water-cooled and
air-cooled condensers, and system and equipment controls.

As the ACTING FOREMAN for the A/C Shop, SUPERVISED and LED a multi-trade team in
the installation, repair, maintenance, testing, and adjustment of air-conditioning, refrigeration,
and HVAC equipment. Supervised preventative-maintenance teams.

SCHEDULED and COMPLETED preventative maintenance on 255 central A/C units 40%
ahead of schedule (9 days instead of 15) and led a team of riggers, electricians, and helpers to
replace a vital commercial 50-ton compressor unit within 36 hours.

TRAINED HELPERS from other trades. Charged time to locations, recorded manual and
computerized time cards, scheduled jobs, and assigned work to mechanics and helpers.

PLANNED and ESTIMATED work; evaluated and rescheduled service desk's priorities based
on job priority and impact on Station personnel.

(continues)

(continued)

ORDERED, INVENTORIED, and ORGANIZED all parts and materials for newly opened A/C parts shop. Kept records for EPA regarding refrigerant types, amounts, and locations used.

05-1984 to 10-1987; 40 hours per week; A/C / REFRIGERATION MECHANIC; $10.00 per hour, Thomas R. Owens A/C and Heating Contractor, Mitchellville, MD; Thomas Owens.

INSTALLED AND REPAIRED air conditioners, heat pumps, oil burners, and refrigeration units.

++ Installed sheet metal and flex ductwork. Used manifold gauges, multi-meter testing equipment, tube cutters, hand tools, electric saws, drills, and sheet-metal cutters.

++ Expert knowledge of all repair skills including brazing, soldering, plumbing, wiring, etc.

01-1979 to 09-1988; 22 hours per week; VOLUNTEER FIRE FIGHTER, GS-0081-5; U.S. Naval Academy Fire Department, Annapolis, MD.
TEAM MEMBER. Experienced in emergency preparedness, safety, first aid, and crisis management. Trained and skilled in operations management, logistics, and equipment repair.

EDUCATION

Certificate, Business Management, Anne Arundel Community College, Arnold, MD, 1994
++ Member, Phi Theta Kappa
Certificate, RETS Electronic School, Baltimore, MD, 1983
Diploma, Southern High School, Harwood, MD, 1970

CERTIFICATES & LICENSES

Certificate, EPA Refrigeration, 1996
License, Refrigerant Handling & Recovery, Universal, 1996
Certificate, Refrigeration, Climate Control, and Clean Air, 1983

PROFESSIONAL TRAINING

Drug Free Workplace, 2 hours, 2002
Asbestos Awareness, 2 hours, 2001
Manitowoc 2000 Training, 40 hours, 2000
Liebert Small Systems / Monitoring Course, 40 hours, 1999
A/C Refrigeration Units, 40 hours, 1998
Carrier Electronics for Technicians, 24 hours, 1998
Carrier Commercial Rooftop Split & Package Systems, 40 hours, 1998
Liebert Environmental Training Class, 40 hours, 1998
EPA Refrigeration Certificate Training, 8 hours, 1996
Carrier Reciprocating Liquid Chiller Course, 40 hours, 1995
Prevention of Sexual Harassment, 8 hours, 1993; 1 hour, 1995

Student Resumix Resume

Scott Hampstead
5555 University Blvd.
Hyattsville, MD 20783
Phone: (301) 333-3333
Email: scotth20202E@earthlink.net

JOB 1
B.S. IN MECHANICAL ENGINEERING HONORS PROGRAM
University of Maryland, College Park, MD
Expected July 2003   Overall GPA: 3.6/4.0   Engineering GPA: 3.7/4.0

HONORS AND ACTIVITIES
National Merit Scholar, Maryland Distinguished Scholar, A.P. scholar with honors, Dean's List (four times), Maryland club lacrosse (1999 to 2000), Maryland intramural soccer (2002)

RELATED COURSEWORK
Calculus, physics, chemistry, differential equations, statistics, dynamics, thermodynamics, introduction to matlab, fluid mechanics, electronics and instrumentation, engineering materials and manufacturing processes, statistical methods of product development, transfer processes, vibrations controls and optimization, product engineering and manufacturing, automotive design, manufacturing automation, technical writing, human resource management, introduction to transportation in supply-chain management.

COMPUTER SKILLS
Word, Excel, PowerPoint, Pro-Engineer, Matlab.

JOB 2
University of Maryland, College Park, MD; 1999 to present

Team Semester Projects:
REDESIGN OF THE DEWALT TRADESMAN DRILL using the nine-step product development process. Directed the testing and building of a prototype cordless/corded drill. Compared results to necessary specifications to determine effectiveness of the design. Gave PowerPoint presentations on project results. Utilized analytical tools such as the House of Quality, Weighted Decision Matrix, Morphological Chart, and Functional Decomposition to redesign drill. 2002

DESIGN OF HYBRID SUV FOR FUTURE TRUCK COMPETITION. In charge of testing of the performance of the electric motor. Analyzed complex schematics to determine connector specifications and location. Negotiated the donation of connectors for the high-voltage system. Researched torque curves for the stock engine and the replacement engine. 2002–2003

DESIGN OF MATLAB CODE TO MODEL AIRBORNE CONCENTRATIONS OF DUST IN TURBULENT WINDS. Modeled winds with force vectors. Displayed results in multiple plots corresponding to different wind conditions. Experimented with different mesh densities to determine the degree of computing power necessary for accurate results. 2001

OTHER PROJECTS HAVE INCLUDED:
Design of portable water pump
Statistical analysis of campus traffic flow
Evaluation of scale wind tunnel testing of a high-rise building
Analysis of stress, bending, and failure in a lug wrench

(continues)

(continued)

JOB 3

University of Maryland, College Park, MD; Team Project Skills

AS TEAM LEADER for more than 10 significant projects, developed skill in analyzing projects, delegating tasks, and establishing timelines. Also developed the following engineering and project management skills:
-Draft project details.
-Devise and recommend alternative methods of standardized analysis as a basis for solving problems.
-Recommend and devise deviations to details.
-Assist in reviews of engineering changes.
-Review compliance to contract during design, development, and production.
-Evaluate control of baseline products.
-Manage and/or witness tests.
-Evaluate quality assurance activities.
-Conduct cost and schedule analysis and estimations.
-Manage engineering data collection and analysis.

JOB 4

Sales Clerk, Village Antiques, 1000 Old Frederick Road, Oella, MD 90909 (1996–1999)
Supervisor: John Jones (410) 444-4444; salary: $12 per hour
Responsible for customer service, sales, and daily operation of store (18 hours per week)

EDUCATION:

B.S. IN MECHANICAL ENGINEERING HONORS PROGRAM
University of Maryland, College Park, MD
Centennial High School, Ellicott City, MD, Class of 1999

AWARDS AND RECOGNITION:

College GPA: Expected July 2003   Overall GPA: 3.6/4.0   Engineering GPA: 3.7/4.0

High School Academic Honors:
Honor Roll; Cumulative GPA: 3.6/4.0; National Merit Finalist/Scholar; A.P. Scholar with Honor

High School Significant Courses:
Gifted and Talented English, Social Studies; Math and Science course work
A.P. Psychology, A.P. Statistics, A.P. English 12, A.P. U.S. History, A.P. Calculus One and Two

OTHER INFORMATION:

Active in basketball, racquetball, and lacrosse throughout high school and college. Attended University of Hawaii, Oahu, for Summer 2002 studying Hawaiian culture, surfing, and golf. Traveled to France and Denmark, Summer of 2003.

Contract Specialist Resume

Seeking General Business and Industry Specialist, GS-1101-12

STEVEN R. TYLER
1725 Greenview Drive
Silver Spring, MD 21209

Home: (301) 233-4333   E-mail: stevetyler@nismic.navy.mil   Work: (202) 789-9874

Social Security No.: 000-00-0000   Citizenship: United States
Federal Status: Contract Specialist (GS-12)   Veterans' Status: N/A
Security Clearance: Secret

OBJECTIVE: General Business and Industry Specialist, GS-1101-12
                        Announcement No. C-138F

EDUCATION:

Master of Arts in Procurement and Acquisitions Management, 1996   **GPA: 3.8**
Wilshire University, Andrews AFB, Washington, DC
Honors: Distinguished Graduate
Thesis: Alternative Dispute Resolution

Defense Acquisition University, 1996   **GPA: 4.0**
Defense Acquisition Workforce Improvement Act—Level I and Level II certified
Honors: Distinguished Graduate for Automated Information Systems
Honor Graduate for Government Contract Law
Distinguished Graduate for Intermediate Contracting

Bachelor of Science Degree in Political Science, 1992   **GPA: 3.5**
Morgan State University, Greenview, MN
Minor in Military Science
Honors: Dean's List
G.T.E. Academic All-American and scholar athlete award in college football

RECENT ACCOMPLISHMENTS:

- Awarded $250 million services contract using new, innovative Blanket Purchase Agreement procedures (BPA). This streamlined process has saved the government hundreds of thousands of dollars and shortened the lifecycle of putting a contract in place. EC/EDI was used throughout the process to simplify the acquisition. Other time- and money-saving tools used were integrated product teams, teleconferencing, oral presentations, and past performance questionaires. Project received praise from national media (copies of press clips available upon request). Agency received the "Hammer Award" from former Vice President Al Gore for its cost-effective use of BPAs. General Services Administration refers to NISMC as the BPA experts when asked by industry or other federal agencies.

- Played an integral role in the highly successful first annual Navy Contracting Intern Training Conference. Received nomination (by immediate supervisor) and was selected by the Department of the Navy leadership to be a team leader for the conference. Served on the committee to organize, plan, and coordinate the conference. Responsible

(continues)

(continued)

Steven Tyler, SSN: 000-00-0000, Gen. Business & Industry Specialist, GS-1101-12, Annct. C-138F

for developing the curriculum, agenda, format, and speakers for over 400 participants. Briefed the Under Secretary of Defense and the Assistant Secretary of the Navy on the progress of the conference. Received award recognizing personal efforts/performance from the Assistant Secretary of the Navy and other top Navy officials.

- Selected for the United States Government "Outstanding Scholar Intern Program." This program was created to attract the brightest students coming out of college. To be eligible, candidate must have a bachelor's degree with a minimum GPA of 3.5 or graduate in the top 10% of their graduating class. Assigned to the 1102 contracting series for a three-year internship. Graduated from program with distinguished honors. Received high performance ratings and grade increases every year in the program. Began as a GS-7 and currently hold a GS-12 rating.

- Solid business and management background gained from experience managing a family-owned 1,000-acre grain and livestock farm. Directed operations (successfully maintaining a rigorous, tight weekly schedule) and facilitated effective communications among the farm owner, agribusinesses, and seasonal employees. Served as team leader for 50 seasonal employees.

EMPLOYMENT HISTORY:

DEPARTMENT OF THE NAVY, Washington Navy Yard, Washington DC   12/93 to present
Contract Specialist (GS-12)   45 hours per week
Supervisor: Tom Hanks, (202) 666-3298   Contact may be made
Starting Salary: $22,717   Current Salary: $46,000

Introduction:

Over three years of contracting experience with the Department of the Navy serving as a Contract Specialist, Cost Team Leader, and Source Selection Evaluation Board member. Currently employed by the Naval Information Systems Management Center (NISMC). NISMC is the central contracting office and center of excellence for the acquisition of Information Technology (IT). NISMC implements the strategic vision of the Department of Defense, Navy, and Marine Corps by providing innovative contracting services and quality customer support. NISMC contracts for and acquires competitive and commercially available products and services for PCs, software, networks, data management, communications, video and data telecommunications, and Internet used worldwide on ships, on military bases, and at headquarters.

Projects:

Currently serve as the cost team leader and senior contract specialist on the ITSS project. This $250 million support services project will be awarded using streamlined Blanket Purchase Agreement (BPA) procedures. Formerly served as contract specialist and SSEB member on the $700 million Tac-4 contract—a tactical and non-tactical hardware/software project. Also worked as the lead contract specialist for three months on the NTOPS contract. This hardware project was worth over $100 million. Completed an extensive rotation administering post-award contracts. During this rotation, successfully managed nine contracts worth over $150 million. Served a six-month rotation with the Fleet and Industrial Supply Center (FISC) with responsibility for managing over 20 contracts from pre-award to contract close-out.

2

Steven Tyler, SSN: 000-00-0000, Gen. Business & Industry Specialist, GS-1101-12, Annct. C-138F

Responsibilities:
- Facilitate integrated product teams and evaluation boards.
- Advise and assist Contracting Officer on the implementation of Federal, DoD, and other agency policy (FAR, FIRMR, DFAR).
- Remain current with and implement Congressional changes to procurement policy (FASA, ITMRA, FARA).
- Implement electronic commerce/electronic data interchange (EC/EDI) into contracting process.
- Use and be highly efficient with the latest IT equipment and software.
- Create contract documents in HTML and upload to agency website for vendor use.
- Analyze Information Technology (IT) market conditions and conduct market surveys.
- Analyze proposed costs and prices and negotiate contract terms and conditions.
- Award Blanket Purchase Agreements (BPA) to GSA schedule holders.
- Evaluate all proposed terms and conditions. Determine competitive ranges.
- Research, prepare, and write position papers for the contracting officer and contract file.
- Communicate with vendor and contractor community on a daily basis.

Professional Development:
Completed the following specialized training: Defense Acquisition University, Small Business contracting, Commerce Business Daily transmissions using the internet, Service Contract Act, Trade Agreements Act, HTML/Internet programming and usage, Defense Acquisition Workforce Improvement Act, Government Ethics, Security in the Workplace, Procurement Integrity Act, Blanket Purchase Agreements, Privacy Act and Freedom of Information Act, Communications with Congress and Department of Defense heads. (All of the above training took place from 1994 to 1997 and lasted from 2 hours to 4 weeks.)

UNITED STATES SENATE, SROB, Washington DC — Fall 1993 — 24 hours per week
Congressional Intern for Senator Donald O'Sullivan
Supervisor: Diana Swinson, (202) 686-8734
- Responded to Congressional inquiries; reviewed and wrote general correspondence.
- Researched and developed Senator O'Sullivan's 1995 Farm Bill Policy.
- Managed 1,000 pieces of incoming constituent mail per day.

SCHOOLDEN'S FARM SERVICE, Schoolden, MN — Nov 1992 to Sep 1993 — 50 hours per week
Custom Applicator/Sales
- Chemical and fertilizer management of 50,000 acres.
- Recommended and implemented nutrient programs for area farmers.

CARLSON HY-BRID COMPANY, Carlson, MN — Summers 1989 to 1992 — 45 hours per week
Harvest Production, Wheelpuller Operator, Construction
- Facilitated and trained inexperienced operators with emphasis on safety.
- Production management of $500,000 in seed corn per day.

C.A. TYLER FARMS, Three Rivers, MN — Summers, 1991, 1992 — 60 hours per week
Farm Manager
Supervisor: Clarence Tyler, (605) 322-8774
- Team leader of 50 seasonal employees.
- Timeline and milestone management of 1,000-acre farm.

3

(continues)

(continued)

Steven Tyler, SSN: 000-00-0000, Gen. Business & Industry Specialist, GS-1101-12, Annct. C-138F

MICHIGAN GAS COMPANY, Three Rivers, MN   Summer 1988
Drafter
- Coordinated gas service maps and assisted installation personnel.
- Provided timely customer support/service for all of Southwest Minnesota.

RELEVANT COURSE WORK:

Information Technology Contracting, Information Systems Security, Computer Resources and Information Management, Contracting Fundamentals, Contract Pricing, Government Contract Law, Intermediate Contracting, Intermediate Contract Pricing, Congressional Research training, Library of Congress training, Negotiations, Logistics, Pricing, Operations Management, Security Management, Analysis of Management Systems, Proposal Preparation

COMPUTER SKILLS:

Internet (Microsoft Explorer and Netscape); HTML (hot dog); Microsoft Word, Excel, PowerPoint, Access, Schedule, Windows 95, Windows 3.01 and 3.11 for WorkGroups; Adobe Acrobat; Harvard Graphics; Lotus 1-2-3; WordPerfect; EBBS; e-mail (cc:Mail and Microsoft Exchange); CA Super Project; Delrina Form Flow; Macintosh

AWARDS:

- Outstanding Performance Appraisal Review System award, 1996, 1997
- Quality Salary (Grade) increase, 1994, 1995, 1996
- Tac-4 Contract Recognition award from Vice Admiral
- Tac-4 Protest Recognition award from Rear Admiral
- Outstanding achievement award for 1995 Navy Contracting Intern Training Conference
- Navy Intern Conference Letter of Commendation from Assistant Secretary of the Navy
- Distinguished graduate for Contracting 201, 211, and 241 courses
- United States Government Outstanding Scholar Program recipient
- Letter of Commendation from FISC executive officer for outstanding customer support
- G.T.E. Academic All-American, all-conference academic team in college football
- College Scholars of America
- Letter of appreciation from U.S. Senator Donald O'Sullivan for outstanding constituent support

LEADERSHIP AND ACTIVITIES:

Civilian Leadership Development Program, College Football team captain for over 100 players, National Contract Management Association, Ice Hockey team captain responsible for organization of 20 teammates, Benevolent and Protective Order of Elks, Friends of the National Zoo, Sons of the American Revolution, NISMC blood drive coordinator, Soil and Water Conservation Society, Government Ethics Representative, High School class president responsible for class reunion of over 300 people, Morgan State University Alumni Association and Varsity Club.

4

Executive Federal Resumes

Deployment Consultant, U.S. Postal Service, Seeking Management Analyst, GS-343-13

BENJAMIN J. KOMINSKI
1008 Juneberry Way
Springfield, VA 22158
Residence: (703) 444-1010
Email: BJKominski@cox.net

SSN: 000-00-0000
Citizenship: U.S.
Veterans' Preference: 5 Points

Military Status: USMC, Sergeant, 6/65–6/70, Honorable Discharge
Federal Civilian Status: Management Analyst, 7/91–7/96, FP-0343-03
Previous Security Clearance: Held Top Secret (TS/CS) for 6 years

OBJECTIVE: **Management Analyst,** GS-0343-13
Announcement Number: **030096921-DEU**

PROFILE:

Results-oriented **management analyst** with strong research, analysis, reporting, and process evaluation skills. Accomplished in problem resolution, administration, and financial management. Outstanding verbal and written communicator, leader, and negotiator. Proficient as a highly skilled **operations manager** and **logistician.** Proven success in providing large, system-wide managed services under performance-based contracts, determining and meeting customer's needs, streamlining workflow processes, and saving projects money. Expert in startup transportation, operations and support, logistics and materials, human resource allocation, quality control, and lifecycle support. Experienced in selecting, training, and leading dedicated, diverse, and high-performing project staffs. M.S. in Project Management. Proficient in project management and spreadsheet software, including MS Excel, Access, and Project.

INTERNATIONAL EXPERIENCE:

Experienced in management of USAID-funded agribusiness and agricultural development projects with private-sector firms and non-governmental organizations. Recruited, assessed, and trained large, culturally diverse, and qualified staffs for projects in five countries in Latin America and Central Africa. Expertise in training counterparts in administrative and financial management. Thorough command of large-scale and special project management, coordination, and development; securing venture capital and business loans; business-plan development; budget execution strategies; and combating hunger.

PROFESSIONAL EXPERIENCE:

Deployment Consultant   10/97–8/02
USPS POS ONE PROGRAM OFFICE   55+ hours/week
475 L'Enfant Plaza, SW, N. Bldg.   Ending Salary: $80,537/year
Room 5322, Washington, DC 20260   Beginning Salary: $71,350/year
Supervisor: Angela Sunil, (202) 555-1312   Contact can be made

Managed the joint nationwide web-enabled deployment of a sophisticated retail point-of-service system with IBM and NCR for the U.S. Postal Service (USPS).

As the single point of contact and key advisor, communicated and coordinated daily operational activities of 45 USPS regional and state coordinators nationwide with IBM and MCI multifunctional field teams and senior USPS program managers, utilizing an online status-management system. Provided liaison with internal, external, and senior-level coordinators, managers, and outside companies.

(continues)

(continued)

Deployment Consultant, continued...

Developed and managed hardware acquisition and deployment schedule with a 120-day site-preparation cycle for the installation of 22,000 computer terminals valued at $400 million to 6,300 facilities affecting over 40,000 USPS retail personnel.

Operated Visual Basic, MS Access, and browser-based front-end deployment-management system connected to Oracle and MS Access backend tool to generate EDI contractual orders for IBM hardware and installation services, and telecommunications orders to MCI for establishing network connectivity to over 10,000 USPS facilities.

Key Accomplishments:
- Met all deployment schedule deadlines during five-year period in face of repeated major schedule changes, database support issues, and a changing deployment criteria baseline.
- Contributed to achievement of 99+% success rate for on-time installation.
- Saved USPS $7.5 million managing a hardware-recycling program.
- Wrote training manual and implemented nationwide training course for 96 USPS regional and state coordinators, and 344 maintenance and contract personnel.

Operations Manager   8/96–10/97
LOGICAL TECHNICAL SERVICES CORPORATION   50+ hours/week
1611 N. Kent St., Suite 200, Arlington, VA 22209   Base Salary: $55,000/year
Supervisor: Tim Booth, (703) 444-5652   Bonus: $2,000

Supervised all aspects of daily operations for USAID-funded international development information clearinghouse in a service-oriented environment. Managed staff of 41 computer hardware and programming specialists and support personnel in three facilities throughout Washington metro area.

Assessed customer issues, analyzed financial reports and performance data on multiple client contracts, linked budget expenditures, and documented problem areas. Took action to overcome performance barriers.

Conducted assessments of employee performance based on individual work plans. Provided timely feedback, and recommended advancement, training, or corrective action to corporate managers.

Key Accomplishments:
- Instrumental in winning five-year, $15 million contract. Awarded bonus.
- Drafted an operational support plan defining policy, procedures, hardware and software requirements, and staff training needs.
- Negotiated work priorities and assignments with senior corporate managers, linking technical operations to customer service and ensuring contract deliverables met client's goals.

Senior Management Analyst   7/95–7/96
OFFICE OF INSPECTOR GENERAL, PEACE CORPS   50+ hours/week
1111 20th St., NW, Washington, DC 20526   Ending Salary: $51,189/year
Supervisor: Jennifer Bettridge, (202) 555-1212   Beginning Salary: $48,465/year

Inspected administrative, programming, training, and security components of Peace Corps overseas operations. Analyzed and documented in-country managements' implementation of Federal Agency's policy, utilization of human resource skill sets in project assignments, internal control systems for funding and material, and soundness of safety and security measures.

Conducted extensive, in-depth interviews with senior U.S. government and Embassy officials, host-country ministers, and non-governmental organization representatives; communicated results directly to and advised the Inspector General.

Senior Management Analyst, continued...

Key Accomplishments:
- Designated team lead for complex country program evaluations involving highly controversial and politically sensitive issues in Kyrgyzstan and Madagascar.
- Drafted formal proposals to resolve deficiencies for Congressional Records ahead of schedule.

Senior Management Analyst
INTER-AMERICA REGION, PEACE CORPS
1111 20th St., NW, Washington, DC 20526
Supervisor: Jennifer Bettridge, (202) 555-1212

7/91–7/95
45+ hours/week
Ending Salary: $48,465/year
Beginning Salary: $34,792/year

Analyzed management of agency's $33 million budget to support field operations in 22 Latin American countries. Evaluated strategic plan and program annual performance plans. Identified areas of deficiency in country operations, recommended changes to Region Director, and coordinated implementation of corrective actions with Agency staff.

Key Accomplishments:
- Developed profiles to analyze internal control systems for improving country operations. Monitored and tracked 167 field projects, 162 private-sector contractors, and the programming and training requirements for 2,300 volunteers and in-country staff.
- Conceptualized and built the only agency-wide cost study for comparing the total cost to support one Peace Corps Volunteer in each of the 107 country programs over a 10-year period.
- Named Acting Administrative Officer for Haiti, responsible for the discharge of $1 million annual operating budget.

Agribusiness Advisor
DEVELOPMENT ALTERNATIVES, INC.
7250 Woodmont Ave., Bethesda, MD 20814
Supervisor: Mike Burleson, (301) 828-4848

4/89–1/90
56+ hours/week
Base Salary: $39,000/year

Promoted venture-capital investments in private-sector agriculture and agribusiness for a $12 million USAID-financed project in the eastern Caribbean region.

Key Accomplishments:
- Discovered U.S. and Canadian specialty and niche markets more suitable for smaller-volume exports from the eastern Caribbean.
- Developed business plans identifying marketing, management, financing, and production needs resulting in startup of three venture-capital processing and export projects valued at $660,000.
- Analyzed financial institutions and foreign investors' preconditions for lending (i.e., feasibility study depth, debt/equity ratios, collateral requirements) and negotiated terms leading to $500,000 in guaranteed loans for construction and rehabilitation of four agricultural processing complexes.
- Wrote business plans for individual farmers and producer associations that captured a total of $420,000 in 14 seed-capital grants.

Project Manager
NATIONAL COOPERATIVE BUSINESS ASSOCIATION
1401 New York Ave., NW, Suite 1100, Washington, DC 20005
Supervisor: Jim Rubenstein, (202) 665-2526

4/86–5/88
60+ hours/week
Base Salary: $34,000/year

Managed $3 million USAID-funded Cooperative Transportation and Extension Development Project in Equatorial Guinea. Planned and supported implementation of first Peace Corps program in Equatorial Guinea. Developed, expanded, and improved strategies and systems for establishing and supporting self-sufficiency and delivering needed food assistance.

(continues)

(continued)

Project Manager, continued...

Key Accomplishments:

- Constructed and equipped $250,000 Cooperative Transportation Service Center with mechanics shop, power-generating facility, warehouses, training classrooms, and administrative offices.
- Recruited, trained, and directly supervised staff of 33 administrators, cooperative educators, mechanics, and drivers.
- Built 12-vehicle fleet system that serviced the marketing needs of 5,000 farmers in 28 village cooperatives whose production furnished over 60% of the country's food requirements.
- Achieved net income objectives, four years ahead of schedule, while guiding project through 30% funding cut and 20% currency devaluation.
- Integrated Center's functions with host government ministries, as well as development activities of IMF; World Bank; and Spanish, French, British, Chinese, South African, and Brazilian projects.

MILITARY EXPERIENCE:

United States Marine Corps   Worldwide Deployments

- **Explosive Ordnance Disposal Technician:** As Team Lead, managed EOD personnel neutralizing and disposing of explosive ordnance that presented a threat to installations, personnel, and material in Latin American and Mediterranean areas of operations. 2/68–6/70
- **Force Reconnaissance Man:** As Company Scout, guided Force Recon Marines in border surveillance operations throughout the Republic of South Vietnam. 6/65–1/68

EDUCATION:

- M.S., Project Management. University of California, Davis, CA 95616. GPA: 3.7, 1984
- B.A., magna cum laude, International Affairs. Florida State University, Tallahassee, FL 32306. GPA: 3.8, 1974
- A.A. with Honors, Economics and Government. St. Petersburg Junior College, Clearwater, FL 33516. GPA: 3.7, 1972

SPECIAL TRAINING AND LANGUAGES:

Administrative Officers Training Course, Peace Corps, Washington, DC, 1991
U.S. Navy Explosive Ordnance School, Indianhead, MD, 1968
U.S. Army Chemical, Biological, and Radiological Corps School, Ft. McClellan, AL, 1968
Fluent in Spanish; Proficient in Guarani; Knowledge of French

COMPUTER PROFICIENCY:

MS Office Suite: Word, Excel, Access, Project, PowerPoint; Remedy; Outlook; and Lotus Notes

AWARDS:

Certificate of Appreciation, POS ONE, 2001 and 1999
Certificate of Recognition and Appreciation, Peace Corps, 1996

PROFESSIONAL AFFILIATIONS:

International Society for Logistics
Society for International Development
Marine Corps Association

Regional Inspector General for Investigations, GM-15, Seeking Supervisory Special Agent, GM-15

TIMOTHY HUTTON
13343 Triadelphia Mill Road
Woodbridge, VA 22191

Home: (703) 744-4324
Timhutton3334@earthlink.net

Work: (202) 709-9874

Social Security No.:   000-00-0000
Citizenship: U.S.A.
Federal Status: Supervisory Special Agent, GM-1811-15, 5/87 to present
Military Status: U.S.M.C., 1967 to 1978
Veterans' Preference: 10-Point Veteran (3 Purple Hearts and 1 Bronze Star WI Combat V)
    Assistant Inspector General for Investigations, ES-1811

OBJECTIVE: Department of Transportation, Washington, DC, Office of Inspector General Supervisory Special Agent, GM-15, Announcement No.: 1-95-30

PROFILE: Twenty years with the General Services Administration, Office of Inspector General. Direct and plan Inspector General investigative activities. Supervise comprehensive and responsive investigative programs. Ensure the integrity of agency programs and personnel. Manage complex investigations involving alleged violations of Title 18, United States Code.

Establish investigative priorities, direct case initiation, and perform case and office reviews. Continually strive to improve investigative techniques and quality and effectiveness of investigative programs and personnel. Represent the office in conferences and meetings with Congressional staff, agency officials, other QIG staff, and high-level governmental officials on investigative matters.

Experienced manager of agents and support personnel. Effective at implementing OIG training and workforce diversity programs. Design training and development programs to implement performance and results initiatives.

EMPLOYMENT HISTORY

GENERAL SERVICES ADMINISTRATION
Office of Inspector General   12/83 to present

Regional Inspector General for Investigations, GM-1811-15   9/90 to present
Washington Field Investigations Office   55–60 hours/week
Regional Office Building, Room 1915   Beginning Salary: $66,125/year
7th & D Streets, SW, Washington, DC 20407   Current Salary: $83,614/year
Supervisor: Charles Vanderbilt, (202) 432-4324; Contact can be made

Manage a staff of professional special agents ranging in grades from GM-14 to GS-7 (FTEs have ranged between 8 and 18), as well as three support personnel. Responsible for hiring, staff and career development, reassignments, and personnel and program evaluations. Management of the regional investigative program in the Washington Field Investigations Office covers both regional and national GSA programs and operations.

(continues)

(continued)

Timothy Hutton, 000-00-0000, Supervisory Special Agent, GM-15, Annct.: 1-95-30

Managed the administrative (budget, personnel, office automation) and operational workload of the office and made long-range investigative plans. Provide technical advice to supervisors and special agents. Promote and require the use of information technologies in the investigative program.

Accept and reject highly complex and sensitive investigative work products. Work closely with QIG headquarters and regional management personnel to enhance and improve the investigative program. Conducted sensitive and complex investigations of the highest-level employee in the agency.

Champion the concept of cultural diversity in the QIG by hiring both minority employees and women. Promoted the first and currently only two female special agents to Assistant RIGI positions.

Accomplishments:

- Participated in a task group with AIGI Henderson and an outside consultant, resulting in the development of the Office of Investigations Strategic Plan pursuant to the Government Performance and Results Act (GPRA), which links budget requests with performance goals and measurable outcomes. It results in mission-driven accomplishments. Issued in May of 1999.

- In May 2001, developed for AIGI Henderson the Office of Investigations, Executive Management Report, an automated report for the Inspector General that reports on quarterly accomplishments.

- In September 1999, following the Office of Investigations Strategic Planning Conference, where downsizing and budget reductions were announced, initiated a training program in the Washington Field Investigations Office in accordance with former U.S. Vice President Al Gore's reinvention initiatives to make the government work better and cost less. Implemented training of the staff in Total Quality Management principles to encourage the use of self-directed work teams and employee involvement and empowerment.

- In order to accomplish personal career/training objectives, became a trainer of a 4-day course by Dr. Stephen R. Covey entitled "The Seven Habits of Highly Effective People" in order to improve staff's personal effectiveness.

- Incorporated a customized Self-Directed Work Team course into the region's staff-development program taught by the Human Resources Office of the Federal Aviation Administration in order to improve teamwork effectiveness and better utilize available staff following downsizing of the agency.

Director, Investigative Support
Programs and Projects Division, GM-1811-15   3/86 to 9/90
    GS Building, 18th & F Streets, NW, Washington, DC 20407   50–60 hours/week
    Supervisor: Alfred H. Henderson, (202) 401-9874

Managed the Office of Investigation's policy development, security, records maintenance, administrative, and ADP technical support to field operations.

Provided technical operational guidance to the Assistant IG for Investigations; advised on a range of subjects including budget/personnel matters, office automation/ADP support, and uses of information technologies in an investigative environment.

2

Timothy Hutton, 000-00-0000, Supervisory Special Agent, GM-15, Annct.: 1-95-30

Accomplishments:

- As the manager of the ADP Division, recognized the need to improve the ADP and management information systems within the Office of Inspector General and sub-offices (Office of Investigations and Office of Audits).

- Helped develop and prototype the Office of Audit's Audit Information System at the direction of the Inspector General; designated as the QIG Project Director for overall development of an OIG Management Information System. This assignment required supervision of the Programs and Projects Division, as well as the QIG Systems Support and Development Division.

Acting Regional Inspector General for Investigations, GM-1811-14   8/85 to 3/86
Washington Field Investigations Office

Managed an investigative staff of 18 agents and three clerical support personnel. Supervised and conducted highly technical and complex sensitive investigations involving the programs and operations of GSA. Provided technical advice to supervisors and agents.

Managed the administrative and operational workload of the office and long-range investigative plans. Developed and implemented budget and personnel actions. Evaluated office, supervisor, and agent performance. Accepted and rejected work products.

Assistant Regional Inspector General for Investigations, GM-1811-14   1/85 to 8/85
Washington Field Investigations Office

Supervised a group of agents and clerical staff in the accomplishment of all investigative activity including prevention.

Assisted the RIGI in managing the office and the investigative program. Analyzed agency regulations, laws, and policies affecting the investigative program. Accepted and rejected work products.

Criminal Investigator Staff Officer Assistant to DAIGI, GS-1811-13   12/83 to 1/85
Office of Investigations
GSA Building, Washington, D.C.

As the staff officer assistant to the Deputy AIGI, helped develop and coordinate nationwide Office of Investigations policies and procedures. Helped develop and prepare budgetary submissions and personnel actions. Analyzed and prepared statistical reports regarding nationwide office accomplishments.

Planned, organized, and conducted sensitive and complex investigations and special projects related to enhancing and developing administrative management processes and management goals and objectives.

3

(continues)

(continued)

Timothy Hutton, 000-00-0000, Supervisory Special Agent, GM-15, Annct.: 1-95-30

Criminal Investigator, GS-1811-13   6/82 to 12/83
Office of Policy, Plans, and Management Systems, Washington, DC

Planned and evaluated functions for the Office of Investigations.
- Developed policy and procedures for that office by preparing the Investigations chapter of the OIG manual.
- Developed a guide for evaluating investigation headquarters and field components. Reviewed legislation, rules, and regulations of the office and agency as the QIG assistant clearance office.

MILITARY EXPERIENCE:

U.S. Marine Corps (various locations throughout U.S. and Far East)   1/72 to 9/78

Conducted criminal investigations pursuant to Chapter 10 U.S. Code and other federal laws to include investigations of fraud against the government, homicide, rape, and narcotics violations. Conducted white-collar crime investigations requiring knowledge of federal laws and federal accounting systems. These investigations required collection and preservation of both physical and testimonial evidence, taking statements and depositions under oath, analyzing questioned documents, and preparing and reviewing highly technical criminal investigation reports.

EDUCATION:

GEORGE WASHINGTON UNIVERSITY, Washington, DC 20006
BS in Political Science, 1980

FEDERAL EXECUTIVE INSTITUTE, Charlottesville, VA, 1999
Studied Economics and Foreign Affairs Management Studies

GEORGE WASHINGTON UNIVERSITY, Washington, DC, 1995
School of Government & Business, Contemporary Executive Development Program

CENTER FOR CREATIVE LEADERSHIP DEVELOPMENT PROGRAM, Greensboro, NC, 1998
GSA Meritorious Service Award, 1999
GSA (IG) Commendable Service Awards (2), 1999, 2000
OPM Honor Graduate, Federal Personnel Management Issues
Executive Management Seminar, 2000

4

Index

Federal Resume Guidebook *CD-ROM*

Federal Resume and KSA Samples/Templates in Word 8.0 format and PDF

Looking for more help with your Federal resume? The winning resumes on this unique CD-ROM will further support you in writing it right and faster.

DON'T WASTE TIME!

In addition to reading this 3rd edition of The Federal Resume Guidebook, consider putting Kathryn Troutman's completely new version of her FedRes Samples/Templates on CD-ROM to work for you. On average, applicants are able to create their Federal resumes 300% more quickly!

WRITE IT RIGHT!

With the CD-ROM, you'll feel more confident that the presentation of your Federal resume will not only fit government requirements, but also catch the eye of the hiring officials. All of Troutman's samples are taken from cases involving successful Federal applicants.

FORMATS AUTOMATICALLY!

A big reason you'll save time with this CD-ROM is that there will be no need to agonize over the formatting of your resume! Using a template on the CD, you can simply replace text with your own information. Automatically your resume will be beautifully formatted with designs based on Troutman's 30 years of experience. Or simply refer to the resumes as excellent models.

IN ADDITION

....to the 24 resumes, you'll also find 25 pages of winning KSAs on this CD-ROM. Your ability to create your own KSA will be strengthened by reviewing the style, length and format of these successful KSAs. Like the resumes, the Knowledge, Skills and Ability statements can be worked with either as templates or samples.

ORDER TODAY!

Don't delay! Enhance your Federal jobseeking skills by ordering the Federal Resume and KSA Samples/Templates now!

Online: http://www.resume-place.com
Phone orders call 888/480-8265, 9 to 5:30 EST.

Includes Resume Templates for:

PROFESSIONALS

COLLEGE STUDENTS

MID-CAREER

EXECUTIVES

CLERICAL

ENTRY LEVEL

THE TRADES

TECHNICAL

ELECTRONIC RESUMES

The Resume Place, Inc. Home of the Federal Resume

Need help with your package? www.resume-place.com

Federal Job Search Consulting and Professional Writing Services

Professional writing, design, editing, and consulting services, including: electronic resumes, private industry resumes, one-page networking resumes, Federal resumes, KSAs, Federal job qualification analysis, professional critiques, and senior executive service applications, interview training, and role-playing.

Full Service Writing and Editing

Need help writing an outstanding professional resume that presents the best experience and skills you have to offer? Want a free estimate for professional services? Not sure what your next step in your Federal job search should be? Send your most recent resume, past applications, position descriptions, and any vacancy announcements to us by mail or e-mail. We will contact you with a complete recommendation and estimate of services.

Federal Job Qualification Analysis

Are you a first-time Federal job applicant and unsure how your private industry experience equates to Federal positions? We will analyze your education, experience, knowledge, skills and abilities, and provide you with Federal job titles, grade levels, and ideas for the best agencies for you. We will review your qualifications against Office of Personnel Management Classification Standards and provide your Federal Job Qualifications Analysis Report.

Professional Editing and Design Services

Have you written your resume already, but would like an editor to review your content and improve your format? Our Edit-Design service to improve your draft is outstanding. Our editors will improve the format, presentation, and readability of the resume; edit and reorganize the content; check verb tenses; highlight any accomplishments that you might not feature as well as you should; make sure your skills are clear in the content.

Professional Critique

Are you sure your resume is focused, written at the appropriate level, clear to the reader? We'll tell you if it is or isn't.

Resumix and Electronic Resume Writing Service

The Resumix resume format, used by the Department of Defense civilian military personnel agencies, can be edited or written by Resume Place writers. We are experienced in all formats: Army, Navy, Marines, Air Force and other agencies. Our Resumix resumes will maximize your success. We will maximize skills and keywords so that you will be as successful as possible with both the database and the selecting official.

SES Services
Consulting, Critique, Interview And Full Service Writing

The Resume Place, Inc. is the leading executive Federal resume-writing firm in the world. We know what's important and how to present your package the executive level. The SES package is a major executive writing project. We are experts in marketing executives and writing about their accomplishments, expertise, and career history in the most impressive, succinct, and persuasive way!

The SES package includes the following components: Cover Letter, Executive Federal Resume, Executive Core Qualification (ECQ) Statements: Leading Change, Leading People, Results Driven, Business Acumen, Building Coalitions, and Technical and Managerial Factors. Total package average: 18 to 25 pages.

Would you like a Senior Executive Service Federal Employment expert to review your materials to determine what it would take to write your SES package? Write to us at resume@resume-place.com. Subjectline: SES service information

Federal Career Corner Newsletter – Free! • Ask your Federal job search questions – Free!
Sign up for a monthly email newsletter by Kathryn Troutman

www.resume-place.com

The Resume Place, 89 Mellor Ave., Baltimore, MD 21228 • E-mail attached files to resume@resume-place.com • Fax: 410-744-0112 • Questions? Call 888-480-8265